OTHER BOOKS ON
COLONIAL AUSTRALIA
BY THE AUTHOR

IN FOR THE LONG HAUL
*The First Fleet Voyage and Colonial Australia:
The Convicts' Perspective*

DOCTOR REDFERN
Mutineer, Convict, Medical Pioneer, Rights Activist

www.annegrethall.com

ANDREW THOMPSON

*From Boy Convict to
Wealthiest Settler in Colonial Australia*

ANNEGRET HALL

First published in 2021.
Revised edition published in 2023.

Copyright © Annegret Hall 2021
www.annegrethall.com

ESH Publication, Nedlands 6009, Australia

All reasonable attempts have been made to communicate with copyright holders of the images reproduced in this book. Any corrections to information provided about these images should be communicated to the author.

This book is copyright. Apart from any fair dealing for the purpose of private study, research, criticism or review, as permitted under the *Copyright Act*, no part of this book may be reproduced by any process without written permission from the author.

A catalogue record for this book is available from the National Library of Australia

ISBN: 978 0 9876292 2 7 (paperback)
ISBN: 978 0 9876292 3 4 (ebook)

Cover design by OzKunstPro
Front cover – 'Andrew Thompson Esq.' oil painting by Syd Hall, 2020
Cover background – 'Governor Bligh's farm Blighton' by John William Lewin ca 1806-1810 (Art Gallery of South Australia: 8910P31)

Text is set in Garamond typeface

Printed in Australia by Ingram Lightning Source

*For all the transported female convicts
who forged a new life in Australia*

Contents

Chapter 1	Great Expectations	1
Chapter 2	A Most Heinous Crime	10
Chapter 3	Beyond the Seas	28
Chapter 4	A New Start	42
Chapter 5	The Young Constable	50
Chapter 6	Newfound Freedom	64
Chapter 7	Entrepreneur	84
Chapter 8	Chief Constable	106
Chapter 9	Settlers' Survival	120
Chapter 10	Eleanor	134
Chapter 11	Bailiff of Blighton	143
Chapter 12	The Loyalist	162
Chapter 13	Rebellion	179
Chapter 14	Loyalist Resistance	199
Chapter 15	Local Hero	214
Chapter 16	First Emancipist Magistrate	231
Chapter 17	A Remarkable Life	254
Chapter 18	Andrew's Legacy	272
Epilogue		295
Maps & Illustrations		viii
Conversion Chart		x
Acknowledgements		297
Bibliography		299
Notes		304
Index		326

Maps & Illustrations

Page

2   Etching of the Church in Kirk Yetholm. (W. Baird, *Memoirs of the late Rev. John Baird*)

7   Wood engraving of a man sitting at a loom weaving stockings. (WL: 30668i)

14 Watercolour by Thomas Girtin of the Jedburgh Abbey from the southeast. (YCB: B2010.23)

21 Andrew Thompson's signature on a 1790 trial document. (NRS: JC12/21 f.81-85)

29 Captain Arthur Phillip prior to the departure of the First Fleet in 1787. Engraving by W. Sherwin in 1789. (NLA: nla.obj-136095976)

33 Etching by John Harris of the transport ship *Pitt* in 1789. (NMM: PZ5921)

44 North view of Sydney Cove painted by Thomas Watling in 1794. (SLNSW DX: DG 60)

46 View of Government House in Parramatta. (NLA: nla.obj-135688446)

54 Engraving of a western view of Toongabbie. (NLA: nla.obj-135681496)

55 Portrait of Chief Constable George Barrington painted by William Beechey in 1785. (NLA: nla.obj-134292248)

55 Portrait of Major Francis Grose. (NLA: nla.obj-136080725)

59 Part of a 1796 map of the settlement in New South Wales. (SLNSW ML: D Q79/60-61)

60 Portrait of John Macarthur painted in about 1850 by an unknown artist. (SLNSW DX: DG 222)

60 Portrait of Colonel William Paterson painted by William Owen. (SLNSW DX: DG 175)

80 Portrait of John Hunter, the colony's second governor, painted by W.M. Bennett (1795-1800). (NLA: nla.obj-134293340)

80 Miniature portrait of Philip Gidley King, the colony's third governor (1800-1806). (SLNSW ML: MIN 62)

89 Etching of Andrew Thompson's Red House Farm Windsor painted by Philip Slager. (SLNSW: D F81/22)

97 Watercolour of Green Hills on the Hawkesbury River painted by John William Lewin in 1809. (SLNSW ML: PXD 388 v. 3 no. 7)

98 Part of a Pitt Town parish map showing Andrew Thompson's properties. (HLRV: AO MAP 263)

99 Part of an 1812 Windsor town plan approved by Governor Macquarie with references to existing land occupied and buildings. (SANSW: SZ 529)

100 Engraving of Windsor by Philip Slager in 1813. (NLA: nla.obj-135298988)

111 Sketch of the Irish convict uprising at Castle Hill in 1804. (NLA: nla.obj-135226428)

124 Watercolour of the Hawkesbury flood in 1816. (SLNSW ML: V1B/Wind/16)

126 Illustration of the plight of settler families in the 1867 Hawkesbury flood. (*Illustrated Sydney News*, 16 Jul 1867)

128 Part of a Castlereagh parish map showing Thompson's farms Agnes Bank, Wardle Bank and Glasgow. (HLRV: AO MAP 203)

130 Map showing the locations of Andrew Thompson's properties.

139 View of Sydney from the west side of the Cove, painted by John Eyre in 1806. (SLNSW DX: XV/201)

144 Portrait of William Bligh, the colony's fourth governor (1806-1808), painted by A. Huey. (NLA: nla.obj-136207002)

150 Watercolour of Blighton Farm painted by George Evans in 1810. (NGA: NGA 94.1418)

157 Watercolour of the Hawkesbury River painted by J. W. Lewis in 1810. (SLNSW DX: DG V1B/3)

167 Town plan of Sydney drawn up by James Meehan at Governor Bligh's request, 31 Oct 1807. (NLA: MAP F 105A)

182 Cartoon portraying the arrest of Governor Bligh during the 1808 rebellion. (SLNSW ML: Safe 4/5)

183 Watercolour of Government House at Sydney Cove painted by John Eyre in 1807. (SLNSW ML: SV/31)

227 A sketch showing the 1816 flood in Windsor. (SLNSW ML: PX*D 264)

228 Part of the Parish map of Melville showing Thompson's farm Creek Retreat. (HLRV: No 14605)

229 Part of the Parish map of Minto showing Thompson's farm St Andrews. (HLRV: AO MAP 250)

233 View of Sydney from the east side of the Cove, painted by John Eyre in 1810. (SLNSW: XVI/1808/8)

235 Part of the Parish map of St James showing Thompson's land grant in Macquarie Place. (HLRV: AO MAP 349)

236 Miniature portrait of Lachlan Macquarie, the colony's fifth governor (1810-1821). (SLNSW ML: MIN 236)

279 Photo of Andrew Thompson's gravestone in St Matthew's cemetery in Windsor taken in 2019.

287 Portrait of Simeon Lord, artist unknown (SLNSW: GN 11/Box 07/p.82)

287 Portrait of Major Henry Colden Antill, artist unknown. (SLNSW: GPO 1-13432)

294 Family Tree of Andrew Thompson

Conversion Chart

For historical accuracy, imperial measurements have been retained in the text.

1 inch (in)	2.54 centimetres
1 foot (ft)	30 centimetres
1 yard (yd)	90 centimetres
1 rod	5 metres
1 mile	1.6 kilometres
1 nautical mile (nm)	1.85 kilometres
1 acre	4047 square metres
1 rood	0.25 acre (1000 square metres)
1 perch or square rod	25.3 square metres
1 gallon	4.5 litres
1 hundredweight (cwt)	50.8 kilograms
1 pound (lb)	450 grams
1 ton	1016 kilograms
1 bushel wheat	27.2 kilograms
1 bushel maize	25.4 kilograms
1 pound Sterling (£)	20 shillings Sterling
1 shilling (s)	12 pence Sterling
1 penny (d)	1/240th of 1 pound Sterling
1 Merk Scots	14 shillings Sterling

For historical authenticity, quotations in the body of the text are given verbatim with original spelling and grammar. To assist comprehension insertions have been made bounded by square brackets.

Chapter 1

GREAT EXPECTATIONS

All the truth of my position came flashing on me; and its disappointments, dangers, disgraces, consequences of all kinds, rushed in in such a multitude that I was borne down by them and had to struggle for every breath I drew.[1]

Andrew Thompson's extraordinary life is difficult to tell in a strictly historical narrative. It is full of hardship, heroism, industry, fortune, determination and redemption – a story better suited to a 19th century novel written for a Victorian audience. Indeed, it is a tale that William Thackeray (1819-75) would have loved to tell – his own fictional characters, Redmond Barry and Henry Esmond, lack the energy and realism of this remarkable man. It is a tantalising possibility that the master storyteller of those times, Charles Dickens (1812-70) may have been inspired by Andrew Thompson's life when he wrote his classic tale of hope and despair, *Great Expectations*. There is a fascinating overlap between the aspirations and disappointments in the lives of Pip and Abel Magwitch and that of Andrew, and it is well known that Charles Dickens and his sons had a strong interest in colonial Australia.[2]

In his rich life Andrew Thompson encountered much more of the best and the worst on offer than most. He had a secure childhood, was educated with high expectations, gaoled for a crime he may not have committed, cast into absolute disgrace and despair, banished to the antipodes, harshly punished, gained respect through industry and honesty, exhibited courage, heroism and leadership, rose to power and prosperity, was appointed to government posts and became the friend of governors. Andrew faced many obstacles in his eventful life but overcame most of them to become one of Australia's most important pioneers. It can be justly claimed that he attained more prominence in the colony to which he was banished than he could ever have hoped for in his native land. Andrew Thompson deserves far greater recognition in Australian history.

Andrew Thompson was baptised on Sunday 7 February 1773 in the Church of Scotland in Kirk Yetholm.[3] He was the sixth child of a successful weaving family living in the Scottish border village of Town Yetholm, the companion village of Kirk Yetholm across the river Bowmont Water. His father John Thompson had married Agnes Hilson from the nearby village of Sprouston in 1760. They had six children but only Andrew and his two brothers, William born in 1762 and Walter in 1765, survived childhood. After the youngest child Robert died at the age of three, Agnes lavished her attention on the newborn Andrew, and he received every benefit a traditional Scottish rural family could afford.

The church in Kirk Yetholm in which Andrew Thompson's parents were married, and where he and his siblings were baptized. It is the site of many ancient Scottish graves.

In the mid 18th century Britain underwent major economic and social changes that affected traditional urban and rural livelihoods. During this turbulent period the Thompson boys were raised in a close-knit protestant household in which a good rural education was provided, both formal and practical. The boys were groomed to become successful young men in a world where advances in mechanised industry and commodity markets in the larger towns trickled down to the small villages as new opportunities. These certainly benefitted educated men who could adapt to changing work practices, but they posed barriers for the unskilled. In many rural districts rising rents on farmland and houses meant that men and their families had to move to larger towns where they became industrial workers, or to villages as labourers on large estates. Others became itinerant workers in occupations such as blacksmithing, carpentry, tailoring and especially weaving.

The twin villages of Town Yetholm and Kirk Yetholm nestle in the sparsely wooded undulating countryside of the Bowmont Water that flows through a valley of the Cheviot Hills. The two Yetholms are less than three miles from the English border and straddle a traditional trade route south to England. In fact, Yetholm's name is Anglo-Saxon for the 'gate village'. For centuries this route was taken by Scots who skirmished and raided English villages, and by English forces attacking Scottish towns in the north. Yetholm's churchyard is the closest consecrated ground to the English border and became the burial place of many border chiefs killed in these conflicts, though scant evidence of these ancient graves exists today.[4]

During Andrew Thompson's childhood, Town Yetholm belonged to the Wauchope family of Niddrie, and Kirk Yetholm to the Marquis of Tweeddale. The population numbers remained steady during this period, and if anything increased, because the lairds of these villages made farming lots available at reasonable rent. The Marquis also allowed limited access to the 200-acre Yetholm Common. By 1786 the populations of the two Yetholms doubled to 1070 people.[5] In addition, Andrew Wauchope, the Laird of Niddrie, offered enterprising farmers land in the village to build a house for a feu lease of 19×19 years.[6] This lease involved an upfront fee, a fixed annual payment and a requirement that a house be built in the village. Obtaining a feu lease, and becoming a feuar, was sought after because it provided long-term land entitlements at a fixed cost. The farming plots outside the village were not feued and still needed to be rented from the Laird. The Scottish Parliament only abolished this feudal type of lease in the year 2000.

Andrew's father, John Thompson, was a feuar. The importance of this within the community is witnessed by the inscription on the gravestone of Andrew's sister Margaret, who died in 1770, and his brother Robert, who died in 1773, it declared 'Here lyeth the children of JOHN THOMSON feuer in Town Yetholm'.[7] This gravestone is one of the few surviving records of Andrew Thompson's family in the Yetholm villages. Other official documents show that John was a farmer-weaver, who sometimes employed additional weavers to make stockings, but we know little beyond this.[8] Specific details of the 18th century John Thompson family in Yetholm, other than those known from court documents to be described later, are few and fragmentary. Such gaps in early Scottish histories are common because births, deaths, marriages and property transactions were not officially recorded until 1855. Prior to this, Scottish churches kept family records only for those who paid, and most village people preferred to avoid the additional cost. Tracing the name 'Thompson' in Scotland is especially problematic. It is a common name with two spellings, Thompson and Thomson, which are used interchangeably within the same family, and even for the same person. This makes the reliable tracing of Thompson genealogies very challenging and highly prone to error.

Other Thom(p)son families lived in Yetholm at the time of John and Agnes Thompson and their three boys. There was William Thompson and Robert Thompson, both weavers. They were probably John's brothers, though there is no direct evidence of this. Andrew, Robert and John Thomson, and their families, were possibly relatives as well. It is entirely likely that Andrew Thompson was surrounded by a coterie of uncles, aunts and cousins in his formative Yetholm years.

Tucked away in the tranquil valley of the Cheviots, the villages of Town Yetholm and Kirk Yetholm managed to avoid most of the mid 18th century industrial and political disruptions, and the young Andrew Thompson would have led a comfortable rural existence assisting his father, attending school and participating in the usual boyhood pleasures. Education was taken more seriously in Scotland than across the border, and every child, independent of means, was expected to be literate and to be able to read the Bible. Although Yetholms' population grew steadily with the influx of new farmers and workers, the small village community would have provided a secure environment for the Thompson boys to grow up in. Today, the Yetholm villages are much smaller, but they still exude the rural charm and tranquillity that makes them a popular stopover for hikers walking the *St Cuthbert's Way*. In Andrew's youth, Yetholm had six merchant retailers as well as bakers, butchers, tailors and shoemakers, masons, millers, thatchers, weavers, wrights and smiths. The weavers were the largest profession with 35 workers.

Another third of the population were day-labourers, ploughmen and shepherds who depended on seasonal farm work.[9] All the cottages in the villages had roofs thatched in straw or heather, with typically two rooms; one for the family to eat and sleep in, and the other for their trade or business. The houses of the more prosperous families had a second floor. Most tradesmen in the village were also small subsistence farmers, keeping cows and workhorses in the barns behind their cottages with access to farmland close by.

Kirk Yetholm was the older but poorer of the two villages. It was distinct from Town Yetholm in that the Marquis of Tweeddale rented out most of its small cottages to rural worker families.[10] Kirk Yetholm was also the traditional place of settlement for gypsies in Scotland. They first came to Scotland in the 15th century and were referred to as 'Egyptians'. In 1570 King James V granted Royal protection to the gypsy leader Johnnie Faa. This was reversed in 1609 by King James VI who declared all gypsies to be vagabonds and thieves, and he ordered them to leave Scotland under threat of death. In any case, by 1700 many had settled in the village of Kirk Yetholm where they were accepted. The location also allowed a quick escape across the border or take refuge in the Cheviot valleys.[11] Most gypsies led a nomadic life, but wintered in Kirk Yetholm where they worked as tinkers, muggers and carters of coal. In 1790 about 50 gypsies resided in the village.[12]

In the 18th century most of Yetholms' prosperity was generated from the manufacture of stockings and textiles. However, being on the border meant that a good living could also be made smuggling goods to and from England. It is reputed that during this period at least a fifth of villagers were engaged in avoiding excise duties – the most lucrative being the trafficking of Scotch whisky into England and gin into Scotland. It is estimated that 20,000 litres of whisky were smuggled across the border annually.[13] Several excise officers lived in the area and their main function was to collect taxes on declared goods at the border. They were also expected to catch smugglers, but the small fines imposed failed to stem smuggling, and locals considered the excise laws unenforceable. Andrew Thompson claimed in later life that he had expected as a youth to become a Scottish excise officer, an aspiration inspired perhaps by his lifelong devotion to Scotland's national bard, Robert Burns, who had been an excise man. Paradoxically, Andrew Thompson was to become a rural police constable in Australia whose duties involved far more dangerous enforcement duties than catching smugglers.

The three Thompson boys, William, Walter and Andrew, were educated at one of the four small schools in the Yetholm villages. It is most likely that the boys attended the Town Yetholm parochial (parish) school administered by local landowners. The other local schools were private.[14] In 1792, prison reformer John Howard wrote that in the southern parts of Scotland it was 'very rare that you meet with any person that cannot both read and write. It is scandalous for any person not to be possessed of a Bible, which is always read in the parochial schools'.[15] Education in parish schools was principally in the traditional subjects of reading, writing and arithmetic, and attendance was encouraged but optional.

The Thompson boys were fortunate to have Mr George Story as their schoolmaster, an educated man very well regarded in Yetholm. He would have certainly had a strong influence on young Andrew and provided him with an additional pedagogical grounding and encouraged a love of books. The school fees depended on the subjects taught – reading, writing and arithmetic with the additional subjects of Latin, Greek, practical mathematics and geography.[16] Andrew appears to have remained at school until his mid-teens, and had, as a consequence, a better education than most local children. He maintained a lifelong interest in books, and as a bright God-fearing youth, his parents John and Agnes would have anticipated a promising future ahead.

In parallel with the school classes, all three Thompson boys were, from an early age, immersed in the family trade of weaving. In 1788, aged 15, Andrew left school to start a weaver's apprenticeship, most likely under the tutelage of his brother Walter. An apprentice spent 4 to 5½ years with the same master before being allowed to work independently or for any other master. Such apprenticeships were highly sought after because they ensured a good income for life. The weaving trade generated most of the paid work in Yetholm, with tenant farmers cleaning and scouring wool in their spare time, womenfolk doing the spinning, and trained weavers producing textiles and stockings on handlooms. The 35 weavers in the village represented the dominant workforce.[17] Their wooden looms each occupied a room in a typical cottage; the small looms for weaving stockings taking a quarter of the space of those used for textiles. Andrew would have spent long hours in his early teenage years sitting at looms weaving stockings and textiles. His father and brothers belonged to the Yetholm weavers' guild, and their banner proclaimed *Industria ditat* – industry enriches. Their banner also included a biblical reminder on the impermanency of life: 'Men's days are swifter than a weaver's shuttle'.[18] *Industria ditat* would remain a guiding principle throughout Andrew's life.

At a time when mechanisation was being rapidly adopted in the major weaving centres throughout Britain, most Scottish rural towns doggedly maintained traditional weaving practices. The introduction of the mechanised flying shuttle in 1733 and the carding machine in 1754 dramatically accelerated the productivity of industrial weaving. These inventions were followed by the spinning jenny in 1765, and in 1774 steam engines were first used to power factories. By 1780, steam engines, water frames, and canals linking major population centres, had made Britain the world leader in high-quality inexpensive textiles.

The industrial revolution propelled by cheap power and mechanical weaving brought great wealth to factory towns, but it devastated the textile manufacturers in rural areas where mills were powered by water. The inexpensive superior textiles made in large factories flooded the market and rural weavers were unable to compete on price or quality. A water-powered fulling mill had been in Yetholm since 1682 but this and the cottage weavers were no match for the new steam-powered factories.

As an apprentice weaver Andrew Thompson would have spent many hours at such a loom making stockings to be sold in his elder brothers' businesses.

However, as is often the case with major workplace disruptions, the demise of some business enterprises led to creation of others. Among the men who benefited from the upheavals created by industrialisation were the enterprising sons of John Thompson. Both William and Walter Thompson established their own textile making businesses in Yetholm and other towns to produce high-quality low-cost muslin cloth. William also started a cloth dyeing business. In 1786, at the age of 24, William married a local girl, Jean Young. Andrew later recalled that his father had wanted William to go into law, but both his brothers had decided to become textile merchants. With two friends, George Sweet and John Gillespie, William established the firm 'Thompson, Gillespie & Sweet' that specialised in the merchandising of muslin textiles, and they exported principally to France.[19]

Following the Seven Years War, the free trade agreement brokered between France and Britain in 1763 opened up the French market to inexpensive British textiles. This trade brought great wealth to British merchants but devastated the garment industry in France. It was in this continental market that the company 'Thompson, Gillespie & Sweet' invested heavily in the export of their high-quality muslin cloth. They would not have foreseen the French Revolution, or the devastating consequences it would have on their business. When the Revolution erupted in 1789, almost all trade into France stopped abruptly and many British trade businesses went bankrupt, including that of William Thompson.

In the summer of 1790, Andrew Thompson's tranquil life was about to change dramatically. For several years Andrew had worked as an apprentice weaver with his brother Walter and during this period was befriended by a journeyman weaver John Aitkin who was also in Walter's employ. Andrew and John resided in Walter's house, as did Eleanor Verdie, a young female servant working for William. Eleanor had become John Aitkin's girlfriend. In June 1790 Andrew suffered poor health and stopped his apprenticeship. He returned to school with the likely intention of pursuing his ambition to be an excise officer.[20] The nature of Andrew's illness is unknown but could have been an allergy, a respiratory problem or musculoskeletal condition – these illnesses were endemic among weavers. J. V. Byrnes suggests in his 1958 thesis on Andrew Thompson that this may have been the early stage of tuberculosis.[21]

Such a debilitating disease seems unlikely, however, considering the vigour and energy he would later exhibit in life.

On returning to school, Andrew moved to his brother William's house in Town Yetholm, where he slept in an adjacent building called a 'byhouse'. During this time John Aitkin had borrowed money from Andrew's mother and accumulated considerable debts. Moreover, he had also become lazy and reluctant to work.[22] This situation, and Andrew's association with John, were to have serious repercussions for their future lives.

A month later, on a cold autumnal day in 1790, we find Andrew Thompson incarcerated in prison in the neighbouring town of Jedburgh awaiting trial on a charge of theft. Stealing was not an uncommon crime in many Scottish border towns where there was widespread unemployment, but it was rare in Yetholm. Andrew, the educated local son of a respectable family in the community, had been accused of theft from his brother and from another local textile merchant. The reason stated in the charge for these crimes was not the usual one of "stealing food" and this, coupled with the prominence of his family and the lack of clear motives for the theft, raised great concern in the community. He was a popular lad with no history of boisterous or rebellious behaviour, and doubts were raised about the veracity of the charge. Nevertheless, the official charge sheets allege that he had committed the thefts with an accomplice, John Aitkin, who had subsequently escaped authorities and had been declared an Outlaw. Andrew alone was listed to stand trial for the thefts, and, considering the substantial value of the stolen goods, he had little hope of remission.

Andrew's future, and indeed his life, now hung in the balance.

Chapter 2

A MOST HEINOUS CRIME

I know very well how I shall be represented among the common people, it is even not unlikely that my name may go down to posterity, in the borders, as that of a hard-hearted unfeeling judge, but there is no help for it & better men have suffered more on account of their zeal for the public safety ... If no lad of fifteen ought to be transported for a capital offence, what will become of this country! And by what examples are young people to be deterred from the commission of crimes.[1]

For hundreds of years the Scottish town of Kelso held a large agricultural market in early August. It was known as St James Fair and was located on the south bank of the Tweed River opposite the grounds of Floors Castle, the traditional home of the Duke of Roxburghe. The Fair provided an important outlet for agricultural produce prior to the onset of winter. It was also a key venue for the weavers and textile makers in the district to display and sell their wares to clientele from all over Scotland and England.[2] Kelso was only eight miles from Yetholm, and merchants and farmers from that community regularly participated in the Fair. With increasing competition from industrial manufacturers in the south, the market also served to inform local textile weavers of the latest materials offered by English merchants, who also attended the Fair.

As established weavers in Yetholm, John Thompson and his family were regular participants in the St James Fair, and on 5 August 1790 they travelled by wagon to Kelso for a three-day round of exhibitions and trade. On this occasion their absence from Yetholm would have unexpected and far-reaching consequences for the family.

On the first evening of the Fair, the Yetholm house of William Thompson, John Thompson's eldest son, then 28 years old, was broken into and burgled. Two flintlock pistols, a gunpowder flask, lead shot, some indigo dye and a pound of tea were stolen. Then, two days later, on Saturday 7 August, the Yetholm shop of Walter Turner, another Yetholm merchant most likely attending the St

James Fair, was burgled. The bolts on Turner's shop window shutter were removed, and the bar between two glass panes broken to make it large enough to admit a man. A large haul of linen and wool cloth, valued at £10, was stolen.[3]

Initially there were no suspects for the burglaries, though it was reported that the weaver John Aitkin had left the village in haste on the following Monday.[4] His rushed departure looked suspicious to the shop owner Walter Turner, and he sought permission to search Aitkin's room. John Aitkin had worked for Walter Thompson, and he occupied a room in his master's house in Town Yetholm. With Walter Thompson's consent, they entered Aitkin's room and found a large, locked chest. After forcing the lid open with a metal bar, the chest revealed items that had been stolen from Turner and from Thompson.[5] Turner immediately reported the incident to the Yetholm constable, George Kerr. A search of neighbouring properties uncovered additional stolen items in the nearby village 'stackyard', and even more buried under cabbages recently planted by Andrew Thompson in his father's vegetable plot.[6]

For the law-abiding residents of Yetholm these thefts caused considerable alarm – burglary in Scotland was seen as a heinous crime. In fact, forced entry into a private dwelling was a capital offence in 18th century Scotland, though non-violent offenders were not always hanged. During this period the frequency of petty crime in Scotland was less than in England, and few people were sent to prison, reputably because of 'the shame and disgrace annexed to imprisonment' and the 'general sobriety of manners' Scottish parents and ministers instilled in the young. Prisons in rural Scotland usually served a custodial function for debtors defaulting on debts, or for serious criminals awaiting transportation.[7]

The Yetholm constable, urged on by the victims Walter Turner and William Thompson, sought to arrest the perpetrators of these break-ins as quickly as possible. The prime suspect John Aitkin had disappeared, presumably over the border into England, where it was unlikely that he would be caught because of slow and uncoordinated communication between local law authorities. He would, in due course, be branded as an Outlaw in Scotland and England and, if ever captured, he was liable to be hanged.

There were immediate suspicions that burglaries on this scale must have involved several people. Attention now turned to John

Aitkin's acquaintances in Yetholm and whether they might have helped him. It was well known that Andrew, William's youngest brother, had been a past associate of John Aitkin. They had worked together and for a time had shared lodgings. Understandably, there was a reluctance to point the finger at Andrew because of his age and his kinship to William – surely, he would not have stolen from his own brother! Nevertheless, constable Kerr could not ignore the fact that Andrew was an acquaintance of Aitkin, and that some of the stolen property had been buried in a vegetable plot that he had recently planted. The evidence against Andrew seemed compelling, and Kerr had no choice but to charge him as an accomplice to the burglary and two robberies.

Nothing is known of how William, or his parents, reacted to this, but the subsequent court proceedings reveal that the shopkeeper Walter Turner had little sympathy for Andrew's plight. It is possible that the Turners, who were business competitors with the Thompsons, were not inclined to help them get off this 'hook' too easily – the Thompson's demise in the village might have been to their advantage. Of course, Andrew's past association with Aitkin contributed to the suspicion that he had some knowledge of the theft, if not a direct involvement. On the other hand, the fact that Andrew had not attempted to flee Yetholm weakened the accusation of his full participation in the crime, or at least suggested his personal involvement was too small to warrant charges.

Two weeks after the burglaries, on Tuesday 24 August 1790, constable George Kerr and his servant Abraham Hogg, accompanied by Walter Turner, took Andrew Thompson to the sheriff in Jedburgh, a larger border town some 14 miles to the northwest. It is unknown if any of the Thompson family accompanied Andrew but since he was still a juvenile it is probable his father was present for the committal. According to a declaration Andrew made to sheriff Thomas Usher the next day, Walter Turner had asked him on the way to Jedburgh 'to tell him all he knew about his goods which had been stolen'. He had replied that 'when he came before a Judge he would tell all he knew by which he meant no more than that'. Andrew also told Turner that when he last saw John Aitkin on Monday, he left Yetholm in a westerly direction and if Turner went in that direction 'he might possibly come up with him'. Following Andrew's statement, the sheriff drew up a charge sheet for the case of 'Walter Turner Merchant in Yetholm against John Thomson Indweller there and his family'. Since Andrew was not yet an adult, his father was named in his place. The wording of the charge sheet would have been of great concern and shame to the proud Thompson family.[8]

During the sheriff's interrogation, Andrew had declared that he knew John Aitkin as a journeyman weaver working for his brother Walter, and that Aitkin had left 'last Monday' (in fact, it was Monday 9 August). Andrew stated that he had worked 'a little in the same place with Aitkin' until nine or ten weeks ago when he returned to school. He claimed that the reason Aitkin had left suddenly was to avoid repaying a debt to Andrew's mother after he 'had turned idle and refused to work'. When Aitkin left Yetholm, Andrew had accompanied him as far as Cavertown Edge near Kelso and as they said goodbye, Aitkin told him he was going to Glasgow, but he did not go in that direction. Andrew informed the sheriff that 'they had no conversation on the road together with regard to Walter Turners Shop having been broke open nor at any time before that he remembers' and that he 'never had any particular conversation on that Subject with John Rae or any other person'.[9] He also stated that his brother William carried a pair of pistols when he travelled with goods for sale, and had told him that these:

> Pistols with some powder in a horn and some had some [*sic*] Indigo and Tea were stolen out of his house on Saint James's fair night the house having been that night broke into but he never heard that his Brother found out who was guilty of that theft[10]

Andrew declared that when he returned from 'setting away John Aitkin he heard that Walter Turner had been making a search and had found part of his goods in a Chest'. He confirmed that he had once slept in the same room as John Aitkin in his brother Walter's house 'but not for six weeks or two months' before Aitkin went away. Since then, he had mostly slept by himself in his brother William's house. Andrew further declared that two weeks ago he had planted some cabbage plants in land rented by his father close to Yetholm, and that there were other cabbage plants in that enclosure planted by his father five weeks earlier. Asked about the cabbages in his father's plot, Andrew stated that he did

> not remember to have seen the Cabbages he planted from the time he set them till Monday last in the forenoon when he observed many of them scarted up as if with a harl [rake/scraper] and some

beans pulled up by the root which the Declarant supposed was done by some malicious person to prevent their growth that he went alone to the park and saw nobody there[11]

After completing his statement Andrew was formally charged and committed to the Jedburgh Tolbooth gaol on 25 August 1790. The charge was to be heard before an Assize Court authorised to administer the full force of Scottish criminal law.

The ruins of the 12th century Jedburgh Abbey viewed from the southeast. The gaol where Andrew Thompson was imprisoned is shown in the right foreground.

In 18th century Scotland long-term imprisonment for petty crimes was rare, and few facilities existed for prolonged incarceration. Serious crimes, such as murder and treason, almost always incurred the death penalty – lawbreakers convicted of minor property or debtor crimes were usually given short stints in temporary lockups. This changed in the 1750s when heightened political concerns about social disruption brought in new laws to discourage theft. The British Parliament reclassified many petty crimes to be capital offences. They included burglary, highway robbery, housebreaking, picking pockets above one shilling, shoplifting above five shillings, stealing above 40 shillings, maiming or stealing a cow, horse or sheep, or breaking into a house or church.[12] The recommended punishment for these crimes was now the same as that for murder – death by hanging.

The Scottish penal code listed fewer capital offences than England. Even so, housebreaking was considered serious regardless of the value of items stolen, though the severity of the punishment could be restricted prior to the trial. Where possible Scottish Judges resisted sending minor criminals to the gallows and used several ploys – just as the English judiciary applied 'pious perjury' – to limit capital punishment. Royal Pardons were also used to commute a capital punishment imposed by a Judge. In the 1780s 79 offenders were executed in Scotland, of whom 73 had been convicted of property crime. The prospects for the young Andrew Thompson were truly grim if he was found guilty.[13]

Prisons in 18th century Britain were old decrepit buildings. In Scotland the prisons and courts were located mostly in tolbooths, which were the main public buildings in towns and burghs. In his 1792 edition of *The State of the Prisons in England and Wales* prison reformer John Howard was also critical of Scottish prisons.

> The following defects may be remarked in the prisons in Scotland. They have no courts belonging to them; generally want water and sewers; – are not clean; – they are not visited by the magistrates; – too little attention is paid to the separation of the sexes; – the keepers are allowed licences for the sale of the most pernicious liquors; the consequence of which is, that the county allowance being paid in money to the prisoners, they generally spend it in whiskey instead of bread. We do not think it possible, that a nation can attain to improvement in science, to refinement of taste, and in manners, without, at the same time, acquiring a refinement in their ideas of justice, and feelings of humanity.[14]

The Jedburgh prison would have been similar to those inspected by Howard, and the young Andrew Thompson was about to be exposed to the harsh miserable existence of a less-privileged felon. The two-storey Jedburgh gaol was, however, relatively new and located south of Jedburgh Abbey next to the bridge on the other side of the Jed Water River.

Jedburgh was a border town with a long and colourful history. Mary Stuart, Queen of Scotland, stayed there during a serious illness in 1566. Years later in 1587 when she was about to be executed by Queen Elizabeth I of England, Mary is reported to have said 'Would that I had died in Jedburgh'.[15] Another catholic royal, Prince Charles

Stuart, bivouacked his army in Jedburgh *en route* to a military defeat by England in 1745. Jedburgh gained a reputation for rough treatment of criminals and 'Jeddart Justice' referred to the practice of hanging someone first and trying them later. This expression took root in 1608 when Lord Home executed some prisoners without trial during a period when cross-border raids by individual clans were rife.[16]

On 31 August, five days after Andrew's arrest, the King's Advocate Norris wrote the prosecution indictment for Thompson and Aitkin to appear before the Jedburgh Autumn Circuit Court. The indictment opens:

> .... Andrew Thomson sometime weaver in Yetholm or Town Yetholm (son of John Thomson – Residenter there) present Prisoner in the Tolbooth of Jedburgh, and upon John Aitkin sometime weaver in Yetholm or Town Yetholm aforesaid. That Albeit by the law of God, and by the laws of this and every other well governed Realm. Theft, especially when repeated acts of Theft committed, and when such acts of Thefts or any of them have been committed under cloud of night, and more especially when perpetrated by breaking into houses or Shops under cloud of night, and also Reset of Theft are crimes of an heinous nature and severely punishable yet true it is and of verily. That the said Andrew Thomson & John Aitkin are both and each or one or other of them guilty actors or art and part of both or one or other of the foresaid crimes aggravated as aforesaid.[17]

This nine-page document states that on 5 and 6 August 1790 Andrew Thompson and John Aitkin did 'feloniously and violently' break into the house of William Thompson and stole 'a pair of Pistols, a Powder Flask, some Powder & Shot, a parcel of Indigo and about a pound of Tea'. The pistols and powder flask were later found among hidden goods that could be connected to Andrew Thompson or John Aitkin. One, or both of them were accused of stealing the items, and that the recovered items would be used in evidence against them.[18]

Additionally, Andrew Thompson and John Aitkin did 'violently invade and forcibly break into the house or Shop of Walter Turner Merchant or Shopkeeper' by removing a bolt fastening the window shutter, breaking out two glass panes and removing the bar of wood between to make the hole large enough to admit a man and 'theftously steal and carry away sundry pieces of cut and uncut

Linnen and Woolen Goods to a considerable amount'.[19]

List of Articles stolen from Walter Turner[20]

	per yard
60¼ yards of Flannell	1s
28¾ yards Tweed plaid	10d
24 yards Red & white Striped worsted stuff	1s 3d
16¼ yards blue checkered	1s
11½ yards light blue stuff	2s 2d
7⅞ yards light blue & white Duffell	2s 4d
9 yards Plaiding	1s ½d
3 yards ditto	9½d
4 yards Linnen	1s 1½d
2¼ yards Linnen	1s 1½d
1⅛ yard grey duffle	2s
2½ yards Striped Linnen	1s 1½d
¾ yard blue Bays	1s 4d
1½ yard Stripped woollen	1s 1d
1 yard blew check ditto	1s 1d
1 yard ditto	1s 2d
⅞ yard ditto	1s
1¾ yard Brown Cloth	2s 6d

The total value of these articles alone, not including the items stolen from William Thompson, was £10 6s (£1520 in today's currency). At a time when the value threshold between a petty and a capital offence was £2, this was a crime liable to punishment by hanging. The various stolen articles were found partly concealed in straw in a stackyard at one end of Yetholm and 'the remainder in a hole dug for that purpose in a park possessed by John Thomson'. Parts of these goods were later removed to a chest in John Aitkin's room where they were found and identified to be the stolen property of Walter Turner. A sack containing another part of the stolen goods was found lying in or near the land rented by Andrew's father, John Thompson. All recovered goods were to be used in evidence against Thompson and Aitkin.[21]

Advocate Norris also wrote in his document of 31 August 1790 about the theft by Thompson and Aitkin (referred to in full as 'Criminal Letters, His Majesty's Advocate against Thompson & Aitkin, Jedburgh Autumn 1790') that:

> John Aitkin conscious of his guilt in the premises and in order to avoid detection & punishment did fly for the same and abscond and secrete himself from justice; and the said Andrew Thomson having been apprehended and carried before Thomas Usher Sheriff – Substitute of Roxburghshire did emit and sign a

> Declaration relative to the premises which Declaration is to be used in evidence against him ...
>
> ... the said Andrew Thomson & John Aitkin or one or other of them are guilty actors or art and part of Stealing or of Resetting or receiving the same – knowing them to have been stolen; all which or part thereof being found proven by the verdict of an Assize before our Lord Justice General, Lord Justice Clerk, and Lords Commissioners of Justiciary in a Circuit Court of Justiciary to be holden by them or any one or more of their number within the Tolbooth or Criminal Court house of Jedburgh upon the Twentieth day of September next the said Andrew Thomson and John Aitkin ought to be punished with the pains of law to deter others from committing the like crimes in all time coming.[22]

In effect, the order stipulates that if Thompson or Aitkin fail to surrender to the court by 20 September in readiness for the next sitting of the Assize Court that they would be declared rebels. Their entire possessions would then be confiscated, and everything would be done to have them prosecuted – the most likely sentence being death by hanging.

A document prepared on 8 and 9 September by the Advocate's messenger, Robert Shortreed, states that on 4 September he had personally presented the charges to Andrew Thompson in the Jedburgh gaol, along with the names of witnesses to be called to the Assize, and the 45 people that were potential jurors at the trial. A copy of this document was also left with Aitkin's girlfriend, Eleanor Verdie, servant to William Thompson. Shortreed reported that an open proclamation was made at the Jedburgh marketplace announcing the full criminal charges against Andrew Thompson and John Aitkin.[23] A fine of 100 Merks Scots (£5 7s or £760 in today's currency) was to be imposed on any of the twenty Yetholm witnesses, including Andrew's brother William, if they did not appear, as requested, at the Assize trial on 21 September 1790.[24]

The Jedburgh court indictment of 31 August 1790 is the sole surviving document detailing the case against Thompson and Aitkin prior to the quarter session of the Assize Court. It fails to stipulate where Andrew was prior to his Jedburgh trial; information that would be useful in understanding his relationships with his brothers William and Walter. We know that he appeared at the Assize Court on 21 September but there is much conjecture on his whereabouts in the ten days prior to the trial. Considering the seriousness of the charges against him, one might have expected Andrew to be incarcerated in the Jedburgh Tolbooth gaol over that period. However, the written requirement that he be at the Jedburgh prison on 20 September implies that he was released prior to the Assize trial. Moreover, in a deathbed statement Thompson later claimed he went to the English town of Workington at this time.

This statement, recorded by his clerk John Howe on 4 October 1810 reads in part:

> ... that he once went to see his brother after his failure, but he avoided him. That Mr. Thompson at that time, from his youthful indiscretion, was not looked upon by his friends, and he then resided at Workington, in the north of England. ... He believed Mr. Thompson was intended for the excise, till he made a breach in his conduct, after which time he was looked upon as an outcast goat, and went to Workington as above. He then corresponded from thence with his father and mother, though only very coolly on their side.[25]

This dictated statement refers to Andrew's interactions with his family and friends at the time of the trial. Together with the court records, this statement is revealing because it alludes to Thompson's relationship with his brothers, and it helps explain his estrangement with the family in later years.

There are some critical gaps in our knowledge of Andrew's trial and prosecution. For example: was he granted bail prior to his trial; if so, who paid for the bail; where did he go; if he went to Workington, why would he travel so far and who did he see? It is 80 miles to Workington and a return trip by coach or horseback would have taken at least 4 days. In his 1958 thesis *An outcast goat or the life and times of Andrew Thompson,* J. V. Byrnes concluded from Thompson's deathbed statement that he went to Workington *following* his sentencing on 21 September. This seems highly unlikely, as it required Andrew to be granted a release to go to England after being sentenced to 14 years transportation 'Beyond the Seas' in Scotland.[26] The court papers state that Andrew should be detained 'in the Tolbooth of Jedburgh till delivered over for Transportation', so such a release would have been nigh on impossible.[27]

If indeed Andrew did manage to get to Workington at some stage, it could only have happened if he had been released around 10 September, with friends or parents paying the bail bond. That he would have then travelled to Workington immediately is questionable; he might have gone to Yetholm and sought the forgiveness of his family, and that William and the family may have refused to see him. Mortified at what he had done, Andrew sought solace in Workington where he probably had relatives or friends in the weaving business.

When the 17-year-old Andrew finally confronted the full Assize Court bench on 21 September, it would have been a truly distressing experience for a young man alone in the dock. The shame of the charges was magnified because he was a member of a respectable family, and he had stolen from his own kin. Yetholm villagers would have been horrified if this had been the behaviour of a member of a Gypsy family, but for a lad who had been given every opportunity, it was deeply disturbing. Nevertheless, Andrew had returned to the Jedburgh Tolbooth gaol on Monday 20 September dreading his Court appearance the next day. If he had travelled to Workington, he may have contemplated skipping bail in England, but he would have baulked at the added shame this would have brought on his family. Andrew faced the charges knowing the resulting sentence may be harsh because of the high value of goods stolen – a capital sentence might automatically apply unless he pleaded guilty.

Andrew would have been well informed that the crime of housebreaking accounted for over half the executions in Scotland, though this was rarely applied if the defendant had no previous convictions and pleaded guilty. In addition, a Scot charged with a capital crime could petition the court prior to the jury being sworn in. In such cases the court would hear the charges before the defence submitted a petition for the consideration of the Advocate Depute (Crown Prosecutor). If the Prosecutor consented to the petition, it mostly resulted in the accused being banished from Scotland or transported overseas. Juries were usually reluctant to convict a juvenile for a major property offence if it resulted in a death sentence. This bargaining process allowed judicial discretion, but it guaranteed that a significant punishment was enforced.[28]

Various court documents show that Andrew Thompson appeared before the Jedburgh Assize Court on Tuesday 21 September 1790. Since the co-plaintiff John Aitkin had not been found, Andrew faced the charges alone. He looked young for his age and in the court report he was described as a 'young boy between 15 and 16 years of age'.[29] The Judge for the Autumn Circuit Court in Jedburgh was Lord Hailes (Sir David Dalrymple). Judge Hailes had a reputation for fairness, and because of Andrew's age, his family expected humane treatment. The courtroom was packed with 25 jurors and 20 witnesses. Among the faces familiar to Andrew were his parents and the 17 witnesses from Yetholm. They included his brother William, Walter Turner, William's apprentice William McDougal, fellow weaver John Rae, John Aitkin's girlfriend Eleanor Verdie and the Yetholm constable George Kerr.[30]

After the charges were read, Andrew was required to plea 'guilty' or 'not guilty' to the burglaries. An excerpt of the court transcript shows the signature of Andrew Thompson on the guilty plea:

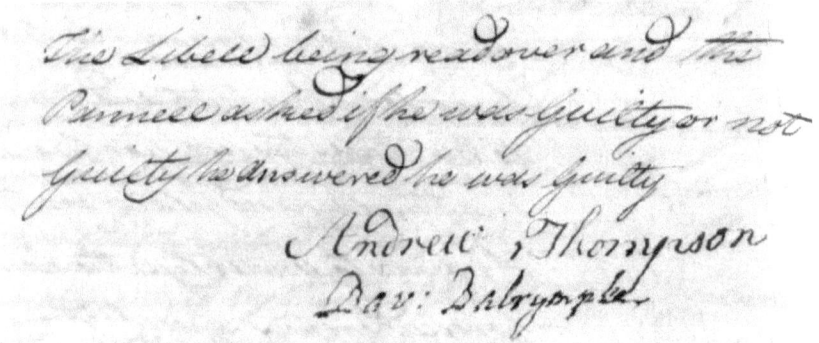

It reads: The Libell being read over and the Pannell asked if he was Guilty or not Guilty he answered he was Guilty   [signed] Andrew Thompson   Dav. Dalrymple[31]

The word 'Pannell' (currently spelt panel or panell) is the Scottish judicial term for defendant. Because of Andrew's guilty plea, no witnesses were called. The Advocate Depute adjourned briefly to consider the sentence the prosecution requested of the court. He declared that on account of the accused's age, 'his former good character and some other circumstances' he would restrict the 'libell' – that is, the charges or the sentence – applicable to these crimes 'to an arbitrary punishment'.[32] This permitted the court to impose a fine, punishment, imprisonment, banishment or transportation.[33] After this declaration, the proceedings read:

> The Lord Hailes having considered the libell against the Pannell Finds the same relevant to inferr an Arbitrary Punishment. But allows the Pannell to prove all facts and circumstances lending to

alleviate his Guilt and Remitts the Pannell with the libell as found relevant to the knowledge of an assize.[34]

Judge Lord Hailes then asked the jury to retire to consider the charges and an appropriate punishment for a first offender. The jury composed of 15 men, 10 of them merchants, announced:

> having considered the Criminal libell raised & pursued at the instance of his Majesty's Advocate for his Majesty's interests against Andrew Thomson Pannell the Interlocutor of relevancy pronounced thereon by the Court and the Panell's judicial confession. They all in one Voice Find the said Andrew Thomson Guilty of the Crimes libelled.[35]

On hearing the jury's verdict, Lord Hailes adjourned the court until the next morning. Andrew may have slept better that night knowing that the Judge was reputed to be a humane man 'at a time when the criminal bench was disgraced by opposite qualities'.[36] The next morning Lord Hailes announced the sentence.

> In respect of the Verdict returned against Andrew Thomson Pannell and in terms of an act passed in the Twenty fifth year of the Reign of his present Majesty entitled an act for the more effectual Transportation of Felons and other offenders in Scotland The Lord Hailes Decerns and Adjudges the said **Andrew Thomson Pannell to be Transported beyond Seas** to such place as his Majesty with advice of his Privy Council has appointed or shall appoint and that **for the space of Fourteen years** with Certification to him that if after being so Transported he shall be found at large in any part of Great Britain during the foresaid space without some lawful Cause, and being thereof lawfully convicted he shall suffer death and Grants warrant for detaining him in the Tolbooth of Jedburgh till delivered over for Transportation.[37]

Andrew and his parents were completely shocked by the sentence – transportation for 14 years was an unexpectedly harsh punishment to be imposed on a 17-year-old youth with no previous offences. The Thompson family had every reason to be distressed at the outcome of the trial, as important questions remained unanswered about the extent of Andrew's involvement in the burglary. After all, he had only submitted a guilty plea on the advice of the council to avoid the possibility of a death sentence. What possible motives did he have to steal, and why would he steal from an elder brother he looked up to? Most people in Yetholm believed John Aitkin had planned the burglary and Andrew had been duped into accompanying him. Furthermore, why would Andrew have helped

Aitkin escape and not absconded himself? Many perplexing aspects of the burglary had not been explored at all in the court proceedings, and in the absence of Aitkin at the trial appeared to place the entire blame for the burglary on the juvenile accomplice.

Andrew's involvement at all in such an act remains one of the most perplexing aspects of the burglary. He was part of a reasonably well-off family, so the thefts were unlikely to benefit him financially. However, the sale of the stolen goods would have motivated Aitkin who was heavily in debt. There is the possibility, of course, that Andrew had incurred debts to Aitkin, though there is no evidence of this. It is also conceivable that Eleanor Verdie, Aitkin's friend and a co-resident in his brother's house, had played some part in this crime. There seems little doubt that Aitkin had planned the robberies and that Thompson had been persuaded to cooperate. So even if Andrew had only been involved in hiding the goods, he was guilty as an accomplice. John Byrnes writes that Andrew's 'astonishing energy, thwarted by enforced idleness, was probably the main reason for his association with Aitkin'.[38] It is unlikely that we will ever know the full story.

The uncertainties surrounding the burglary strengthened the resolve of Andrew's parents to challenge the court verdict and the harshness of the sentence. They had braced themselves for a short prison sentence but not for him to be transported to a distant land for fourteen years. This seemed a ridiculous punishment for a young lad who had never had a previous brush with the law. Their anger intensified when the burglary trial was published in the widely circulated *The Scots Magazine*.[39] This publicity caused many in the border towns who knew the Thompson family to denounce Lord Hailes as a hard-hearted unfeeling person.

The first ships to take British convicts to New South Wales had not included Scottish prisoners. However, within months of his sentence, Andrew was told that he was to be transported on the *Pitt* that would soon sail for New South Wales. Immediately on hearing this news, Andrew's parents petitioned the local Laird, Andrew Wauchope of Niddrie, to appeal for mercy on their behalf. In May 1791 this action led to a petition by the Duke of Buccleuch to the Home Office Secretary asking for the King's mercy. The parents sought a reduced sentence for their son, and possibly a full pardon.

No reply had been received by July 1791 when the *Pitt* departed Portsmouth with Andrew on board.[40]

But the Thompson family persisted and in October the local MP for Roxburghshire, Sir George Douglas, made another plea for the King's mercy. When there was no response to either plea, the family once again petitioned the Laird of Niddrie to write to Judge Lord Hailes requesting clemency. The Judge's reply on 4 December 1791 was unfavourable.

> It may be remembered how happy Andrew Thompson and his parents were when I consented to relieve him from the imminent hazard of capital punishment and when I made his transportation for a term of years and not for life, and yet all this is forgotten and their wish now is to diminish a punishment already small enough for the offence; if no lad of fifteen ought to be transported for a capital offence, what will become of this country! And by what examples are young people to be deterred from the commission of crimes![41]

Lord Hailes regretted that the Thompsons had given the Laird 'so much trouble' and he pitied these 'poor people'. He understood that his reputation among the commoners of the border villages might go down in posterity 'as that of a hard-hearted unfeeling judge' but he said he could bear this as 'better men' had suffered more in order to keep the public safe. Andrew's sentence was to set as an example to deter others.

John and Agnes Thompson had claimed in their petition to the Laird that Andrew's case had not been represented properly. Lord Hailes responded in the same letter to the Laird of Niddrie that

> I hear that the Petitions have some time or other interested the Duke of Buccleugh & the Duke of Rokesburgh [Roxburghe] in their favour, they are worthy & honourable men, & I presume that they act upon grounds that satisfy themselves. I hope, however, that the case has been truly represented to them. I have learnt by another channel that Thompson is said to have been convicted of resetting of stolen goods & that by the evidence of an accomplice. But he seems indicted for a crime of shop-breaking & he pleaded guilty, so, no witness was examined in his cause. It was a bold thing thus to assert in contradiction to the Reason of Court.
>
> I have been told that Andrew Thompson can give an account of a gang of thieves with which he was intimately acquainted, which by the way, removes every plea arising from his good character if he soon gave such intimation as may lead to the conviction or punishment of the gang it is possible that the Kings Advocate may

> be induced to apply for some mitigation of his sentence. But this is a matter quite out of my line of examining(?) & on which I cannot interfere at all.[42]

This suggests that if Andrew had revealed the names and details of the gang members involved in the burglary, there was a chance of a reduced sentence. Since there was no indication of anyone but Thompson and Aitkin being involved, this was an empty gesture. Lord Hailes clearly considered this now to be a matter for the King's Advocate and, in any case, the defendant was already aboard a convict transport ship sailing to the other end of the world. Best let sleeping dogs lie!

It was not until 7 February 1792, when Andrew Thompson was a week away from disembarking in Sydney Cove, that the Duke of Roxburghe received the response from the Home Office Secretary, Henry Dundas.

> On an application made on behalf of Andrew Thompson in May last, and on another made in his behalf by the Duke of Roxburgh in October two several References of Thompson's Case were sent to the Lord Justice Clerk, and I am sorry to inform you that from the Reports made by his Lordship on both Occasions, it appears that the Circumstances of Thompson's Case were of so unfavourable a nature that I did not then, nor should I now think myself justified, in recommending him to the King as a fit Object of His Majesty's Mercy.[43]

Andrew's fate as a transportee was now sealed, and there would be no further pleas to reconsider his case – from now on he was on his own. However, it is relevant to note here that Henry Dundas' reply is hardly surprising. As a Scottish Tory member of the British Parliament, he had the reputation of never showing mercy to the underprivileged, and it is justly claimed that he had been single-handedly responsible for delaying the abolition of the British slave trade from 1792 to 1807.[44] It is a cruel twist of fate that Andrew Thompson's appeal for mercy was to be decided by this man – in 1806 Dundas was the last person in Britain to be ever impeached from public office for the misappropriation of public money. Although acquitted, he never held public office again.

The transportation sentence had been devastating for Andrew's parents, not only because they believed he had been badly advised to plead guilty in the trial, but they, and others, were convinced that the sentence was far too harsh for a young accomplice to an adult burglar who was not tried. Andrew's father John Thompson was by then aged 64 and his wife Agnes was 58. This was a time when people rarely lived beyond 60 years, so there was little prospect they would ever see Andrew again. The tyranny of long distances and slow communication would compound their anguish – no record has survived of Andrew ever being in contact with his parents again. One hopes that this was not the case, considering the affection Andrew held for his mother and the likelihood that he would try to tell his parents of his experiences in the colony. On the other hand, as his life story will reveal, the severity of the family's shame was considerable and there was a clear lack of forgiveness on the part of his brothers – the Thompson family may well have cast Andrew completely adrift.

The loss of their youngest son was not all the Thompson parents had to endure. Shortly after Andrew's trial, his elder brother William, his wife, children, servants and tenants received threats from the local weaver John Rae, his wife Isobel Wright and their dependants. William Thompson sued Rae and the others in December 1790 for threatening his family with violence. The outcome of this action was that three Yetholm locals, Surgeon John Walker, William Jordan and weaver Robert Cairns were appointed as executors and cautioners to guarantee that William Thompson and his family would not be molested by John Rae and his wife. Any non-conformances would incur a penalty of 400 Merks Scots.[45]

Regrettably, the court papers do not reveal the reasons why Rae had threatened the Thompsons, and we are left to speculate on what these might have been. There is considerable documentary evidence that in later life Andrew displayed great skill in engaging with people, with an 'even Tenor of his Way and acquitted himself with mildness, moderation and wisdom'. [46] He was respected for his approachability, honesty and fairness in dealing with everyone. It seems likely therefore that his personality and demeanour as a youngster was not dissimilar, and that many of his friends in the Border Towns were appalled at his treatment and Lord Hailes' sentence. As one of the accusers, his brother William may well have been pilloried in the district. For many in this close village community this theft was considered a 'family matter' and should have been dealt with as such – why would William let his own brother be convicted, and then transported? Surely John Aitkin, the adult instigator of this theft, should have been assigned the bulk of the guilt, and Andrew, a gullible juvenile accomplice, severely reprimanded and fined. The Thompsons ought to have been sorted this out financially with the plaintiff Walter Turner – this is what families do!

Of course, there may have been quite separate reasons why John Rae threatened William Thompson. William's firm 'Thompson, Gillespie & Sweet' exported muslin to France, with local weavers supplying the cloth on commission. The French Revolution sent many of the British textile merchants into bankruptcy and William's firm incurred serious financial losses. Their share value plummeted from £1 to only 3s 6d.[47] It is entirely possible that John Rae supplied muslin to Thompson's company and had lost his money and livelihood as a consequence. The collapse of the company would have affected other businesses in Yetholm, and this would have been highly embarrassing for the Thompson family. Sometime after the 1791 losses, William Thompson, his wife Jean and their two children left the village and moved to Glasgow.

Chapter 3

BEYOND THE SEAS

In selecting the convicts who compose the present embarkation care has been taken that no persons but such as are likely to be useful in the settlement will now be sent out.[1]

In May 1791 forty-six convicts were selected to be the first Scottish prisoners transported to New South Wales. Andrew Thompson and eight others from Jedburgh gaol were among them.[2] The notification that they were to be sent to the other side of the world would have shocked them, as it was generally believed that Caledonian authorities opposed the Botany Bay Scheme. It is likely that Andrew promptly sent a letter to his parents telling them of his imminent fate and was asked by illiterate transportees to help them do the same.

The British government had instituted the Botany Bay Scheme for the transportation of prisoners to New South Wales in 1786 in an attempt to reduce the riots in overcrowded prisons. There had been an avalanche of petty crimes in the mid 18th century due to massive unemployment from major industrial and agrarian changes. Many rural labourers had moved to industrialised towns in search of work, but few had the required skills and the consequent unemployment and poverty led to a proliferation in property crimes. Communities across Britain demanded harsher penalties for petty felons. Until 1775 convicts were routinely transported to the American colonies where they were sold as indentured servants. The American Revolutionary War put an end to this lucrative trade, and within a decade, British gaols overflowed with convicts awaiting transportation to an overseas' destination.

In August 1786, after years of debate and indecision, the British government announced that Botany Bay in New South Wales would be the site of a new penal colony. Nine months later, on 13 May 1787, a flotilla of eleven small ships, known as the First Fleet, transported 750 English convicts from Portsmouth to Botany Bay.

After an eight-month voyage across largely uncharted seas, the ships arrived in Sydney Cove in Port Jackson, and on 26 January 1788 Commodore Arthur Phillip was proclaimed Governor of the New South Wales colony. The establishment of a colony on the tranquil shores of Sydney Cove would ultimately be successful but it had a very difficult beginning. The soil around the Cove was poor and the settlement suffered from severe food shortages. Better farmland was eventually discovered inland close to a river flowing into Port Jackson and farms there became the colony's first agricultural success. But food shortages persisted for years, during which time the colony relied on provisions being shipped from England.

Portrait of Captain Arthur Phillip painted prior to the departure of the First Fleet from Portsmouth. He became the first Governor of New South Wales (1788-1792).

Despite the setbacks Phillip remained optimistic that the colony would one day become self-sufficient. More fertile land had been discovered in the western regions close to a large river that he had named after Lord Hawkesbury. Phillip noted that large merchant ships could easily navigate this 'noble' river.[3] He told the Home Office that he would defer settlement at the Hawkesbury until he received a small boat and men with better farming knowledge.

> The river Hawkesbury will, I make no doubt, offer some desirable situations, and the great advantages of a navigable river are obvious; but before a settlement can be made there proper people to conduct it must be found, and we must be better acquainted with the country. Settlers may be sent there hereafter, but then we must have small craft to keep up communication.[4]

This letter to the Home Office was sent just three months after Andrew Thompson had been sentenced to 14 years transportation. Arthur Phillip also requested they send him 'proper people ... acquainted with the country'. Raised in rural Scotland, Andrew certainly fitted the bill and as time will tell, he would eventually become the largest grain grower in the Hawkesbury district and the colony.

Until the mid-19th century prisoners awaiting transportation to New South Wales were routinely gaoled in decommissioned naval ships, called 'prison hulks', moored in London, Portsmouth and Plymouth harbours. By early 1791 some Scottish convicts had already been transferred to the *Dunkirk* hulk in Plymouth and to the *Lion* hulk in Portsmouth, in readiness for transportation. The majority of these convicts were semi-skilled young men from the larger Scottish towns. And, importantly, most were literate, which was not the case for the majority of English convicts.

Although he read widely, it is possible that Andrew Thompson knew nothing about the colony he was about to be sent to. In 1787 he may have read in Scottish newspapers about convict ships sailing to Botany Bay, and perhaps of the establishment of a convict prison colony at Sydney Cove.[5] Newspaper articles in 1789 and 1790 often gave quite optimistic accounts of progress in the penal colony. In March 1790, on Governor Phillip's orders, Philip Gidley King sailed from Sydney Cove to London to convince the government that the colony was in the midst of a serious food shortage. King arrived in December 1790 and told the Home Office Secretary that provisions were so scarce in the colony that famine was imminent. The seriousness of his report appeared in *The Chester Chronicle*: 'At Botany Bay there prevails a sense of the most perfect equality, since hunger, like the grave, levels all distinctions'.[6] Heated debates in Parliament followed with statements condemning the sending of 'more convicts, or rather victims, to such a place'. Transportation was branded as 'repugnant to humanity and expedience'. MPs told the Parliament that Sydney Cove was 'under the apprehension of famine' and they 'were as much cut off from communication with mankind, as if they were stationed in the Moon'.[7]

Other articles about the inappropriateness of convict transportation appeared in newspapers. On 2 February 1791, *The Evening Mail* demanded that the laws in Britain be better regulated:

'Many criminals are transported for a first offence, and several whole cases seemed to be of a very trivial nature, are transported to Botany Bay for life'. The article highlighted the class bias in sentences by citing the case of two well-off women, 'who were not driven by want to temptation, and yet were sentenced to only 14 days imprisonment'.[8] It declared that there was apparently no threat of being transported if you had money or influence.

While debates raged in the House of Commons about the viability of the colony, the shipment of convicts continued unabated. In early 1791 over 2000 convicts were loaded onto the eleven ships comprising the Third Fleet. Although this fleet departed before news of the Second Fleet's dreadful mortality rate had been received in England, the conditions for convicts on these ships were much improved. At this time Andrew Thompson was still being held in Jedburgh gaol but he may have heard about the food shortages in the colony. Despite this, he and other prisoners in old rural gaols may have seen transportation to a new land as being better than their current hardship. Indeed, from the start of the Botany Bay Scheme in 1786, many prisoners were convinced that anything was preferred to lingering for years in dark, filthy gaols or in hulks with poor food and sanitary conditions. An article published in *The Public Advertiser* on 5 January 1791 gives some insight into these views when 24 Bristol convicts arrived in Exeter *en route* to ships in Plymouth harbour destined for Botany Bay.

> On Thursday evening last arrived here, under the care of the Gaoler of Bristol, on their way to Plymouth, to be shipped for Botany Bay, twenty-two convicts, in an open waggon, and two who are stiled gentlemen convicts, in a tilted cart. They had each of them an iron collar, and an iron chain run through a ring in each collar, which fastened them all together; the next morning, at eight o'clock, they set off again in the same manner, and though there was a violent storm of wind, hail, and rain, they were singing and hallowing as they passed through the streets, with great glee and jollity. Whilst these convicts were passing the streets of Exeter in the manner above mentioned, a woman, struck with their hardened conduct, called out to them, "Ah you wretched creatures, how can you be so merry in your dreadful situation?" "Merry, mistress" replied one of them, "why bless your sunny heart, if you was in our situation, you would not only be merry, but actually *transported*!"[9]

Such feelings may be hard to comprehend today but so were the hardships prisoners faced. Pestilence, back-breaking labour and high death rates made transportation an inviting alternative, and convicts often pleaded to be shipped to the 'Thief Colony' as there was 'no Place in the whole World that would be so agreeable for them to be sent'.[10] Prisoners in Newgate prison rioted when they learnt that this option would not be available to them. But, in reality, transportation was not as favourable as some envisaged – many convicts would not even survive the long sea voyage to the colony.

To facilitate the shipping requirements of convict transportation, the British government continually sought out merchant ship owners who were willing to charter their vessels as convict transports. In early 1791 a contract was signed with the East India Company to hire the merchant ship *Pitt*. Owned by the London Alderman George Mackenzie Macaulay, the *Pitt*, with a burthen of 775 tons, 139 ft in length and 36 ft in width, was the largest ship ever contracted to transport convicts. The height between decks was between 6 ft 1 in and 6 ft 6½ in, much more room than previous transport ships – an adult could actually stand up below decks.[11]

In early April 1791 the conversion of the *Pitt* into a convict ship was progressing well and the government summoned transportees from the Newgate prison in London. Because the *Pitt* was still not ready to house convicts by mid-May, these prisoners were moved to hulks moored on the Thames.[12] This delay renewed press criticism of overcrowded gaols, and *The Stamford Mercury* claimed that a local police force would be a better solution than transportation.

> Must we ever thus periodically send two or three thousand men and women out of the kingdom? Is not this curing an ulcer by cutting off the limb? Would not internal medicines, a police regimen, answer better?[13]

But the government remained fully committed to transportation, and, as soon as convict cells were ready on the *Pitt*, she sailed down the Thames from Deptford to Woolwich and embarked her first convicts.[14] On 5 June 1791 the *Pitt* sailed for Portsmouth where more convicts were waiting. Seven days later she arrived at Spithead outside Portsmouth, where she moored to prepare for the voyage to New South Wales.[15]

No records have survived explaining how the Jedburgh prisoners were sent to the *Pitt*. It is likely they made the same journey taken two years earlier by Thomas Watling.[16] He and other prisoners left the Edinburgh port of Leith and sailed directly to Spithead where they were placed on the hulk *Lion*. An iron collar would have been placed on Andrew's neck and a chain attached to the collar to prevent his escape on the 50-mile journey to Leith in an open wagon. One suspects that he was not as 'jolly in wind and rain' as the Bristol prisoners were observed to be when passing through the streets. At Leith the men were herded aboard one of the ships that regularly carried soldiers to and from Portsmouth.[17] With guards already on board, the convicts were quickly and roughly confined to cells below decks. Fortunately, when this ship finally sailed into the Spithead waters the convicts on board did not have to endure further imprisonment on the decrepit hulk moored there. Andrew and the other convicts were transferred ship-to-ship by a longboat rowed directly to the *Pitt*.

A 1789 etching by John Harris of the convict transport *Pitt* owned by George Mackenzie Macaulay. The *Pitt* departed Portsmouth for New South Wales in June 1791 with Andrew Thompson among the transported convicts.

Most of the 443 male and female convicts confined on the *Pitt*, including the 18-year-old Andrew, were brought aboard in filthy prison slops (loose course clothing).[18] Their iron collars were removed and replaced with a chain to a ring on the ankle, which could be used when needed as a link to other convicts. New slops would have been issued to Andrew after he had washed and shaved off his hair to remove the lice.[19] The diary of William Noah, written in 1797 about his transportation to Sydney Cove, gives some sense of the appalling conditions the convicts endured.

> ... these Men are truly Deplorable so Rag'd & Alterd that the several [who] went from Newgate I hardly [k]new them & for Vermin they was Eat up with these to us was no very Agreable Companions having never experienced the Hardships of the Hulks which by Account is very Miserable. But kind Hope Paints in our mind a Better Day & leads us thro the Most Disagreable Pangs and Misfortunes of Life which Death would Otherways be a Happy Relief[20]

Because of the state of prisons, it is not hard to understand why convicts saw transportation as preferable to incarceration in gaols and hulks, even when they had no idea of what awaited them on the voyage ahead. They could not imagine anything worse than prison.

In Portsmouth the *Pitt* also took aboard a detachment of the recently formed New South Wales (NSW) Corps, with their commanding officer, Lieutenant Governor Major Francis Grose. These soldiers were being sent to relieve the Royal Marine regiment that had been guarding the colony since the landing of the First Fleet. Major Grose had recruited the NSW Corps officers and men in Britain and had found it difficult to enlist suitable men due to the remoteness of the posting. The recruits were often rejects from more established regiments, or deemed too old for active service, or had been criminals, deserters or mutineers. Because the regiment was being established to mostly guard convicts, it was of little interest to professional soldiers – they sought active service in exotic and lucrative places such as India. However, not all Corps recruits were military cast-offs. Many joined with the aim to make their fortune in a new land, and, indeed, some achieved this. Among the NSW Corps soldiers was Captain Joseph Foveaux – he would play a leading role in the governance of the colony and over the years became a close acquaintance of Andrew Thompson, who was on the same ship but below decks as a convict.

On 21 June 1791, after the last convict had been loaded onto the *Pitt*, the Home Office received a complaint that the ship was overcrowded. An anonymous writer 'JW' condemned 'the natural horror of screwing such a number of miserable objects within so small a compass' and that this would result in the death of a third of these 'wretches'. JW argued that the heat conditions below decks was almost suffocating convicts and that this would get worse in the tropics, resulting in contagious illnesses that would spread among convicts as well as crew and soldiers. The complainant advised that

150 convicts be taken off the ship; particularly sick convicts and old men over the age of 60 who were of 'no possible use' in the colony.[21] Whoever JW was, he had considerable prior knowledge of the voyage ahead and that the NSW colony needed healthy convicts capable of doing a hard day's work.

On 23 June 1791 Home Office Secretary Henry Dundas convened an inquiry into the overcrowding, and the method of paying ships' masters. Dundas wanted contractors to only carry convict numbers that could be properly accommodated and fed, and to make payments to masters for the number of convicts landed alive in the colony, not for the number originally taken on board.[22] This was exactly what Governor Phillip had requested after the shameful 25% mortality rate of the Second Fleet voyage. It is more the pity that Henry Dundas did not apply the same moral standards to the hideous slave trade in which Britain played such a dominant role in the late 18th and early 19th centuries.

An inspection of the *Pitt* quickly established that JW's allegations were correct – the ship could not accommodate more than 410 convicts. The inspectors found that a space of only a 'cube of 6 ft' (6 cubic metres) had been allocated to eight men. In such a space 'every berth of 18 inches' (46 cm) would have been occupied, and, if any sickness occurred, sick and healthy people would be in contact with each other. The ship had three female compartments; 27 women were accommodated in a room of eleven square metres, and two smaller rooms of five square metres each held ten women. This space was suitable for only 47 women, whereas 58 had embarked. Following the Inspector's report, 33 sick convicts were re-landed.[23] This reduced the Scottish contingent from 46 to 39 (31 males and 8 females); seven male prisoners from Jedburgh remained on board. In the next month at the mooring, eight more convicts had either disembarked or had died.

These reductions improved the conditions for remaining convicts but space on the ship was still cramped because of the large amount of cargo needed for the voyage and the destination. The *Pitt* was the first transport ship to carry private merchandise to the colony. When the *Pitt* finally docked in Sydney, Governor Phillip complained that far too much of the cargo, valued at £4000, were items Corps officers and merchants planned to sell in the colony. He later wrote to the Home Office about the 'evil' of private traders' goods occupying a quarter of the stowage to the detriment of the colony's vital provisions. The shortfall in food supplies was severely felt in the colony following the arrival of the *Pitt*.[24]

The *Pitt* also conveyed despatches from the Home Office Secretary Dundas referring to the request for better-skilled prisoners. Phillip was informed that the convicts on the ship had been carefully selected to be 'useful in the settlement'. Indeed, prisoners such as Andrew Thompson would eventually prove to be more than 'useful' to the new colony. Additionally, the *Pitt* carried a partially constructed vessel that, when assembled, would become the schooner *Francis* for use on the Hawkesbury River.[25]

When the *Pitt*, under the command of Captain Edward Manning, finally departed Portsmouth on 17 July 1791 she carried 402 convicts (349 males and 53 females). The exact complement of the ship is uncertain, but there were also 80 soldiers and 28 wives, children and free men. Additionally, a large ship such as the *Pitt* was typically manned by a minimum of 30 seamen, bringing the total ship's complement to about 540.[26]

The first port of call was the port of Praya (Praia) on Cape Verde Island off the coast of West Africa, some 2550 nautical miles from Portsmouth. The *Pitt's* departure from England had been delayed and it entered the tropics in mid-summer when the temperatures and humidity were extreme. Despite medical checks in Portsmouth, smallpox was present among the convicts and by the time they reached Cape Verde on 16 August, fifteen convicts and two children had died. While the ship replenished its supplies of food and water, seamen, soldiers and their families were permitted to go ashore. This proved fatal for many who contracted a deadly sickness that was likely to have been epidemic typhus.[27]

The *Pitt* departed from Praya on 20 August 1791 and set sail to Rio de Janeiro, 3250 nautical miles away. For nearly a month the ship was becalmed in heavy rains and oppressive tropical storms. Captain Manning claimed that he had never witnessed such severe weather and was thankful that the *Pitt* had lightning rods on the masts. For a month the ship made little headway, and, without wind, the conditions below deck were stifling.[28] For security reasons, all portholes had been blocked so that the convict areas were dark, even by day. To improve airflow, a grating hole to the lowest deck was made on both sides of the ship, and soldiers and convicts slept as close as possible to those.[29] However, the stench of the bilge water (at the ship's bottom) and the effluent coming from the 500 people below decks permeated every corner of the ship. It was unbearable even for convicts accustomed to conditions in hulks and filthy gaols. Even the non-convict personnel who could go freely on deck found it almost as intolerable.

When the stifling weather finally abated convicts were allowed to exercise on deck. But soon high winds and heavy seas started to batter the ship, with enormous waves breaking over the gunwales. The hatches had to be battened down again to stop flooding below decks. Similar conditions were experienced six years later by convict William Noah, who described his crossing of the Equator in a diary.

> Could I here Describe the Misserable situation of Upwards of two Hundred of my fellow prisoners many of them was persons brought up well who for trifling Offences had been Banish'd from their Familys and Homes and now invold into a State of Wretchedness & Misseray Staring on one another not noing One Moment but that we might be plung'd into the Arm of Death so Loosey so full of Diseases the poorness of Living short of Water in a Hot Country with no Nourishment made our Situation truly Deplorable It was one would think enough to softing the Heart of most inhumane Being to se us Irond Handcuft & Shackeld in a Dark Nasty Dismal Deck without the Least Wholesome Air.[30]

Drinking water and fresh food soon ran low, and ship's rations were restricted to salted meat, dried peas, oatmeal and biscuits. Confinement below decks in the bad weather meant that 'malignant epidemical fever' spread rapidly among the sailors and soldiers. Within two weeks of departing Praya, 30 seamen, soldiers, their wives and their children were buried at sea. Captain Manning thought it extraordinary 'that the fever never touched the convicts, among whom, one might naturally have concluded, that it would have been most fatal'.[31] He may have not appreciated that most convicts had survived far unhealthier conditions, and that they had probably acquired a degree of immunity to the fever. However, the convicts did suffer mercilessly from flux and scurvy because of a lack of vitamin C in their diet. At one point over 150 convicts were sick, but not one died.[32]

Sailing on a southerly route the *Pitt* continued to encounter enormous seas and continuous gales. Having already lost seven experienced seamen from fever, the depleted crew was unable to keep the ship on course. The *Pitt* was driven close to the South

American shoreline and was in danger of being wrecked or of foundering. When only five sailors were fit enough to be on deck, and most unable to go aloft, Captain Manning was 'compelled to liberate many of the convicts and trust to their assistance to relieve the ship'.[33] He requested that young men, with shackles removed, climb the masts and set the sails. Was the 18-year-old Thompson one of the convicts who volunteered for this dangerous task? Unfortunately, no names were recorded of the men who braved work in the rigging in weather that even experienced seamen feared. However, we do know that in later life Andrew risked his life to rescue others in floods, so it is entirely possible that he was one of those convict volunteers. Of course, these men would have realised that the survival of the *Pitt* was in their best interests, and most would have done whatever was needed to get safely back onto *terra firma*. Even the authoritarian Major Grose later commented that the convicts behaved 'themselves with great regularity'.

> It is very remarkable that amongst the convicts who are confined there is not a sick man, and of those who were released for the purpose of working the ship when the sailors could do their duty no longer, not any have been so severely afflicted as to lose their lives.[34]

It was with much relief and celebration that the *Pitt* finally entered Rio de Janeiro harbour on 8 October 1791. Soon after dropping anchor urgent priority was given to replenishing the food and water for all on board. Rio would be the main port-of-call for victualling the ship and for the purchasing additional food supplies for the colony. The Viceroy of Rio de Janeiro welcomed the ship and ensured that the purser had access to as much beef and fresh fruit as needed. Supplies were cheap and plentiful, and everyone was allotted a generous fresh food ration.[35]

Sick soldiers and crew on the ship were transferred to hospital, and sick convicts were attended to on a nearby island, probably Enchados. One convict tried to escape the island, but he drowned; another, who received permission to go ashore, was killed. Captain Manning, who knew many of the convicts personally following their help on the ship, gave more trustworthy convicts permission to use small rowboats for ship-to-shore transfers. However, once their fetters were removed, seven men escaped and were never seen again. William Tweedie from Jedburgh gaol was one of the escapees.[36] It is entirely possible that Andrew helped on these rowboats, but he had respected the confidence of the captain.

The fresh food quickly restored everyone's health and vigour. On the morning of 1 November, the *Pitt* set sail for Cape Town on the southern tip of Africa, 3300 nautical miles away. After a speedy passage of 26 days, they reached Table Bay harbour on 27 November.[37] Moored to the northwest of the Cape of Good Hope, the ship was relatively unprotected from strong winds and heavy seas coming off the Southern Ocean. Two British naval ships, HMS *Providence* and HMS *Assistant*, were also anchored in the Bay. Under the command of Captain William Bligh, a future Governor of New South Wales, the two warships were on another breadfruit expedition to the Pacific Islands, and later the West Indies.

The *Pitt* was moored close to the Cape Town shoreline, and escape was always on the minds of some convicts, especially as they could now walk on deck without chains. In the first month of anchorage, at least one convict drowned attempting to swim ashore.[38] However, a maritime drama was about to distract all on board. On 17 December the Dutch merchant ship *Waaksamheyd*, commanded by another future Governor of New South Wales, Captain John Hunter, attempted to moor in Table Bay during a violent storm. The ship was returning Hunter and his crew to England after his ship HMS *Sirius* had been shipwrecked on Norfolk Island. Hunter now feared that another ship under his command would be lost. The *Waaksamheyd* wallowed after losing two anchors when mooring and was driven out to sea for several days. On 22 December Hunter realised that without heavy anchors his ship risked being grounded on reefs, and he hoisted a distress flag.[39] Immediately the *Pitt*, HMS *Providence*, HMS *Assistant* and several whalers sent their long boats out to tow the ship into the harbour.[40]

Interestingly, if Andrew had been one of the *Pitt* rowers in the *Waaksamheyd's* rescue, he may have met John Hunter and William Bligh. Much later these two naval officers would, as Governors of New South Wales, become important to Andrew Thompson's life and career. In 1797 John Hunter would grant Andrew an absolute pardon, and William Bligh would employ him as his farm bailiff. Early encounters in Cape Town harbour may have played some role in these later events. The young energetic Scot must have impressed Joseph Foveaux, the NSW Corps Captain on board the *Pitt*, because he would later contribute considerably to Thompson's advancement in New South Wales.

Not everyone on the *Pitt* was involved in the recovery of the *Waaksamheyd*. In the excitement of the rescue effort, six more convicts managed to escape. Three males boarded the whaling boat *Duke of Clarence*, which had sheltered alongside the *Pitt* during a hard squall. The convict Ann Collin disappeared in a small boat with the *Pitt's* quarter master, John Ely, during his watch on deck. A fifth escapee, Dominicus Dorlong, a mathematical instrument maker, had gone ashore at the request of Captain Bligh to repair his sea barometer but never returned. The sixth and most famous escapee was Thomas Watling, a Scottish professional draughtsman from Dumfries who had been transported for forgery.[41] The *Pitt* sailed without him. A month later he was recaptured by the Dutch, imprisoned and taken on board the convict transport *Royal Admiral*, which was *en route* to New South Wales. On arrival in Sydney Cove in October 1792, Watling was assigned to Chief Surgeon John White and Judge Advocate David Collins to draw botanical, zoological illustrations and landscapes. Today his early colonial landscapes and natural history drawings are very highly regarded.

The *Pitt* remained in Cape Town until 24 December before setting sail for its final destination of Sydney Cove.[42] This would be a long 7000 nautical mile passage through treacherous southern oceans, with no possibility of replenishing supplies on the way. Pelting rain and heavy gales gave them their first taste of the fabled Roaring Forties, and it would not have been a happy Christmas Day for most on board. Driven by gales, the heavily laden *Pitt* tossed and rolled in the violent seas. Fierce winds screamed through the riggings; waves were often over 10 metres high as the *Pitt* plunged and ploughed through interminable icy storms. The conditions were fearful for veteran seamen; for landlubber convicts it was the most frightening experience of their lives. Seasickness was rife even among the experienced crew and in the drenching storms everyone was bitterly cold and wet for most of the time. Convicts stayed in their bunks to keep warm, but their poor clothing offered little protection against the icy cold of the southern seas.

The *Pitt* eventually rounded the southern coast of Van Diemen's Land and bore north towards the colony at Sydney Cove. On 14 February 1792, after a voyage of almost seven months, the *Pitt* finally sailed into Port Jackson and saluted Sydney with a 13-gun salvo.[43] Most on board had little idea what to expect in Port Jackson, but when they sailed into the harbour, they saw a large deep-water harbour surrounded by wild and uncultivated woodlands – a vista that still delights experienced travellers arriving in the harbour today. Andrew had just turned 19, and he and his fellow convicts eagerly anticipated walking on land after eight months on the ship. The *Pitt* quickly disembarked its 319 male and 49 female convicts and their five children. The 120 sick convicts were sent to hospital.[44] Andrew Thompson and the healthiest *Pitt* convicts were immediately sent inland to Parramatta, fifteen miles west of Sydney.

Although Governor Phillip was unhappy with the large number of sick aboard the *Pitt*, he was satisfied that 'those who have been received from the *Pitt* [were] less emaciated, and in appearance fitter for labour, than most of those who have been hitherto received'.[45] Phillip's request to the Home Office for healthy convicts and their better treatment aboard transports appeared to have been acted upon. The death rate due to illness on the *Pitt* was about 8%, an improvement on the Second and Third Fleets, but still far higher than the 2% on his First Fleet voyage.

Phillip had expected the *Pitt* to bring more food provisions for the colony, not goods for sale by private traders. The colony would experience a shortfall in rations because of this selfish enterprise. The salt meat brought on the *Pitt* was supposed to provide for ten months of rations, but it lasted only 40 days, and desperately needed flour supplies had not been shipped at all. The Home Office continued to believe the colony grew enough grain for its own consumption, but this level of self-sufficiency would not happen for another decade.

Chapter 4

A NEW START

> *His new country, which he was later to adopt as his own, provided the outlet for his remarkable personality. To those qualities which are common to the Border Scots, independence, reliability, frugality, sobriety and practicality, he added an astounding energy, an exceptional ability to organise, intelligence of a high order and, above all, a great humanity. If the transportation system gave future Australians nothing else to admire, it gave them Andrew Thompson.*[1]

When Andrew Thompson disembarked from the *Pitt* in Port Jackson in early 1792, the New South Wales colony was still reliant on food supplies from England. Founded in 1788, Sydney Cove had grown into a bustling town of 1100 inhabitants, with some officials already living in brick houses and the convicts sharing wattle and daub huts. Governor Phillip had brought a measure of stability to the settlement, but the shortage of food remained a major problem and this meant that finding new food sources, both locally and overseas, was almost his sole focus. Because he personally shared in the reduced rations being distributed equally, independent of class, rank or station, there was a minimum of grumbling about food shortages. Other government supplies were also shared, so there was no question of preferential treatment – everyone suffered in equal measure. This lack of distinction between social classes was rare in the 18th century – privileged members of society expected, and usually received, special concessions. In a British famine, the poor usually fended for themselves and starved if they could not.

Despite the lets-pull-together attitude in the struggling colony, the persistent hunger inevitably led to increased food theft. Many convicts, especially those doing hard labour, were so famished they stole from the vegetable gardens of fellow convicts. The colony's first Judge Advocate, David Collins, noted that most crimes were to procure food, and that violence was rare. Even so, the harsh punishments imposed for food theft, which included hanging, failed to stem crimes driven by starvation.[2]

To increase grain production, Phillip established a new

government farm at Toongabbie, five miles north of Parramatta. Anyone, convict, soldier or freeman, caught stealing was flogged and sent to do hard labour at this farm. Although the Toongabbie farm was not as brutal as later punishment camps, it was feared because of its remoteness and the separation it imposed from the rest of the settlement. Most new convict arrivals in the years 1791 to 1795 were sent directly to the Toongabbie Farm. By 1792 over 500 men worked there clearing trees and tilling land for cropping.[3]

In March 1791 to encourage the cultivation of wheat crops that could be used to mill flour Phillip granted freehold lots in the Parramatta and Ponds districts to as many men as possible who were prepared to farm the land. Somewhat controversially he even granted land to well-behaved convicts. For men who had completed their sentences, his rehabilitation policies created a growing body of men and women, known as 'emancipists', who would become the productive mainstay of the colony. With uncharacteristic foresight the British government realised the most compelling incentive for emancipists to remain in New South Wales was the ownership of land. It not only gave them an investment in the future, being a property owner encouraged their law-abiding participation in the colony's life and their cultivation of land contributed to the much-needed food production. The British also saw other benefits in possessing land – it was a disincentive for ex-convicts to return to England, where, it was assumed, they would resume a life of crime.

In February 1792, the same month Andrew Thompson set foot in the colony, Governor Phillip registered the first colonial deeds for the 69 allotments granted to convicts and emancipists in the previous year. This egalitarian distribution of land made the colony look quite advanced to newcomers. Major Francis Grose and Richard Atkins, who also arrived on the *Pitt*, were most impressed by what they saw – though the expectations of these two men were probably not high to start with. Grose claimed, somewhat prematurely, that the colony had become so self-sufficient that it only lacked a ship bringing 'corn and black cattle'.[4] Neither man would have appreciated, nor cared, that the livelihoods of convicts were far from enlightened – they laboured long hot hours on short rations and were desperately hungry most of the time.

Even so, for freemen and emancipists the prospects for advancement were apparent, and businesses and farming in the colony offered energetic men and women many opportunities. Richard Atkins, the newly appointed Registrar of the Vice-Admiralty Court and Justice of the Peace, recorded this view after visiting settlers' farms. He wrote that many residents were comfortably housed with plenty of vegetables for their families and had already cleared land for sowing wheat.

> In short they are in every particular much better situated than they could possibly be in England. Indeed too much praise cannot be given to the Governor for ... the paternal care and encouragement he give[s] to all and each of them who deserve it.[5]

Phillip's fair and impartial rule encouraged the cooperation of both convicts and marines with his administration. The First Fleeters quickly saw themselves as the pioneering settlers of the colony, and that fair and equal justice was an entitlement for their efforts – an aspiration that commoners in Britain still found hard to achieve.

A 1794 view of the Sydney Cove settlement painted by Thomas Watling, who was a transported Scottish convict aboard the *Pitt* with Andrew Thompson.

The combined population of the two principal towns in the colony, Sydney and Parramatta, had grown to 3068. The governor, his administrative officials, and most of the NSW Corps, resided in Sydney. As did 742 convicts who laboured at building sites, at the brickfields, attended to the storehouses, manned fishing boats and worked as servants for various officers and officials. Sydney's market gardens produced enough vegetables to feed its inhabitants, but the rocky terrain was quite unsuitable for the much-needed grain crops. The colony's main cereal crops were now concentrated in and around Parramatta, where the land was more fertile and there was a reliable water supply. A contingent of 87 Corps soldiers guarded the 1723 convicts working in the Parramatta district, and they cultivated most of the grain grown in the colony.[6]

The town of Parramatta was established in mid 1790. It had a 205 ft (62 m) wide main avenue, now called George Street, which ran for one mile from the river wharf to the residence where the governor resided during his frequent visits. Convict huts straddled this avenue on both sides and various side streets contained huts for women and families. The lath-and-plaster governor's house still sits at the top of the hill in Parramatta today, though it has been modified by successive governors.[7]

In 1792 there was no road from Sydney Cove to Parramatta other than a bush track through hilly terrain and dense bushland. Andrew Thompson was taken to the Parramatta open prison in a ferry, the fastest and safest means to reach the settlement. The scene when he disembarked at the Parramatta wharf was described by one of the accompanying Corps soldiers.

> On your ascending the wharf appears a row of huts on each side, and a spacious road to the distance of a mile; at the upper end, Governor Phillips erected his country seat. The garden that surrounds it is beautiful, abounding, in the season, with grapes, melons, pumpkins, and every other fruit and vegetable. The florist may also amuse himself. In short, the country may well be called Botany Bay; for the botanist, I believe, may here find the most beautiful shrubs and evergreens that produce very fragrant flowers. The Governor's garden at Parramatta is so situated by nature that, in my opinion, it is impossible for art to form so rural a scene.[8]

Thompson and fellow convicts would have experienced something similar when they disembarked, though probably not with the same enthusiasm. They were placed in simple huts along the main avenue, each housing fourteen to eighteen men, without beds or blankets. Some men built their own beds from bush timber, others just slept on the floor. In any case, all were hardened to cold damp prisons, where, if fortunate, they had straw to lie on. Every convict hut had an adjacent garden for growing vegetables and a female hut keeper was assigned to keep the hut clean and cook for the men while they were working. Spoons, knives and bowls had to be made for each newcomer from the local green wood. The convicts worked from 5am to 11am with a break for lunch, and from 2pm until sunset.[9]

This would have been an exhausting new regime for a young 19-year-old. Most male convicts were assigned to labouring in the fields to grow cereal crops on land around Parramatta and Toongabbie. In these districts they cleared massive eucalyptus trees, dug out their stumps and tilled the soil with spades and hoes in preparation for seeding. Some convicts were employed constructing buildings in Parramatta. These were men who had experience as brickmakers, bricklayers and stonemasons. All tasks involved hot exhausting physical labour. Phillip's main concern about the health of men arriving on recent convict ships was that they were incapable of working in such conditions, and not strong enough to build the much-needed new hospital in Parramatta.[10] The fit young Andrew Thompson was assigned to 'serve as a labourer in the stone-masons gang at Parramatta'.[11]

A view of Government House in Parramatta. In 1792 Andrew Thompson was housed in one of the huts on the side of the main road.

In the early days of the colony convicts were often allocated work without taking into account the wide disparity in their skills and experience – this was frustrating for the men and wasteful for the government. Later Phillip made sure men were assigned work that was appropriate to their ability and physical strength. It seems that Andrew was initially allocated labourer jobs because his weaver apprenticeship was unfinished, and no account was taken of his literacy – even though both were useful skills for a convict to have.

Over time Andrew's abilities were recognised and he was assigned more appropriate work. However, for months he toiled at hard manual labour from dawn to dusk, like the rest of his hut mates. Exactly how his talents were discovered is uncertain. Phillip had a passion for town planning and buildings, and he personally supervised some work in Parramatta. Perhaps it was in this capacity that the governor met and assessed that the young Scot working as a stonemason on one of his projects needed to be reassigned.

In April 1792 a virulent disease raged through the settlement and convict deaths occurred daily, mostly among the weak men from Third Fleet ships and the *Pitt*.[12] The nature of the illness is unknown, but dysentery, cholera and typhus existed on convict ships. They all took their toll at various times, with no known way to combat them. Food rationing was still in force, and recently landed convicts were in such an emaciated state that they were incapable of recovering, let alone working, on the meagre food rations. Within three months of arriving, 59 of the 368 convicts from the *Pitt* had died. A total of 81 died during the year.[13] Among the deaths were five Scottish convicts. Only Andrew Thompson and James Agnew had survived from the Jedburgh prison.

This high death rate put additional pressure on Phillip to increase local food production and remediate the hospitalised convicts. Food shortages had become a threat to the very existence of the colony and all able-bodied persons capable of using a hoe or a spade were ordered into the fields. Since late 1789 Phillip had sent urgent requests to Under Secretary Evan Nepean for the immediate shipment of more provisions. He reminded Nepean that convicts could not work effectively unless they were adequately fed.[14] Phillip gave special attention to improving the diet of the ill, and the death rate in hospitals fell significantly after patients received more fresh meat and vegetables. Only when the long-awaited store ships finally arrived, did Phillip reinstate full rations to others in the colony.

The shortage of food was not the only issue tormenting the governor. The NSW Corps officers were starting to impose their considerable influence over colonial matters, both commercial and administrative. The military declared that the direct supervision of convicts was below their station; they had been recruited as soldiers, not as overseers. This forced Phillip to appoint overseer and storekeeper posts to anyone capable of taking these responsibilities. If there were no suitable freemen, trustworthy convicts were put in charge. It was a common practice for store assistants to steal provisions and severe punishments failed to stem these thefts. The problem became embarrassing when Major Grose informed Phillip that he had heard about the pillaging of Sydney stores while on board the *Pitt* in Cape Town. Someone on the *Waaksamheyd* claimed that during his stay in Sydney he could purchase anything from two storekeepers. These two men had returned to England after their sentences had expired, paying their fares with the profits of illegal food sales. Phillip promptly wrote to the Home Office demanding these men be arrested in England for their 'nefarious practises'.[15]

The in-store theft of food made Phillip determined to appoint men who could honestly supervise the stores. In October 1792 Judge Advocate David Collins reflected on the governor's actions, 'that the people employed about the stores, if not free, should at least have been so situated as to have found it their interest to resist temptation'. Many of the men who currently served in the stores were replaced with convicts 'to whom he promised absolute emancipation at the end of a certain number of years'.[16] Andrew Thompson was one of the convicts employed 'in a situation of trust, having committed to him the charge of the men's provisions'.[17] One would like to believe that his appointment was made in recognition of his demonstrated honesty, but it is much more likely that Andrew sought and gained this post solely to shorten his 14-year sentence. His job in the Parramatta store was to allocate food rations to other convicts. This was a difficult task because it involved the accurate proportioning of salted meat, flour, rice, corn and vegetables for each ration, often under the watchful eye of the recipient. It needed a person who was methodical, numerate and courageous – someone who could withstand the fierce scrutiny of a hungry convict watching every step of the process.

Governor Phillip's final days in the colony were approaching fast. For several years he had suffered kidney pains, and they were now so severe that he found it difficult to sleep. This affected his ability to govern, and he needed to return to England for expert medical treatment. He had requested leave several times from the Home Office, but it had not been approved because the Home Office saw his leadership in the young colony as essential.[18] Arthur Phillip was a stoical man with considerable fortitude, and he continued his duties despite the acute discomfort. But by October 1792 his health had deteriorated so badly that he could no longer wait for approval. To the great concern of all at the settlement, he announced he would return to England on the *Atlantic* departing in December.[19] Phillip was reluctant to leave without an official sanction, but he believed that this was the right time. In keeping with his general lack of interest in personal kudos, Phillip was more than willing to let future governors gather the bountiful fruits from the colonial tree he had planted and nurtured. He remained steadfast in his belief that the colony would eventually become self-sufficient and prosperous.

On 10 December 1792 Governor Phillip boarded the *Atlantic* and departed a settlement that he had almost single-handedly created.[20] He would never return. The whole colony was greatly saddened by his departure and his leadership would be badly missed in the coming years.

After his arrival in England, Phillip formally resigned as governor and recommended the lieutenant governor of Norfolk Island, Philip Gidley King, as his successor. Instead, Whitehall selected the more senior naval Captain John Hunter.[21] The British government was preoccupied with the war with France, and it would take another two and half years before John Hunter departed for New South Wales. In the meantime, the Commandant of the NSW Corps, Major Francis Grose, became the lieutenant governor until John Hunter arrived, and he and his fellow Corps officers set about undoing much of the good work and goodwill that Arthur Phillip had cultivated in the colonial community.

The young and energetic convict Andrew Thompson seems to have made a favourable impression on Arthur Phillip, and he mentioned this to Major Grose before he left for England.[22] Phillip's recommendation would prove important to the 19-year-old's advancement in the colony.

Chapter 5

THE YOUNG CONSTABLE

> *Governor Phillip, on leaving the Colony, recommended him [Thompson] to the notice of his successor, who finding him useful and deserving, continued him as Constable of the different districts in his neighbourhood.*[1]

Arthur Phillip's abrupt return to England on 10 December 1792 greatly troubled the convicts. They respected the governor for his fair treatment on the First Fleet voyage and his efforts to improve convict conditions in the colony. And it was their support that had largely determined the spirit and temper of the settlement. In return Phillip had been resolute in ensuring that New South Wales was much more than just a penal colony. His discipline had been strict and punishments severe, but he administered justice fairly and equitably. It was widely recognised that Phillip treated the convicts as unfortunate men and women who had had none of the privileges he or his officers enjoyed, and he acted more as a guardian than a gaoler. Convicts and emancipists appreciated his personal concern for their rehabilitation, and they behaved accordingly. Their cooperation made his administration more effective and enabled widespread acceptance of Phillip's firm edicts despite the persistent food shortages. Under someone else's leadership, the genesis of the European settlement of Australia might have been quite different.

The convicts' apprehension at Phillip's sudden departure was justified – the colony was about to get a lesson in the importance of good leadership. The 35-year-old Major Francis Grose of the NSW Corps would, as lieutenant governor, take charge of the colonial administration. When Grose accepted the commission of lieutenant governor in England, he would have seen the post as largely ceremonial – few incumbents expected this position would require serious governmental decisions to be made.

Major Grose's administrative experience was limited. He understood how things worked in the army and had been financially successful at a personal level in the granting of commissions in the

NSW Corps – a lucrative practice in the British military at a time when officer ranks were purchased rather than earned. From the outset of his appointment Grose showed no interest in the subtleties of governance and was a person prone to rash judgements. On the same day he took office, Grose abolished the civilian courts and gave the Corps officers legal authority over all civil and military matters. Under Phillip, the military's principal roles were to guard convicts and protect government facilities. This changed totally. Previously a civil magistrate investigated all complaints concerning convicts, but this now fell to Corps officers. Grose placed Captain Joseph Foveaux in charge of the convicts at Parramatta, and his appointment would later benefit Andrew Thompson, who he knew from the *Pitt* voyage.[2]

Next, Grose cancelled Phillip's equal-rations-for-all policy. Freemen, watchmen, overseers and storemen would now receive a larger ration than convicts.[3] Andrew Thompson's appointment to a government store had raised his status above that of a convict labourer, and he now received the larger ration. Ex-convicts who had completed their sentence or had been pardoned continued to receive the smaller ration of serving convicts. Grose had, in a few days, reimposed the privileges expected in a British class-driven society – he did not believe that the Corps should equally 'partake of whatever miseries assail the colony'.[4]

The power and influence of the NSW Corps was already a worry in Phillip's time, especially when Major Grose sought special privileges and increased food rations for his men. Phillip resisted most Corps demands, confining officers to minor administrative roles, prohibiting rum imports and denying requests for land grants to be worked by convict servants.[5] With Grose in charge, the devil was unleashed. Ignoring the threat of widespread drunkenness, he permitted in the same week that Phillip departed, the sale of alcohol to convicts. His decision went even further; he allowed the Corps to pay for goods and convict labour in rum. The consequences were immediate and tragic. Judge Advocate David Collins observed that 'the peaceful retreats of industry were for a time the seats of inebriety and consequent disorder'. It did not help when Grose appointed Lieutenant John Macarthur as the Inspector of Public Works to oversee storekeepers, overseers and convicts in the Parramatta and Toongabbie districts. He was also in charge of the most important food depository in the colony, the public granaries.[6]

Almost overnight the trafficking of spirits became widespread. An American cargo ship anchored in Sydney Cove started selling alcohol to civilians, military officers and superintendents with intended resale to convicts. David Collins expressed alarm at the deleterious effects a constant alcohol supply had on the population, observing that many men sold all that they owned for a drink.[7] A shortage of coinage at the time accelerated the use of rum as currency. The payment of wages in rum now became routine, and it was difficult to transact purchases in coins or in other goods.

Grose protected the Corps' monopoly on rum sales by punishing convicts who traded in alcohol. The penalty for reselling rum without a licence was the confiscation of the items sold and the alcohol, and the demolition of the offender's hut. Through official intimidation, the Corps' control of the rum trade was complete.[8] Grose reduced the government's involvement in farming, instead offering vast tracts of land to Corps officers, officials and free settlers. He considered them to be more reliable and better qualified to grow cereal crops than convicts and emancipists. Additionally, Phillip's plan to develop Sydney and Parramatta as the colony's major towns was abandoned, and John Macarthur, in his capacity as Inspector of Public Works, transferred convicts from the government farms at Toongabbie to work on other construction projects and on Corps officers' land.[9] The diminution of government farms greatly reduced grain production, and made the goal of self-sufficiency more remote than ever.

Prior to departing, Phillip had recommended to Grose that Andrew Thompson, 'in Consequence of his good Conduct' be considered for positions of increased responsibility. In early 1793, Grose assessed Thompson's abilities and 'finding him useful and deserving, continued him as Constable of the different districts in his neighbourhood'.[10] He made him a constable at the government farm at Toongabbie. It is also likely that the senior Corps officer in Parramatta, Captain Joseph Foveaux assisted in his promotion.

Convicts working on the Toongabbie Farm were housed in huts with gardens, laid out in a grid pattern similar to that in Parramatta. The huts were located on the bend of the Toongabbie Creek between what are now the Old Windsor and Oakes Roads. The overseers, constables and military resided in separate huts of wattle-

and-daub with gabled thatch roofs, not unlike those Andrew had lived in when arriving in Parramatta as a stonemason labourer. He was now housed with the overseers and, as a serving convict, he was given free time to do paid work elsewhere. This was an important concession since convict constables received no pay.

The Toongabbie government farm was established in 1791 to bolster the colony's food production, and by the time of Phillip's departure it had become the largest grain producer.[11] In 1792, food theft had reached such a level in Parramatta that it was decided that anyone caught stealing would be first flogged and then sent to the Toongabbie farm. The remoteness of the farm was more dreaded by convicts than the flogging, as it meant the loss of their huts and gardens in Parramatta and separation from the rest of the colony.[12] During Grose's reign, Lieutenant John Macarthur, as Inspector of Public Works, administered Toongabbie farm with superintendents Thomas Daveney and Richard Fitzgerald. Daveney was often drunk and treated convicts so badly that, after repeated claims of abuse, Grose eventually dismissed him.[13]

Incarceration at the infamous Toongabbie farm is synonymous today with cruel punishment. Grace Karskens, in her book *The Colony*, suggests that this reputation is undeserved, and convicts feared Toongabbie more for its isolation than its brutality.[14] Unquestionably conditions at Toongabbie were extremely hard; convicts had inadequate tools to clear and till land, and because they lacked harness animals to pull the few ploughs in the colony most of the tilling was done with spade and hoe. It was exhausting work in hot summers, especially for men on short food rations. Many of the weak convicts collapsed and died. Such conditions existed across the colony and heavy manual labour on these farms overwhelmed the fittest of men. Phillip knew only too well that hungry convicts could not work in such conditions, and he had tried where possible to provide better rations for hard-working labourers.

Toongabbie's reputation for brutality, real or otherwise, was widely accepted in England where the horror stories about Botany Bay always had a willing audience. George Thompson (not related to Andrew) arrived as a freeman in Port Jackson in May 1792 on the transport *Royal Admiral*, and he subsequently published a book on his experiences, entitled *Slavery and Famine, Punishment for Seditions*. The preamble to Thompson's stories, which included graphic and blood-curdling accounts of the colony, was written by the anti-transportation advocate George Dyer. His claim that 'of 450 [convicts] that came from England in the *Pitt*, only 29 were alive six weeks since' is complete nonsense.[15] There were illnesses among convicts on the *Pitt*, but only 81 had died by the end of 1792.[16] In fact, over 180 *Pitt* convicts were still alive twelve years later. His account of conditions at Toongabbie was mostly factual but he grossly exaggerated the severity of the punishments.

A western view of the Toongabbie Farm where Andrew Thompson was a constable from 1793 to 1795.

When the 20-year-old Constable Andrew Thompson arrived at Toongabbie Farm in 1793, it was already known in the colony as a place for punishing convict reoffenders. Policing these recalcitrant men was extremely challenging, especially for a young man who was a serving convict himself. He was fortunate to have Chief Constable Barrington in charge at Toongabbie to guide him in his early duties. George Barrington was a convicted pickpocket from Ireland who arrived in Sydney on the transport ship *Active*. Before his arrest Barrington had been a popular London socialite, who had lived the high life stealing from his influential friends. But his luck ran out; he was caught red-handed stealing a gold watch from an acquaintance and was duly sentenced to seven years transportation.

Portrait of George Barrington, chief constable and supervisor of Constable Andrew Thompson at Toongabbie Farm.

Portrait of Major Francis Grose of the NSW Corps and Lieutenant Governor following Arthur Phillip's departure.

Barrington exuded confidence and charm, and shortly after his arrival in Sydney in September 1791, he convinced Governor Phillip, not a man easily hoodwinked, to make him the principal watchman at the Toongabbie government stores and in November he became chief constable at Parramatta. Captain Watkin Tench knew Barrington and described him as lively and active, though without the 'elegance and fashion' he was famous for in England. Since his arrival in the colony, Tench judged his conduct to have been irreproachable, and his temperament to 'eminently fit him for the office' of chief constable. In November 1792 Barrington received a conditional pardon because of his good behaviour, and his admirable diligence as a constable. He was a larger-than-life figure, and, undoubtedly, he had a very positive influence on his new constable. As the 'prince of rogues' Barrington was credited with numerous publications and theatre pieces, though there is little evidence to support these claims. Even so, his quick wit and ability to convince even the hardest of men to do it "his way" would have served him well in policing the Toongabbie Farm.[17]

Under Barrington's tutelage there is every indication that young Andrew's abilities to lead, and to make friendships, flourished – attributes that would later help him excel in his agrarian and business pursuits. But Thompson's initial police duties at Toongabbie were difficult in the extreme. Convict labourers particularly disliked convict overseers, and especially a Scottish 'pup' who ought to have been sharing their hard labour in the field. Andrew would have stepped very gingerly in the early years of his apprenticeship and left the really gritty policing jobs to his chief.

The increased availability of rum in the colony was doing enormous damage in all the settlements, and even the remote Toongabbie Farm was affected. Convicts there were allowed to do paid work on local farms after their assigned hours, and because Grose had given land grants to Corps officers in the district, convict labour was in high demand. Rather than be paid in coin, many convicts accepted rum. The Toongabbie constables and watchmen now had to supervise drunken convicts, and the stores and granaries had to be doubly secured. Violence arising from drunken convicts became common at the farm, but the most serious problem for the constables remained the theft of grain from the ripening crops.

With Grose's abolition of civil courts, judicial authority now rested in the hands of the military, and the magistrates in Parramatta district were Captain Foveaux and Lieutenant Macarthur. They, and fellow Corps officers, adjudicated on all charges made in Parramatta and Toongabbie. It was the duty of Thompson and other constables to take men charged with theft to the Parramatta court. John Macarthur was seen by constables as a very abrasive magistrate, and it is relevant to note here that the activities of Thompson and Macarthur were to overlap many times in future. However, in 1794, Thompson would have been just another junior constable to John Macarthur, indistinguishable from all the other prison rabble passing through his court. Even when Andrew later became a successful and wealthy emancipist businessman, the indelible convict stain was never expunged for Macarthur. In contrast, Joseph Foveaux would in later years collaborate with Andrew Thompson, and rely on his support. He seems to have always maintained a positive opinion of the young Scot.

The possibility of escape was never far from the minds of convicts, especially at Toongabbie. Irish convicts proved to be the most ingenious absconders. A number escaped from Parramatta in 1791 and hid in the bush to steal from local gardens at night. One group planned to walk to China, believing it was just over the horizon. Other Irishmen repeatedly attempted escape by boat – in

April 1794 a number were captured sailing down the Hawkesbury River. With no constables in that district, Andrew and other constables from Toongabbie had to capture and bring these men to court. In 1794 a special convict work gang was formed in Toongabbie 'for the employment and punishment of all bad and suspected characters'. These Irish convicts had to work in chains.[18]

Convict escapes were not the most frequent or the greatest challenges facing police at Toongabbie – food theft and Aboriginal hostilities were much more of a problem. The clearing of land for farms displaced and harassed the indigenous people, and conflicts with settlers increased. The Aborigines' nomadic lifestyle was based on a deep knowledge of the land and the climate, and they moved from place to place to gather food according to the seasons. The permanent clearing of land for crops and stock was anathema to them, as it prevented access to waterways and other food sources. The white farmers were occupying their traditional lands and were hunting their birds, kangaroos and fish. To compensate, the Aborigines stole corn to replace lost food sources – they treated the settlers just as they would have any other tribe infringing on their territory. For the indigenous people retaining food sources was a matter of life and death, and intertribal battles over such issues had been part of their existence for thousands of years. Most European farmers did not comprehend their nomadic lifestyle or food gathering practices, and they defended their crops vigorously. Armed men were sent to drive them away and 'to throw a few shot among them' but were ordered 'to be careful not to take a life'.[19]

From the very beginning, the correct way to treat indigenous peoples in New South Wales was an enigma for the government. Arthur Phillip had sought to be friends with the local Gadigal people of the Eora Nation in the Port Jackson region, and in some respects he was successful. During his tenure, Europeans and Aborigines coexisted moderately well in and around Sydney Cove. Importantly, Phillip insisted that contact with indigenous people be minimal and friendly, and any colonialist violating this rule was heavily punished.[20] As inland areas were inhabited, contact between farmers and Aborigines became more common. The government's declaration of 'Terra Nullius' did not help because it encouraged settlers to believe that vacant land was theirs to occupy. Naturally, Aborigines saw them as invaders. To them the concept of 'owning land' made no sense; the land, water and sky belonged to everyone.

In the Parramatta and Toongabbie district Aborigines camped near settlers' farms and raided their crops, sometimes burning their huts. In retaliation farmers often fired on them, taking Aboriginal children as hostages and using them as forced labour. When the raids escalated to the spearing of settlers and the taking of reprisals, Corps soldiers were called in to protect some farms.[21] Additional attacks on settlers travelling between the settlements amplified the overall hostility. In December 1793 'a large party of the natives attacked settlers who were returning from Parramatta to Toongabbie, and took from them all the provisions which they had just received from the store'. Judge Advocate Collins believed these Aborigines were from the 'Hunter's or Woodman's tribe, people who seldom came among us, and who consequently were little known'.[22] Over time the raids increased in frequency, becoming bolder and involving larger numbers.

In early 1794 famine again threatened the colony and the need to grow more grain became critical. Grose promoted the establishment of a new farming settlement at the Hawkesbury River, about 25 miles north of Parramatta, where soils were known to be fertile, and farming promised higher grain yields. He granted the first land in an area known as Mulgrave Place, and the township of Green Hills was established on the banks of the Hawkesbury River overlooking rich undulating land.

Despite Grose's declared mistrust of the convicts' farming skills, he issued grants to a number of emancipists at the Hawkesbury River but made sure that their allotments were small. One of the attractions for farmers to settle in the area was the minimal presence of the Corps. The abundantly fertile soil and the lack of Corps' interference encouraged a steady migration of settlers from farms around Parramatta. Access to this remote area was helped by a new track from Sydney to Green Hills that reduced a two-day trek to an eight-hour walk.[23] Because this new district had no police force in 1794, the young Scottish constable from Toongabbie would have walked to Green Hills on the bush track that had been widened and cleared for wagons. If policing was needed in the Hawkesbury area the constables from Toongabbie and Parramatta were regularly called in to help and the journey would have taken at least half a day. Through regular contact with Hawkesbury settlers Thompson appreciated the much harder daily challenges faced by settlers on the small remote cropping farms, compared to grazing duties on the larger estates, where mostly Corps officers had an abundance of free convict servant labourers doing most of the work.

Part of a 1796 map showing settlements in the various districts surrounding the Parramatta and Hawkesbury Rivers.

In December 1794 a real sense of relief pervaded the colony when Major Francis Grose resigned as lieutenant governor and departed Sydney. His administration had been largely dysfunctional and his belief that Corps officers were the best farmers was delusional – favouring them over emancipists had left the colony close to starvation. Grain yields had plummeted, and the British government now needed to ship more food to the colony at a time when England itself was on the brink of famine. If Grose had given small settlers the same opportunities and concessions he gave to the Corps, they could have produced the required food at a fraction of the cost to the motherland.

However, Grose's reign had made many in the military wealthy. The rum trade, the large land grants and generous access to convict servants had been a bonanza for the Corps. These perks left problems and expectations that Grose's successors would struggle to solve. Richard Atkins recorded the damage caused.

> It is much to be lamented that the health, peace of mind and every thing that could conduce to the alleviation of the situation of the convict is sacrificed to the avarice of a few individuals. Major Grose notwithstanding any thing that individuals may say, who from Gratitude ought to speak well of him, has done more harm to this colony, than it will be in the power of any Govt. to do good for many years. All subordination is at an end, the morals of the people destroyed, Idleness and drunkenness have taken the place of Industry and sobriety. The sole object of a man's working for himself is solely for the purpose of getting Liquor.[24]

Captain William Paterson of the NSW Corps replaced Grose as the government administrator until Captain John Hunter RN (Royal Navy) took up the post of governor in September 1795.[25] Under Paterson's watch, the trading of rum by the Corps flourished and Lieutenant John Macarthur was promoted to Captain. The increased rank would enable him to exert even more influence on colonial matters in the future.

Portrait of Captain John Macarthur of the NSW Corps, and inspector of public works in Parramatta. He was a constant thorn in the sides of all governors.

Portrait of Colonel William Paterson of the NSW Corps. He was lieutenant governor from Dec 1794 – Sep 1795 and from Jan – Dec 1809.

The rich soils along the Hawkesbury River attracted many settlers. In March 1795 the population of the district had grown to

385 people and the farms spread for 30 miles on both sides of the river. The duties of the ten NSW Corps soldiers guarding the Green Hills granary were about to become more difficult.[26] An extremely dry summer, coupled with the expansion of farms in the district, meant that the local Aborigines had reduced access to waterways and food at a time when they needed it most. As at the Toongabbie farms, the ripening maize attracted foraging Aborigines, and the Hawkesbury farmers vigorously safeguarded their crops. Aborigines seeking access to water attacked the farms on the river, destroying their stores and huts. Men on both sides were killed.[27]

Five settlers were fatally speared in the Hawkesbury district, and several were wounded. By May, open hostility existed in a large area and Lieutenant Governor Paterson feared that settlers might abandon their farms when food was most needed. He set up a Corps garrison in Green Hills and Corps soldiers were sent on punitive expeditions to drive Aborigines away from settlements and farms. An additional detachment of soldiers was sent from Parramatta to confront Aborigines 'in the hope of striking terror' in them. They even erected hangman's gibbets in Green Hills as a visual threat. A number of indigenous men, women and children were taken prisoner, but were later released.[28]

This concerted military action led to a pause in hostility. But instead of seeking a way to satisfy the need for both sides to access water, Paterson irresponsibly rewarded his soldiers with additional land grants close to the Hawkesbury banks. This meant the military now had a vested interest in keeping the Aborigines out of the area.[29]

On 7 September 1795 Captain John Hunter RN arrived on HMS *Reliance* to become the second Governor of New South Wales. The 58-year-old Hunter was a First Fleet naval veteran, and the colony, in the main, welcomed his return. The Registrar Richard Atkins declared 'How happy is it for this Colony that we have at last a Governor who will make the good of the community at large his particular care, abstracted from all party and dirty pecuniary views'. Atkins believed that Hunter 'will do every thing for the general good', but observed that reform would 'not easily be brought about, as the very people whose interest it is to prevent it, have the C. [NSW Corps] ear'.[30] Judge Advocate David Collins was also pleased with Hunter's appointment, and assumed that Phillip's policies would soon be reinstated and the Corps' influences curtailed. This proved to be overly ambitious.

John Hunter had received thorough briefings from the British Home Office on what to expect in the colony, but he was shocked at what he found. When he had returned to England in March 1791 the settlement was struggling on short rations but under Phillip's benevolent rule it had remained a stable and orderly settlement. Hunter now found a largely frustrated community dominated by the military. He immediately resolved to rectify the damage by curtailing the power of the NSW Corps.

Governor Hunter's first administrative action was to restore civil authority to the courts. He reinstated the civil magistrates and the Judge Advocate David Collins. For the time being John Macarthur remained Inspector of Public Works and Hunter listened carefully to his advice. Macarthur claimed that the government farms were inefficient, and recommended private individuals be put in charge of food production. Macarthur's mantra was that if the government farms grew cereal crops, it disadvantaged industrious settlers and discouraged the breeding of cattle. He also tried to convince Hunter that the farms of Corps officers should retain their current allocation of assigned convicts at government expense, and, if necessary, more convicts should be sent from England for this purpose.[31] What Macarthur did not say was that these officers profited greatly from these concessions, and Hunter, foolishly, was impressed enough to reappointed him. Later, after talking to civil magistrates and non-military officials, the governor realised the colony's economy was in a decrepit state, and was embarrassed he had reappointed an official who, along with other Corps' officers, was largely to blame. He should have immediately fired Macarthur but hesitated because of his sway among Corps officers. Hunter would later greatly regret this indecision.

In order to better understand the colony's employment, production and commercial activities, Hunter conducted a General Muster (census), in which every inhabitant was questioned on their dependents, status, wealth and property. The muster revealed that Grose and Paterson granted 10,674 and 4965 acres of land, respectively. They were extraordinarily generous compared with the 3389 acres granted by Phillip over a much longer period. It was to take Hunter three years to reconcile, and to reclaim, some of these grants. Later in his governorship he realised that land ownership was a key incentive in making farming attractive, and in subsequent years he issued title deeds for much of land that Grose and Paterson had granted. Hunter's own land grants in the years 1795 to 1800 were to exceed 28,200 acres.[32]

Increasing grain production remained the top priority. To assist in this Hunter restricted the convict servant assignments to Corps officers on large estates and had more convicts work on government enterprises and small farms growing cereal crops. This closed off a labour market that had, for the past three years, been controlled by the Corps. They reacted angrily and threatened noncooperation. Captain Macarthur, as Inspector of Public Works, saw his power being eroded and resigned declaring he had lost confidence in the governor. John Macarthur, once again, actively cultivated civil disobedience against the government.

Macarthur's resistance suited Hunter and he quickly appointed Court Registrar Richard Atkins as the new Inspector of Public Works.[33] Several of the governor's new reforms were about to impinge on the duties of Constable Thompson. Hunter sought to lessen petty theft in the settlements by removing disorderly and vagrant people roaming the streets. Constables were ordered to stop loiterers and check if they had authorisation to be in the district. If not, that person was to be brought before a magistrate.[34]

Increased drunkenness in the colony was the prime motivation for the governor to try and improve civil order. He was determined to stop payments in rum and prevent the importation of alcohol. Hunter mandated that the distillation of alcohol now required a permit issued by a magistrate, and constables were instructed to find and destroy any unlicensed stills.[35] Reverend Samuel Marsden was made the new civil magistrate in Parramatta where Constable Thompson brought offenders for judgement. In his role as magistrate Marsden proved to be a sadistic moralist, who abhorred convicts and detested Catholics, especially if they were Irish. He routinely sentenced offenders to hundreds of lashes and would become known as 'The Flogging Parson'.[36]

Chapter 6

NEWFOUND FREEDOM

No man contributed more to the well-being of the penal colony during the first ten years of the last century than did Andrew Thompson.[1]

The importance of the Hawkesbury farming region to grain production increased rapidly, and by early 1796 it was the single most important food source in the colony. To the surprise and chagrin of many in Sydney, it emerged that almost all of the grain coming from the Hawkesbury was grown on the small allotments of ex-convicts. The high yields of these farms were in stark contrast to those of the larger estates, which were either uncultivated or used to graze cattle. These grazing estates were mostly properties granted by Grose and Paterson to officers of the NSW Corps. The enormous disparity in food production between small and large farms was a source of concern and embarrassment to the government, as the latter had access to the majority of subsidised convict labourers. The Corps officers tried to dismiss this disparity as being due solely to the higher fecundity of soil on the smaller farms close to the river. Nevertheless, the previous assertions by Francis Grose that Corps officers 'made better farmers' became the source of much ribaldry in the settler community.

As a form of payback the large estate owners promoted the belief that emancipists at the Hawkesbury were all heavily in debt owing 'to a disposition to indulge in drunkenness', and that their 'labour of a whole year had been thrown away for a few gallons of a very bad spirit'.[2] Indeed alcohol was a problem in some districts but most indebtedness among farmers arose from land costs, flood losses and the high cost of provisions.[3] Hawkesbury settlers also routinely suffered grain theft by hungry convicts and Aborigines. In any case these settlers knew from the experiences of fellow farmers that selling grain for alcohol was a certain pathway to ruin. Drunkenness spawned debt and moneylenders were always ready to service arrears at high interest rates, which led to bankruptcy and the forced sale of farmland. By such means unscrupulous traders acquired cheap land and became very wealthy. In an attempt to stem this exploitation and usury, Governor Hunter mandated that farmers should now sell their wheat harvests directly to the government stores, and that it was illegal to buy alcohol with grain.[4]

It was the rapidly increased grain production at the Hawkesbury that had forced Paterson in 1795 to build a store, granary and a military barracks at Green Hills.[5] But this granary quickly proved too small for the harvests, and a year later Hunter had new granary barns built on Green Hills land between the South Creek and Hawkesbury River. These barns were constructed from large timber logs to prevent stealing. A weatherboard house was also built for the local commanding NSW Corps officer – it would become known as Government House.[6] This building and the government store, wharf and granaries were located on a central plot referred to as the 'government precinct' or 'government domain'. The precinct was bounded in the east by Samuel Wilcox's land grant, now Arndell Street, to the west by James Whitehouse's land grant, now Baker Street, and from the bank of the Hawkesbury to the South Creek.

The growing importance of the Hawkesbury district meant that the Green Hills residences and granaries needed to be more secure. Governor Hunter issued a General Order inviting convicts to apply for constable positions at Green Hills. It sought men 'of the best character' who would be rewarded for their 'very fatiguing duties' and 'their exertions' with a special uniform for 'a more respectable appearance'. In addition to being eligible to the food ration of military and non-convict men, they would get a pint of spirits each week. Most importantly, well-behaved convict constables were eligible for a reduction in their sentence; a fourteen-year sentence could be reduced to seven years after satisfactory service. Each constable was entitled to three convict servants to assist him and to mind his house and property.[7]

Andrew Thompson saw the announcement of the Green Hills police posting and was immediately interested. He was especially attracted by the offer of a sentence reduction and, having served as a constable at Toongabbie for three years, he had sufficient training. He obtained references from Chief Constable Barrington and the Toongabbie superintendents and applied for the Green Hills position. In about mid 1796 it is recorded that 'Thompson was removed to Windsor [Green Hills], where a Constable of sober habits, and of a good character in other respects, was wanted; and here he took up his permanent abode'.[8]

The young Scot may not have seen this as a promotion, but the new post promised a shorter sentence for good service, and an opportunity to serve in a more attractive part of the colony. Whereas Toongabbie was a prison farm for reoffenders, Green Hills was an emerging hub of an important farming district. This change in duties and location would turn out to be an excellent move. Andrew was assigned a small, whitewashed cottage in the government precinct next to the log granary, with an orchard and garden on the banks of the Hawkesbury. From his cottage he could oversee both the grain handling facility and the boat movements. It was an idyllic location, close to the broad expanse of the river winding down through green fields, backgrounded by the Blue Mountains in the distance. The 23-year-old quickly settled into his new policing role, with three convict servants minding the house and garden and securing the cottage during his absences on patrol. He policed the district mostly on foot, or by small boat on the Hawkesbury River and South Creek. Horses were rarely used; there were only 57 horses in the colony and 43 belonged to the military.[9] For urgent police business one of the military horses could be borrowed but for routine patrol duties travel was by boat or on foot.

Shallow-draft sailing ships were the most economical means of transporting goods to and from Green Hills to Sydney. In 1796 the only ship capable of navigating the Hawkesbury River was the *Francis*, which had been prefabricated in England and brought to the colony in pieces by the *Pitt*. By August 1796 the greater Green Hills community had grown to about 600 people, including a battalion of 48 NSW Corp soldiers.[10] In such a small place, the residents and settlers in the district quickly came to know the approachable young Constable Thompson. Because the Corps mostly ignored Hunter's ban on the rum trade and other policies, constables had to enforce most government regulations. Policing was often difficult work; constables had to be fit and strong as their duties were arduous and dangerous, and assaults were common. Investigating complaints over such a large district was also slow and meant that constables might be absent from Green Hills for days. Also, if a magistrate needed to adjudicate on an arrest, offenders had to be taken to Parramatta, or even Sydney, to stand trial.[11] Occasionally an ox-drawn or horse-drawn wagon was used for transport but otherwise it was a slow journey on foot with a chained prisoner in tow.

By the end of 1796 the civil administration of law had become so important to the security of the colony that a professional police force was mandated. Full-time constables were to be selected from the 'most decent and respectable men' in the colony and elected annually by a majority of a district's male population. Candidates for the post had to be literate in order to read government orders and be able to write reports for their superiors.[12] Again Andrew Thompson saw this as an opportunity, and he put his name forward. He was elected in the first batch of new police officers to become constables in the district. These men were responsible to magistrate Reverend Samuel Marsden who had assessed Andrew Thompson as 'a remarkably active & Intelligent man in Detecting Robberies, He cd read & write'.[13]

The elected chief constable for the Hawkesbury was the emancipist Thomas Rickerby (Rickaby). In England he had been a coachman to a noble house but was transported for seven years for the excessive use of his employer's hay for his own horses. After receiving a 30-acre land grant in 1794 from Lieutenant Governor Grose at Argyle Reach on the Hawkesbury, he lived and farmed there with his family. Besides Andrew Thompson, two other constables had been elected, David Brown and John Soare.[14] Brown was a Scot from Glasgow who had served as a soldier in the American Revolutionary War, and later sentenced to transportation for life for house breaking. He and Andrew arrived in Sydney on the *Pitt*, and both had been constables in Toongabbie. The other constable, emancipist John Soare, arrived in 1790 on a seven-year sentence for stealing clothing. In 1794 Soare received a 30-acre land grant from Francis Grose on the South Creek. He supported his wife and two children on his constable wages – the farm did not bring in enough money to sustain his family.

Well before Andrew Thompson arrived in Green Hills, hostility had been simmering in the Hawkesbury district between Aborigines and settlers. Three settlers had been killed in February 1796 and the Corps soldiers were itching to respond. Governor Hunter resisted any military action by proclaiming that the security of the district should sit squarely with the inhabitants, and settlers had to give each other assistance if there was an attack on a farm. Nevertheless, he stipulated that anyone with a firearm should 'not wantonly fire at or take the lives of any of the natives, as such an act would be considered a deliberate murder, and subject the offender to such punishment as (if proved) the law might direct to be inflicted'. The governor also warned settlers 'from giving any encouragement to the natives to lurk about their farms'.[15] This was a difficult edict because many settlers had reached an understanding with local Aborigines that, provided they remained friendly, they could have some corn when it was ripe. Most settlers wanted to preserve this fragile peace, and Hunter's order was largely ignored.

Constable Thompson encountered few indigenous people in his daily rounds of Green Hills. His main duties were to check the papers of strangers in the district, deal with drunks and family violence, and investigate thefts. Vagrancy was common in the town because convicts who had completed their sentence were no longer eligible for food rations and needed to earn money to survive. Most could not afford to return to England and those without work lounged about the town. This kept the police busy, and if the Vagrancy Act needed to be invoked, a magistrate may send the men to the Toongabbie government farm to work for food.

Thompson proved a proficient and popular police officer, and, on 17 October 1797, Governor Hunter gave the 24-year-old Scot an absolute pardon. This was awarded for 'the diligence and particular good conduct of Andrew Thompson as a Constable for six years'.[16] The pardon dissolved his sentence and restored his legal rights to those of a free man. As an ex-convict, he would now be designated as an emancipist. The pardon was a significant reward, as he had served only seven years of his fourteen-year sentence – for five of these years he had worked as a constable. Andrew was now free to leave the colony and he probably celebrated his first day of liberty with his friends at the pub!

Andrew Thompson had faced many challenges since his Yetholm days, and he was now a confident young member of the Green Hills community. With this newfound freedom, what ambitions would have dominated Andrew's mind? Clearly, it was a pivotal moment on which to decide his future directions. Most importantly, should he now go back to Scotland? Where to spend the rest of his life was a critical matter he certainly would have discussed with his friends and fellow constables. Most of the emancipists he knew had decided to stay in the colony and take advantage of the opportunities offered in a growing prosperous community. This had been the case with George Barrington, Andrew's superior in Parramatta. Governor Hunter had promoted Barrington in 1796 to high constable and superintendent of convicts to entice him to remain in the colony. He never returned to England.[17] Similarly, Chief Constable Rickerby and Constable Soare decided to stay in the colony with their young families.

But everyone's circumstances were different, and Andrew would have pondered the 'leave or stay' question for many weeks. Andrew knew that returning to Yetholm was fraught with difficulties. He had disgraced his family, and there was the dreadful uncertainty of whether they would welcome him back. There is no record of him corresponding with his family over his first six years in the colony. The lack of letters is surprising considering his parents' strenuous and well-documented efforts to have his sentence expunged. Unfortunately, the true extent of correspondence between parents and son may never be known – none of Andrew's private letters have survived – they were probably burnt after his death.

Andrew's ultimate aim appears to have been to seek success and respect, as these two attributes would enable his acceptance back into the Thompson family. This is speculation of course, but, considering his affection for his family, and particularly for his mother, it seems the most likely ambition of the homesick young man. Nevertheless, Andrew would have also realised that he had been very fortunate in the colony. His duties as a constable had given him insights into how the government works and what was needed to get things done in a farming community. And he saw lots of business opportunities. Green Hills was plagued by an unreliable and out-dated transport system, and goods were outrageously expensive to import and export. Andrew could see no impediment to improving the supply of goods and materials, and, as his future business ventures would show, his assessment was well founded.

The pardoning of his convict sentence was the watershed moment in Andrew Thompson's life. He decided, after much introspection, to remain in the colony and to make his fortune in the new land. Although he was now free to go anywhere and do anything, Andrew remained a constable in Green Hills and continued to live in the cottage by the Hawkesbury performing his daily policing duties. His immediate working life changed little, though in addition to his government rations and three servants, he now received a wage – his first regular income.

Andrew's off-duty interests and endeavours were about to blossom. The locals had embraced this articulate young constable and he was widely considered a spokesman for emancipist farmers in the district. Many of these settlers had been granted land, a right their parents in Britain could never have contemplated, and they were anxious that these privileges would not be eroded by future governors or political decisions. Also, the ex-convict farmers who rented farmland – something they could never have afforded in the old country – formed a group who were ready to fight the vicissitudes of governors and the prejudices of elitists in Sydney. Farmers in the district were now well aware of their importance as the major food producers in the colony, and they wanted to protect their future rights and livelihoods. The Hawkesbury settlers decided to unite and present their collective views to the governor as a single voice. To do this effectively they needed a literate spokesman who could represent their best interests in future communications with the government.

Since Andrew Thompson's arrival in Green Hills, he had become fully conversant with the problems of farming in this remote area. He routinely listened to settlers' complaints on the many issues affecting their land and their lives. He had good ideas on how to do things better in the community but needed money to make them a reality. The thrifty Scot began to save every penny he could.

One of the most burdensome problems facing all Hawkesbury farmers was the prohibitive cost of transport and consumables. The distance that goods had to be shipped from Sydney and Parramatta was not the main reason for the exorbitant prices levied on settlers – retailers made ridiculous profits from sales in remote localities. The price of commodities was a constant complaint in the colony and Hunter was well aware of the unfair usury practises of traders, and how this was threatening the farmers' livelihoods. He ordered officials to tour the farming districts and solicit suggestions and remedies. It was the first time in the colony's history that settlers were invited by the government to express their views and to submit proposals to the governor. In January 1798, Hunter received petitions claiming that the prices charged by traders were 'out of all reason exorbitant' because of the high profit margins placed on goods purchased from ships.[18] The petitions pointed out that government stores carried little stock because private retailers bought goods from ships at higher wholesale prices. Hunter sympathised with the settlers in a letter to the Home Office.

> The settlers are so frequently ruined, their crops mortgaged, their persons imprisoned, and their families beggared, and falling back upon the public store to prevent starving through the heavy debts they contract, …. their ground by this means becomes useless for the want of strength to work it.[19]

He ordered Reverend Samuel Marsden and Surgeon Thomas Arndell to carry out a survey of the settlers' grievances in the farming districts. In submissions to Marsden and Arndell, the farmers accused the traders, dealers and publicans as being 'the engines of our destruction' and claimed that the colony was now 'infested with dealers, pedlars, and extortioners it is absolutely necessary to extirpate them'. Settlers were particularly aggrieved that wealthy merchants should claim that tea and sugar were luxuries to which 'a settler ought not to aspire'.[20]

Of course, private traders strongly disputed claims that the widespread indebtedness was due to high retail prices. They argued that most debts were caused by alcohol consumption, and that this had led to the ruin of many settlers. Marsden and Arndell disagreed, saying that in most cases these arose from the high cost of goods, and concluded that indebtedness facing small farmers was often not their fault.[21] The settlers were buoyed by this strong repudiation of the profiteers, and assumed that the governor would act promptly. They were to be disappointed – the settler's grievances had been fairly recorded, but the influence of the Corps on the commercial activities in the colony was far too strong for them to be acted upon without recrimination. This had eroded Hunter's resolve to try and prevent exploitation, and nothing happened.

Other malpractices in the grain trade also hindered the viability of settlers. When the smaller farmers wanted to sell their grain, the larger landholders thwarted sales by falsely claiming the granaries were full. Farmers were then forced to sell their produce at bargain prices to someone of influence who could demand storage rights. It had also become common practice for some dealers to use false weights when buying grain. In an attempt to circumvent such skulduggery, Hunter had special agents validate weights used by dealers. This slowed the practice, but, without Corps cooperation, the fraudulent practices continued.

Hunter's apparent weakness when faced with Corps opposition slowly corroded his support in the colony. He failed to curb the Corps' insatiable appetite for profits in the rum trade, and this damaged all aspects of his administration. Hunter's intention to govern justly was not in question, but John Macarthur opposed him on every issue – even when the interests of the Corps were unaffected. Macarthur set out to ruin the governor, and his ability to do this was reinforced because he had the receptive ear of the Duke of Portland, the Home Office Secretary. Macarthur frequently wrote to Portland about Hunter's interference in Corps matters, not mentioning that his own profits were involved. He complained about excessive government spending, the granting of land to lazy and incapable settlers, and of moral degradation in the colony. The governor was unaware of the contents of Macarthur's letters until the Home Office demanded a response to the allegations. Hunter probably knew his authority was being undermined, but he lacked either the courage, or the political agility, to combat it. The actions of his administration were guided by the belief that the government needed to tread judiciously otherwise the security of the colony might be jeopardised by the military.

In early 1797, Hunter had requested the Home Office Secretary to replace the NSW Corps with a contingent of regular marines. Records show that the British government considered putting a detachment of marines on the next transport to New South Wales.[22] Unfortunately for the colony, these orders were cancelled owing to the war with France, and the designated marine regiment was stationed elsewhere. The Rebellion in Ireland further impeded the possibility of a new military contingent being sent to the colony in 1798. The Home Office had other concerns and Hunter's request to replace the NSW Corps was forgotten.

By 1798 the Hawkesbury district had six public houses (inns) licensed to sell alcohol. One of these public houses, the 'Coach and Horses Inn', belonged to Chief Constable Thomas Rickerby, and another, the 'Cross Keys Inn', was run by the emancipist John Harris. These inns sold goods as well as alcohol, but they were more pubs than stores. Innkeeper Harris was the only person other than Andrew Thompson permitted to reside in the government precinct with the military and civil officers. Harris had been a constable in Sydney and on Norfolk Island before coming to the Hawkesbury and was a good friend of Andrew Thompson. In January 1798 he had received a lease of 6½ acres of land in the government precinct. The proximity of the Cross Keys Inn to the military barracks meant it was the main watering hole for the soldiers, and John Harris was a well-known and popular publican.

In late 1798, Lieutenant Anthony Kemp became the Corps commandant for the Hawkesbury district. Like many of the Corps officers, he was an arrogant man who considered himself socially superior to most of the locals. Kemp and Harris were neighbours in the precinct, and they soon crossed swords. Pigs from Kemp's plot regularly trespassed onto Harris's ground and trampled down his corn crop. One day it got too much for Harris and he ordered one of his servants to set the dogs on the pigs to drive them off his property. This infuriated the Commandant who demanded that the servant be punished with 25 lashes. When Harris responded that 'he had better not do that as the man had acted by his order', Kemp threatened to lash him instead. But Harris, knowing his rights from his days as a constable, told Kemp that he 'could not do that as he [Harris] was a free man' and 'as free as Mr Kemp', indeed 'a citizen of the world'. Kemp took this as an insult, finding it inconceivable that such a person could challenge him, and he promptly gaoled him in the watch house.

Harris was quickly released when magistrate Samuel Marsden and Chief Constable Rickerby intervened. But their attempts to settle the dispute were fruitless and, shortly after, Harris sued Kemp for assault and false imprisonment. Harris successfully argued in the trial on 10 June 1799 that his emancipation meant he could no longer be treated like a convict. For the first time in colonial history an emancipist had won a civil rights case – an astonishing achievement considering that military officers sat on the court bench.[23] It was seen as an important test case for the emancipists as it gave precedent for future civil cases against the NSW Corps' iniquitous dealings. This was also a valuable lesson for Andrew Thompson, and for the rest of his life he never hesitated in exerting his and other settlers' rights to challenge injustice.

After his court success, John Harris moved to Toongabbie where he opened another inn, and became an agent for John Macarthur. This led to his downfall when in December 1800 the new Governor King found that Harris had contravened government orders by purchasing convicts' rations with rum – an action deemed illegal because it encouraged food theft. Magistrate Marsden put Harris in custody, cancelled his spirit licence and destroyed his alcohol casks. Deprived of a livelihood, he left the colony.[24] Thus, John Harris had provided emancipists with another lesson: cooperating with Corps officers was not always beneficial.

Relations between settlers and Aborigines in the Hawkesbury district had been relatively tranquil between 1795 and 1798. The Corps commanded by Lieutenants Edward Abbott and Neil McKellar had avoided any action that might lead to violence. This sensible approach changed when Lieutenant Kemp took command, and the attitude of the military towards Aborigines became much more aggressive. Aboriginal raids on farms also increased when land was granted on the outer perimeter of the settlement. Andrew's close friend constable David Brown had moved to his new 30-acre allotment at Wilberforce on the Hawkesbury – it was one of the most isolated farms in the settlement. Brown was speared while carrying water from the river to his stock. Fortunately, the wound was not life threatening, but the following day another farmer was killed in the same area. These incidents led to threats by settlers to abandon their productive farms unless something was done to improve security.[25]

In August 1799 Lieutenant Thomas Hobby, was appointed to replace Kemp as the new Commandant of the Hawkesbury detachment. Hobby had landed in the colony only two months earlier and knew little about the settlers or the Aborigines.[26] Moreover, the discipline of the soldiers he commanded was low because they were incensed by the Aboriginal unrest and their own inaction. Several had instigated revenge attacks on a local tribe. Immediately confronted with settler complaints, Hobby was too inexperienced to appreciate the subtlety of the interactions or how to arbitrate peaceful solutions. He believed that a major attack was imminent and escalated hostility with Aborigines across the district, involving both the constables and the Corps soldiers.

When a settler reported he had been attacked on the Parramatta Road and but for a firearm he would have been killed, Hobby promptly went to Sydney and informed Hunter. The next day, Constable Thompson arrived in Sydney with news that ex-Sergeant Goodall, a settler on the Hawkesbury Road, had been wounded by several Aborigines on his farm, and was not expected to live. In fact, he later recovered quickly. Hobby asked the governor to send out a 'party of the military to kill five or six of them wherever they were to be found'. Hunter refused and told Hobby to 'act discretionally against the Natives' and to return to the Hawkesbury.[27]

In August 1799 the Hawkesbury settler, Thomas Hodgkinson, went hunting into the western hills with three Aboriginal youths he had hired as scouts. However, when the youths saw that settler John Wimbow would join the hunting party, they absconded and were replaced by two Aboriginal men, named Major White and Terribandy. Two weeks later, the settlers Hodgkinson and Wimbow were found dead.[28] Wimbow lived with Terribandy's daughter, and the killing appeared to be a family dispute.[29] Lieutenant Hobby sent soldiers and settlers to recover the bodies, with orders 'that if they fell in with any Natives .... to fire in upon them'. Shortly after the settlers encountered the three Aboriginal lads first hired as scouts by Hodgkinson – they had been sent by their tribe to return the dead settlers' guns. The three blameless youths were seized and imprisoned on a farm. One escaped, but the other two were murdered and buried.[30]

The following day, 19 September 1799, Mary Archer, a partner of one of the search party, told Chief Constable Rickerby of the murders. She followed her conscience and named the five men who had killed the youths. She also stated that three other settlers were not involved in the killing. Constables David Brown and John Soare, led by Chief Constable Rickerby, recovered the boys' remains, and the five named men were taken into custody. On 14 October, settlers Powell, Freebody, Metcalfe, Timms and Butler were tried for murder. Judge Advocate Richard Dore headed a court bench with three Naval and three NSW Corps officers. The accused were found 'generally Guilty of Killing two Natives' but the bench was split in deciding the sentences; the Naval officers recommended corporal punishment, whereas the Corps officers and the judge advocate recommended the case be referred to a British court. This meant the judgement and sentences effectively bypassed Hunter, who was appalled by the murders. The five men were released on the condition that each paid a surety bond of £100 and a bail bond of £200. Powell was also dismissed as a constable.[31] The court action was a shameful example of the calibre of justice applied to indigenous people.

What Mary Archer had not foreseen when she reported the

murders, was that her courage would initiate major changes to the laws involving Aborigines in the colony. It would take almost two years before the new judicial instructions arrived from England and by then Hunter had left the colony. On 30 January 1802 the Home Secretary, Lord Hobart wrote to the then Governor Gidley King:

> I cannot help lamenting that the wise and humane instructions of my predecessors, relative to the necessity of cultivating the goodwill of the natives, do not appear to have been observed in earlier periods of the establishment of the colony with an attention corresponding to the importance of the object. The evils resulting from this neglect seem to be now sensibly experienced, and the difficulty of restoring confidence with the natives, alarmed and exasperated by the unjustifiable injuries they have too often experienced, will require all the attention which your active vigilance and humanity can bestow upon a subject so important in itself, and so essential to the prosperity of the settlement, and I should hope that you may be able to convince those under your Government that it will be only by observing uniformly a great degree of forbearance and plain, honest dealing with the natives, that they can hope to relieve themselves from their present dangerous embarrassment.[32]

In future, anyone killing an Aboriginal person would be fully accountable and 'any instance of injustice or wanton cruelty towards the natives will be punished with the utmost severity of the law'.[33] Mary Archer paid a price for following her conscience; her partner left her and returned to England, but only after signing over his land in her name. It was a token reward for her honesty and bravery.

From January to March 1799 the colony experienced a severe drought. Most tributaries of the Hawkesbury dried up and fierce fires threatened bush around Parramatta and Sydney. In late March the drought broke with days of heavy rain. The waters of the vast Nepean-Hawkesbury catchment area roared down the Hawkesbury River and the connected creeks. The local Aboriginal people had warned settlers of flooding when heavy rain fell in the mountains, but few had listened. The river rose 50 ft (15 m) and was so powerful 'it carried all before it' and 'the whole country here appear'd like an immense ocean'.[34] This happened so quickly that settlers on the low-lying land were unprepared. The government storehouse, huts, crops and animals were swept away. Although only one life was lost, many people needed to be rescued from the roofs of their houses and trees by the few boats in the district. The constables and settlers manned the rescue boats and Andrew Thompson coordinated the recovery effort. When the floods receded, settlers were confronted with scenes of utter devastation, and the loss of about 20,000 bushels of wheat.[35] Many in the district had lost almost everything they owned and had to start all over again. Most settlers promptly set about recovering as much as possible and rebuilding their homes. This included Constable Andrew Thompson, who had to rebuild his heavily damaged cottage in the government precinct.

The flood of 1799 was a pivotal event in Andrew's life. His brave rescue and recovery efforts were the principal reasons why Governor Hunter granted him on 1 October a fourteen-year lease for the acre of land on which his white cottage stood. The grant was proclaimed as recognition of his loyalty to the governor, his diligence as a Hawkesbury constable and his rescue actions during the recent flood. The annual rent for the lease was set at 2s 6d and the land was 'let for the purpose of building on'. A lease condition permitted a public road of 100 ft width through his land; it would be called George Street.[36] The plot would become the focus of Andrew Thompson's future business activities.

Prior to the flood of 1799 Andrew Thompson was the only constable in the district not farming when off-duty. The losses from the recent floods meant that many settlers at the Hawkesbury faced serious financial hardship. They had taken out loans to replace seeds, stock and homes, and some creditors wanted immediate repayment, threatening imprisonment unless settlers sold their farms and repaid their debts. The emancipist settler Henry York found himself in this situation. Francis Grose had granted him a 30-acre plot on the South Creek, close to Green Hills, shortly after completing his sentence.[37] When creditors demanded repayments of debts from York, Thompson stepped in and offered to buy York's property so he could pay his creditors. As a frugal Scot, he had saved enough from his wages to offer a reasonable price for the farm. It was the first land he had ever owned, but he knew from his rural upbringing that good land was always a worthwhile investment.

Henry York's farmland had already been cleared, so Andrew and his servants were able to quickly cultivate it and sow wheat. His first crop looked promising until heavy gales swept the area and flattened every stalk of wheat. Many settlers in the area who had survived the floods were now destitute, and grain prices rocketed to new highs.

Those farmers whose crops had survived the winds were astonished when the government offered to buy their meagre wheat harvests for 20% less than last year's price. Hunter was attempting to keep food prices low after he had been criticised by the Home Office for being too generous last year. The farmers were further incensed when Hunter demanded that settlers pay their outstanding debts to the government before their grain could be stored in the granaries. The outraged farmers simply refused to sell their wheat at a price that did not reflect the shortfall in supply, and they maintained their boycott for three months until there was a flour crisis in the colony and the previous year's price was matched.[38] Hunter later justified this to the Home Office by sending them the submissions of settlers stating that the initial low grain prices were 'intolerable'.

The storm-depleted 1799 harvest and the settlers' boycott caused the government to question if the colony's grain stocks would be adequate to feed the colony's growing population. Governor Hunter decided to carry out a survey of the grain growing and grain storage capacity in the major farming areas. Knowing the respect that Andrew Thompson's rescues had gained him in the Hawkesbury community, he asked him on 19 November 1799 to conduct the survey in that district. Andrew was to be assisted by constables David Brown, John Ryan and Richard Hill.[39] As farmers themselves, Andrew and his fellow constables were well acquainted with the problems of growing grain and getting it to market in the district. Additionally, in their policing roles these men regularly encountered the duplicitous practices of some of the grain traders.

The flood-devastated farmers were also active. The calamities of 1799 had brought them together, and they jointly petitioned the governor for more humane treatment. At a meeting on 14 January 1800, the settlers appointed Andrew Thompson and thirteen other district representatives to present a petition to the governor on the cost of farming and living in the Hawkesbury district. They reported that the cost of growing 25 bushels of wheat was £13 5s 9d, whereas this could only be sold for £12 10s. Moreover, they were charged double the Sydney prices for tea, sugar, soap, linen, shoes and clothing. This petition was Andrew Thompson's first involvement as an official spokesperson for the farming community.[40]

A month later, 181 Hawkesbury settlers, including Thompson, presented another petition to Hunter that complained of the ridiculously high prices in the district. This petition overlooked the traditional diplomatic niceties and went straight to the point, making their complaints in eight emphatic statements.[41] It also stated bluntly that the government had not done enough to rectify their situation. Hunter heatedly refused to accept such a brusque missive, claiming he had been more than generous with the settlers. Realising that they had not been respectful enough, the settlers submitted a more tempered petition, and this was favourably received. Hunter assured the settlers that he would rectify any aggravation within his power.[42] It was a lesson in diplomacy for the settlers, and Thompson learned from it – future petitions to authorities were much more flattering. However, it soon became clear to the petitioners that Governor Hunter was no longer prepared, or perhaps able, to act on their complaints. Reducing prices was apparently beyond his control.

In March 1800 many farms along the Hawkesbury were again inundated with water. The river burst its banks and flooded crops in the lowlands that were ready for harvesting.[43] Widespread bankruptcy threatened many in the farming community and some gave up completely. The timing of these floods coincided with the imminent change of governors. On 15 Apr 1800 the ship *Speedy* docked in Port Jackson with Captain Philip Gidley King on board. Dispatches from the Duke of Portland proclaimed King as the new governor and that John Hunter was recalled to England. The repeated complaints of John Macarthur, and others, had destroyed Hunter's reputation at the Home Office, and his failure to show strong leadership meant many in the colony now considered him ineffective. Although Hunter had sent letters to the Home Office refuting the charges against him, they failed to arrive before Captain Philip Gidley King was appointed as his replacement.

Despite Captains King and Hunter being familiar colleagues on the First Fleet, the handover of governorship was neither smooth nor swift. The 63-year-old Hunter had no intention of departing the colony unless he could command the warship HMS *Buffalo*, due to arrive in Port Jackson soon, for his return to England. Because of this and other demands he remained governor for another five months. Over this time cooperation between the two deteriorated badly. While awaiting the handover, Philip Gidley King reported to the Home Office that a feeling of 'vice, dissipation, and a strange relaxation' had invaded the colony. Alcohol 'that fiery poison' was everywhere, in the cellars of the 'better sort of people' and with the 'blackest character among the convicts'.⁴⁴ King predicted that his duties over the next five years would be laborious and highly discouraging. He also noted that the prices for the most common necessities were even too high for *him* to pay, and that many other disagreeable issues had been left for him to sort out.

Portrait of John Hunter, the colony's second governor (1795-1800).

Portrait of Philip Gidley King, the colony's third governor (1800-1806).

King let it be known that when he assumed the role of governor, many of the longstanding malpractices in the colony would be eliminated. Based on his experience as lieutenant governor on Norfolk Island, he believed that he knew how to deal with the NSW Corps. In 1794 King had faced unfounded Corps allegations that he punished soldiers too severely and ex-convicts too lightly. He had sent ten Corps soldiers 'under the charge of mutinous behaviour' to be tried in Sydney by court martial. They had disobeyed their commanding officer's orders and had been drunkenly insolent to him. Although Corps officers on Norfolk Island mostly supported King, Commandant Grose defended the Corps soldiers' interests irrespective of the charges, and he heavily rebuked King.⁴⁵ Grose later apologised, but King never forgave him, or the Corps, for this episode. King vowed that once he became governor, he would deal with the Corps' intransigence directly.

Even so, King realised that his first priority as governor would be to implement trading reforms that would lower the price of essential goods and regulate land transactions in the colony. To provide some benchmarks for making these reforms, he ordered a General Muster be held. King was a good administrator who was suspicious of anecdotal data; he wanted to know the demography of the colony as a whole. In July 1800, a General Muster was conducted of all residents, their dependants, land holdings and livestock. 4958 people now lived in the colony and every third person was a convict. The Hawkesbury had a population of 964, including 145 women and 190 children, with an adult gender ratio of four men to each woman.[46] It was certainly not easy for men to find a wife in the colony, and this led to anti-social and criminal behaviour.

The 1800 muster records show that Andrew Thompson had 26 pigs, 25 acres of wheat and 12 acres ready to be planted with maize and had delivered 100 bushels of wheat to the government store this season. Thompson, his three male servants and one female convict housekeeper were all on government provisions. He employed a second female on wages, but her role in the house is unlisted. According to the muster, Thompson was already among the top twenty Hawkesbury grain producers. Of these, fourteen emancipists had larger farms and more stock than the young Scot.[47] The emancipist John Stogdell was by far the largest landowner in the district with 565 acres and had delivered 3000 bushels of wheat to the stores. Stogdell was a successful farmer and businessman, but he drowned during the 1801 floods trying to reach his farm on horseback, aged 38.

On 25 September 1800, the 42-year-old Captain Philip Gidley King RN became the third Governor of New South Wales. Three days later, John Hunter sailed on HMS *Buffalo* to England. Hunter had been a faithful servant of the Crown, but he struggled in his role as governor. His recall was needed, but the strong censure of the Home Office was undeserved. Few could have provided strong leadership in the colony where the power lay in the hands of the military, and Hunter was simply not up to it. Even so, there was much to admire about John Hunter as a person and a naval officer. He had been Arthur Phillip's reliable right-hand man in the first years of the settlement. A naval command was quite different from running a government; naval orders were executed without hesitation or severe punishment ensued. Hunter strove to achieve many worthwhile goals as governor, but he was simply unable to cope with the politics inherent in his position, particularly against the ruthless behind-the-scenes manoeuvring of John Macarthur.

Governor King wanted to initiate the much-needed reforms quickly. Using the data from the 1800 Muster, he issued a series of governmental edicts designed to remove the principal abuses of previous administrations. He refuted rumours in the Hawkesbury district that the government would not buy this year's grain crops – this would have resulted in total ruin for small farmers. With the backing of the Home Office, King launched a campaign to eradicate the rum trade and imposed regulations that prohibited government workers from trading in alcohol. When the expected opposition to his reforms surfaced among the Corps, King wryly observed that 'the greater their rank is the more I shall be the object of their resentment'.[48] He then limited the number of convict servants assigned to Corps officers and civil personnel, such as constables, to two men. Next, he stopped anyone, except authorised officials, from boarding incoming cargo ships and required that the government be given first choice in purchasing imported goods. Private retailers were only allowed a 20% mark-up on the remaining items.[49] He also created public warehouses that sold the imported articles at a low profit, and this immediately reduced retail prices. King knew these changes would further infuriate the profiteering Corps officers, but he had learnt from Hunter's demise – he kept the Home Office fully informed of all his actions.

During Governor King's regular visits to Green Hills, the 27-year-old constable and grain assessor, Andrew Thompson, must have favourably impressed him. The Corps still resisted cooperating with the government, and King needed competent men to take up additional administrative positions. He observed that Thompson was not only enforcing the law as a constable and assisting grain productivity as the assessor of harvests, but he had also become a major wheat grower in the area. On 13 November 1800, only one month after taking office, Governor King appointed Andrew Thompson as the Registrar of Agreements for the Hawkesbury district.[50] The hapless land-granting practices of Grose and Paterson were still, years later, causing property disputes, and King needed someone honest and numerate enough to help sort these out. Land had often been granted without being officially registered, and, in some instances, Corps commanding officers had issued a handwritten note stating that the named person 'has my permission to settle'. At the time this had been deemed sufficient authority to occupy land without an official survey.[51] Land sales had even been sanctioned by a handshake, without any deeds or documents at all.

Governor Hunter had tried to correct these irregularities by reissuing deeds for 20,000 acres but many grantees had no official purchase records. To reduce property disputes King ordered that no claims could be made to the civil court unless the buying and selling parties had entered into a written agreement. This had to be registered and signed by responsible officials in either Sydney, Parramatta or Green Hills. In the last district, the Registrar of Agreements Andrew Thompson, was entitled to sixpence (6d) 'for his trouble' for each entry in his register. Every Saturday Andrew travelled to Parramatta to have his register countersigned by Reverend Samuel Marsden. In July 1803 Andrew Thompson was reappointed as Registrar of Agreements.[52]

In eight short years, the boy convict Andrew Thompson had become a free man, a respected police constable and leader in the colony's most important farming district and had been appointed to a position of trust by the governor. His appointment as the Registrar of Agreements significantly increased Thompson's stature in the colonial civil hierarchy and also improved his finances. But in the eyes of the colonial elite, he was still seen as an emancipist whose social status was very low indeed. The freemen of John Macarthur's ilk were, of course, well aware of the rapid rise of this young emancipist official and would be more than willingly interact with him over land transactions or other business dealings. But they would have nothing to do with him socially. The government post provided the young constable with additional status and income, but his wider acceptance by the sort of people his family aspired to be part of was still a long way off.

Chapter 7

ENTREPRENEUR

No finer stamp of early Australian manhood is to be found in the historical records of New South Wales than that exemplified by the hard-headed, shrewd young Scotchman, Andrew Thompson.[1]

By the close of the year 1801 Hawkesbury settlers had come to realise that this was truly a land of drought and flooding rains. Three successive floods occurred over four months and by March 1801 many of the productive farms in the district were ruined and the farmers exhausted, physically and financially. The river and its tributaries had risen over 40 ft (12 m) and inundated settlers hung on 'trees and pieces of floating wood, until the floods subsided'.[2] The ghastly ordeal of clinging to the roofs of their huts in the high winds and incessant rain was for many more frightening than the voyage from England. Rescuers in small rowboats worked through the night responding to calls and received a hero's welcome on reaching the inundated farms.

Governor King declared the floods a natural calamity. He wrote to the Home Office that Hawkesbury settlers were 'exhibiting such a state of woeful misery that is but seldom seen or heard of'. They had lost their possessions, houses, wheat and corn harvests and nearly all of their animals. King regarded this as a disaster for the entire colony, since over half of the grain and most of its pork meat came from the Hawkesbury. Without this food, the colony faced massive food shortages and King contemplated sending ships to India to supplement the grain supply.[3]

Natural disasters invariably bring out the best, and the worst, in people. A lamentable consequence of the floods was that some traders used the flood losses to foreclose on the loans of insolvent and ruined settlers. This led to forced land sales, from which the creditors often benefitted greatly because of the low prices. Such exploitative practices infuriated settlers. A joint petition was sent to the governor requesting that he delay the loan-repayment demands until they had time to recover.⁴ King acted swiftly and gave settlers a year's suspension of civil court actions by creditors.⁵ Despite this reprieve, many were so disheartened by their losses that they gave up cultivating their own farms and worked as labourers for other settlers who managed to retain their properties. The Hawkesbury constable, John Soare, had a farm that was severely affected by the floods. His farm bordered on the land Andrew Thompson had bought from Henry York two years earlier. Some months after the flood Thompson purchased Soare's 30-acre farm, increasing his holding to 60 acres.⁶ Soare remained a constable in Green Hills and farmed on a small, rented plot.

In July 1801 the annual General Muster was held and everyone in the Hawkesbury district was required to assemble at Government House in Green Hills. The muster shows that Andrew Thompson had 60 acres of land; 40 acres had been cleared of which 34 acres were sown in wheat and maize. He owned two horses, five goats and 24 pigs. Apart from Commissary John Palmer in Sydney, Thompson was now the largest employer in the colony. Palmer had 22 assigned convict servants fully provisioned by the government, whereas Thompson had only two, but he employed 20 people on wages.⁷ It is not known if his servants included any females.

After the floods few settlers had enough money to employ workers, and many men were in need of paid work to feed their families. On his constable rounds Thompson encountered destitute cases regularly and because of his own experiences as a convict, he tried to employ as many of these struggling men as he could. He paid them enough to keep food on their table and to prevent theft being the only alternative to starvation. The families he helped never forgot his kindness and they would repay his generosity in later years by supporting his police work and business enterprises.

In recognition of his outstanding service to the community Governor King appointed Thompson as the chief constable of the Hawkesbury district in 1801. A later governor, Lachlan Macquarie, would recall that Thompson had worked 'to the perfect satisfaction of all his superiors, and particularly the [succeeding] Governors. Thompson was a sober, industrious, and enterprising man'.⁸ Andrew was appreciative of this promotion and of Governor King's praise, and thereafter gave him unerring support in his efforts to curb the power of the NSW Corps. Predictably, Thompson's loyalty to King earned him the sustained wrath of the Corps officers.

King's principal reforms targeted the two greatest evils in the colony: alcohol trading and the high cost of imported goods.[9] His crackdown on the rum trade, and the relaxation to access rights for inhabitants to buy 'dry goods' from ships at regulated prices, met with strong Corps resistance because it undermined their monopoly. Government restrictions on activities from which the Corps profited also meant an inevitable clash between the governor and John Macarthur. King was well aware of the Corps' power when their entrenched commercial interests were threatened, and he made sure not to repeat Hunter's mistakes. He reported Macarthur's every action to the Home Office, adding that 'One thing I shall remark, that the arts and intrigues of a man you have heard so much about (I mean Captain McArthur) will one day or other sett this colony in a flame'.[10] His prediction would prove to be true.

In an attempt to isolate the governor socially, Macarthur insisted that Corps officers refuse any social engagements with Government House. When the Corps' commandant, Lieutenant Colonel Paterson, ignored this impertinent demand, Macarthur threatened to release some personal correspondence. Paterson was affronted and challenged him to a duel. This took place in September 1801, and Paterson received a wound that was thought to be fatal. Macarthur was arrested but released when Paterson recovered. To rid the colony of this troublemaker, King appointed Macarthur as Corps Commandant on Norfolk Island. He declined the post, demanding instead to be court martialled. Governor King knew that John Macarthur exerted too much power on the Sydney court benches to be prosecuted and he referred the matter to the Home Office.[11] He made it clear 'that if Captain McArthur returns here in any official character it should be that of Governor, as one-half the colony already belongs to him, and it will not be long before he gets the other half'.[12] King banished Lieutenant Macarthur to England to face court martial charges.

In mid-November 1801, Macarthur sailed for England aboard the *Hunter*. The *Anna Josepha* sailed soon after with King's dispatches detailing the charges against him. However, when the ship docked in England the governor's dispatches had mysteriously disappeared. An associate of Macarthur's aboard the *Anna Josepha* almost certainly removed them, but no inquiry was held into their disappearance.

The loss of the governor's evidence prevented any meaningful prosecution of the court martial, and Macarthur was simply censured for bad conduct and released. For the next four years he remained in England, returning to Sydney in 1805.

With Macarthur out of the colony, Governor King addressed other malpractices with renewed vigour. The NSW Corps still controlled the rum trade, and he was resolute in eradicating this once and for all. The Corps was equally determined to resist his edicts and was not averse to slighting him in public. Philip Gidley King had experienced this before. During his tenure as lieutenant governor of Norfolk Island from 1788 to 1790, he had observed that ex-convict settlers were more law-abiding than Corps soldiers who he believed were responsible for most ills on the island. Now, a decade later, the indignant arrogance and outright disobedience of the miliary meant his reforms were either ignored or laxly applied. He reacted by excluding Corps officers from any decision-making and cultivating strong links with the emancipist and free settler communities. Nonetheless, King knew that the convict colony needed the military for its security, so he diplomatically exercised his civil authority while finding a working relationship with the Corps. On more than one occasion he needed to remind Corps Major George Johnston that the British government had not intended convicts to be in 'Oblivion and Disgrace for ever' and that all emancipists were 'as Free and Susceptible of every Right as Free Born Britons as any Soul in this Territory'.[13]

Progressively, the governor reinforced his support base by pardoning large numbers of well-behaved convicts, and in doing so created an influential emancipist block of men and women who were loyal to the government. Many of these men gained important official roles in the colony and became his political backers and advisors. King even appointed emancipists to his bodyguard. A former officer in the East India Company, George Bellasis, who had been transported for killing someone in a duel, was made commandant of the governor's cavalry, and of the artillery unit at Dawes Point. He appointed emancipists, Andrew Thompson, Richard Fitzgerald, David Mann, James Meehan, Reverend Henry Fulton and Father James Dixon, into official positions. As we will see later, all these men would achieve prominence in the colony but, because of enticements offered by the Corps, they would later divide into two political camps – one for the governor, the other against.[14]

King was the first governor to offer convicts a ticket of leave. This ticket excused a convict from government work for a defined period and was awarded to those who were well behaved and could support themselves.[15] It also allowed convicts to seek out their own employment within a specified district, though they could only leave that area with a magistrate's permission. In effect, the ticket allowed a convict much more freedom and lightened the government purse by not needing to pay for their support.

When his police duties allowed, Chief Constable Thompson invested time and energy into his farm. By early 1802 he had increased his South Creek farm to 120 acres by purchasing the adjacent Peacock farm and West farm. He consolidated the four properties and named it West Hill farm. This land, bordering on the South Creek, was low lying and frequently waterlogged, but it was fertile and provided abundant grain yields. The south side of this property rose to McGraths Hill and here Andrew built a spacious two-storey deep-red brick house, which was well above the reach of floodwater. This 'incomparably beautiful little Estate' was referred to in Green Hills as 'the Red House'.[16] Over time, a granary, barns, offices and outhouses were added, and West Hill became one of the most productive farms in the colony. A year later, King agreed to consolidate the 120 acres of land into one deed. This farm and its distinctive red house close to the South Creek could be seen from the government precinct in Green Hills was simply known as the Thompson or West Hill farm.[17]

Although the proximity of the West Hill land and buildings to the Hawkesbury River made shipping of grain to Sydney reasonably straightforward, Andrew saw that better access to the government stores in Green Hills would greatly reduce his transport costs. These granaries were particularly important because of the need to protect grain storage from floods – the very survival of the colony depended on their security. He believed a new bridge across the South Creek was needed, and he embarked on his riskiest business venture yet. With it his entrepreneurial inclinations were initiated.

Thompson applied for governmental approval to build, at his own expense, a floating toll bridge over the South Creek that would connect his farm to Green Hills. King readily supported the project, contributing £15 and two men for three months towards the construction of a bridge connecting his West Hill farm to the grain stores and wharf in Green Hills.[18] King's support for the bridge spawned the even-more-ambitious goal of realigning the connecting roads. The Old Hawkesbury Road from Parramatta ended on the northeast boundary of the West Hill farm. To give other grain growers access to his toll bridge Thompson had a new road laid through his farm to connect with the Old Hawkesbury Road. This had major benefits for the district as it provided a direct route to Parramatta without having to ferry across the South Creek.

Etching of Andrew Thompson's Red House Farm on the South Creek in about 1810. The rider on the horse is probably intended to be Thompson.

The new access road to Green Hills passed Thompson's Red House near the south end of the bridge. Prior to the opening of the toll bridge traffic from southern farms to the storehouses and granaries in Green Hills was relatively light; the bulk of goods and people being carried on small boats. The toll bridge meant that many more pedestrians, carts and carriages crossed the South Creek from Thompson's land. For farmers living further along the waterways, small boats remained the cheapest way to transport goods and people. Indeed, for many farmers these small vessels were the only means by which grain could be shipped to the granaries.

The bridge across the South Creek was completed in May 1802 and was the first toll bridge in the colony. Thompson was granted a fourteen-year licence to impose tolls on travellers, horses, carts and carriages crossing the bridge, but not on convicts, constables, soldiers or officials. Foot passengers paid 4d, or 10s per year; a horse could cross for 2s 6d, or £2 10s per year, while every cart or carriage had to pay 1s 6d, or £1 10s per year. Thompson was responsible for maintaining the bridge. His licence prohibited others from operating a competing barge to cross the South Creek – offenders were fined £5.[19] In December 1805, the bridge was 'instantaneously immersed' by a lightning strike. Thompson promptly had it repaired, and the bridge licence was renewed in March 1806.[20]

The success of the toll bridge whetted Thompson's appetite for other business ventures. In April 1802 William Cox, the Corps Paymaster, asked Thompson if he was interested in managing his Argyle Farm for two years. Cox offered him half the net proceeds of the farm, with a mutual cancellation penalty of £100. Unfortunately for Cox, he was quickly bankrupted, and Thompson needed to recover his surety by auctioning Cox's farm.[21] This particular financial arrangement is instructive because it shows that business transactions between emancipists and Corps officers often took place. Andrew had regular dealings with the Corps, but outside of commercial interactions there was no contact – doing business and socialising were two entirely separate matters.

Thompson's business interests now extended beyond his transport and farming ventures. He organised regular property auctions, both at his government precinct cottage and his private residence, the Red House. In June 1803 the auction of William Cox's estate was held 'at the House of Andrew Thomson, Hawkesbury'. This transaction had the double benefit of providing an auction fee as well as the recovery of his contracted penalty fee of £100.[22]

Thompson's farms and businesses provided work for many men in the district. The August 1802 Muster shows that he had become the largest private employer in New South Wales, and the second largest grain producer in the Hawkesbury district. The 29-year-old chief constable and farmer owned 120 acres land of which 94 acres had been cleared for growing wheat, barley and maize. He still had three assigned convict servants, but his paid workers had increased to 32. Again, these lists show no females.

Employing so many men meant that Andrew was in the "good books" of Governor King, who desperately needed to reduce the number of people on rations, and their cost to government. Most of Thompson's workers were ticket of leave men who no longer received rations. As someone who had personally suffered under servitude, Thompson was a firm but fair employer who avoided imposing harsh punishments. In any case, most of his employees sought to keep out of trouble to protect their ticket entitlements. And his workers who were assigned convicts always preferred working for ex-convicts because they were more humane but knew that misbehaviour meant dismissal and return to the government.

The 1802 Muster shows that Thompson had increased his stable to six horses, the largest number in the district. Each horse was worth a small fortune – equivalent to the cost of a farmable plot of land.[23] The horses were for riding and to draw carriages; they were far too valuable to pull heavy carts or ploughs. Oxen were the main draft animals in the colony, and they could be hired from the government herd. Thus far on his farms Andrew had concentrated on growing grain crops, but he clearly appreciated the practical importance of cattle and in 1804 he bartered one of his horses for two cows and an ox from the government herd.[24]

Governor King's farm concessions had benefitted many settlers. At 30 years of age, Andrew Thompson reached the zenith of his industry and ambition, and his businesses enterprises grew at astonishing speed. His entrepreneurship coupled with a reputation of being the friend of the governor, made him someone to be reckoned with in the Hawkesbury community and, in turn, this support enhanced his standing with the governor. King continued to assist small farmers with predictable grain prices, limits on retail prices, fixed workers' wages and set hours for assigned convicts. The government had also tried to eliminate the forgery of promissory notes by providing printed promissory forms, but these were not widely adopted.

To further assist farmers, the governor built a new storehouse and brick granary at the top of the government precinct in Green Hills.[25] The settlers appreciated his support, and in January 1803 Governor King received a letter with over 200 signatures, thanking him 'for the many fold blessings we freely enjoy from your determined, just, and salutary Government'. The settlers were particularly grateful that the governor had suppressed 'the infamous and ruinous monopolies'.[26]

> You have, by your impartial and just Government over those under your command, brought to us that sense of liberty which we never felt before. By your administration of justice, the rich, the poor, the free, and the bond[ed], enjoy the same privileges as if in our mother country, where no distinctions are made.[27]

Under King's leadership the colony approached self-sufficiency. In line with his promotion of emancipists, the governor encouraged freedom of expression in the colony, and this led in March 1803 to the establishment of the colony's first newspaper, *The Sydney Gazette and New South Wales Advertiser*. Emancipist George Howe was responsible for the weekly printing of *The Sydney Gazette* and as the official government journal it contained all announcements of new orders, laws and regulations.[28] Howe was trained as a printer in the West Indies where his father and uncle ran the government press. In 1799 he was sentenced to death for shoplifting in England; later commuted to transportation for life. With a wife and son, he was shipped to NSW in 1800 but his wife died on the voyage. Soon after his arrival in Sydney he was made the government printer and in March 1803, after being granted an absolute pardon, he became responsible for *The Sydney Gazette*. George Howe was an admirer of Andrew Thompson's achievements and over the years he praised him in numerous articles. Both these men enjoyed books and literature, and much of the information about Andrew's activities comes from the writings of this editor and journalist.

Andrew Thompson's attention now shifted to transportation. As the second largest grain producer in the district, he stood to benefit significantly from cheaper bulk shipping to Sydney. In the 1800s all goods were sent to and from Green Hills on the Hawkesbury River, and the small schooner *Francis* was one of three small sailing boats involved in this trade. Prior to 1797, the private ownership of large sailing boats was prohibited in the colony, so as to prevent convict escapes and protect the monopoly of the East India Company. But the conveyance of goods by the *Francis* was slow and expensive, and in 1798 Governor Hunter had permitted the first trading ship to be built in Sydney. Governor King decided it was now time to promote the building of ships specifically for the Hawkesbury River trade.

In 1802 Andrew Thompson commissioned the local shipwright John Kelly to build his first trading ship. Kelly had arrived in 1790 on a seven-year sentence for stealing magazines and books, and in

1799 he was granted 30 acres of land at Canning Reach on the Hawkesbury River. John Kelly shared the property with ex-convict William Cosdale, who farmed while Kelly built boats at the river's edge of his land. Other shipwrights, John Grono and James Webb, also had shipbuilding sites along the Canning Reach.[29]

On 18 October 1802, Andrew launched his new boat the *Hope*, a single-masted sloop of sixteen tons with a crew of three. Loaded with wheat, barley, oats, fruit and vegetables, the *Hope* sailed several times a month between Green Hills and Sydney.[30] The sloop's shallow draft permitted direct access to the West Hill farm dock on the South Creek, and to the Green Hills wharf on the Hawkesbury. On 8 May 1803 the *Hope*, loaded with maize, potatoes and melons was wrecked near Broken Bay at the mouth of the Hawkesbury River. *The Sydney Gazette* attributed the loss to a skipper who had 'professed himself capable of piloting her to the WORLD'S END.' The sloop had been driven ashore and 'dashed to pieces by the violence of the surf' and editor Howe sympathised with Andrew Thompson: 'the proprietor, we are sorry to add, sustains a heavy loss'. However, the *Hope* could not have been too badly damaged because she sailed into Sydney harbour with a load of corn only three weeks later.[31] Encouraged and enriched by the *Hope's* success, Andrew commissioned Kelly to build a much larger trading vessel of 40 tons. On 17 September 1803, Andrew's second sloop, the *Nancy*, was launched.[32]

The ships' names, *Hope* and *Nancy*, appear to have originated from Thompson family attachments. *Hope* presumably reflected a desire to return to Scotland one day and be reconciled with his family, and *Nancy* was the nickname for his mother Agnes. On her maiden voyage the *Nancy* shipped grain from the Cornwallis government farm to Sydney. Skippered by the builder John Kelly, she docked in Port Jackson on 1 October 1803 loaded with 1160 bushels of wheat. Two weeks later she sailed to the Hunter River to load 40 logs of cedar timber, each at least six metres long and one metre in diameter. The *Nancy* was now a formidable competitor for the Sydney shipowners Henry Kable and James Underwood. Their sloop, the *Surprise*, could only carry 17 logs of cedar.[33]

Governor King showed confidence in the seaworthiness of the *Nancy* when, on 1 January 1804, he sent food and despatches to Lieutenant Governor Collins on Van Diemen's Land (Tasmania). Renewed hostilities with France had led Governor King in August

1803 to establish a new settlement in Port Phillip Bay on the south coast. It would be governed by Captain David Collins, previously the First Fleet judge advocate to Governor Phillip, who had been sent out from England. On his arrival in Port Phillip Bay, Collins found the area unsuitable and with King's approval, he sailed to Van Diemen's Land to establish the settlement Hobart Town, named after the Colonial Secretary Lord Hobart.[34] The *Nancy* transported provisions to the Hobart settlement and on her return carried sealskins and whale oil from Bass Strait.[35]

In February 1804 Andrew Thompson launched his third ship, the 30-ton sloop *Hawkesbury*, from the same shipyard. Loaded with 700 bushels of grain, the *Hawkesbury* was escorted on her first voyage to Sydney by the *Speedy*, owned by Jonathan Griffiths.[36] Andrew's three ships became essential to the colony's commerce. The *Hope* mainly shipped farm produce on the Hawkesbury, whereas the larger sloops *Nancy* and *Hawkesbury* sailed to Coal River (Newcastle) and the Bass Strait.[37] By early 1804 there were 22 major private vessels trading in the colony. Like Thompson, Commissary John Palmer and the firm of Henry Kable & James Underwood each owned three boats.[38] Thompson's competitiveness in the shipping on the Hawkesbury was enhanced because he also owned a barge that assisted the loading of his vessels at Green Hills.[39]

Thompson's time was not totally confined to business pursuits; he had many personal interests as well. As a Scottish Presbyterian, the establishment of a school and church at Green Hills were a high priority for him. The first settlers had tried to build a school in the area, but it proved too costly. In late 1804 the government established a public school for boys at Green Hills, which could also be used as a chapel. To pay for a teacher and clergyman at the school, settlers were charged an annual levy of 2d per acre on any land granted by the crown for the period of fourteen years. Six men elected by the settlers, two magistrates and a clergyman oversaw the administration of the school. As one of the wealthier men in Green Hills, Thompson was likely to have been an elected administrator.[40] His own education had been in the parish school of the Scottish border town Yetholm, where reputedly every child owned and read a Bible, and he was a firm advocate for education and literacy being compulsory for all children.

With more and more convicts arriving from England, the shortage of food remained a constant concern. In 1803 Governor King established a new farming area on the Nepean River, upriver from Green Hills. Except for one granted land lease, Andrew had always purchased his land freehold. In 1804, in recognition of his assistance to the colony, Governor King awarded Thompson two land grants. The first, in May 1804, was 78 acres of land between the Nepean River and the Yarramundi Lagoon.[41] And soon after, Andrew purchased the adjoining 200 acres from John Howell.[42]

In August 1804 King amalgamated the granted and purchased lands into one plot of 278 acres with an annual lease after five years of 5s. The consolidated farm, called Agnes Bank in memory of his mother, was situated on the eastern side of the Nepean River near the confluence of the Grose, Nepean and Hawkesbury Rivers.[43] The second land grant made by Governor King in August 1804 was for 260 acres south east of Andrew's West Hill farm on the South Creek and bordered the Old Hawkesbury Road and the Nelson Common Ground.[44] This property crossed the Chain of Ponds, which after heavy rain joined up and ran into the South Creek. This became known as Killarney farm. At age 31, Andrew Thompson now owned 658 acres of cultivable land, making him one of the largest private landowners in the colony, apart from several Corps officers. The Sydney elite were increasing aware of the influence this affable young emancipist wielded in the colony, but none were inclined yet to invite him to dinner – the prevailing social etiquette excluded ex-convicts from their circles.

In 1803 Governor King set aside land on the Cumberland Plain for common use by farmers to feed their stock. Settlers welcomed this, as most small farms were unsuitable for grazing stock animals. Adjacent to Andrew's new Killarney farm, Governor King gazetted 5650 acres of the Nelson Common to be shared by farmers raising cattle, sheep and breeding stock. Andrew Thompson, Thomas Biggers and Thomas Tyler were elected by settlers to be the Trustees of the Nelson Common and were approved by the governor. Later Andrew would also be elected to be a Trustee of the 5130-acre Richmond Common bordering on his farms on the Nepean River.[45]

One of the most impressive aspects of King's administration was that his official appointments drew little distinction between freemen and emancipists. This reinforced the sense of equality and meritocracy that was starting to permeate the colony at every level – these changes were greatly welcomed by most in the colony but not all. In the remote townships such as Green Hills inhabitants relied on each other, and social distinctions had almost disappeared. Free settlers might not mix socially with ex-convicts but in the course of their daily interactions, class distinctions were ignored. Some freemen and Corps officers had even started to acknowledge Thompson socially; he was now too prominent in the area to ignore without repercussions. Then, as now, money and power tend to lower any perceived social barriers!

Further evidence of Andrew Thompson's changing social aspirations is shown in an 1804 record of purchases from Rowland Hassall's well-stocked shop at Parramatta. The articles listed in this purchase order confirm that Andrew started to entertain lavishly at the Red House. This was something he would become well known for. Rowland Hassall was a former missionary in Tahiti, and his store stocked a diverse range of items. Thompson's name appears multiple times in his sales book: in July, he bought three yards fine black cloth for £6 2s 6d, as well as hem silk for 2s, most likely for a suit or jacket. Raised in a textile manufacturing family, Thompson would have only bought the finest material. In November he bought six decanters for £1 14s and two unknown items for £8 each. Thompson spent the large sum of £32 in Hassall's shop (£3150 in today's currency).[46] To buy so many glass decanters in one purchase was a rare extravagance in the colony – most inhabitants could hardly afford a pound of tea. In any case, purchasing these items from Hassall appears to have triggered a decision by Andrew to open an equivalent store in Green Hills.

In 1803 and 1804 Thompson commissioned the construction of several new buildings on his one-acre lease in the government precinct. He built a single-storey retail shop; later adding a three-storey warehouse with workshops and stables to the southwest of his white cottage. The shop would sell imported goods at reduced prices, and for this reason Governor King supported it. An 1807 painting of Green Hills by G. W. Evans shows both buildings.[47] Together with his white cottage, these became the chief constable's police station and business hub. The retail store would sell a wide variety of goods: sugar, tea, soap, candles, tobacco, clothing and shoes, pots and pans, crockery, window glass and tools.[48] The items stocked in his shop depended on cargo aboard ships visiting Sydney and on items sent by his London agent John Braddick.[49]

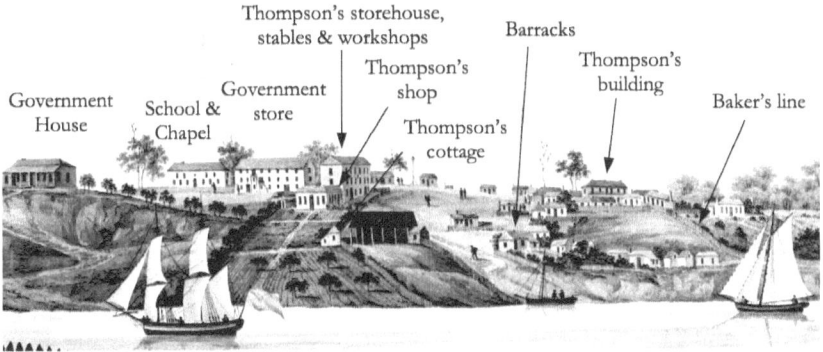

Part of an 1809 painting showing the government precinct at Green Hills looking from the north bank of the Hawkesbury River. Andrew Thompson's whitewashed cottage and orchard are to the left of the log granary in the middle of the painting.

Most items sold were everyday consumer articles available throughout Britain. Although the needs of most of his customers were for basic goods, the store also offered some luxury items. These were extravagant goods intended for special occasions, such as women's outfits. A store-bought dress was a rare and expensive treat for women, most of whom wore homemade clothes. The women's dresses would have been a source of much fascination for the hardworking farm women and servants. Since it was customary for colonial stores to also serve as licensed inns offering beer and spirits, it meant Thompson was now a publican as well.

Thompson's store accepted payment for goods in coin or grain. Wheat was considered the most secure currency substitute; other barter goods such as meat needed salting and went putrid even in winter. More importantly Thompson knew that grain stored in his granary could be easily sold later to the government store, often at a profit. It could also be used to feed and pay his workers, or as seed for next years' crops. Additionally, grain provided a convenient means to purchase animals or make large government or private commercial transactions. Thompson's construction of the new warehouse on the government precinct included, on its upper floors, rooms for hire to government and private enterprises. Such facilities were needed as Green Hills lacked suitable places to transact business. In Parramatta, James Larra, another enterprising emancipist, already offered equivalent facilities. Thompson's offices catered to estate auctions, land and goods sales, debt collector agents and government officers collecting the annual 'Quit Rents' for granted or leased land.[50] The prominent Sydney merchants Robert Campbell and Simeon Lord conducted auctions in these buildings.

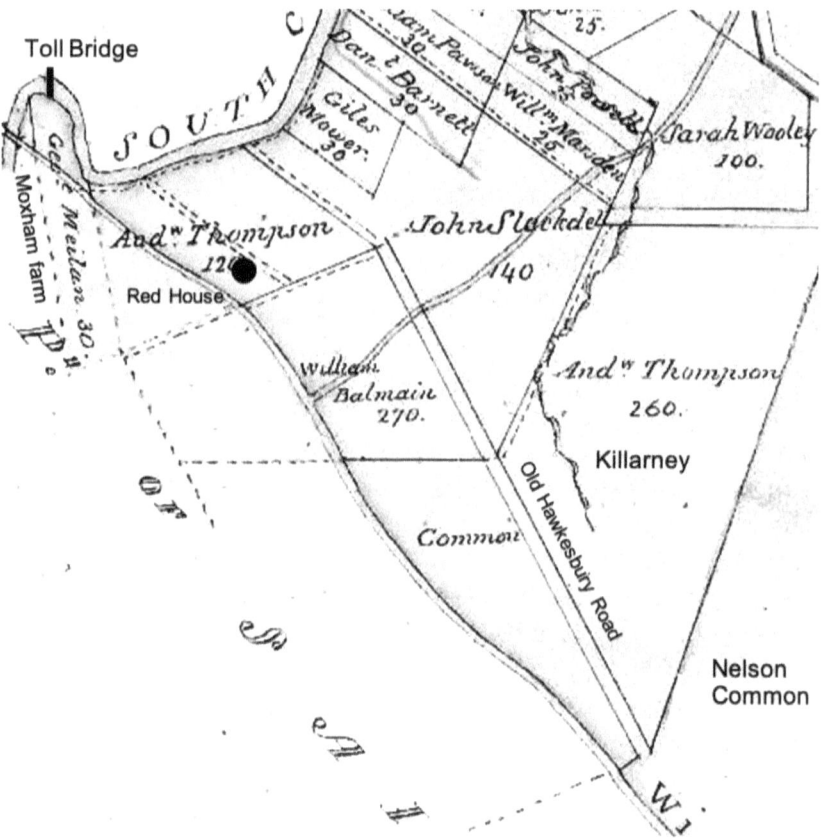

Part of a Pitt Town parish map showing Andrew Thompson's *West Hill* and *Moxham* farms on the South Creek and *Killarney* bordering on the southwest on the Old Hawkesbury Road. The public road ran along the border of the *West Hill* farm through Thompson's land to the South Creek and Thompson's toll bridge. In 1807 he leased Balmain's land, to the south of *West Hill*.

Robert Campbell and Andrew Thompson were Scotsmen of a similar age and education, and well acquainted. Campbell was a partner in the Calcutta-based trading house Campbell & Co and had arrived in Sydney in 1796 on his own cargo ship. He believed the NSW colony had a promising future and he bought land at Dawes Point of the Cove harbour in 1798 where he built a house, warehouses and a wharf for his ships. The stone warehouses still stand today. Despite Governor King's criticism of him for importing spirits, Campbell secured government contracts and became a successful merchant in Sydney with a reputation for fair-trading and generous credits.[51]

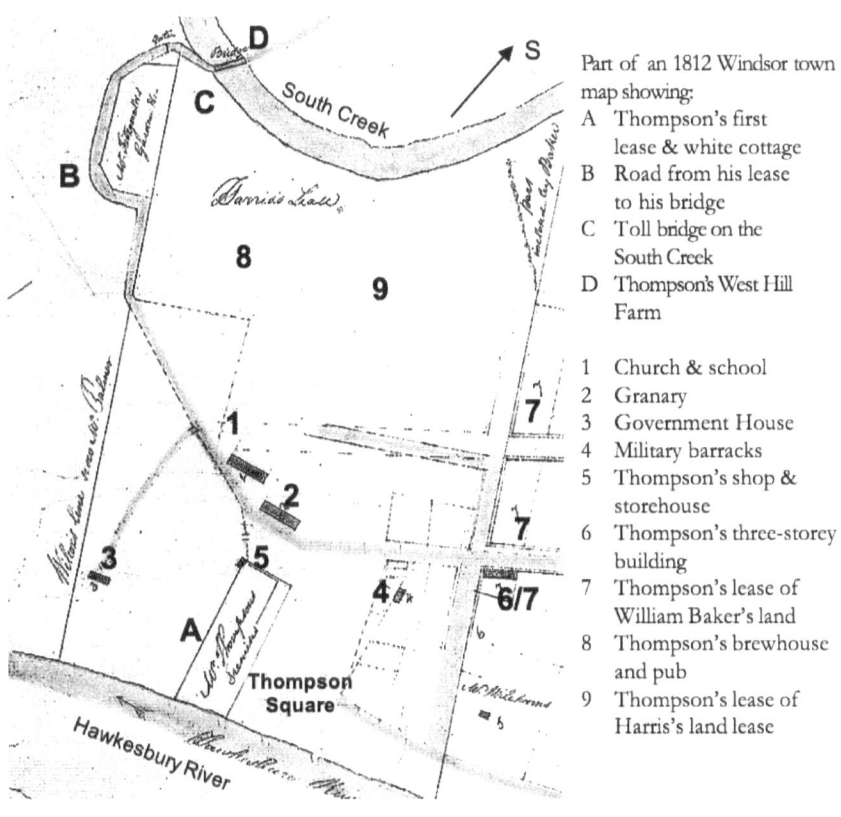

Part of an 1812 Windsor town map showing:
A Thompson's first lease & white cottage
B Road from his lease to his bridge
C Toll bridge on the South Creek
D Thompson's West Hill Farm

1 Church & school
2 Granary
3 Government House
4 Military barracks
5 Thompson's shop & storehouse
6 Thompson's three-storey building
7 Thompson's lease of William Baker's land
8 Thompson's brewhouse and pub
9 Thompson's lease of Harris's land lease

In November 1804, Thompson added a fourth ship to his fleet, the brig *Speedwell*, a two-masted sailing vessel with a burden of 18 tons and a crew of six. A month earlier the *Speedwell* had been grounded in Broken Bay near Lion Island and was abandoned by her owner John Grono who was unable to finance the ship's recovery.[52] Grono was a free settler and shipwright, who had settled with his family at the Hawkesbury in 1799 and, until 1801, had skippered the *Francis* to transport goods between the settlements. In 1804 Grono's infant daughter had been assaulted and Chief

Constable Thompson arrested the two men thought responsible. They were released when no evidence could be found to charge them. But Thompson persevered with the case and in March 1804, he arrested Henry Wright, who was convicted, flogged and spent three years in hard labour, including being placed in public stocks every Saturday for two hours.[53]

With the loss of the *Speedwell* John Grono faced financial ruin, and he approached the chief constable for help. Thompson agreed to buy and salvage the stranded *Speedwell*. However, the salvage effort was delayed for several weeks when a huge fire threatened many farms in the district. It was the start of a hot summer and men were being employed to clear and burn off scrub. On one of the farms the fire got out of control and spread to the surrounding grain farms. Andrew was one of the first to see the smoke and 'He gave an instant alarm, and followed by all the inhabitants in that quarter, pressed forward to render every possible aid'. It was only his organisation and effort that prevented the fires from destroying many 'valuable Government lands at Cornwallis Place'.[54]

Part of an 1813 view from the north bank of the Hawkesbury River looking south towards Green Hills. Trading ships for transporting grain and goods to and from Sydney are shown in the river; the buildings to the left are in the government precinct.

It was not until early December 1804 that the *Hope*, the *Hawkesbury* and another smaller boat, with 20 men, freed the *Speedwell* and were able to sail her back to Green Hills. To fund this salvage effort John Grono was forced to sell all his property and effects, and he asked Thompson for immediate payment on the purchase of the *Speedwell*. This bill came at a time when Thompson was committed to acquiring another ship and to building a salt making plant on Mullet Island. In order to pay Grono for the *Speedwell* he sold his favourite sloop the *Nancy* to Henry Kable & Co. Months later the *Nancy* was lost at sea.[55]

Thompson then enlisted Grono to sail the *Speedwell* to the South Island of New Zealand to hunt seal furs. John Grono acknowledged Thompson's friendship and generosity when naming a number of fjords that he discovered during his various trips to the South Island. These included: *Bligh Sound, Doubtful Sound, Grono Bay, Elizabeth Island* (after his wife), *Milford Sound, Nancy Sound, Thompson Sound* and *Eleanor Island*.[56]

Thompson's salt boiler on Mullet Island (now Dangar Island) at the mouth of the Hawkesbury River started to produce salt in early 1804. Salt was the essential ingredient needed to preserve meat and hides, and until then was mostly imported at high cost. Since his sealskin trade required salt to preserve skins, Thompson knew this venture would reduce costs for his other businesses. In any case, with Governor King promoting enterprises that would reduce expensive imports, he leased Thompson crown land on the island for the initiative. The installed salt boiler could produce about 200 lb (91 kg) of salt per week. Enthusiastically, *The Sydney Gazette* reported on 9 December 1804 that the process 'must prove a successful undertaking'.[57]

> This will doubtless be attended with much utility, from the possibility of accommodating private stock growers with such proportion of that valuable article as may not be required for his own use; and from the liberal sanction and encouragement shewn by Government to every worthy project that promises public advantage, it may almost be wondered that the scarcity and necessity of salt to individuals has not induced others to adopt the means of a certain self supply.[58]

However, since Mullet Island was at the mouth of the Hawkesbury River, it was not an ideal location to extract salt. The men operating the salt boiler probably did not understand the evaporative process and when it failed, they were inclined to believe the devil was at work. *The Sydney Gazette* reported that one operator was astounded that, after four days of topping up the boiler, no salt appeared.

> As the solution of the mystery was superior to his natural talents, he readily coincided with Quixote's systems of enchantment; and was about to abandon the place to the undisturbed possession of Lucifer himself, when a boatman acquainted him of the impossibility of extracting salt from fresh water, the very judicious use of which had occasioned his disappointment.[59]

The operators had not understood that the Hawkesbury estuary at certain times of the year was mostly fresh water flowing from the huge river. Byrnes says in his 1958 thesis on Andrew Thompson that the article in *The Sydney Gazette* was unlikely to have been written by the editor George Howe; his writing style was different.[60] As the Gazette's representative in Green Hills, it is quite likely that Andrew wrote the article. If so, it provides a glimpse of a man with a sense of humour, who could tell a good yarn.

There are an abundance of documents and newspaper articles recording Andrew Thompson's political and business activities but remarkably little is known of him personally. We are reasonably certain that he was nicknamed 'Long Harry' because of his height – he was taller than 6 foot – and that he spoke with a mild Scottish-border accent that was more understandable than that of a Highlander.[61] Beyond this, little is recorded about his personal characteristics. Since he was a police constable, it can be assumed that he was robust in stature and his business successes suggest significant mental astuteness and a gregarious approachability.

No written material has survived that gives any real insights into his private life. Did he have a close female friend, for instance? At the age of 32, he was in his prime and there are strong indications that he was interested in female company. So, is there specific information on personal relationships with particular women? For his first ten years in the colony the answer is NO. However, from his late twenties onwards he had well-recorded associations with a widow, reputedly for business reasons, but they seem to have been much more than that. Of course, there can be a multitude of reasons why there is no record of Andrew having a girlfriend at an earlier age. Being a convict for much of his youth, he would have had little contact with females. They were few in number on the ship, or in the colony – men outnumbered women in New South Wales four to one. Moreover, most female convicts were older than Andrew and they would have preferred long term attachments to mature men who could give them security. Another likely reason is that the majority of women in the colony were uneducated, and this might have been a factor in discouraging Andrew from forming a close relationship.

There is ample evidence that Andrew was a conscientious young man who probably set high standards in his associations with the opposite sex. Of course, it is possible he had sexual contacts of a casual nature from time to time, though there is no record of this, and nor is there likely to be. He was certainly not the only prominent man in the colony whose female acquaintances were unknown. Colonial records and newspapers contain remarkably little about females in general, and even the names of the wives of important officials and businessmen are omitted. This may have been intentional of course, but it was probably because there were few female letter writers and authors in the colony. Even in Britain, women were often not named in legal transactions involving their family. Females were also expected to play a lesser role in society and rarely considered newsworthy by male newspaper editors and reporters. Nevertheless, there is good evidence that Andrew Thompson had a close female friendship over a prolonged period, and we will expand on this later in the story.

Regardless of his physical attributes or interests, Andrew had a reputation for honesty, reliability and astute business acumen.

> ... he uniformly conducted himself with that strict regard to morality and integrity, as to obtain and enjoy the countenance and protection of several succeeding Governors; active, intelligent and industrious, of manners mild and conciliatory, with a heart generous and humane.[62]

Thompson clearly had an attractive way of engaging with people, in the 'even Tenor of his Way and acquitted himself with mildness, moderation and wisdom'.[63] He was admired for his approachability and fairness in dealing with everyone – freemen, convicts and Aborigines. In business circles he was respected for his shrewd and successful investments.

The distinction of class or rank was fading in colonial society, especially among pioneer settlers. As a chief constable, a major grain producer and successful businessman, Andrew may have already exceeded the social standing held by his parents in rural Scotland.[64] In the Hawkesbury district, where everyone shared similar hardships and status rarely mattered – floods, the vagaries of weather and seasons, a dependence on neighbours, and the importance of marriages eroded such differences. Thompson's Red House was known to welcome 'Civil and Military Officers and other respectable Inhabitants of the Colony' and his involvement with men of all levels and professions helped mitigate the prejudices of social class prevalent in even the most elite circles.[65]

Andrew Thompson had a lifelong love of literature, and his large library grew with increasing prosperity. The passion for books is evidenced by the fact that in early December 1804 he sought to recover books he had lent to others. Andrew must have shared his collection – good books were rare in the colony – but from time to time these had to be recalled in order to keep his library intact. To do this, he placed a notice in *The Sydney Gazette*.

> The Books herein undermentioned were at different times borrowed from the house of Mr. Andrew Thompson, at the Green Hills, Hawkesbury, but from forgetfulness have neglected to be returned, viz.
> . Two Volumes of the *Spectator*, Andrew Thomson written on the 15th page of each Volume.
> . Milton's Paradise Lost complete
> . Sterne's Work's including his Sentimental Journey.
> . Three Volumes of the Works of Mr Robert Burns, the Scottish Bard.
> . Thompson's Seasons.
> . Hervey's Meditations and other Works.
> . Two Volumes of the Newgate Kalender.
> It is earnestly requested, nor is it doubted, that any persons who upon looking over their books may find either of the above among their number will be kind enough to return the Interlopers to their Owner, at Hawkesbury, or cause them to be left at the house of Mr. Larra, at Paramatta, or Mr. Kearns at Sydney; as by their detention complete sets are destroyed and those valuable works rendered incomplete and consequently useless.[66]

Although these books represent only a fraction of his library, one wonders how he had time to read so much and so broadly. The books and magazines listed reflect his wide interests, and most are unexpected reading for a police man at that time. The *Spectator* in his list was a London daily publication that was read mainly by English middle-class merchants and traders. The *Spectator* was supposedly politically neutral, but it promoted Whig (liberal) values and interests. *Paradise Lost* is a collection of ten books of poems by John Milton. Lawrence Sterne was an Irish born novelist and clergyman who incorporated aspects of his trip to France into the novel *A Sentimental Journey Through France and Italy*. Robert Burns, a famous Scottish poet and lyricist, was a pioneer of the Romantic Movement. After Burns' death in 1796 his work inspired liberalism and socialism in Scotland. Robert Burns had visited Jedburgh in 1787 where Andrew had been imprisoned awaiting transportation.

Seasons is a book of poems by the Scottish author James Thomson and *Meditations and Contemplations* was written by the English clergyman and author, James Hervey. The most unusual book in the list is the *Newgate Calendar*. This described the fates of murderers, fraudsters, robbers, and traitors in Newgate Prison in London. The punishment of notorious criminals was popular literature in England, but it is an unexpected reading for someone who had personally felt the severity of the law.

The encyclopaedic nature of Andrew Thompson's book collection is consistent with him being an inquisitive individual. As with other educated people in the colony, reading of good books would have helped compensate for the lack of a theatre and other erudite pursuits. J. V. Byrnes puts a different interpretation on the scholarly nature of Thompson's borrowed books. He suggests they were lent not only to literate emancipist friends but also to educated freemen and Corps officers, so as to form 'another strong bond between readers whether bond [bound] or free and must be considered as a powerful factor in social levelling.'[67] This view rather overlooks the fact that many influential inhabitants, and particularly emancipists, were illiterate. In reality, many of Thompson's close acquaintances probably found it difficult to comprehend news articles in *The Sydney Gazette,* let alone a book of Milton's poems.

Chapter 8

CHIEF CONSTABLE

Soon after my arrival here, I found Mr. Thompson to be, what he always had been, a man ever ready and willing to promote the public service, for this was the character he had obtained from all my predecessors.[1]

Thompson's daily life as chief constable brought him into contact with a broad cross-section of Hawkesbury inhabitants – officials, convicts, settlers, soldiers and Aborigines. By all accounts he was well respected by all for his fair and intelligent handling of his duties.[2] As the fixer in the district who resolved complaints by convicts and masters with equal alacrity, his cottage on the Hawkesbury was often full of people seeking his advice on matters outside his official jurisdiction. Most of the contentious matters in the area would eventually reach him for adjudication or rectification. However, since he was paid to keep law and order in the district, this remained his, and his constables', first priority. By 1804 about 1700 people resided in the Hawkesbury district, an area that encompassed the town of Green Hills and the farms along the Hawkesbury and Nepean Rivers, as well as those along the South and Eastern Creeks.[3] Most inhabitants in the remote district were law abiding but the ruggedness of the pioneer farmers with uncertain property boundaries meant that there were always issues that needed to be sorted out by police.

The constables under Thompson's command were also farmers in the district. These men often joined the police force solely to supplement their farm income and to pay off debts incurred from floods or land purchases. A police constable's life was hard, but it provided both a regular income and assigned servants who were provisioned by the government. The Scot David Brown, a married man with a family, was a constable who had known Andrew for years, first in Toongabbie and he later joined him at Green Hills. The 60-year-old Richard Burman was a constable who reached the colony in 1790 on the notorious second fleet ship *Neptune* to serve a seven-year sentence for stealing 20 lb of lead. In 1799 Burman was granted land on the South Creek and remained as a Hawkesbury constable until 1805. Another constable, Matthew Lock, sentenced to seven years for stealing goods valued at 39s, received a land grant on the Hawkesbury and farmed there with his family. Years later, Thompson would recommend Lock to be the next chief constable.

Some convicts were granted a magistrate's permit to travel in the colony and to rent land. This might suggest that their movements and work were loosely administered. Nothing was further from the truth. Every serving convict was required to report regularly to a local authority and do their assigned government jobs before private work could be undertaken. In such a regime, convicts were subject to strict regulations, and reoffenders incurred heavy penalties. The colony was administered as an open prison in which convicts were rarely placed behind bars. Nevertheless, reoffending convicts were routinely flogged and often made to work in chain gangs. Serious recidivists were sent to do hard labour on farms on Norfolk Island or in the mines at the Coal River settlement. A typical sentence for a convict who assaulted a free person was 200 lashes and twelve months in a work gang. On the other hand, assigned-convict servants had to be treated fairly by their masters, and private punishment was forbidden. A free person striking a convict was fined £2 for the first offence and a £50 security bond; a second offence incurred a fine of £5 and the new bond was doubled.[4]

The chief constable's cottage in the Green Hills government precinct was where complaints on such matters were lodged. It was at Thompson's discretion that serious matters were reported to a magistrate, and he adjudicated the seriousness and assigned the penalty. A typical complaint was that a convict servant failed to do assigned duties, or that a settler gave a convict work he or she was physically incapable of doing. Some convicts were worked to death, and for this reason assigned convict servants preferred masters who were emancipists – they provided a much fairer workplace.[5]

Employment was tightly regulated. Everyone had to carry a certificate showing his or her status: free, ticket of leave or convict. Employers needed to examine this certificate or incur heavy fines. Settlers wishing to employ a convict servant had to apply to the local magistrate or, in the case of the Hawkesbury district, Chief Constable Thompson. Servant working hours were from sunrise to 8am and 9am to 3pm on weekdays, and from sunrise until 9am on

Saturdays. Sunday was free of labour. If a convict was required to work longer hours, he or she had to be paid overtime.[6] Governor King announced in 1804 that assigned servants should be fed, clothed and paid £10 a year in wages. Since many small farmers could not afford cash wages, this was waived if assigned convicts were paid in kind. In such cases, convicts usually farmed part of their master's land in their free time to raise crops and animals for their own food.[7] For a well-behaved convict servant with a fair employer, life would have been quite tolerable. Otherwise, it could be extremely hard, and work disputes often became matters for Chief Constable Thompson to resolve.

As the colony advanced in age and size, more and more convicts completed their sentences and were taken off government rations. Released ex-convicts who had not yet found work became a major vagrancy problem in some districts, and constables were ordered to arrest persons found idle or disorderly and bring them before a magistrate. Depending on the charge and subsequent conviction, offenders might be fined or sent to labour gang for up to a month.[8] In such cases Chief Constable Thompson worked closely with the Parramatta magistrate Samuel Marsden up until 1804, and after that with Thomas Arndell who became the Hawkesbury magistrate.

Thomas Arndell had arrived on the First Fleet as an assistant surgeon and was in charge of the Parramatta hospital until 1792 when he became a farmer and practiced medicine privately. In 1798 Governor Hunter appointed him as a magistrate in Parramatta. Arndell's female companion was the convict Elizabeth Dalton (Burley). In 1804 Thomas and Elizabeth moved to their Cattai farm on the Hawkesbury River, and in 1807 they married. Thompson worked closely with Magistrate Arndell on legal matters in the district. Although Thompson's emancipist status supposedly separated the two men socially, their personal and political interests were similar, and they eventually became friends and allies in the fight for the rights and conditions of Hawkesbury settlers.

Judge Advocate Richard Atkins presided over all court cases in Sydney. He had no legal training and was appointed temporarily in 1796 after David Collins returned to England unexpectedly. In 1798 attorney Richard Dore became the new permanent judge advocate, but he died two years later. Atkins was reappointed in an acting capacity until the British government confirmed his position in

1802. Prior to coming to the colony, Atkins had borrowed heavily on an expected inheritance from a rich cousin. When this failed to materialise, the possibility of debtor prison loomed and Atkins, with his wife and son, boarded the *Pitt* sailing to Sydney in 1791. During this eventful voyage, he became acquainted with the boy convict Andrew Thompson. On arrival both men were sent to Parramatta under quite different circumstances. Atkins became the magistrate and court registrar, and Andrew laboured as a convict stonemason, and later became a constable at Toongabbie. Richard Atkins was a heavy drinker and his long-standing battle with alcohol kept him in debt. Periodically Atkins was censured for his behaviour and poor legal judgements, but when sober he was a humane man who showed sympathy for convicts and small settlers.

Arresting absconding convicts and protecting the lives and property of settlers were the core duties of the Hawkesbury police. Most official documents detailing Thompson's involvement in early police criminal cases have not survived. However, a police action involving him was reported in the 5 March 1803 issue of *The Sydney Gazette*.[9] Capturing offenders was dangerous and often involved weapons. Even when not armed, criminals would resist arrest with anything they could lay their hands on. This was all part of the rough and tumble of law enforcement in an open prison – though, it is important to point out, not all offenders were convicts. The constabulary were always prepared for violence and, even when others were prepared to assist in remote localities, the work was often life threatening. By 1803 Andrew was wealthy enough not to need his police wages and could have resigned, but either he felt obliged to continue helping settlers, or he simply enjoyed the police work and the prestige the post entitled him to in the community.

One of the few surviving records of cases involving Chief Constable Thompson occurred in May 1803 when Charles Palmer, a free settler and brother of the Sydney Commissary John Palmer, was robbed and violently assaulted on his Hawkesbury farm by masked men. He and his wife were bound, hooded and threatened with drowning in the nearby river unless money was handed over. But there was no cash in the house, and the men stole clothing and other items. Chief Constable Thompson took charge of this high-profile case. Initially Palmer's convict servants were suspected but no evidence was found. Thompson persevered and after a tipoff he arrested Lawrence Holding, Thomas McLaughlane and his son, and Mary McLane. Female clothing belonging to the Palmers was found in their house, and although McLane had resewn these into men's clothing, Thompson easily recognised this. A court in Sydney found both of the McLaughlanes guilty and sentenced them to death. Lawrence Holding was acquitted, whilst Mary McLane was sent to Norfolk Island. Soon after Governor King converted McLaughlane Junior's death sentence to life. McLaughlane Senior was returned to Green Hills and hanged on 3 October 1803 at the back of the Old Store.[10] This public event would have been organised by the chief constable, but he was not the executioner – a hired hangman would have carried out this dreaded task.

By 1801 the land at the Toongabbie Farm, where Thompson had been inducted as constable, was infertile from overcropping and a new government farm was established at Castle Hill, fifteen miles south of Green Hills. Convicts who misbehaved at the new farm were the responsibility of both the Green Hills and Parramatta police. The hard-core political prisoners of the 1798 Irish Rebellion transported to Sydney were sent directly to the Castle Hill prison farm. These convicts soon plotted a return to Ireland, and several escapes were initiated. Following one attempt, Judge Advocate Atkins and Magistrate Marsden had an Irish escapee to be flogged mercilessly until he divulged hidden weapons. Marsden was known to routinely sentence convicts to over a hundred lashes.

Another escape from Castle Hill was attempted in February 1803 when fifteen Irish convicts terrorised neighbouring settlers before being captured. They had ransacked farms for clothing, food, alcohol and firearms, and seriously injured a convict servant. The police and NSW Corps soldiers at Green Hills were requested to help Parramatta constables pursue the absconders. Two days later, Thompson, with a party of soldiers and John Jamieson, a superintendent from Parramatta, captured Patrick Gannan and Francis Simpson. Aided by Aborigines, the constables and soldiers arrested the remaining Irish convicts a few days later in bush between the Hawkesbury River and the western mountains. Fifteen convicts from Castle Hill were arraigned before a magistrate, committed and brought under guard to Sydney for trial.[11]

Thompson and Jamieson gave evidence at the trial of the two men they had arrested. These men were found asleep and had resisted arrest. Stolen silver spoons were discovered near where the men slept. The judge advocate sentenced the two men to death. A second group of prisoners whom constables Thompson, Lock and Brown had arrested, met the same fate. Within days Gannan, Simpson and Macdermot were returned to Castle Hill to be executed in front of their fellow convicts. Macdermot received a last-minute reprieve from Governor King.[12]

Artist's impression of the Irish convict uprising at Castle Hill in 1804, showing Major Johnston and 25 Corps privates firing on the armed rebels. Twelve rebels were killed.

Undeterred, the Irish convicts were soon planning another major escape. On 4 March 1804, 330 Irish forced a mass breakout from the Castle Hill Farm. The rebel leader Philip Cunningham had earlier sent a scout to tell Irish convicts working along the Hawkesbury that there would be an uprising, but he was arrested before spreading the word. Unaware of the arrest, Cunningham ordered that the rebellion should begin – it was to be 'Death or Liberty'. They raided houses in the Castle Hill area for weapons and planned to march on Parramatta and Sydney. On hearing of the revolt, Governor King proclaimed martial law and sent a company of NSW Corps soldiers commanded by Major George Johnston to confront the rebels at Vinegar Hill, ten miles south of the Hawkesbury. Johnston offered them the governor's mercy if they surrendered. They did not, and the soldiers opened fire, killing twelve men and wounding many more. The ringleaders were arrested at gunpoint.[13]

Some rebels initially escaped but gave themselves up when they heard the leaders had been captured. The Irish convicts had assumed that Green Hills would be easy to overrun, as a third of the inhabitants were convicts and only eleven soldiers guarded them. However, they underestimated the resolve of the police and the settlers, and the presence of 95 soldiers in Parramatta.[14] Chief Constable Thompson was not specifically mentioned in these arrests, but the uprising caused frenetic activity in the Hawkesbury area and the constabulary were heavily involved. *The Sydney Gazette* gave particular praise to the courage of the settlers in this respect.

> The energy and activity of the Settlers and other inhabitants of the Settlement of Hawkesbury, in pursuing and apprehending the ill-advised and equally ill-disposed miscreants who fled towards the Mountains in wild and terrible despair, was highly meritorious and praiseworthy; and the ardour with which they exerted themselves in the cause of Loyalty, while it gives an indisputable testimony of zeal and attachment to a much loved MONARCH and a happy, envied Constitution, will have some influence in deterring the rash, unprincipled, and deluded, from future efforts of intemperance and folly.[15]

Had the Irish uprising succeeded, it might have been a serious problem for the colony and the governor. The rebel leader Philip Cunningham was given a brief court hearing, together with seven others, and then hanged at the staircase of the Green Hills' public store – a store Cunningham had boasted earlier he was going to plunder. Nine rebels were given 200 to 500 lashes, and the rest were sent in chain gangs to the re-established Coal River settlement to mine coal and cut cedar logs.[16]

Following the uprising, heightened security was applied to all convicts, and the uprising remained a painful memory for many farmers of Irish descent in the Nepean and Hawkesbury districts. The 1804 Irish uprising was probably the most dramatic event that constables at the Hawkesbury had to face in their careers but was certainly not as dangerous as other arrest they made.

During the Irish uprising several armed convicts had attempted to seize a boat on the Hawkesbury River and sail it down to the ocean. This, and the growing number of boat thefts by run-away convicts or Aborigines, prompted Governor King to order that every 'Person possessing Rowing Boats on the Banks of the Hawkesbury are to have them Numbered and Registered by Mr. Andrew Thompson, Head Constable, in the course of the ensuing Week'. Henceforth rowboats without registration papers would be seized; boat owners were not allowed to row boats after dark; boats had to be secured by a chain and lock, and oars had to be stored separately. All boats rowed at night were to be examined, the rower to be detained and a constable was to be informed.[17]

Since 1799 Andrew Thompson had held the position of Assessor of Grain in the Hawkesbury district. This, together with his new role as the Registrar of Boats and his police responsibilities, required the constant upkeep of registrations, documents and statistics for the government records. The importance of this duty was evident in a January 1804 court case when three of the leading emancipists in the colony – Andrew Thompson, Simeon Lord and Richard Fitzgerald – were involved in a government compensation claim. Although Simeon Lord and Andrew Thompson were quite different in character and political views, they had become firm friends. They were the same age and had both been transported to New South Wales for stealing cloth. Simeon Lord arrived in 1791 on the *Atlantic* with some money of his own and had been assigned to Corps Captain Thomas Rowley as a convict servant. Rowley had advised Lord to invest in the retailing of spirits and merchandise bought in bulk from ships by Corps officers. The business proved lucrative, and Simeon Lord eventually became the head of a merchandising firm trading from a large house in Bridge Street, Sydney.[18]

The other emancipist involved in the 1804 court action was Richard Fitzgerald. At the age of fourteen he was sentenced to seven years transportation in 1787 and reached Sydney in 1791 with some material assets. He was sent to the Toongabbie Farm where he became acquainted with Andrew Thompson. Successive governors appointed Fitzgerald to various farm management roles, reputably because of his agricultural knowledge, but more likely because of an alleged connection to Lord Edward Fitzgerald. Even John Macarthur gave him patronage. Managing his numerous grants and land purchases meant Fitzgerald had little time for official duties.[19]

Thompson, Fitzgerald and Lord appeared in the compensation court case in different capacities: the first as the Assessor of Grain and the second as the Superintendent of the Cornwallis government farm on the Hawkesbury. Simeon Lord was the plaintiff who had bought two stacks of grain on a farm adjacent to the Cornwallis Farm, where, while burning off stubble, these stacks were destroyed. Lord sued the government for £330 compensation for lost grain, naming Supervisor Fitzgerald as the defendant. In court Fitzgerald stated that the wind had shifted and 'a hurricane unexpectedly came on'. Several witnesses were called to verify the damage, but Andrew Thompson's evidence determined the verdict.

> The Court being now desirous of ascertaining as nearly as possible the true amount of the damage, and several witnesses who spoke in that particular differing in their opinion, recourse was necessarily had to the quantum of Wheat specified by Mr. Andrew Thompson in his Returns officially made to His Excellency on an Inspection and Survey some short time prior to the accident, in which he estimated the contents of the larger stack to be 600 bushels; and the other had been since erected, and was computed at 100 bushels more; and Mr. Thompson being questioned by the Court whether he had at any time known damage to be awarded under similar circumstances, declared that he had himself paid damage in a similar case.[20]

Thompson had prior experience in such matters. Much earlier he had been sued for a fire that had destroyed grain on a neighbour's farm and had settled out of court. In the 1804 case, no blame was attached to Fitzgerald, as the Court determined it was an unforeseen event. The court returned a verdict for the plaintiff – damages £280 'with Costs of Suit, to be paid in Wheat'.[21] It was not, however, the first or last fire to occur on Fitzgerald's watch. A year earlier, Andrew had stopped a fire spreading from the Cornwallis Farm and this had delayed his salvaging of the *Speedwell*. Six months after the claim by Simeon Lord, Governor King dismissed Richard Fitzgerald from his supervisory role for 'gross neglect of duty'.[22] He then moved to the Hawkesbury where he became John Macarthur's fulltime agent.

By 1805 Andrew was employing over 100 men on his farms. They were assigned servants on government provisions and ticket of leave holders on wages. Records show that behavioural problems were rare on his farms, and few attempted to escape or to steal. Except, that is, for one major disruption on 19 May 1805.

> A robbery has been recently discovered to have been committed on the property of Mr. A. Thompson at Hawkesbury, on account

of which several persons were sent down for Examination. Wheat, corn, and live stock to a considerable amount are missing; and we are sorry to say that several of his own servants are suspected as principals in the felony.[23]

Four of Andrew's servants, Richard Clifton, James Perkins, John Mealing and Thomas Bryan were charged with stealing or receiving stolen pigs. At a trial on 1 Jun 1805 Judge Advocate Atkins sentenced Mealing and Bryan 'to corporal punishment and the gaol gang' for stealing, and Clifton and Perkins were committed for trial 'as receivers of the property at various times'. At their trial John Spital, who was in charge of Andrew's pigs, was examined and admitted that the charged defendants had purchased pigs from him. Their delivery had been an open transaction in the presence of several persons to the value of 35s a pig. After hearing all evidence Clifton and Perkins were acquitted.[24]

In this trial Judge Advocate Atkins had shown leniency when he announced that 'salutary influence' and his 'fair character' had saved Clifton from prosecution. Andrew Thompson would have pondered on this verdict, since in Scotland his own exemplary past behaviour had not saved him from prosecution. Richard Clifton was transported with Andrew on the *Pitt* in 1792 and, having served his sentence, he was now working for his former inmate. This time the court was on Clifton's side and a year later he received a land grant and was able to cultivate his own farm.

The majority of matters the police dealt with were relatively minor. This was as true in Chief Constable Thompson's time, as it is today. He adjudicated on matters such as the supervision of workers, the treatment of convicts, settlers' complaints about assigned servants and *vice versa*. Less frequently the constabulary investigated thefts, robberies, assaults and rapes, and occasionally murders. A particularly gruesome instance of the latter occurred in 1805 when labourer William Miller was arrested for the murder of Bridget Kean. After the murder Miller had run to the constabulary and confessed that he had cleaved open Bridget's head with a hoe. When Thompson and magistrate Arndell arrived at 'the place where the deceased lay' they discovered the 'unfortunate object, a spectacle the most shocking'. The court of criminal jurisdiction was set for a week later in Sydney, when Miller confessed to murdering Kean during an 'unbridled momentary rage'. After hearing the witnesses,

Judge Advocate Atkins returned the inevitable verdict: Guilty. Miller was hanged the next week, but he was truly repentant of what he had done, wishing to atone 'by yielding blood for blood' and declaring that 'life was no longer desirable'.[25] This particular case certainly did not test the investigative abilities of the police, but it was indicative of the brutality of the times – life was cheap. Violence was a constant companion of the police and being a constable required both physical strength and mental resilience. Most men in the colony did not see policing as a desirable occupation.

Since the 1800 murder trial of the two Aboriginal boys, the relations between the Aboriginal community and the settlers had been reasonably calm. Governor King was determined to implement the instruction of the Home Office Secretary Robert Hobart 'to conciliate the Goodwill of the Natives'. However, by 1803 relations with the indigenous tribes had become strained by increased land grants along the Nepean River and further down the Hawkesbury River at Portland Head. These new farms on the periphery of the Hawkesbury district prevented some Aborigines from accessing water and traditional food sources; a problem made more critical by the 1803 drought. The Aborigines were incensed at the new land clearing and cultivation, and conflicts with settlers ramped up in the districts between Castlereagh and Portland Head. A Hawkesbury Aboriginal tribe headed by an elder named Major White joined other tribes to drive settlers off land that had been their traditional home for millennia.[26]

Governor King was reluctant to involve the military in these conflicts because he knew that it would result in more bloodshed. Instead, he instructed police to forbid Aborigines from trespassing onto settler's farms. This was never going to work, as the concept of 'trespassing' was not something Aborigines understood – moreover, this was *their* land. In further clashes at Portland Heads, the remotest settlement in the colony, three settlers were speared. King sent additional soldiers to Magistrate Arndell in Green Hills and ordered the constables to support settlers at Portland Head. At the same time two Aborigines were shot in a conflict with Corps soldiers near Green Hills.[27] Notwithstanding the increasing hostilities, in December 1804 King refused settlers permission to shoot at Aborigines, and he personally questioned indigenous men from the Hawkesbury to get their views on the grievances.

> On questioning the cause of their disagreement with the new settlers they very ingenuously answered that they did not like to be driven from the few places that were left on the banks of the river, where alone they could procure food; that they had gone down the river as the white men took possession of the banks; if they went across white men's grounds the settlers fired upon them and were angry; that if they could retain some places on the lower part of the river they should be satisfied and would not trouble the white men. The observation and request appear to be so just and so equitable that I assured them no more settlements should be made lower down the river.[28]

Based on the concerns raised in this interview, Governor King granted no new land in the Hawkesbury River area during 1805.

Nevertheless, in autumn 1805 Aborigines burnt huts and killed several settlers at remote farms along the South Creek and the lower Hawkesbury River. Different groups of Aborigines had banded together, and their raids now involved hundreds of warriors. The expansion of the settlement on *Cowpastures* land along the Nepean River may have been a trigger for the combined attacks.[29] Apparently oblivious to the loss of water access for Aborigines, Governor King concluded the settlers were not to blame and that the indigenous people had suddenly turned against them.[30]

The settlers' deaths were then followed by Aboriginal attacks on boats plying the Hawkesbury River, and on the salt boiler workers on Mullet Island employed by Andrew Thompson. In April 1805 *The Sydney Gazette* reported that two boiler workers were missing and thought dead, as their guns had been found. In fact, the men had escaped death by giving up their possessions and wandering through the bush for two weeks until rescued by other Aborigines. A week later the men returned to Sydney with their Aboriginal rescuers, 'two friendly natives joined in their route by four others, who appeared equally anxious in their preservation'. The men had invited the Aborigines 'to continue their friendship' by coming to Sydney to be hosted at their expense.[31]

Because of the persistent indigenous attacks, armed boats from Green Hills patrolled the waterways and more military were posted to remote settlements. Governor King felt he had no option but to issue a General Order forbidding Aborigines from approaching settlers' houses until those responsible for the murders were 'given up'. Settlers were required to refuse native visits, and anyone found harbouring Aborigines would be 'prosecuted for the breach of a public order intended for the security of the settlers'.[32] Soldiers were sent to the outer settlements to hunt for those responsible, and Chief Constable Thompson was instructed by Magistrate Arndell to lead an armed party of settlers and constables into the western mountains on an similar mission.

The chief constable headed a well-equipped group that included ex-soldiers and Aboriginal trackers. It had rained heavily, and because the Nepean River was overflowing the men used a boat to travel west towards a known camp. This was found deserted and the pursuit would have ended there had it not been for the trackers who were Richmond Hill Aborigines. Their tracking skills led the party to another camp at the junction of Shaw's Creek and the Nepean River where Aborigines were found making spears. With little warning, the group attacked the camp killing several warriors and wounding many more. Among the dead was Yaragowhy, who Andrew had 'left the day before at the Green Hills under every assurance of strict friendship'. Wearing a dead settler's clothes Yaragowhy had gone to the camp to warn his kinsmen of the search party's presence in the area and to expect reprisals.[33]

While some of the search party set about destroying the 'several thousand spears, frightfully jagged' others tried to follow the retreating warriors. In this chase their 'faithful guides' rescued the party by warning them that warriors were waiting in ambush to 'hurl stupendous rocks upon their heads'.[34] Before returning to Green Hills, Thompson left several guards at the farm of ex-Corps officer Obadiah Ikin on the western side of the Nepean. That evening an Aborigine named Charley went to the farm, but because he was 'well known and little suspected' the guards remained hidden. However, more warriors were waiting in the bush and when Charley demanded the firearms in the house, the guards shot him. Hearing the shots, the other Aboriginal warriors fled. They returned the next day, only to be driven off again.[35]

Most people in Green Hills had thought that the two Aboriginal men killed, Yaragowhy and Charley, were their friends and these events spread much unease in the community. If one could not separate friend from foe, what hope was there for a peaceful end to these conflicts? The destruction of a large quantity of spears – each of which took days to make – was expected to at least delay the prospect of future attacks.

The government proclaimed that from June 1805 Aborigines in

the Sydney and Parramatta districts would be permitted onto farms again. However, this ruling did not apply to the Hawkesbury district where boats continued to be attacked from the banks.[36] In September 1805 Aborigines threatened one of Andrew Thompson's salt-boiler workers on Mullet Island while he was collecting water for the saltpan in a small boat. He was rescued by one of Thompson's sloops, the *Hawkesbury*, that was shipping grain to Sydney. Shortly after, a group of Aborigines boarded the *Hawkesbury* but were 'prevailed on by presents to leave the vessel'. Later, when the boat crew was resting below another group boarded, and a fight broke out. Just as the shipmaster was about to be speared for a second time, a boiler worker shot the intruder with a pistol and the other Aborigines fled.[37] This and other problems led Andrew Thompson to abandon Mullet Island and establish another salt plant on Scotland Island in Pittwater.

Throughout 1806 Aborigines continued to try and torch wheat crops on farms along the Hawkesbury River. Andrew Thompson was well known to be on speaking terms with some of the local Aboriginal elders and when repeated efforts by magistrates and settlers failed to stem the unrest, the chief constable was commissioned by the government 'to enquire into their grievances'. The elders told Andrew they had 'no subject of complaint' but admitted to burning the crops that they were not permitted to share in. The Aboriginal elders promised Thompson that they would halt the raids if there was some sharing of food.[38] They kept their word, and for a year there were no reported attacks.

Chapter 9

SETTLERS' SURVIVAL

Andrew Thompson, in one of his own boats, saved the lives of 101 persons, which he took from off the tops of houses and rafts of straw.[1]

The year 1806 would be a formative one for Andrew. He was now 33 years of age and had been in the colony for fourteen years, the duration of his original transportation sentence. Since his release from servitude eight years ago he had achieved a great deal. He was a successful farmer and businessman, and, as the chief constable of the Hawkesbury district, he had become a highly valued member of the Green Hills community and held several official positions. Governor King had given Andrew considerable responsibility in the district and relied on his support at a time when his administration was heavily censured by both the Corps and the business elites in Sydney. In mid-year William Bligh would arrive to replace Philip Gidley King as governor, and this would have immediate ramifications for all inhabitants, none more so than Andrew Thompson. From that point on, for better or for worse, his life and livelihood would be closely aligned with Bligh's government and farming interests. In 1806 the chief constable achieved hero status for his brave efforts in rescuing farmers from the massive Hawkesbury floods – his heroism was widely lauded, but his actions were to have grave and long-lasting repercussions for his health.

Much to the relief of Hawkesbury settlers, the grain yields in the summer of 1806 were abundant, despite a parched spring season. Most farmers in the district had major debts from the preceding year and they could now repay these from the bonanza harvests. But the repayment process itself was cumbersome. Most payments in the colony were in either pounds Sterling or Spanish silver dollars, but there was a shortage of coinage in these currencies because overseas merchants had removed most of it with their transactions. This meant that barter, or payment in grain, was the only feasible means of exchange, and this practice became the preferred way farmers would settle their debts. Promissory notes could also be used but were less popular because they involved a degree of risk for both parties due to forgery, which persisted despite printed forms being issued by Governor King.[2] Transactions in grain played a particularly important role in the Hawkesbury district where most of the wheat was grown. Settlers routinely exchanged wheat in their transactions, even for buying small items from the government stores. This suited the stores because they accumulated grain that could be reissued as food rations. Many convicts, soldiers and officials, including the Hawkesbury constables, were still dependent on the food rations from the government stores.

In June 1805 John Macarthur returned from England in his part-owned whaling ship *Argo*. Macarthur's court martial in London had been quashed because the documents prepared by Governor King detailing his behaviour in the colony had been stolen from the dispatch box on the *Anna Josepha* while sailing to England. Quite unfairly, the Colonial Office (the new name for the Home Office) rebuked Governor King for wasting the time of the court. In England Macarthur had resigned his NSW Corps commission and had also been informed by the Colonial Office that Philip Gidley King would soon be recalled as governor. Macarthur's hand-in-glove relationship with English authorities had borne him other fruits – Lord Camden, the Colonial Office Secretary, granted him 5000 acres of land to be used for sheep breeding in the colony, as well as assigned convicts to attend the animals.[3]

The location of Macarthur's land grant was not stipulated, and on arrival in Sydney he insisted that Governor King grant him the Cowpastures property just west of the Nepean River, the finest grazing land in the colony. For the past decade Governors Hunter and King had zealously protected these pastures for the government herd of cattle. King refused and sought clarification on the grant provisions from Lord Camden.[4] Macarthur had also requested a large number of assigned convict servants on full government rations to farm his new land. Again, King refused it on the grounds that the colony was short of able convict workers.[5]

The heaviest blow for Governor King came when he learned that Macarthur had convinced the Colonial Office that he was incompetent and was disrupting the duties of the NSW Corps. The former was nonsense, as King was certainly one of the most diligent administrators the colony had seen so far. But the latter was certainly true – King had made repeated efforts to try and stop the Corps' profiteering. In November 1803, Lord Hobart informed King that because of 'the unfortunate differences which have so long subsisted between you and the military officers of the colony' he would be replaced as soon as 'some person competent to exercise the duties' was found.[6]

Governor King received the official dismissal letter from the Colonial Office in August 1804 and was infuriated with the reasons given for his sacking. He immediately requested leave to return to England and respond to the allegations. He also needed to get some specialist treatment for the severe gout he had suffered for years. The request was denied.[7] Twelve months later, in England, Captain William Bligh RN was commissioned to be the new governor of New South Wales. Until Bligh could get to Sydney, Philip Gidley King carried on; continuing to govern the colony diligently and make further efforts to improve the colony's food production.

John Macarthur had returned to the colony with a cargo of novel items for sale. The merchant Simeon Lord purchased many of these to be auctioned at his warehouse in Sydney.[8] Macarthur also carried a much more contentious cargo on the *Argo*, a large quantity of spirits. Governor King immediately placed these into bonded storage until the custom dues were paid. In December 1805 Andrew Thompson purchased some of the spirits, most likely for his retail store in Green Hills. As payment he made out a promissory note stating: 'whenever demanded (and that to be before next June)' from his granary at the Hawkesbury '428 bushels of good wheat on condition of receiving 60 gallons of Rum from the *Argo* Stores lodged in Government Bonded Stores'.[9] This was a normal business arrangement. Thompson certainly would not have jeopardised his good standing with Governor King to make any illegal deals, especially with someone like Macarthur.

It was well known in Sydney circles that John Macarthur regarded Andrew Thompson as an upstart of no social importance. However, when it came to making money Macarthur would trade with anyone, even with ex-convicts. In this instance he desperately needed money to pay the duty on his imported spirits. Knowing that King would soon be recalled, Macarthur maintained that the importation of spirits should be tax-free because the governor's embargo had not yet been sanctioned by Parliament. Governor King disagreed in 'the most decided manner'.[10] In the meantime, Thompson's purchase of the spirits went ahead.

Most of the large estates in the colony, especially those owned by free settlers and Corps officers, were for raising cattle and sheep, and they grew few cereal crops. Wool was an increasingly important export to the textile industry in England, and meat fetched a high price in the colony. Governor King supported some livestock breeding but the milling of flour from cereal crops remained his highest priority – without locally grown wheat the colony would starve. In later years Thompson would increase his livestock numbers to keep pace with rising meat consumption but he understood all too well the importance of flour and bread to the colony's diets, and his farms cultivated mainly cereal crops.

One of the original reasons given to Parliament for establishing a colony in New South Wales was its suitability for growing flax and hemp. These commodities were much needed for making sails and ropes for the navy. In February 1788, just two weeks after the First Fleet arrived in Sydney Cove, the then 30-year-old naval Lieutenant Philip Gidley King was sent with a contingent of convicts to Norfolk Island to grow additional food for the NSW colony, and, if possible, to establish a flax and hemp industry.[11] For a variety of climatic and logistical reasons the venture failed, but now, sixteen years later, King sought to grow these fibrous crops on the mainland in sufficient quantities to make linen for clothing and for sails.

In early 1804 King ordered hemp to be planted on the government farm at the Hawkesbury. Thompson supported the effort and 'applied himself to the cultivation of hemp' using a small quantity of English flax seeds sourced from the government. By December 1805 he had raised four acres of flax with plants reaching almost 18 ft in height.[12] Being a shipowner, Thompson had a special interest in the local production of canvas and ropes, and he strongly supported King's call for farmers in the district to grow hemp.[13] By March 1806, convicts were assigned to public works at the Green Hills 'House of Correction' refining flax, hemp and wool, using them to make ropes, sails and clothing.[14] Green Hills and its neighbouring districts had progressed from being a backwater village to a relatively prosperous business and manufacturing hub.

Despite crop losses from blight, smut and rust diseases,

successive wheat harvests in the area had been bountiful, and farmers had good reason to assume this was the norm for this fertile district. The most productive farms were located in the low-lying areas of the Hawkesbury tributaries where they were susceptible to flooding. There had been some flooding in 1801 but a reoccurrence was considered unlikely. Farmers felt confident that floods would not affect their future, and in any case good rains were always welcome. They even ignored the recent flood damage done to Thompson's toll bridge on the South Creek.[15] This complacency would be short lived. After very heavy rains in March 1806, the normally placid Hawkesbury River became a raging torrent that inundated valley farms and vast tracts of land along the South Creek. For cereal farmers the timing could not have been worse, as rapidly rising water drowned abundant wheat and maize crops ready for harvesting. When the Hawkesbury River rose over 50 ft (15 metres) settlers realised that not just their livelihoods were at stake, but life itself. Those with boats tried to evacuate to higher ground, but most were trapped on their farms by the rising floodwater.[16]

An 1816 painting of the flooded Hawkesbury River and South Creek at Windsor. In the 1806 and 1809 floods Andrew Thompson's men rescued many settler's families.

By 23 March the entire Hawkesbury area was a 'scene of horror and misery'.[17] Magistrate Thomas Arndell prepared an emergency plan to save lives, which was 'actively carried into execution by Mr.

Thompson, Chief Constable'.[18] Thompson, with constables Lock and Green, set out with four other district constables in three boats to rescue stranded settlers. The emancipist Thomas Biggers, John Palmer's farm manager, joined the search with several other settlers.[19] Flooded farming families clung to the roofs of their huts for several days, accompanied by pets, farm animals and the occasional snake. Others found refuge in trees or on haystacks. Water covered enormous stretches of remote farmland and settlers had to discharge their muskets to gain the attention of the rescue teams. Many families had 'a night of horror', pierced with the 'dismal cries' of those calling for help. Drenched rescuers had little rest over three days, rowing through the surging waters to look for survivors. Thompson and Biggers, in particular, manoeuvred their small open boats to make many miraculous night and day rescues. Nearly 300 people were 'saved from the deluge by the humane perseverance and incredible exertions of the rescuers'. *The Sydney Gazette* praised their efforts:

> Mr. Thompson, Chief Constable; who in one of his boats saved the lives of a hundred people, whom he rescued from the tops of houses, and rafts of straw floating on the deluge. He had two more boats employed in the same humane work, and by means of these also a number of lives were saved. Mr. Thomas Biggers, often at the risque of his own life, saved upwards of 150 men, women, and children; and others who possessed boats, particularly the District Constables, were very active in this benevolent duty.[20]

Remarkable stories of survival were recorded. A woman was immersed up to her neck in water for three days in a house thought abandoned. Her 'piteous cries' were eventually heard, and she was saved. Another woman with her newborn twins was rescued at the last moment from a heap of straw that was separating and rapidly floating down the river. Others escaped after taking refuge in a barn washed away in the flood – they were rescued by Thompson's boats just seconds before it sank.[21]

Some were not so fortunate. Three settlers and a child had fled to the farm of William Chalker on higher ground. But the flood rose so quickly that Chalker, three adults and a five-year-old boy had to jump into a boat, which overturned in the fast-flowing water. The three adults could not swim and drowned. Chalker, with the boy's arms around his neck, swam for one mile (1.6 km) to reach dry land. Throughout the ordeal the boy tried to be brave and 'occasionally to cheer him [on] with the assurance, that they were almost out of danger'.[22] Both lived to tell the tale.

William Chalker must have been a strong swimmer to survive in a churning river with a child on his back; it was a heroic act at a time when most people could not swim. A few days later, he was one of the eight constables appointed to keep law and order in the devastated region. To assist with the welfare of flood victims, Andrew Thompson distributed food from his stores to those worst affected. He also stored salvaged grain free of charge until a settler's land was dry again.[23]

Another hero of the 1806 floods was Thompson's friend, former seaman Thomas Reibey. He had just saved eight people in a boat steered by John Morris, when it was holed by a floating bough and began to sink. As the only swimmer aboard, Reibey dived under the boat but failed to plug the hole. He immediately swam ashore, tore down a long sapling and managed to pull the boat and four people to safety. John Morris and another man drowned.[24] Five people lost their lives during the flood. Years later Thomas Reibey and his famous wife Mary would become neighbours of Andrew Thompson at his Sydney house.

Illustration of the typical plight of families during a Hawkesbury flood. Many families would have been in similar situations when Andrew Thompson and his men in small boats rescued them from the rooftops of their farmhouses and floating debris.

Governor King responded immediately to the disaster by sending extra provisions to the district, and by assigning 125 convicts to help with the relief. Over 42,000 acres of farmland in the Hawkesbury, Nepean and South Creek districts had been flooded, ruining most of the wheat and maize crops, and drowning 4000 pigs.[25] King also rewarded the men involved for their rescue effort. He gave the leaders Thomas Biggers and Andrew Thompson 40 gallons of spirit each and told Magistrate Arndell and Chief Constable Thompson that if more alcohol was needed by flood victims, it would be sent directly from Parramatta.[26] Today this offer sounds odd but at that time alcohol was considered by the Royal Navy to be the best way to combat the cold and fatigue.

The Hawkesbury floods had serious repercussions for everyone. This area was the colony's breadbasket and the loss of an entire harvest threatened starvation. Two weeks later King was compelled to commission ships to import grain from overseas. The most productive farms in the low-lying areas suffered the most extensive losses, despite strenuous efforts to recover as much grain and animals as possible. But remarkably, the overall optimism of the farmers prevailed; they maintained that 'One good Crop will repay two bad ones'.[27]

King appointed the magistrates Arndell and Marsden to survey what was lost in the flood and, with the assistance of Thompson and his constables, determine how much grain had been saved.[28] A week later Reverend Marsden presented a detailed report to the governor. One of the entries in this report shows that Andrew Thompson still had 200 bushels of wheat that would be used for next year's seeding, but he had lost 200 bushels of corn and 105 pigs.[29] Although Thompson had suffered severe crop losses and his toll bridge over the South Creek had been badly damaged, his granary store on higher ground had been spared.

The floods had severely impacted most Hawkesbury farms and many settlers in the district were now financially destitute. In an act of generosity without avarice, Thompson offered liberal credits to many settlers that could be repaid in grain from their next harvest. Debts owing to him for the goods purchased in his store amounted to over 3000 bushels of grain.[30] The value of this debt with wheat priced at 9s 3d per bushel came to £1387 (£125,000 today).

Thompson incurred additional losses from the flood. A new ship being built at a Hawkesbury shipyard had been badly damaged. In late 1805 he had commissioned the construction of the second largest ship in the colony, capable of carrying 100 tons. *The Sydney*

Gazette reported this as a 'colonial achievement' that would 'prove a valuable acquisition to our list of colonial vessels'. Only the whaling ship *King George*, owned by Henry Kable & Co., was larger.[31] His other three ships, the *Hope, Hawkesbury* and *Speedwell*, were undamaged because they were trading elsewhere. To finance the construction of his damaged vessel and make repairs to his farm buildings, Thompson sold his sloop *Hope* to Garnham Blaxcell.[32]

A Castlereagh parish map showing Thompson's three farms on the Nepean River, *Agnes Bank* (278 acres), *Wardle Bank* (80 acres) purchased from William Baxter and *Glasgow* (150 acre) purchased from John Bayliss.

The pitiful aftermath of every flood was the hounding of farmers for the repayment of the loans taken out for the previous season's seeds and labour. With no income from their crops, many settlers had no choice but to sell their land. On 1 May 1806 David Bevan held an auction at Thompson's house to sell 20 allotments. One of these belonged to ex-constable Rickerby. A month later another 30 lots were offered for sale.[33] The sales were devastating for settlers, but they had no other option to pay off debts and to find work elsewhere in the district to feed their families.

In May 1806 Thompson bought three of the auctioned farms adjacent to his existing property. There is no evidence that he foreclosed on debts to achieve these purchases but there is little doubt that land prices at the time were low. He bought the 30-acre Moxham farm just east of his West Hill farm on South Creek and two plots adjacent to his Agnes Bank farm on the Nepean River, paying £180 for the 150 acres of Joseph Bayliss and £128 for the 80 acres land of William Baxter. He called the farms Glasgow and Wardle Bank, respectively.[34] Some in the community exploited the destitute settlers and they added cheap land to their estates. Byrnes writes that Thompson 'had no such reputation – rather the opposite'.[35] And a statement made by Reverend Marsden in 1822 indicates that Andrew Thompson gave liberal credits and refrained from taking legal action to recover these debts.

> To his other employments, he added those of constable and public house keeper, and through liberal credit and forbearance, he acquired a great deal of influence amongst the class of smaller settlers in the neighbouring districts of the Hawkesbury.[36]

But the snobbish Marsden, who was often envious of the business successes of ex-convicts and deemed anyone without a degree from Cambridge University, his *alma mater*, as uneducated, added:

> To a considerable share of natural shrewdness he added great activity of mind and body, and though quite uneducated when he arrived in the colony, he succeeded afterwards in acquiring the ordinary knowledge of a retail shop-keeper.[37]

Throughout his tenure as governor, Philip Gidley King tried to have colonists drink beer instead of rum. To promote this, his administration established a brewery in Parramatta in 1804. But the venture was not a success and in March 1806 the brewery was leased to ex-convict Thomas Rushton to make his own beer.[38] Somewhat awkwardly for King, shortly after leasing the brewery to Rushton, a large shipment of brewing equipment ordered a year earlier, arrived. Rushton was not interested, and King desperately needed to find someone who could take this expensive gear off his hands.

Enter Andrew Thompson, who would soon meet with the governor in his capacity as the Registrar of Agreements. The wily King quickly realised that this was just the sort of young man who could build and run a brewery at Green Hills, and to do this, he would need new copper vats and tanks. Andrew, as always, was open to new business opportunities and he gladly took the bait. On 11 May 1806 King announced that Andrew Thompson would be awarded, for his 'repeated useful and humane exertions' in saving lives and property, a permit to establish a brewery on the banks of the South Creek. This would 'provide a wholesome permanent Drink for the Settlers and Labourers in that extensive Settlement'.[39] Thompson purchased the new copper kettle and other brewing utensils from the government with a 50% advance payment and contracted to supply 'good Beer at not more than One Shilling per Gallon, and Small beer at sixpence'.[40]

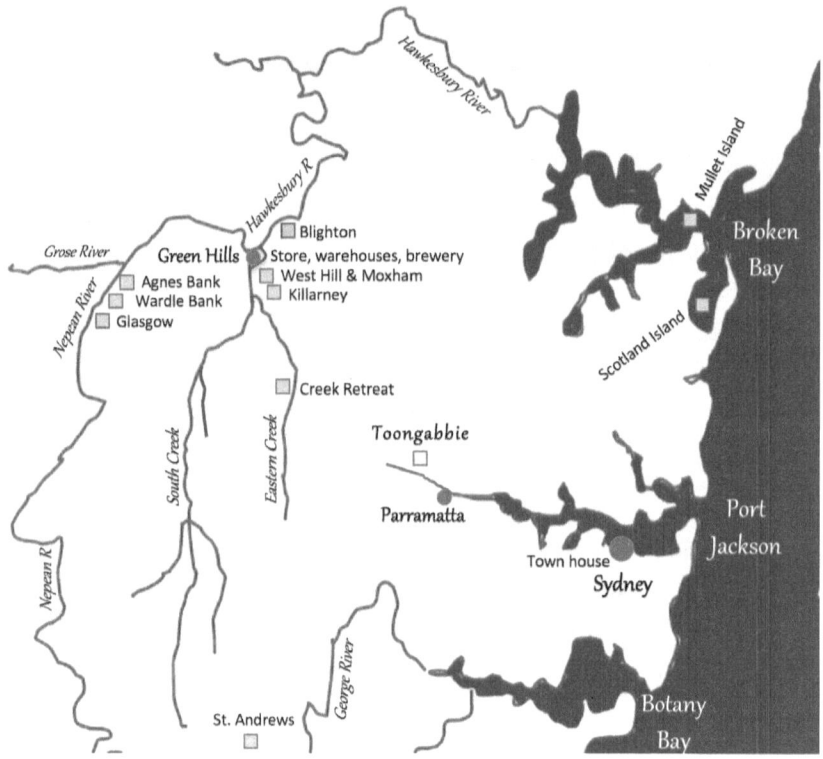

A map showing the farms, premises and salt works belonging to Andrew Thompson.

Near the present Court House in Windsor, Andrew Thompson built a two-storey building, a malt kiln, granary and cooperage.[41] Andrew now needed someone who knew how to brew beer. Not too much in the district escaped the notice of the chief constable, and when he heard that the recently arrived convict Richard Woodbury, serving seven years for stealing brandy, had brewing experience, he had him reassigned from the Castle Hill farm to be his convict servant. Woodbury was put in charge of the brewery, and his beer was reported to be 'very good'.[42] The brewery was the first in the district and also served as a public house or inn. The pub was generally known as 'Thompson's house' and on the second floor had rooms for hire to travellers. Because of its central location in Green Hills, close to the military garrison, it soon became a popular and much-frequented local watering hole.[43]

While Governor King was more than prepared to permit licensed breweries from which taxes could be earned, he was determined to stamp out home brewing and the distillation of spirits. Anyone reporting the use of stills was rewarded: a convict received £10 and a pardon; others received livestock to a value of between £28 and £56.[44] The rewards led to the confiscation of many private stills, and heavy penalties for distillers.

On 6 August 1806 Captain William Bligh RN arrived on the *Sinclair* to become the fourth Governor of New South Wales. Bligh's daughter Mary accompanied him, and her husband, Lieutenant John Putland, commanded the escort ship HMS *Porpoise*. The appointment of William Bligh as governor was largely at the recommendation of the eminent botanist Sir Joseph Banks. Bligh had joined the Royal Navy at the age of seven and by 1776 was the master of HMS *Resolution* on James Cook's third and last voyage. Joseph Banks had been on Cook's first voyage to Australia. In 1787 Lieutenant Bligh of HMS *Bounty* led an expedition to Tahiti to procure breadfruit for the West Indies. The reluctance of sailors to resume naval duties after five months in Tahiti ultimately led to a mutiny in which Bligh and eighteen others were cast adrift in a seven-metre open boat. Bligh's skilful seamanship enabled them to reach Timor after 41 days at sea. On return to England Bligh was court-martialled for the loss of HMS *Bounty* but acquitted. The accusations that his tyranny had caused the mutiny were dismissed when some sailors maintained that he was no crueller than most other commanders of Royal Navy warships.

William Bligh was a veteran mariner with a reputation for stern leadership and an intolerance of disobedience. He did not hesitate to use strong naval invective to make a point. His patron, Sir Joseph Banks, was aware of his brusque manners and regarded Bligh's 'severity of discipline' necessary for the task ahead and he recommended him as governor both for his 'Merit & Ability' and a 'firmness & Integrity' of character.[45] Before leaving England, Bligh was fully briefed on the NSW Corps' commercial interests and their uncooperative attitude to past governors. He was confident he could sort out their discipline problems. However, Bligh might not have known that he was about to face serious resistance in the colony from more than just the NSW Corps officers.

On arrival Bligh quickly established a cordial relationship with Philip Gidley King and the transfer of leadership went smoothly. Bligh was informed of the current governmental challenges, and the obstacles the Corps officers were likely to place in his way. As was customary before the official handover of leadership, Captain Bligh accepted three land grants from Governor King – 240 acres at Camperdown near Sydney, 105 acres at Mount Betham near Parramatta and 1000 acres at Copenhagen on the road to Green Hills. Bligh's daughter Mary Putland received 600 acres at Frogmore bordering on Mary King's farm on the South Creek. And, on taking up office in August 1806, Governor Bligh's first action was to grant King's wife, Anna, 790 acres of land at the South Creek. This farm bordered on the 2340 acres that King had previously granted to his own children. The generous exchange of land grants was apparently a traditional benefit with the interchange of governors.

One of King's last duties as governor was to hold a General Muster of the colony in August 1806. This showed that the population had grown to 7148 inhabitants, with 1576 children. More than 85% of the adult population were either convicts or ex-convicts.[46] The muster records that, apart from Commissary John Palmer, Chief Constable Thompson was the largest grain grower in the colony. With 918 acres of land, Thompson was certainly not the largest landowner – many military and civil officers had bigger estates, but these were for cattle and sheep grazing. Significantly, of the fifteen private landowners with over 300 acres, seven were emancipists: Simeon Lord, James Squire, Andrew Thompson, Isaac Nichols, Richard Fitzgerald, George Crossley and Matthew Kearns.[47] Unlike in England, the ownership of large properties in New South Wales was not confined just to the gentry. Such class entitlements were fast disappearing in the colony and there was a growing expectation that men should be promoted according to their abilities and productivity.

Andrew Thompson's land included 703 acres in pasture, wheat, maize, barley, as well as fields in oats, peas and potatoes, and an orchard. In addition, he had increased his animal herd to nine horses, 26 cattle, 252 sheep, 40 goats and 96 pigs. The muster data shows that Thompson was one of the most prosperous farmers and businessmen in the Hawkesbury district. He had, in fact, become the biggest private employer in the colony, paying the wages of 124 emancipists, convicts and freemen.[48]

All of Thompson's employees were paid wages and none received government rations. His workers were categorised as shop assistants, clerks, storekeepers, bakers, brewers, pub attendants, bricklayers and carpenters for the many building works, shipwrights, seamen, farm overseers, convict overseers, salt boilers, farm labourers and female housekeepers and washer women. Thompson was also known to have given work to destitute settlers trying to recover after the flood. His generosity increased his popularity in the district, and this contributed to his business successes. Andrew's personal convict servant Richard Wright was the only employee to receive government food rations but was paid no wages. Instead, he was provided with six acres of land on which he grew wheat and raised pigs.[49]

Chapter 10

ELEANOR

Q: Was he a man of immoral Habits of Life?
A: Yes I think he was. He lived with a woman of very Infamous Character, who is now alive.[1]

The 1806 General Muster showed that the demographics of the colony, particularly with respect to gender and family, had changed markedly in the eighteen years since the arrival of the First Fleet. Reverend Samuel Marsden used this information to compile a 'Female Muster' of women and children in New South Wales. He was particularly critical of the prevalence of unmarried females and expressed moral indignation at the large number of what he described as 'concubines and illegitimate children' inhabiting the colony. Whereas the General Muster recorded the status of females in a variety of ways, 'wife of', 'housekeeper of', 'servant to', 'self-employed', 'lives with', etc., Marsden classified females in his muster in only two categories, 'married' and 'concubine'. If a single woman lived in her employer's house, as many servants did, Marsden labelled her as a concubine. Because he only considered a marriage in the Church of England to be legitimate, all women betrothed as Catholics or Jews were also designated as concubines.[2]

The high number of unmarried couples living together should not have been a surprise. Many convicts had been married in England before transportation and were unable to get a divorce in the colony. What is more, Reverend Marsden refused to sanctify 'mixed religion' weddings, and this certainly contributed to the high incidence of *de facto* relationships. On his return visit to England, Marsden submitted his Female Muster to the British Colonial Office as evidence of the preponderance of sinful unions in the colony. His righteous and widely publicised criticism of these females, based solely on his personal interpretation of the muster data, exaggerated the false belief in England that most women in New South Wales were immoral. Such ridiculous views persisted into the 20th century, with female transportees routinely portrayed in novels and histories as slatternly members of a criminal class, and as promiscuous whores.[3]

The colony's official birth and marriage registers contain no evidence of Andrew Thompson being married or having children. The only significant record of him having a relationship with a female appears in a much later British government report on the administration of the colony by Governor Macquarie. The report tabled by Commissioner Thomas Bigge in 1822-1823, examined Macquarie's governance of the colony in terms of being an effective deterrent to petty crime in Britain. He visited the colony in 1819. The primary intent of Bigge's investigation was to reverse Macquarie's enlightened treatment of emancipists, and the veracity of his findings is highly questionable. The British Tory government instructed Bigge to prove that Macquarie had mismanaged the administration of convicts and ex-convicts. The Tories wanted the sentence of transportation to be a severe punishment for petty criminals, not to be an avenue for rehabilitation. Because Macquarie treated convicts humanely and encouraged ex-convicts to re-enter society, Bigge denigrated his efforts relentlessly. His observations on Macquarie's allies – of which Andrew Thompson was certainly one – were also prejudicial. Equally, Bigge flattered Macquarie's enemies, who included Macarthur and Marsden. Bigge's reports must be interpreted with their prejudicial intent in mind.

In one of the three Bigge reports, Reverend Samuel Marsden refers to Andrew Thompson's domestic life 'as immoral'.[4] This is not surprising, since Marsden considered any prolonged association with a single woman as 'immoral'. He also had an unfortunate trait of vilifying anyone he considered socially inferior and was especially critical of ex-convicts. It was the main reason Governor Macquarie disliked Marsden so much and had dismissed him as magistrate. The only useful information that one can draw from Marsden's comment, assuming it to be a true record, is that Andrew Thompson was a friend of, or perhaps lived with, a woman who was not his wife. Various aspects of Andrew's social and business life indicate he had a companion, or close female friend, who resided in his Sydney house in later years.

The Bigge reports also contain a remark attributed to the shipwright Thomas Moore about Andrew's personal life. Bigge claims that Moore told him that Andrew lived 'with a woman of very Infamous Character'.[5] This observation has contemporary significance only. In parlance of the era, the phrase 'a very Infamous Character' was often used to describe someone with a criminal past.[6] Moore's remark confirms that Thompson almost certainly cohabited with a female ex-convict, however, there is an ironical twist in his reply. Moore was a very close friend and neighbour of Thompson and was himself married to an ex-convict. It seems likely Moore had responded to Bigge's questioning about Thompson's private life with an intentionally provocative tongue-in-cheek description of Thompson's partner, who, as it will be revealed, was a very successful businesswoman in the colony. Bigge would not have known of the status of Moore's wife, and since he was only interested in slandering Thompson, he recorded Moore's sarcastic reply as a denunciation.

A statement made by Alexander Riley in 1819 to the Select Committee of the British House of Commons suggests that Thompson 'had illegitimate children'.[7] Extensive searches of the colonial birth register, and other records, provide absolutely no evidence for this. There were certainly many children belonging to families on Thompson's farms, but it would be stretching credibility too far to link any of the tenant farmers' children to Andrew.

The Bigge reports, and inferences in other colonial papers, indicate that Andrew had a close female friend. Unfortunately, her identity, and the precise nature of their relationship, is never stated explicitly in any written communications. A thorough search of females living and working in the Hawkesbury district reveals no sensible matchups. However, a study of eligible females residing in Sydney in the early 1800s does suggest one likely candidate – her name is Eleanor (Ellen) Moore. In his thesis on Thompson, J. V. Byrnes draws the same conclusion, but suggests that Thompson 'must have had as little time for Romance as for reading'.[8] In reality, Andrew appears to have had time for both.

As already stated, no documents survive indicating a private liaison between Ellen and Andrew, but there is evidence of a close business relationship. As an educated and successful member of the business community in the colony, it can be presumed that Andrew would have been attracted to a female with equivalent interests. From what is known of his meticulous habits and character, he was unlikely to form a lasting relationship with anyone who did not share his energy and intellect.

The emancipist Eleanor Moore was a fashionable woman with her own millinery business in Sydney. She was born in about 1767 in Cork, Ireland where her father was a respectable merchant. Ellen later lived in Dublin where she married and had a daughter. But the early death of her husband brought hardship to the young widow and, to support herself and her daughter, she worked as a seamstress doing 'plain work for persons of distinction and respectability in Dublin'.[9] In December 1798 she was found guilty of pawning clothing belonging to George Grierson and was sentenced to seven years transportation.[10]

While imprisoned in the Kilmainham gaol Dublin, she sent two petitions pleading for the mitigation of her sentence.[11] Her first petition to Lord Castlereagh, the Chief Secretary for Ireland, stated that her father was a respectable merchant in Cork. Her handwritten petition is informative for several reasons. First, it is written in a stylish educated hand and the composition of her plea demonstrates considerable literary skill. Also, her plea explains that her employees had, in lieu of wages, pawned the 'stolen' articles from her business. Her crime was that she had attempted to conceal the pawning of items by making matching replacement garments. Her plea reads, in part:

> Your Humble Petitioner was the Daughter of a merchant of respectability in Cork and educated to every principle that was good and had every reason to obtain share of the parents honest Industry but for an unfortunate marriage your petitioner made with a person far beneath her Situation and who from a long and painful sickness was deprived of perusing his Trade and by the addition of want and distress left your Petitioner a widow with one Daughter and the entire Substance spend in the pangs of a tedious sickness. Your Humble Petitioner being so reduced and only enable then to reap the advantage of her education was encouraged to undertake work and was thereby making an honest livelihood until that Your petitioners attention and time was so engaged by some who employed her in messages and Business irrelevant to what she honestly endeavoured to pursue that she ... lost some Customers and being so unable to attend to her business and to satisfy the women whom she employed they in her absence took and pawned some Valuable Articles for their wages. Distress accumulating in your unfortunate Petitioner and ... the horrors of a prison and desirous of preserving such things as were Pawned your Petitioner with hard labour paid the Interest and preserved the Articles from being disposed of and delivered the Duplicates

to the Owner of the Goods in order to redeem them, who ungenerously seized your unfortunate Petitioner and put her into Confinement and by the Goods and the Duplicates she gave up furnished her unfeeling prosecutor with sufficient proof to prosecute your miserable Petitioner to Conviction and had her Sentenced to Seven Years transportation and since her Trial has been affected with a severe illness without the means of obtaining the Common necessaries of life and declared by the Physician attending the prison then unfit to go with the other prisoners.[12]

On 20 May 1800 Ellen sent a second petition, along with character references from nine of her customers, to Lord Lieutenant Charles Cornwallis, Governor General of Ireland. No reply had been received when, a month later, Ellen was taken by open wagon to Cork and placed aboard the transport ship *Anne*, which departed for New South Wales on the 26 June 1800. Her father and daughter were most likely at the harbour to say goodbye. Ellen's daughter was not allowed to accompany her to the colony, and both would have been heartbroken. This was the last time Ellen would see her daughter, who presumably was raised by her grandparents. It was cruel justice for her crime of trying to rectify the actions of her staff.

The convict transport *Anne* of 384 tons departed Cork on 26 June 1800 with 171 Irish convicts on board, 147 men and 24 women, as well as 7500 gallons of spirits.[13] The voyage to New South Wales was not without danger and hardship; 20 people died on the journey. Three weeks before reaching Rio de Janeiro, the male convicts mutinied and attempted to take possession of the ship. They surrendered after one convict was shot and two wounded. To prevent any further unrest, one of the ringleaders, Marcus Sheehy was executed by firing squad in front of the convicts and crew, and another, Christopher Grogan, received a flogging of 250 lashes. Sheehy has the dubious distinction of being the only person ever executed on a convict ship.[14] The *Anne* sailed into Port Jackson on 21 February 1801. In a letter to the Colonial Office, Governor King described the convicts on the *Anne* as 'the most desperate and diabolical characters that could be selected' for transportation to his colony. King was a man of strong opinions, and one can safely assume that this was an exaggeration as far as the majority of convicts, and particularly the females, were concerned.[15]

An 1806 view of Sydney from the west side of the cove. On the east side of the harbour is Ellen Moore's small house located between Simeon Lord's large 3-storey residence next to the Tank Stream bridge and the large government storehouse on the left.

The 34-year-old Eleanor Moore quickly adapted to her convict duties and within a year had received a ticket of leave from Governor King, which permitted her to work for herself.[16] In the 1806 Muster Ellen is recorded as having completed her sentence and was self-employed as a milliner in Sydney.[17] However, it is interesting and relevant to note that Reverend Marsden omitted her name from his Female Muster. As a widow living by herself, she simply did not fit his criteria of being married or a concubine. Regardless, Ellen's business successes were unusual for a female at the time, especially as Governor King had such a poor opinion of the Irish. During this period Mrs Moore had even been granted a land lease in the centre of Sydney near the Cove harbour.[18]

We can only speculate on the reasons for Ellen's meteoric rise in the business community at a time when opportunities for both emancipists and women were extremely limited. It is entirely possible that in Ireland Lord Marquis Cornwallis had responded positively to Ellen's second plea, but his reply had arrived after she had departed for New South Wales. If a copy of his reply recommending a pardon or leniency for Mrs Moore had eventually reached Governor King, it would certainly account for the rapid granting of a ticket of leave, and the land lease. Another avenue for Ellen's swift promotion may have been through her skill as a milliner of fashionable hats and dresses for society women. Her business would have brought her into contact with many of the colony's elite, and perhaps even with the governor's wife, Anna Josepha. Such associations were valuable in the settlement, and the influence of wives on husbands was probably as significant then, as it is now. These interactions may also explain how she met Andrew Thompson, who moved in similar business circles and regularly conferred with Governor King as part of his official duties.

If Governor King had encouraged Ellen Moore to apply for the highly valued Sydney lease close to the waterfront, then it is quite possible that Andrew Thompson assisted her in its acquisition. They were both relatively young; he was six years her junior. When the two met is unknown – it may have been as early as 1802. We know that sometime in 1805-6, John Grono, the skipper of one of Thompson's ships hunting seals in New Zealand, named a small island on the southwest coast of the Fiordland region of the South Island, close to Thompson and Nancy Sounds, Eleanor Island. Grono was responsible for naming a number of new localities he discovered on these trips. Eleanor Island was close to the sounds Grono named after Andrew and his mother and it signifies the close personal relationship that had existed between the two for several years. It is also likely that Andrew called his new property on the Hawkesbury, Killarney farm, after the Killarney Lakes in Ireland. This was probably at the suggestion of Ellen, as Andrew would have had little knowledge of Ireland except through her. So, despite the lack of specific written evidence that Mr Thompson and Mrs Moore were established partners, there is considerable circumstantial evidence that this was the case. In Sydney they would have made an impressive fashionable young couple; two strong, influential and energetic emancipists.

Although Ellen was likely to have been Andrew's companion for a number of years, there are good reasons why they never married. She was an Irish Catholic, and he was a devout Scottish Protestant, holding pew No. 2 in the Hawkesbury church. Even if Ellen was prepared to change her faith, it is unlikely that Reverend Marsden would have married them. In any case, not marrying had advantages for cohabiting couples in the colony as it enabled a woman to retain her name, property and children. After a church marriage, a couple became one person in law and the female lost rights to her wealth and possessions.[19]

For these reasons alone, common-law marriages were *de rigueur* for the middle and lower classes. The upper classes and clergy criticised such arrangements, quite hypocritically in view of the behaviour of British Royals at the time, but they were ignored. Military officers were particularly at ease with *de facto* relationships. Major George Johnston had a large family with his partner, the ex-convict Esther Abraham. Others with unmarried female partners were Thomas Arndell, Richard Atkins, David Collins, John White and Philip Gidley King. Joseph Foveaux's partner Ann Sherwin had arrived with her husband Sergeant William Sherwin on the *Pitt*. She left her husband after a year to move in with Foveaux and they married nineteen years later. Andrew's close friend Simeon Lord saw no problem in living with Mary Hyde without being married.

However, it was also true that these unions were rarely acknowledged in the social circles of the colony, and that *de facto* wives were seldom mentioned in letters, diaries or other documents sent to England. The lack of detail about females in the colony applies to all groups – free and emancipist, married and unmarried. Even the identity of prominent men's wives is deplorably sparse. Domestic duties and child rearing were women's work, and in a male-dominated world, such matters were rarely considered newsworthy. The missing information about females is a serious impediment to fully recounting early histories, and as a consequence there is disproportionally less written about females, whether they are convicts, emancipists or free women. Official birth, death and marriage registers provide some details of colonial females, but they are often incomplete.

It was a special tribute for a female in the colony to receive a land lease, such as that received by Mrs Eleanor Moore. Under English law, married women were denied property rights, but in New South Wales the governor had discretionary powers to permit a female to own land.[20] Because Mrs Moore ran a business and leased land, there are more documents containing her name than for most females in the colony. This was at a time when even the property transactions of married couples might omit the wife's name. It was not until the mid-20th century that the practice of referring to a married couple as 'Mister (Mr) and Mistress (Mrs) *Husband's Name*' was replaced by both partners' names. Prior to then, the addressing custom of 'Mr and Mrs *Man's Name*' concealed a female's identity and destined married women to historical obscurity.

The lack of written evidence of Andrew Thompson's romantic attachments has led to some speculation over the years. More than a century after his death, George Reeve suggested in an article for *The Windsor and Richmond Gazette* that Thompson might have been a 'veritable Brigham Young', the Mormon polygamist with 55 wives. Reeve cited as evidence the large number of women who lived and worked at Thompson's various farms and businesses. It is a fascinating and quixotic description of Andrew's contributions to the district. Reeve quotes other reports that 'praised Thompson to the highest pinnacle as the Hawkesbury's greatest citizen, and look upon Thompson as the personification of all the attributes of the Archangel Michael'.[21]

Of course, there is no evidence to support this polygamist theory and it is highly unlikely that Andrew had heavenly aspirations. Polygamist relationships always leave a myriad of family connections and recriminations, and as none exist, we can safely conclude that Thompson was neither a polygamist nor an angel – he simply kept his private life very much to himself.

Chapter 11

BAILIFF OF BLIGHTON

From his first arrival in this country he uniformly conducted himself with that strict regard to integrity and morality as to obtain and enjoy the countenance and protection of several succeeding Governors; active, intelligent, and industrious of manners, mild and conciliatory, with a heart generous and human.[1]

On 13 August 1806 Philip Gidley King and his family boarded HMS *Buffalo* for the voyage to England but because of a severe attack of gout he had to disembark. The King family went to Parramatta until the pain had abated but a later departure was also delayed because there was insufficient grain to make bread for the voyage. During this six-month delay, King witnessed a rapid deterioration in the relationship between William Bligh and John Macarthur. In February 1807, the King family finally left Sydney on HMS *Buffalo*. Reverend Samuel Marsden and his family, who had been granted temporary leave, accompanied them. The Reverend would return to Sydney in 1810.

Philip Gidley King had been an efficient and popular governor who had worked hard to give the colony self-sufficiency in food. He believed in convict rehabilitation and encouraged emancipists to participate in private enterprise. Overall, King had achieved much for the small settlers and emancipists, and under his guidance both penal reforms and private enterprise coexisted. Unfortunately, his continual disputes with the NSW Corps and John Macarthur weakened his resolve, and this tarnished his reputation with the Colonial Office. Most people in the colony considered him a good and fair governor, and they were saddened at his dismissal and the departure of this popular family.

When William Bligh was proclaimed governor on 14 August 1806, he was presented with a welcoming letter signed by Major George Johnston for the military, by Judge Advocate Richard Atkins for the civil service and by John Macarthur on behalf of the 'free inhabitants'.² Bligh gladly accepted the tribute, but after it had been published in *The Sydney Gazette*, 135 Sydney inhabitants and 244 Hawkesbury settlers sent a separate welcoming letter to Bligh.³ The letter made it clear that John Macarthur had represented the free inhabitants without their authority and, while they truly welcomed the governor, the first letter was an 'infringement made on our rights, privileges, and liberty by John McArthur, Esq,' and had been done 'without our previous knowledge, consent or authority, public or private'.⁴

Portrait of William Bligh, the colony's fourth governor (1806-1808). His efforts to abolish the trading in spirits and other illicit practices of the NSW Corps officers and John Macarthur resulted in the 'Rum Rebellion' and his arrest in January 1808.

The Hawkesbury settlers then petitioned the governor for a bill of rights that would grant freedom of trade, rights to buy and sell on the open market, a reduction in monopolies and extortions, justice to be administered by free inhabitants and not only by the military, and debts to be payable in a legal currency or government orders. They pledged their loyalty to Bligh and declared they would risk their lives and fortunes for his protection and the welfare of the colony.⁵ The petition and welcome was signed by most of the major Hawkesbury grain growers, and it sought a fair and fruitful relationship with the new governor. The lead authors were the Hawkesbury settlers John Bowman, Matthew Gibbons, George Crossley, William Cummings and Thomas Pitt. Neither Thomas Arndell nor Andrew Thompson signed the petition, most likely because they were now both government appointees. It is also possible that Thompson thought the letter might be seen as indirect criticism of Governor King's administration, under which he had fared so well.[6]

William Bligh had arrived in the colony shortly after the devastation of the 1806 Hawkesbury flood, and he offered to help affected farmers. On 31 August he asked two magistrates to form a committee of ten respected Hawkesbury settlers to report on the consequences of the flood and how the government might assist.[7] The committee members are not recorded, but as the largest wheat grower in the colony and the Chief Constable, Andrew Thompson was almost certainly a member. Within days, the governor visited the flood area and arranged for the distribution of maize seeds for the next year's harvest. Over 320 farmers benefited from this relief effort.[8] In addition, farmers with surplus seeds were encouraged to distribute them to the needy, which enabled much larger crops of wheat to be sown after such a destructive flood. Bligh understood only too well that the colony's future hinged on the success of the next harvest at the Hawkesbury.

Prior to the March 1806 floods when grain supplies were plentiful, settlers used the government store price as the basis for most grain sales. Because of a lack of coinage, farmers were often paid with promissory notes. Andrew Thompson preferred to make his notes payable in grain, valued at the current government store price. In early 1805, he had made out a promissory note to Thomas Rickerby for 99 bushels of storable wheat. This was later possessed by John Macarthur through his wife Elizabeth, who had sold 44 ewes to Rickerby while John was in England. Rickerby paid for the sheep with 308 bushels of wheat and part of his payment included Thompson's promissory note. In 1805, the wheat price had been 7s per bushel, so the note had a value of £34 13s.

Thompson's promissory note was not redeemed before John Macarthur returned from England. As was his practice, Macarthur held onto notes until he could maximise their return. He waited until grain scarcity caused wheat prices to soar and he then sought payment at the current value of the stated number of bushels of wheat, thus benefiting from its inflated price. On 18 September 1806, Macarthur served a court order for payment of £341 10s; the valuation based on the wheat price of about £3 10s per bushel, not on the original 7s per bushel.[9] He stood to make a tenfold profit. The court case was heard on 27 October 1806, adjudicated by Judge Advocate Richard Atkins and assisted by Thomas Moore and

Reverend Henry Fulton. The plaintiff John Macarthur insisted that the payment be made in wheat, pointing out that he requested this because Thompson could easily afford to deliver this grain from his granary. Thompson agreed to make payment in wheat but only for the number of bushels that could be purchased at the original value of the note. Macarthur refused the offer.

Within the wider community, this case was much more than a dispute between a wealthy grazier and a wealthy cereal farmer. The court ruling would set a legal precedent for many other outstanding promissory notes. If Macarthur won the case, men who had issued similar notes in grain would face immediate ruin. The trial also had implications for a government trying to fix prices and keep the colony's treasury bills low. The court proceedings reveal that Magistrate Arndell supported the defendant by pointing out that Thompson had lost 'the amount of 3000 bushels in debts that were owing' because of the floods. Thompson added 'all wheat notes brought before the last civil court since the flood' had been 'ordered to be paid in money at their original value, that is at storehouse price'.[10] He claimed that he had just enough grain in his granary to feed his 160 workmen and, if the case were not settled in his favour, many of these men would have to be dismissed.

Macarthur was well versed in court tactics. He asked one of his witnesses, Garnham Blaxcell, a question: 'In the occasional visits to the Hawkesbury when you put upon the defendant's house do you eat wheat or corn bread?' Blaxcell replied that he ate 'bread of the best quality', meaning wheat bread. Then Macarthur asked, 'When you visit me at my house what bread do you there eat'? 'Maize bread' Blaxcell replied. The court bench understood the intended message of Thompson's superior table and circumstances, but the case was then adjourned until 4 November. When the court sat again, it had decided that if the person being sued had been adversely affected by the flood, the pre-flood price would be payable, but if the defendant had not been harmed, the post-flood price was applicable. Since Thompson's fields had been damaged by the flood, the plaintiff would receive payment of only £34 13s, computed on the original price of 7s per bushel.

It was an important victory for the government's economic policy, and a reversal for John Macarthur. He was not used to being denied in court and he immediately appealed the verdict.[11] It would be several months before the appeal was scheduled for a hearing.

Although Governor Bligh had not intervened in the court action, he announced three days before the judgment, that from 1 January 1807 all promissory notes had to be drawn in pounds Sterling and not in wheat or other goods. Debts could still be paid in grain provided the note was drawn up in Sterling.[12] A day after the trial Bligh wrote to Sir Joseph Banks that promissory notes were an evil in the colony that had 'been drawn up with every act and chichanerry [chicanery] … I have very satisfactorily checked these proceedings & the value of the Notes will become recoverable without any litigation'.[13] When the promissory note regulation came into effect, Bligh proclaimed that it had been done 'in consequence of the undefined manner in which notes' had been given and 'the many evils and litigations which have resulted therefrom in the colony'.[14] The Hawkesbury settlers had found in Governor Bligh a staunch ally and this further strengthened their support for his policies.

Bligh wanted to protect farmers against the profiteering of the NSW Corps and their cronies, and he promptly set about reassigning officials within his administration, and in doing so replacing many of the military officers with civilians. These posts were influential in the colony and part of the military's power base – the Corps were furious and complained bitterly. Undeterred, in October 1806 Bligh began to eradicate other malpractices. He issued new port regulations that exerted control over incoming ships, including cargoes, crews and passengers. Heavy fines and embargoes were to be imposed if convicts escaped on these ships.[15]

At the close of November 1806, *The Sydney Gazette* reported that Governor Bligh had visited Green Hills for two weeks.

> His presence has had the most salutary operation in influencing the Settlers to industry and exertion, and in maintaining amongst the labourers a due subordination, and ready obedience to the commands of their employers. His Excellency has already visited the farms above the Green Hills; and this day extends his excursion down the River.[16]

It would have been entertaining to see the governor encouraging harvest workers, presumably with a mixture of colourful language and ribaldry. During his stay, Bligh listened sympathetically to the settlers' complaints about the high cost of labour, and he agreed to fix the wages of farm labourers.[17] As someone who knew every farm and person in the district, Andrew Thompson most likely accompanied William Bligh on his tour of the Hawkesbury, Nepean and South Creek farms. Both the governor and the settlers enjoyed the visit and Bligh developed a fondness for the 'industrious settlers' of the Hawkesbury, seeing them, rather than the graziers on the large estates, as the backbone of the colony. In return, the small settlers became Bligh's most loyal supporters.

In all likelihood Andrew Thompson made a positive impression on the governor during the visit. Bligh had resided at the Government House in Green Hills and the view from that building included the impressive Red House farm on the South Creek, Thompson's brewery, store and warehouse. Even so, it is unlikely that the governor would have considered personally entertaining Thompson or accepting an invitation to visit his Red House. Instead, Thompson's brewery-inn, with its large meeting rooms on its upper floors, is where Bligh would have met settlers during his stay. This was the only venue in the district suitable for such gatherings and for the post-meeting celebrations of eating and drinking. At these events Bligh would have been the centre of attention and adulation. As a military man he loved the camaraderie and company of men, and it is easy to understand why he later cared so much for these rugged farmers, and they for him. These men worked hard and acknowledged his ability to help them.

During Bligh's visit it is entirely possible that Andrew reminded him of the storm recovery of the *Waaksamheyd* at the Cape of Good Hope in 1791. Bligh certainly would have recalled the rescue and probably told an expansive tale about his involvement. Whether he would remember the efforts of a Scottish boy convict named Andrew Thompson on that occasion is quite another matter.

The farms Governor Bligh visited in the Hawkesbury district at the close of 1806 greatly impressed his touring party. They admired the energy and teamwork of the settlers, but several noted that many of the farming techniques employed were somewhat antiquated. This was partly due to a lack of agricultural implements commonly used in Britain, but some practices reflected unfamiliarity with standard agrarian techniques. Such observations, coming from desk-bound men and a naval captain who had spent most of his life at sea, probably caused some ribaldry among the settlers, but also some indignation. Without doubt Bligh and his touring party were being influenced by the views of King George III, who was currently advocating major improvements to farming practices in Britain to combat a food shortage. The King had established 'model farms' in England where the latest agrarian techniques were being trialled and taught. Because of his farming interests King George had become affectionately known as 'Farmer George'.

The growing New South Wales colony still needed more food, so any ideas that would enable settlers to improve their crop yields were always welcome. Increasing food production was essential and Bligh gave it a much higher priority than the wool industry or overseas exports. Other ventures had to wait until the vital food supply was secure.[18] With this in mind the governor directed Reverend Marsden to purchase land in the Hawkesbury district suitable for a model farm that could be used to teach settlers to be more productive farmers. Bligh strongly believed that improving the profitability of individual grain growers benefited the colony as a whole. On 1 January 1807, he bought two adjacent allotments for £150 from settler Thomas Tyler, who was returning to England. The 220-acre plot, to be named *Blighton*, was on the banks of the Hawkesbury River six miles northeast of Green Hills. Blighton would be an experimental teaching farm where emancipists and convicts, the future farmers, were taught soil conservation and planting techniques for improving grain yields. He appointed Andrew Thompson as the Blighton farm manager and bailiff.[19]

The cereal harvests in the Hawkesbury area were poor in early 1807. Some grain varieties failed to germinate, and in general crop yields were well below those normally expected. Moreover, because of low grain prices farmers were discouraged from selling their meagre harvests, there was a shortage of wheat in the colony and most granaries were almost empty. Bligh's appeal to the settlers that the colony's survival depended on their grain supply, and without it much more expensive grain would have to be imported, got little support. His argument only strengthened their resolve to be paid a fairer price. Bligh then took an innovative tack; to give 'every Encouragement to the industrious Farmer' he offered settlers who would sell this year's grain to the store, a premium price for next year's crop. The government then raised the current price of wheat to 14s 9d per bushel and maize to 6s per bushel and offered cattle in exchange for wheat. For the next season, Bligh promised 10s and 5s respectively to those who sold this year's grain to the government now.[20] Bligh knew that a guaranteed price would attract settlers, who understood only too well that the overseas grain ordered by Governor King would, when it arrived, significantly reduce prices. The farmers needed to decide quickly whether to take up the offer.

An 1810 painting of the Blighton model farm where Andrew Thompson was the bailiff.

Andrew Thompson, who had been advising Bligh during the grain supply crisis, arranged a meeting of the Hawkesbury settlers at his pub to consider the government offer. The assembled crowd acknowledged Thompson's leadership and for his 'exertions on the occasion' he 'received the warmest thanks'. After considerable discussion the settlers unanimously agreed to support Bligh, 'whose kind and solicitous attention to the interest of the Settlement had on all occasions manifested itself'. The governor's earlier assistance to flood-affected farmers had gained him a strong following and at the meeting 200 settlers agreed to sell 5000 bushels of wheat and 15,000 bushels of maize to the government store.[21]

On 29 January 1807 the Hawkesbury settlers sent Bligh a letter promising grain delivery to the stores, stating 'We have subscribed all the grain we can possibly spare from our own support to be carried to the Public Stores, at your stipulated price, rejecting far greater prices, in money, which we could receive from the present market sale'. They also thanked him for his help during the 'dreadful crisis of general calamity' and pledged to risk their lives and property to support him. In the event of any future grain shortages, they offered to supply their produce at a fixed price. Thomas Arndell, Thomas Hobby, John Palmer, Andrew Thompson, George Crossley and 152 other settlers, signed the letter.[22]

In February a ship bringing rice and wheat from overseas docked and the price of grain in Sydney halved. This bankrupted traders who had held out for higher prices, but it benefited the farmers who had signed Bligh's agreement.[23] The fixing of grain prices frustrated the business community who believed market forces alone should determine prices. Government interference in the grain market opened up a serious political rift between the trading elite of the colony and the emancipist settlers, who were the majority of grain farmers. It was an early demarcation in colonial politics, where the prosperity of the large grain growers in the colony competed with the profits of the merchants who depended on an unregulated market. From this point on, the political and commercial ambitions of these two groups diverged.

The marketing regulations of the government strengthened Bligh's support in the farming districts but made him powerful enemies in Sydney. For the past four months John Macarthur had demanded that Bligh grant him the Cowpastures property. In one confrontation Macarthur alleged that Bligh, in refusing to grant him the Cowpastures land, used abusive language to describe his sheep breeding efforts. Some historians dispute the authenticity of this account. H. V. Evatt writes in *Rum Rebellion* that it was a story 'which was deliberately created in order to hurt Bligh and help Macarthur'.[24] Bligh certainly would have argued that Macarthur's use of Cowpastures for sheep breeding was unacceptable at a time when the colony was in desperate need of more grain. He agreed with King on the unsuitability of the Cowpastures land for this purpose.

On 7 February 1807 Bligh wrote to the Colonial Office Secretary Windham, asking that the location of Macarthur's grant be changed.[25] However, because Viscount Castlereagh was replacing Windham, he did not respond until late 1807, and by then Bligh was no longer in charge.[26] Eventually Castlereagh agreed with Bligh's recommendation, advising that land be granted elsewhere so as to protect the wild cattle. He asked that no further land grants be made west of the Nepean River. Throughout these exchanges, Macarthur badgered Bligh. Macarthur saw the Cowpastures as the jewel in his grazing empire and he would not let it go without a fight.

In the meantime, Bligh pressed ahead with other reforms. He banned all rum trafficking and chipped away at the Corps' monopoly on the retail sale of imported goods. The Colonial Office had instructed Bligh to normalise trading conditions in the colony and on 14 February 1807 the government banned bartering and payment with spirits for grain, labour hire or any other products. The importation of distillation equipment was also prohibited. Severe penalties applied for violations of these regulations: convicts to receive 100 lashes and twelve months of hard labour; emancipists a £20 fine and a three-month prison sentence. A free person was fined £50 with a loss of privileges. The unexpected twist to these new regulations was that a portion of the fines imposed would be paid to the informant.[27]

Bligh's restrictions proved effective, reducing both the rum trade and the Corps' profits. They were incensed; especially as a reward was given to a convict or emancipist who had informed on a soldier. Bligh's persistence with these reforms further outraged Macarthur who now slandered the governor in public. With the judiciary and the military still on his side, Macarthur was confident that his insults and criticism would not incur a legal challenge. Bligh was not unfamiliar with Macarthur's corroding tactics and constantly updated the Colonial Office on the progress of his reforms. A year on, King George III himself wrote of his approval 'to put an end to the barter of spirits which appears to have been abused to the great injury of the morals of the colony'.[28] Bligh had Royal support for his actions, but by the time the letter reached him, local law and order enforcement of the new regulations by the Corps had deteriorated badly.

Predictably, most small farmers backed Bligh's efforts. They had suffered badly under past trading practices and appreciated that the new regulations would improve grain sales and reduce the cost of retail goods in remote areas. On 25 February 1807, 546 Hawkesbury settlers sent a letter to Governor Bligh supporting his efforts and pledging their loyalty in the event of any future difficulties.

> Beg leave to return our sincere thanks for your wise and unwearied Solicitude over the public welfare at all times, … under a just, equitable, and gracious government, which we impress with the strongest desires to support with our lives as also a bounden duty in all loyal subjects, have willingly according to Your Excellency's order enrolled our names for the defence of the country, in which we will readily participate, at all times of need; but sincerely hope

that your Excellency, in your wisdom, by judging from the real and presumptive proofs exhibited in this country now and for many years past, by those disaffected people of their relentless and incorrigible spirit of rebellion, murder and atrocity keeping liege subjects in constant alarm, that you will be graciously pleased to dispose of the ringleaders and principals so as to prevent future conspiracy amongst them and to restore public tranquillity.[29]

The signatories were mostly ex-soldiers, freemen and emancipist landholders. By then Andrew Thompson was the wealthiest resident at the Hawkesbury but he was the sixth signatory on the petition, following the five freemen Thomas Arndell, Thomas Hobby, James Cox, George Evans and William Baker. Thompson understood the social protocols that were still in force here and the importance of not appearing to transgress them. He knew, all too well, how to play the politics of being the modest populist.

However, Andrew Thompson's private life was far from humble. His businesses were flourishing, and his burgeoning wealth lent respect and power to his daily dealings. With a fine splendidly furnished house and rich farming estates Andrew appeared to any casual observer to be living the life of a rural gentleman. And befitting such a role, he had taken to breeding and racing horses. Races in the district began with the arrival of the first Corps officers stationed in Green Hills in 1795. They were the only ones who could afford a horse and over time the sport became very popular. With a price tag of between £50 and £100 per carriage horse, and £190 for a racer, it was strictly a pastime for the well off.[30] In 1806 Andrew raced nine horses at the 'Race Ground' in the Nelson Common to the east of his Killarney farm. The track was not comparable with today's racecourses, being a roughly levelled circuit in a paddock. Later it became the Killarney Racecourse.[31]

Prior to the March 1806 flood, Andrew Thompson had bought for £120 (£10,900 today) a grey gelding, called Kangaroo, from Corps officer Nicholas Bayly. It was 'well known to be the fastest Horse in this Colony either to ride or to drive'.[32] The racehorse was evidently not as fast as expected; a year later Thompson sold Kangaroo at an auction in Green Hills, listing it as 'a remarkable good lady's horse'. He also offered for sale a 'capital Grey Horse with an elegant Chaise, & Harness, brass mounted; also an excellent Bay Gelding, with good Cart and Harness', a six-year-old brown stallion called Oman, a very large bullock called Boxer, a few ewes and lambs, four working bullocks with harnesses and two strong carts, a plough, a harrow, two cows and calves. Also offered for sale was 'a quantity of strong Men and Women shoes'. Bartering in goods and produce other than spirits was allowed, and settlers used this means to purchase animals or clothing. Payment to government stores could be made in wheat, maize, pork or coins, and buyers were allowed three months credit.[33]

Thompson's store gave customers the same conditions, and his encouragement to use grain to pay for purchases frustrated traders who had, until Bligh's reforms, bartered in spirits. Some businessmen of the community, and particularly John Macarthur and the Corps officers, were exasperated by this young emancipist's successful efforts to garner support for the governor, and they vowed to take this upstart down at the earliest opportunity. Thompson was certainly aware from friends and colleagues of these vague threats, but he was probably far too busy to be really concerned – there were not enough hours in the day to manage his retailing, brewing, shipping and farming businesses, or to carry out his chief constable duties and responsibilities as bailiff to Governor Bligh's and Mary Putland's farms. This was a gargantuan workload, even for someone with Andrew's organisational skills and drive. He was clearly eager to accept every opportunity to serve the governor, and, of course, to make a profit from that association. For someone with so much business sense it seems odd that he had not yet appointed a manager to coordinate his activities. He did employ three clerks: James Smith, Abraham Youler and John Speed; but they appear to have been no more than bookkeepers. What he really needed was someone who could share the day-to-day responsibilities and assist in the decision-making.[34]

Unquestionably, the invitation to become the governor's bailiff at Blighton was a singular honour, especially for an emancipist. It was a managerial post that carried privileges, not the least of which was routine access to the governor. Byrnes writes: 'From conviction to the trusted servant of the King's representative; this was indeed the greatest honour that had ever been given to any settler in the colony, bond or free'.[35] Thompson hired the emancipist William Haydon as the onsite overseer at Blighton. Haydon wrote frequent reports for Thompson about activities on the farm and the costs incurred. In March, the ticket of leave convict Thomas Bundle replaced Haydon as farm overseer, though Haydon still countersigned the reports. The reason for this is unknown; perhaps a stricter man was needed to motivate the labourers. Thompson supplied most of the materials and equipment used at Blighton from his own farms and frequently consulted with Bligh, who gave instructions on the animals to be stocked and the grain to be grown. Farm transactions were invoiced for the governor's attention, even for the stock obtained from the government herd.[36]

Andrew's shipping interests continued to expand. At the end of February 1807, his sloop *Speedwell* arrived back from the Bass Strait, and the *Hawkesbury* returned from Tahiti after taking missionaries there for the absent Reverend Marsden. Two weeks later, Thompson sold four horses with saddles, several good chaises and 400 lb of salted pork and 30 gallons of coconut oil imported from Tahiti. He then put the *Hawkesbury* up for sale. These sales helped finance Thompson's new ship the *Governor Bligh* that was launched on 21 March 1807. She was the second largest vessel built in the colony and would be captained by John Grono and crewed by eighteen men.[37] The editor of *The Sydney Gazette* enthusiastically described the launch:

> Mr. Thompson's fine vessel was launched from the Green Hills; numerous spectators attended on the occasion, which afforded to that part of the country a spectacle as pleasing as it was nouvelle. She went off in very good style, and as she darted across the stream was honoured with the appellation of "The Governor Bligh".[38]

It was about this time that Thompson invested in another commercial venture; a tannery that would manufacture leather from locally sourced seal, sheep and kangaroo skins, and cattle hides. Tanned leather was vital for making everyday items such as shoes, belts, harnesses and saddles. The scarcity of local hides had made leather expensive in the colony, and almost all leather goods were imported. Since Thompson's small fleet of ships was already engaged in the profitable seal hide trade, the shrewd Scot took the opportunity to add value by also tanning the hides. He already owned a salt works on the lower Hawkesbury that made enough salt to cure skins. The tannin needed for the commercial tanning process was extracted from the bark of native eucalyptus trees, such as the Blue Gum. On his West Hill farm, close to the South Creek, Thompson built an extensive tanning yard with pits, sheds and a weatherboard house for the workers.[39] These hides were then used to produce a variety of leather goods that could be sold in his shop in Green Hills.

On 26 March 1807 Thompson presented Bligh with an inventory of the Blighton farm. This is the earliest document written by him to have survived. It lists the farm equipment, the number of animals and workmen, the work performed and the overseer's requests for tools and articles.[40] The report reveals Thompson to be an accomplished scribe with a flair for journalism, and for flattery.

> I hope your Excellency will be pleased to observe by the inclosed returns that every attention is paid to your own estate; which, in improvement and produce, will, I am certain give your Excellency every satisfaction and profit that can be expected from it; and more so, in my humble opinion, should you be pleased to approve of some further plans which I will take the liberty of waiting on your Excellency shortly to explain; and, with due submission to your Excellency's great wisdom and attention to farming and improvement, which the Sovereign was pleased to practise at Home, might not be unworthy of his grand representative here, as an example for all others, exciting them to that in which the riches and prosperity of states must depend. Craving your Excellency's pardon for this liberty and digression, I beg leave, with all due respect, to subscribe myself.[41]

A catalogue of Andrew Thompson's manifold undertakings at this time reflects the man's enormous industry and ambition. But not all his activities show his motives and achievements in a particularly favourable light. His early business ventures certainly exhibit a preoccupation with profit making and land acquisition. These may have been simply his early frantic attempts to recover the respectability he had lost in Scotland. In any case, criticism of them must be tempered by the knowledge that he had acquired his wealth solely through his own endeavours. This contrasts with almost all his neighbours on their large estates, who had become prosperous from large government grants and free convict servants. Andrew had purchased most of his property from his earnings and had amassed his holdings without disadvantaging fellow settlers. Few successful men in the district could make an equivalent claim.

When an opportunity arose in April 1807 to lease from the estate of the late William Balmain's two properties bordering his own land, Thompson took it up. The first one was the 270-acre property bordering his West Hill farm, and the second the 6½ acres in the government precinct at Green Hills. The precinct plot had originally been held by the emancipist John Harris, who had owned the Cross Keys Inn in 1798 and sold the lease to Balmain before he returned to England. For both leases Thompson paid £35 per year.[42] This meant that Andrew Thompson now held the only two private leases in the government precinct.

A view of the Hawkesbury River in 1810 showing the farms around Green Hills.

He then advertised in *The Sydney Gazette* for 'a person or persons to make and well burn 30,000 Bricks'.[43] What he was building at the time is unknown, as he always had multiple projects in train. By 1807 Thompson had erected another house in Green Hills: 'A Brick Building of two stories, comprising eight Tenements of two Rooms each'.[44] The building stood on land Thompson had leased from William Baker, the government storekeeper at the Hawkesbury since 1795, whose land marked the western side of the government precinct.[45] The purpose of the building is uncertain, but it seems to have been a luxurious inn catering to wealthy visitors to the region. Thompson's houses were well known for their hospitality 'equally partaken of by the same Officers and Gentlemen'.[46] This cordiality was also true at his private Red House residence.

The seemingly endless expansion of Thompson's enterprises appears to have had Bligh's approval and, indeed, throughout his career Andrew had had the strong backing of governors. This may have been because he took care to comply with government regulations, and to get official advice before making a major move. Colonial businessmen who fell short on compliance issues suffered the consequences. His respect for authority and the latest regulations meant the Corps found it difficult to pin even minor misdemeanours on the shrewd Scot. Nevertheless, Bligh's right-hand man at the Hawkesbury would eventually feel the sting of his envious and irritated opposition.

Bligh's insistence that his reforms be followed to the letter had galvanised opposition among an elite accustomed to the compromises of past governors. Professional men who had once sided with Bligh now defected to the Macarthur camp. This included the military surgeon John Harris (not related to the Cross Keys Inn lessee), who had been one of the few Corps officers friendly with Governor King. In May 1807 Bligh dismissed Harris as a magistrate for trafficking rum, and Robert Campbell replaced him.[47] Harris became a fierce critic of Bligh, and surgeon D'Arcy Wentworth and businessman Simeon Lord soon joined the opposing cabal.

Accusations that Bligh gave preferential treatment to Thompson and his business ventures were rife in Sydney. And they were accompanied by the usual assertions of bribery and corruption, of which there was no evidence. Thompson was careful to keep meticulous records of every transaction, and this annoyed his opponents, who often did not. Nevertheless, it was agreed in elite circles that somehow Thompson had to be taught a lesson, if necessary, by chicanery. In May 1807 Thompson was accused of distilling spirits contrary to government regulations. No details of the accusation have survived, and in any case, the governor refused to accept the charge, and no investigation followed. But more such attempts to implicate Thompson in some sort of misdemeanour were to follow.[48]

A few days later, on 27 May 1807, Thompson forwarded a report on the Blighton farm to Bligh that listed the returns of stock and labour, the length of timber cut and the cost of developing the farm.[49] In his report Thompson stressed the need for extra care in restocking from the government herd at Toongabbie in order to avoid further recrimination. He refused to stock Blighton with more animals until he received orders from the governor.

> I would also beg leave again to hint the benefit of the Flock of Ewes when you might have leisure to give Order for them, and I would come into Toongabbie to choose and bring them safe out. Sincerely begging leave gratefully to assure your Excellency that every exertion shall be used in my part to promote your Excellency's wishes and real Interest in every Shape, of which I hope in due time to give the fullest proofs, I have took the liberty of sending One hundred and twelve Dollars, and 1s. the price of 93½ Bushels of nett Maize at 6s. per Bushel of yours put in Store to my Name, in a little Box with the Vouchers in it, not telling the Bearer what he carried, as the lure of Money however trifling often excites peculation in this Country.[50]

This excerpt of his note also reveals the complexities that Thompson faced regarding the sale of the Blighton harvest. He had sold the maize in his own name and then 'took the liberty' of sending Bligh £120 'in a little Box' and 'not telling the Bearer what he carried' in case the transaction is misinterpreted. Bligh believed the British government would not pay treasury bills made out in his own name and Thompson, who, as a bailiff could not refuse the governor's request, had become a middleman in the transaction. Whether Bligh was profiteering without proper disclosure is unclear, as presumably the farm was government owned. However, if these transactions were later considered in a court of law, Thompson's defence would certainly not have been helped by the note below thanking Bligh for his support with the distilling accusation.

> I am gratefully thankful to your Excellency for your justice and goodness respecting the insinuations made against My Character in telling you that I was then concerned in distilling. To which I again beg leave to pledge My life and property *is false*, defying any Person in existence to prove that I ever spoke or Acted against Your Excellency's Order on this head since the day it was published up to the present moment. But your Excellency is or will no doubt be convinced that the Slander of this Country would deprive you of honest Men if your Excellency's just Wisdom and penetration did not counteract such destructive Plans.[51]

In mid-June 1807 Bligh made another two-week visit to the Hawkesbury district and inspected Blighton with Thompson.[52] Shortly after Bligh's return to Sydney, Thompson wrote to the governor on how he would purchase sheep from Parramatta and Sydney for the farm. This was important, as Thompson had been informed of rumours circulating that Blighton was being stocked illegally from the government herd. He advised Bligh that 'it might not perhaps appear so well' to take too many animals from the government stock.⁵³ Perhaps Thompson was getting nervous at his involvement in the Blighton acquisitions from the government herds, and he thought it wise to say so in writing.

In early July 1807 John Macarthur appealed against the court verdict on the value of Thompson's promissory note. Critical of this action, *The Sydney Gazette* published an article attacking Macarthur and supporting the original verdict.⁵⁴ On 11 July the Court of Civil Appeals heard that the plaintiff insisted on being paid the inflated price for the grain, despite the newly enacted promissory note law. When making the appeal Macarthur expected the Corps officers sitting on the court benches to back him up – he had not appreciated that the governor was to preside over the sitting. Bligh promptly refused to accept Macarthur's arguments for an appeal and dismissed the case.⁵⁵

The Sydney Gazette editor George Howe relished the opportunity to tell his readers of the appeal proceedings, though he did not mention names. This editorial upset Macarthur and two weeks later a vociferous letter from 'An Oculist' praised Macarthur and his action – it was a letter that had all the earmarks of the man himself. This triggered a fusillade of opposing letters that continued for several issues, with George Howe playing the mediator highlighting various important moral aspects of the court findings. Macarthur persisted with these exchanges and in his article on 2 August 1807 he viciously attacked Thompson as a man without honour who was well able to afford to pay his debts in full.

> Am I to forego my right with the man who has escaped the calamity, and only resists my claim that he may sell his wheat at a tenfold price, or employ it in some doubtful speculations?⁵⁶

To be sued by Macarthur was seen by most settlers at the Hawkesbury as a singular badge of honour, and the court case would have boosted Thompson's popularity even more. During the first court appearance Thompson had maintained that he could not pay the promissory note in grain without dismissing a large number of employees and suing settlers who were destitute from the floods to pay their debts. In fact, he had withheld such actions until the settlers had recovered. In March 1807, a year after the flood, and following a successful harvest, Thompson requested the prompt return of loans, hoping that court actions would not be necessary.⁵⁷

H.V. Evatt wrote in his book *Rum Rebellion* that Governor Bligh had, in dismissing Macarthur's appeal, acted correctly and the judgement was a 'distinct setback to those who had taken advantage of the scarcity to press unexpectedly onerous demands on small settlers'. Evatt, a lawyer and judge by profession, believed that 'Macarthur was legally wrong, and Bligh was legally right' and Macarthur may have deliberately brought on the case 'to test Bligh's courage and tenacity'.[58]

The appeal and the verdict had consequences for *The Sydney Gazette* and its editor. After publishing the court proceedings on 30 August 1807, the paper ceased publication. It was announced that this was due to a lack of printing paper, but Howe later revealed that the government store had enough paper.[59] It is likely Bligh did not want the newspaper to become a propaganda platform for those opposing the government.

After his rebuff in court, Macarthur was openly disrespectful of the governor, refusing to meet him socially and encouraging others to do the same. However, the widening schism between the government and the business community seems not to have diminished Bligh's resolve to have his reforms complied with. As he saw it, the Colonial Office had demanded the removal of the trading iniquities in the colony, and he was acting on those instructions. His opponents had not appreciated yet that this naval veteran, hero of the Battle of Copenhagen who had been praised by Admiral Horatio Nelson, had more broadsides to fire in his campaign to rid the settlement of business malpractices. Thus far, he had attacked only the resistance to his new reforms; he now embarked on eliminating unlawful interpretations of longstanding regulations.

Chapter 12

THE LOYALIST

> *We ... express the fullest and unfeigned Sense of Gratitude for the Manifold, Great, and Essential Blessings and Benefits we freely continue to enjoy from your Excellency's Arduous, Just, Determined, and Salutary Government over us, ... And, while enjoying such inexpressible Benefits from Year to Year under Your Excellency's Auspicious and benign Government, We feel and hold ourselves gratefully bound, at the risque of Our Lives and Properties, at all times, as liege Subjects, to support the same.* [1]

Governor Bligh maintained that the Blighton farm was a government workplace and as such it was entitled to use convict servants. Their assignment to the farm coincided with his decision to reduce servant entitlements to Corps officers. Until then, the Corps and other favoured inhabitants depended heavily on free assigned convict labour. D'Arcy Wentworth, the Surgeon in charge of the Parramatta hospital, had for some time directed 'invalid' convict patients to work illegally on his farm. Instead of returning a recovered patient 'to Government labour or to the poor Settlers from whom they came', he or she was put to work for him for months before being discharged.[2] When Bligh learnt of this practice, he immediately stopped it, and Wentworth was charged with using the labour of sick convicts for his private advantage.

Wentworth was nonplussed by the charge, as he knew his friends would be sitting on the court bench and his case would be heard before the lax Judge Advocate, Richard Atkins. He was right; the court found him guilty, and Atkins sentenced him to a 'public reprimand'.[3] Bligh was furious and suspended Wentworth from hospital duties until advice was received from the Colonial Office. The sacking of such a prominent member of the colonial society shocked many in the settlement, and they sent a flood of protest letters to the Colonial Office. But Bligh was unrepentant; he had intended it as a clear signal that social rank would no longer protect a person from prosecution. It was a startling wakeup call for the military and business elite, who were known contemporaneously as the 'exclusives'.

Opposition to the governor now became noticeable in business circles. In August 1807 Simeon Lord and his partners Henry Kable and James Underwood wrote a blunt letter to Bligh demanding permission to transfer goods directly from one ship to another. This was in contravention of port regulations, and Bligh saw their clumsy letter as insulting his authority. Permission was denied and the men arrested, gaoled for one month and each fined £100.[4]

Improvements to the Blighton model farm continued. At the end of July 1807 Thompson sent another detailed report to the governor. The farm now had two houses, one for the overseer and one for the stockmen, a barn and a shed for animals. There were 60 cattle, 67 sheep and 60 pigs, total value of £2032. This was a surprising number of animals for a farm that had been operating for six months. Thompson had donated fowls, turkeys, ducks and geese from his own flock.[5]

The progress at the farm so impressed Bligh that he decided to make further improvements and increase his holdings. In October Thompson purchased the 110-acre adjoining farm from James Simpson for £100. The land was paid for with a promissory note in Thompson's name, to be repaid in produce from the Blighton farm.[6] The new land was to become a dairy farm. On his last visit Bligh had expressed dissatisfaction with eight cows received from the government herd at Toongabbie, and he requested that they be exchanged for better stock. Thompson was sent to the Toongabbie yard to swap the eight 'inferior cows' and bull with the best he could find in the herd.[7] The rejected cows had already calved, and the calves remained at Blighton. Using the government herd in this way raised a few eyebrows among officials and elsewhere. Bligh undoubtedly believed such actions to be legitimate. When he was offered the governorship in England, Sir Joseph Banks advised him that 'the whole of the Government power and stores' would be at his disposal for his financial benefit.[8] In any case, Bligh saw improvements to the model farm as being in the colony's best interests. What is puzzling, however, is that there are no documents showing that Blighton was used for its intended purpose, namely, to educate settlers in the latest farming techniques. Possibly this was happening, but no evidence has survived to verify the involvement of other farmers. On the other hand, the convicts working at

Blighton were trained in agricultural practices, and would, when their sentences expired, become the future farmers.

Thompson's next letter to the governor on 16 October 1807 exhibited a new familiarity when he wrote about sending fresh fish to Bligh's son-in-law Captain Putland, who was gravely ill.

> I delivered you the transfer of Simpson's estate, and that your Excellency put it, with other papers, I think, into a desk on the bedroom table upstairs, and has no other papers of consequence relative to estates up here except the enclosed agreement of the overseer's, which I had kept with a design of settling with him myself, if pleased. ... I will take the liberty of waiting on your Excellency in a week's time with the little curiosities, &c. I have taken the liberty of sending a few, just caught, live fresh-water fish, hearing Captain Putland had a desire for such, and would be glad to send more at any time if acceptable.[9]

This communication indicates that Andrew now had the confidence of the governor and was comfortable in his position of authority.

Relations between Bligh and the business community were now at rock bottom, and they bombarded the Colonial Office and politicians in England with letters attacking his administration. Free settlers John and Gregory Blaxland complained that Bligh had no interest in supporting their enterprises and had failed to give them the assistance promised by the British government. The letters also included criticisms of the Blighton farm, accusing Bligh of improperly removing cows from the government herd. They also claimed he was selecting the best convict labourers for his farm, while leaving the invalids and other 'atrocious characters' for the rest in the colony.[10]

Bligh appeared indifferent to this far-from-secret sniping and set about overhauling Sydney's town planning, knowing full well that this would pit him against the colony's most powerful landholders. In his view, Sydney was 'sinking into decay' and its public buildings and storehouses were 'in a state of dilapidation'. He wanted to restore order to a town that had grown too quickly without adequate planning.[11] Governor Phillip had zoned a large area of land behind Government House and St Philip's church as a public domain, but Governors Hunter and King had granted leases there. In fact government regulations stipulated that leases may not exceed five years but King had, at the conclusion of his tenure, granted a number of fourteen-year leases to influential inhabitants.[12]

Thompson's good friend Mrs Ellen Moore was one of those who had received such a lease.

Governor Bligh was determined to correct these irregularities. He deemed many of the leases to be invalid, and that houses without leases should be demolished. This action fuelled another flurry of furious letters to the Colonial Office. Both Hunter and King had attempted similar planning reforms, but they had eventually caved into opposition. But, on this occasion, the exclusives were about to be reminded that Bligh was made of sterner stuff. A number of prominent inhabitants were evicted, and although they were offered land elsewhere as compensation, not one was prepared to willingly hand over their central property.[13] Some had no legitimate lease at all, while others hastened to get 'some person of respectability and character to accept a friendly assignment of their leases' in the hope this transfer would protect their property from confiscation.

> Let me also observe, that the lower class in New South Wales looked up to the few independent and respectable inhabitants, as their only protectors against the violence with which they were threatened, and the tyranny with which they were beset. Thus, when Gov. Bligh threatened to pull down their houses, they were in the habit of requesting some person of respectability and character to accept a friendly assignment of their leases, flattering themselves that the superior station of these persons would be respected, and their property thus secured. But when it became known that of this class of society seven individuals were at once to be imprisoned and sentenced to death or banishment, every hope seemed at once to vanish, and despair with all its attendant feelings seemed to take possession of every mind.[14]

The battles for central leases developed into the sort of combat Bligh had expected with exclusives all along. Many elite squatters were about to lose their Sydney leases entirely and controversially others, including Commissary Palmer and Chief Constable Thompson, were about to receive new leases. These lease vicissitudes would have long-term consequences for the colony.

The precise circumstances by which Andrew Thompson received a new lease to a central Sydney allotment are unclear. Governor King had in 1806 given Andrew's friend Ellen Moore a fourteen-year lease on land near the mouth of the Tank Stream, and here she had built a house and garden. Her small plot of 19 perches (480 square metres) sat in between the land leases of Thomas

Randall and William Chapman.[15] Bligh may have known that Mrs Moore was Thompson's *de facto* partner, as they were both among the diminishing number of businesspeople supporting him in Sydney. It seems probable that Andrew had agreed to accept a friendly assignment of Ellen's lease on the assumption that his good standing with Bligh would protect it from confiscation or alteration. The details of the assignment between Moore and Thompson have been lost, but there is a record of the sale a year later.[16] In any case, from that point on, this property, which sits at the heart of Sydney's business district, is recorded as belonging to Andrew Thompson. Presumably Ellen continued to reside in the house. There is no record of Andrew staying there on his frequent visits to Sydney, but it seems a likely arrangement.

An alternative explanation is that Thompson took advantage of the turmoil surrounding the reallocation to land leases to purchase the house and land directly from Moore. He could certainly afford it. The property registers show, however, that the purchase of the house took place a year later. Another possible explanation of Thompson's new lease is linked to his employment as the Blighton bailiff as there is no record of him being paid for these services, so Bligh may have granted him the lease for managing his farm. But this would have been politically dangerous for the governor, and in any case, Bligh did not favour free land grants or leases. The most probable explanation is that Ellen Moore assigned the lease to Andrew on mutually agreeable terms, and that Bligh accepted it in recognition of Thompson's service to the government. Such an arrangement matches comments written in a letter by Surgeon John Harris, a declared enemy of Bligh, to Mrs King, the wife of the former governor:

> Governor Bligh is turned a great farmer and has plenty of stock at the Nepean. Andrew Thomson is his Director and right hand man. ... he has given Thomson 3 cows for his attention to his concerns and has also given him that place opposite Lords (Mrs. Moore's) to build on and tho' he says King had no authority to give leases, he continues to do so to his favourites.[17]

Quite apart from the romantic implications of the house transfer, Thompson would have fully appreciated the importance of this lease to his businesses in Sydney. The land was directly at the harbour's front, adjacent to the house of Simeon Lord, another prominent businessman, and close to the Tank Stream Bridge.

Naturally, the granting of this lease would have fuelled even more claims of Bligh's preferential treatment of his bailiff, and further gossip of Thompson's relationship with Mrs Moore. Such gossip was common; many other prominent residents in Sydney were known to have similar arrangements. In any case, the Bligh loyalists in the colony probably viewed Thompson's receipt of a new lease in Sydney as entirely legitimate – after all, he had received grants from Governors Hunter and King for his policing and rescue efforts. Surely Governor Bligh was entitled to do the same.

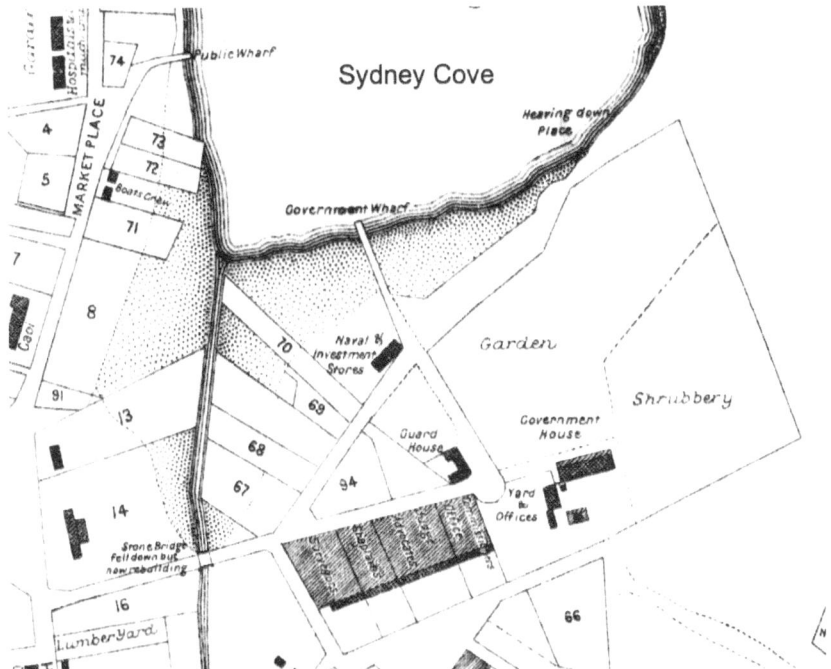

Part of surveyor James Meehan's plan of Sydney in Oct 1807. Bligh granted Thompson Mrs Moore's lease, part of the unlabelled land between lots 68 and 69. The Dec 1808 land grant to Thompson from Foveaux encompassed the unlabelled lot and lot 69.

By now Bligh was either oblivious to, or defiant of, the increasing hostility to his administration in some segments of the community. In his letter to Sir Joseph Banks on 11 October 1807, he appears to infer that his opponents were becoming more compliant. He told Banks that the colony had recovered from a 'most deplorable State' and 'the town altogether is become what has not been seen before in this Country'.[18] Sensing, incorrectly, that his opponents were softening Bligh now embarked on ambitious reforms intended to remove the blatant bias and prejudice from the law courts. He wanted everyone to 'enjoy a just and upright Government' and wrote to Joseph Banks about the 'very unfit & very disgraceful' Judge Advocate Atkins, a 'disgrace to human Jurisprudence'. He wanted him removed without delay. Bligh sought the regulations for the criminal and civil courts to be identical to those in England, and that an Attorney General, who should be a qualified Judge and a trained lawyer or solicitor, attend every trial.[19] Two weeks later, in a letter to Colonial Secretary Windham, Bligh wrote:

> With respect to Mr. Atkins, more particularly, he has been accustomed to inebriety: he has been the ridicule of the community; sentences to death have been pronounced in moments of intoxication; his determination is weak; his opinion floating and infirm; his knowledge of law insignificant and subservient to private inclination; and confidential cases of the Crown, where due secrecy is required, he is not to be trusted with.[20]

Because of Bligh's mistrust of Atkins' legal abilities, emancipist George Crossley, an attorney and solicitor, was made his legal adviser. Crossley was asked to assist Atkins in preparing the case against Macarthur for allowing a convict to escape the colony. Crossley had worked as an attorney in London for 25 years before being charged with forgery and sentenced to seven years transportation. He arrived in Sydney in 1799, was pardoned by Governor King in 1801 and became a Hawkesbury farmer where he had been helping other settlers with legal matters.[21]

Bligh now had 'a full head of steam', or to be more metaphorically correct, he hoisted 'a full set of sails with a following wind'. He sought to radically change the colony's law regime by having the Colonial Office disband the NSW Corps or transfer them to India. He pointed out the absurdity of the current situation in which the virtues of 'plain sensible farming Men' clearly exceeded those of the military who were responsible for maintaining order in the community.

> If Government supports my Dignity & determinations, things will go on right, & let them be aware of this, as I am not here for my ease or comfort but to do justice and relieve the oppressed poor Settlers who must be the support of the Country and are honester Men than those who wish to keep them under.[22]

To reinforce his previously voiced disgust of the NSW Corps, Bligh wrote another letter to Secretary Windham two weeks later, warning him that they might become 'a dangerous militia' unless removed from the colony. He reminded Windham that a governor 'must be determined and firm in his measures, and not subject to any control here'.[23] Unfortunately for Bligh, the British Tory government were becoming increasingly disillusioned with his rigid reform agenda. The latest letters to the Colonial Office from Sydney residents requested he be replaced with the previous Lieutenant Governor Francis Grose, who was now a general in the Royal Marines. The NSW Corps would certainly have welcomed Grose's appointment, as he had been most generous to them.[24] Fortunately for the colony, the Colonial Office declined.

John Macarthur continued to inundate the Colonial Office with letters demanding Bligh's dismissal, the same lobbying actions that had been successful against previous governors. But support for Macarthur among the Corps was waning, as the military became increasingly unsure whether opposing the governor might be a treasonable offence. Even so, Macarthur remained a persistent thorn in the governor's side and in November 1807 Bligh saw an opportunity to get rid of him. He had known since June that a convict had escaped to Tahiti on the schooner *Parramatta* owned jointly by John Macarthur and Garnham Blaxcell. To deter such escapes, ships' masters had to lodge bonds that were forfeited if a ship carried a convict.

When the *Parramatta* returned to Sydney Cove in late November, officials demanded the owners forfeit a bond of £900, and the ship was impounded. Macarthur not only refused to pay the fine, he announced the ship's crew would no longer be paid or fed, forcing them ashore in breach of landing regulations. Moreover, Macarthur refused to respond to the charge and said that the government could keep the ship. He said he would abandon the ship rather than pay the £900 fine.[25] Bligh was convinced Macarthur was implicated in the escape and referred the matter to Judge Atkins, requesting that Macarthur be brought to court.[26] Atkins issued a warrant for him to appear before the magistrate court on 16 December 1807. Macarthur refused the court order and 'fell into a great rage' saying that 'he would never submit until there was blood shed'. He declared that the governor and justice officers would 'soon make a rope to hang themselves' and called Bligh 'a tyrant'.[27]

Macarthur was arrested, given bail, and required to appear for trial on 25 January 1808. Skilled in the deflection and obfuscation of legal matters, Macarthur produced a 15-year-old promissory note in the name of Richard Atkins and demanded that he repay £82 before his trial – the original loan was for £26.[28] Atkins agreed to do so, but later reneged. At that point Macarthur declared that Atkins could not be impartial in judging his case. There had been a long-standing friction between the two. In 1792, Macarthur as the NSW Corps commander at Parramatta took exception to a ruling of Atkins when he was magistrate. Since then, the men had been in continuous disagreement and exchanged slanderous letters.[29] Governors King and Bligh were fully aware of the feud. In any case, even if inclined to do so, Bligh had no legal power to replace Atkins, who would have to adjudicate in the *Parramatta* escape case.

In late December 1807 Andrew Thompson was charged with an offence of illicitly selling spirits that seriously called into question his propriety. The case also tested the judgement and impartiality of Governor Bligh. This offence is puzzling because it only came to light as part of an English trial four years later. In early December 1807 a man (name unrecorded) in the possession of a barrel of rum, claimed that he had bought it from Andrew Thompson. This rum was from the government store and had been intended for distribution to the Hawkesbury settlers.[30] The matter went to court before Magistrate Robert Campbell, a known business friend of Thompson. Campbell gave evidence about the case at the 1811 trial of George Johnston in England, when he stated that:

> Thomson proved before the Bench that the spirits had been received from the Government stores; and although the person in whose possession the spirits were found, when he was brought before the Bench, insisted that Thomson had sold him the spirits, and not lent them, to the best of my recollection Thomson brought evidence which disproved that; but as I knew the spirits had been entrusted to Thomson for distribution among the settlers at the Hawkesbury, I considered that whether the spirits were sold or lent, it was a breach of good faith on his part, and therefore I was of opinion that he should be fined the hundred pounds.[31]

Magistrate Campbell considered Thompson to have been careless rather than dishonest but, nevertheless, ignored his unblemished record and imposed the substantial fine of £100. But, knowing of the campaign in Sydney business circles to besmirch him, Campbell also expressed some doubts about the validity of the accusation.

However, based on the statements made by William Bligh at the Johnston 1811 trial in England, there is an odd twist to this tale. When Bligh was asked if he remitted the £100 fine imposed on Thompson for selling the puncheon of rum, he claimed that he had dismissed Thompson from his service and that he had actually been personally responsible for bringing him to court in the first place. Bligh said at the 1811 hearing:

> Andrew Thomson was the man who had charge of a little farm of mine; it was through my rigid impartiality that he was detected in the offence of making an improper use of a quantity of spirits which had been intrusted to his care for distribution among the settlers in the interior; and it was by my order to the Judge Advocate that he was brought to trial; and I would have nothing to do with him afterwards; he was in the hands of the magistrates, and I had nothing more to do with him.[32]

Asked again if he remitted the penalty, Bligh responded emphatically:

> No; I recollect nothing of the kind, of remitting the penalty; I was so incensed, I thought the penalty too light; he had been guilty of a breach of faith, which I thought deserving of the highest punishment.[33]

When asked if he had dismissed Thompson, Bligh replied:

> I dismissed him from my service so far, that I never allowed him to come near me afterwards; the usurpation came on very soon afterwards, and there were several things he had to account for, but he never came into my confidence again, though he supplicated in the strongest manner; but there were some circumstances of my affairs which I had to settle with him, and he was obliged to come to me for that purpose, and I saw him upon that occasion.[34]

It is important to appreciate that at the 1811 rebellion trial of George Johnston, William Bligh also needed to defend his record as governor, and demonstrate to the court that he was completely unbiased in adjudicating the law. Bligh would have realised that defending the bailiff of his farm against this charge, trivial as it was, would weaken his claim of impartiality. Moreover, as a military man, he knew when to strategically retreat. He was quite prepared to sacrifice Thompson's reputation for the greater good of the office. In an act of blatant political expediency and hypocrisy, Bligh showed no mercy for the man who had been his supporter and dedicated bailiff at the Blighton farm for years. His performance at the trial revealed the ruthlessly pragmatic side to the ex-governor.

Precise details of the charge against Thompson at the 1807 trial in Sydney heard before Magistrate Campbell are unknown – a record of the proceedings is missing from the court archives. We do know, however, that Thompson was found guilty of selling the rum illegally and fined £100, and that he protested 'in the strongest manner' against the finding. The fine itself would have meant nothing to him but being found guilty of stealing from his fellow settlers would have hurt him deeply.

The most troubling aspect of this whole episode is that the actions taken by William Bligh following this 1807 trial do not agree at all with what he stated in England in 1811. First, there is no record of Thompson paying the £100 court fine. Furthermore, colonial records for the years 1807 to 1809 do not support Bligh's claim that he had nothing more to do with Thompson, who continued to be the chief constable at the Hawkesbury and the bailiff at Blighton farm. Perhaps Bligh's confidence in his bailiff had diminished, but numerous records show that Thompson continued to manage the Blighton farm and report regularly to the governor. Both men may have realised that after the spirits charge their meetings needed to be less frequent, but Bligh's claim in 1811 that he 'had nothing more to do' with Thompson was blatantly untrue. Andrew Thompson continued to be a Bligh loyalist, and this would prove critical for the governor during the turbulent rebellious years ahead. In fact, Bligh later asked Andrew to come with him to England to defend him at the same 1811 trial he had castigated him at. Bligh's later blatant perjury would have appalled Thompson, but he never witnessed it – he was no longer alive when this dismal episode took place.

Bligh's vacillating allegiances and faulty recollections are not the only matters of interest here – the charge that Thompson sold spirits illegally is important in assessing the character of the man. He routinely handled alcohol in his brewing establishment, having a licence to do so, and he would have been fully aware of any illegalities. It is therefore baffling that such a smart individual would endanger his future by such a foolish action. Was there a special reason for the trade, or were more deep-seated motives at play here? Considering his personal wealth, it seems incongruous that a quick profit was the reason for the trade, though Byrnes implies that the sale was perfectly in keeping with Thompson's incessant drive for greater riches.[35] A separate question also needs to be asked: does this misstep have the same psychological origins as the crime committed in Yetholm? The theft from his brother and a neighbour by an educated youth with a promising career ahead is in some respects just as inexplicable as this charge. Neither this nor the handling of someone else's alcohol makes any sense hundreds of years later.

Frayed tempers and damaged egos may have dominated the Sydney courts in December 1807, but the efforts of Hawkesbury farmers were totally focused on the next harvest. What is more, Thompson needed to get his own farms ready, as well as those at Blighton. At the close of 1807 Thompson submitted another report to the governor on the Blighton farm. The dairy had made a profit of £60 from only two months operation. The number of horses, sheep, pigs and poultry had increased; all fences, farmhouses and stockyards had been finished, and a new maize crop had been sown. The farm was now valued at £3678 and had yielded £589 in profit. Thompson assured Bligh 'humbly begging leave to assure and point out to your Excellency that I ever have and will use every means in my Power (and I trust none could or would do it better) towards the Improvement of the Estate and Stock'. He estimated that Bligh's profit for next year would double. However, Thompson made an intriguing, and somewhat dangerous, comment:

> But it may be observed that a common Farmer who has to pay for everything would by no means have such profits.[36]

This implies that Bligh had not paid for all his acquisitions, and Thompson hoped he would 'pardon the Liberty of these private hints'. Anticipating his report would incur Bligh's disapproval, Thompson added that future instructions from him would 'be carefully obeyed by His Excellency's Devoted Servant'. Despite the success of Blighton, Thompson knew his position was vulnerable.

> I have taken the Liberty to make a kind of private Testimony inclosed wherein I would hold myself responsible in every Shape and bound in my own Person and Property that there has [been], nor shall be, no error, impropriety, debt, or incumbrance on the Management of your Excellency's Estate; with a desire to Show that everything was done only with a genuine desire to serve and please your Excellency, having ever felt the most grateful Pleasure and satisfaction in being able to render myself in the smallest degree serviceable or acceptable in your sight, and nothing could cause Me more compunction and grief than the Idea of having offended your Excellency.[37]

Thompson understood better than most that Bligh was under enormous political pressure. At that time sixteen Corps solders were stationed at Green Hills and each evening they would have come into Thompson's pub and discussed their latest orders. Information overheard there would duly be passed on to the chief constable who would relay it to Bligh. Settlers in the area were anxious to avoid Corps interference in their farms and businesses – the memories of the disruptive practices of Major Grose and Lieutenant Colonel Paterson were still fresh in their minds.

The financial underpinnings of the Blighton model farm, which had initially been supported by government funds, were problematic for Bligh. Thompson foresaw this and warned him by suggesting that, as King George's representative, he had every right to advance the prosperity of the colony 'by such a noble, laudable, and public example'. In a separate declaration Thompson certified that Blighton had 'been managed without impropriety or known Error' and that there were no debts, or encumbrances outstanding or belonging to the management of the estate.[38] In a letter to the Colonial Office Secretary in 1808, Bligh admitted that he had received Thompson's regular reports but the seriousness of 'the public concerns of the Colony' at the time prevented him from attending to farm matters or reading the letters from his bailiff.[39]

The trial on the *Parramatta* convict escape was scheduled to start, and much to John Macarthur's annoyance he realised that the support of Corps officers on the bench could not be assured. Their allegiances were now fragmented; some officers stood by Macarthur, others by Bligh. For the first time Macarthur would face a court without guaranteed support on the benches. It seemed likely that a verdict might be reached based only on the evidence presented, not on the status of the defendant.[40] This would be a new experience for John Macarthur and nervous members of his cabal held their collective breath.

The nervous tension pervading the colony on Christmas Day 1807 was palpable. With rumours abounding that John Macarthur would soon remove the governor from office, the Hawkesbury settlers anxiously discussed on what could be done to prevent it. Almost to a man the settlers were ready to support Bligh and defend his government. Andrew Thompson, despite recent differences of opinion with Bligh, was prepared to help oppose his overthrow – the prospect of Macarthur gaining power again strengthened his resolve to assist the governor. Some settlers were in no doubt that an armed revolt against the governor would take place and that the Corps would be involved. Paradoxically, and quite mistakenly, Bligh dismissed these rumours believing that Major George Johnston would remain loyal to the government.[41] This was a serious error of judgement, and he would soon pay for it dearly.

During this period of hostility and uncertainty, the chief constable worked to shore up support for the government through a declaration of the settlers' loyalty. It was intended as a conspicuous signal to the rest of the colony that the Hawkesbury community would aid and abet the government in the event of any unlawful disruption. The declaration, in the form of a 'Loyalty Address', would also demonstrate 'the popularity and high Estimation' in which the governor was held by all 'respectable inhabitants' in the colony. On New Year's Day 1808 Thompson informed Bligh of an impending submission from the Hawkesbury settlers, which, once signed, would be delivered by Magistrate Arndell as evidence of their 'full and loyal adherence' to his government. At the end of his letter to Bligh, Thompson wrote that the Blighton farm flourished but, under the circumstances, he thought it best not to send a detailed assessment just yet. Instead, when a future opportunity arose, he would give him a verbal update on the farm activities. Thompson closed the letter with a declaration of his own personal allegiance, knowing this would please Bligh. He wrote that he had 'no greater gratification or ambition in the World than essentially serving your Excellency'.[42]

Having informed Bligh of the impending Loyalty Address, Andrew Thompson and George Crossley set about completing the final draft. When it was finished, the Chief Constable, Commissary John Palmer and Surgeon Martin Mason shared the task of taking the address document to almost every settler in the district for their signature or mark. Macarthur would later claim that Palmer and Thompson had pressured Hawkesbury settlers into signing, and that getting the support of this cohort 'of so low and of so thoughtless a description of persons' was easy as 'the greater part of them being deeply indebted to Mr. Campbell, Mr. Palmer, and this Andrew Thomson'. He implied that these sorts of people would sign any document put in front of them without inquiring into its contents.

There is no evidence of coercion; in fact, Surgeon Mason claimed the contrary. When he travelled the district collecting signatures, he 'was most cordially met' by the people who 'expressed the greatest satisfaction in having an opportunity of acknowledging their gratitude for the protection they had received under Gov. Bligh's administration'.[43]

The Loyalty Address expressed the settlers' appreciation of Governor Bligh for improving their lives and they pledged their loyalty at the risk of their lives and lands to support a 'Wise and Patriotic Government'. The pledge also made two requests of the governor. First, that they be permitted to trade directly with visiting ships and, second, that the courts adopt the same trial by elected jury process as in England.[44] The document presented to Bligh had 833 signatories. Most were freemen and emancipists from the Hawkesbury, and they included ten women. The principal signatories were Judge Richard Atkins, Merchant Robert Campbell, Magistrate Thomas Arndell, Commissioner John Palmer, former-Lieutenant Thomas Hobby, Surgeon John Harris, Nicholas Devine, Reverend Henry Fulton, William Gore and Thomas Moore. Further down the list was Surgeon Martin Mason, followed by settlers Andrew Thompson, George Crossley, John Bowman, William Cummings, Thomas Pitt and George Suttor from Baulkham Hill.[45]

The signatories encompassed a complete demographic of the district, from small farmers to large landholders, and included labourers, dealers, merchants, professional men and skilled tradesmen. Contrary to the opinion of Bligh's critics, it proclaimed that his reforms were beneficial and aimed at eradicating abuses harmful to the colony. The Address was, first and foremost, intended as a widely circulated public declaration of the strong support Governor Bligh had in the colony. It was a conspicuous demonstration of early colonial political lobbying at play.

The main opposition to Bligh's administration came from Corps officers and wealthy businessmen who claimed it neglected private development in the colony and only served the small farmers. These critics asserted that Bligh's blunt language and poor manners better suited the illiterate settlers than the educated people of Sydney. But the majority in the community kept their opinions to themselves and were quite ready to switch sides if need be. Bligh's adversaries soon came to know of the Hawkesbury Loyalty Address, and many found it unsettling because it fully backed the reform of their business practices. The Address also called for the opening up of retail trade and trial by jury but were considered less of a concern because they had been previously rejected by Governor King. Nonetheless, there was a worry that if Bligh agreed to these reforms, the commercial power of the Corps and other traders would be severely curtailed.

The relentless efforts of the Macarthur cabal to bring down the governor continued unabated. There was an expectation that it would take only one more major aggravation to convince the Corps that Bligh must go, and some believed the lease cancellations in central Sydney might provide the tipping point. Macarthur had been offered land in exchange for his central plot and had selected three allotments close to the harbour wharf, knowing full well that Bligh would never agree to the swap. When his selection was rejected on 14 January 1808 Macarthur refused to give up his prime allotment, and, in defiance of the prohibition on building on the leased land, he had Corps soldiers fence off his leasehold. The fence denied public access to a well on his plot and Bligh had it pulled down.[46] This certainly aggravated the leaseholders, but it was not enough to incite anyone to storm Government House.

Macarthur had more cards to play. The night before his trial for aiding and abetting the escape of a convict on the *Parramatta*, the acting commandant of the Corps, Major George Johnston, hosted a dinner party in the officers' mess of the Sydney barracks. John Macarthur was not present, but he was in the vicinity and represented at the dinner by his son and his nephew. Johnston would subsequently claim that, after a boisterous dinner party with plentiful alcohol, he fell out of his chaise going back to Parramatta and suffered minor injuries. In his book *Rum Rebellion* H. V. Evatt observes 'Thus, on the day before Macarthur's trial, the anti-Bligh alliance was sealed in a little blood and a great deal of rum'.[47]

On 25 January 1808, Macarthur's trial proceeded with Judge Advocate Atkins adjudicating and six Corps officers on the bench. At the opening of the proceedings Macarthur addressed the officers and demanded that Atkins be barred from presiding over the case. With 'a great Torrent of Threats and abusive Language' Macarthur asserted he was about to sue Atkins for an unpaid debt, and he was therefore unfit to adjudicate.

Atkins immediately withdrew from court, declaring that the proceedings should not continue without him. In his hurried exit, he left his court papers behind. On realising this, Atkins sent a constable to retrieve them but Captain Kemp on the bench refused to hand them over. The bench officers then sent a letter to Government House demanding that another judge be appointed. Bligh responded that he had no legal power to do so and reminded the bench that the court could not sit without a judge advocate. A standoff ensued. The Corps officers refusing to attend court with Atkins presiding and they then released Macarthur on bail. If refusing a governor's order was not mutinous enough, the release of Macarthur certainly was.[48] Bligh immediately sent a courier to Parramatta instructing Major Johnston to come to Sydney to control the actions of his officers. Johnston refused, claiming he was disabled by his fall from the chaise.[49]

Sunday 26 January 1808, the twentieth anniversary of the colony's foundation, would be a day of drama and high dudgeon. With the judicial impasse needing urgent resolution, Bligh ordered Macarthur to be re-arrested and gaoled. He then summonsed the court bench to Government House for the next morning and ordered the court hearing to be resumed. Macarthur's cabal saw this summons as a ploy to arrest the six court bench members Captain Kemp and Lieutenants Brabyn, Moore, Laycock, Minchin and Lawson for treason. The mood of the military now turned hostile. Further inflaming the situation, Corps Surgeon John Harris announced, without foundation, that 'an insurrection of the inhabitants was to be feared'. Major Johnston miraculously recovered from his injuries and set off for the Sydney settlement.[50]

Knowing that he now had the full backing of the military, Macarthur immediately drafted a proclamation calling on Major Johnston to arrest the governor and take charge of the government on the grounds 'the present alarming state of this colony, in which every man's property, liberty, and life is endangered'.[51] The arrest petition was nothing more than a hastily scribbled note, initially signed by Macarthur and six other men. Whether other names were added to the petition before or after Bligh's arrest is still disputed. In its final version, 151 people signed the arrest petition. Some residents, whose names were added *after* Bligh's arrest, claimed they were coerced at the point of a bayonet by soldiers going from house-to-house demanding signatures. Unsurprisingly, Bligh later observed that the men named on the petition were 'inhabitants of all descriptions, some of which are the worst class of life'.[52]

Chapter 13

Rebellion

Macarthur was his inveterate enemy. We can well imagine what must have been the state of Thompson's mind. What would Macarthur endeavour to do in the way of vengeance? Was his life in danger? Whether he went free or not, it must have been obvious that the one thing he prized above all else – his good name – was once more in jeopardy.[1]

In the early evening of 26 January, a troop of 300 Corps soldiers, with colours flying and bayonets fixed, marched the short distance from their barracks to Government House, accompanied by a band playing 'The British Grenadiers'. With Macarthur's arrest petition in his hand, Major Johnston led the troop followed by John Macarthur, Simeon Lord, Henry Kable and D'Arcy Wentworth. Inside Government House, Bligh was hosting a formal dinner to celebrate the colony's twentieth anniversary with John Palmer, James Williamson, Robert Campbell, Thomas Arndell, William Gore, Reverend Henry Fulton and Secretary Edmund Griffin.

The soldiers quickly surrounded the building and forced entry.[2] The only resistance came from Bligh's small personal guard and his defiant daughter Mary Putland, who had just lost her husband to tuberculosis. Ignoring her own safety, and with 'extreme anxiety to preserve the life of her beloved father prevailed over every consideration', Mary blocked several inebriated soldiers carrying fixed bayonets. William Gore reported that 'She dared the traitors to stab her to the heart, but to respect the life of her father'.[3]

One of the dinner guests, Reverend Fulton, stopped the soldiers from forcing the hall door, but they came through another entrance and quickly arrested everyone except Bligh. He had left the room promptly and ordered his servant to saddle a horse in readiness for him riding to Green Hills where he knew the settlers would defend the government. But Bligh first locked himself in a secluded bedroom and ripped up sensitive documents so as to prevent them falling into rebel hands.[4] Soldiers searched the house and eventually found the governor. They would later allege that he was found hiding under a bed quivering with fright. It was an accusation totally inconsistent with Bligh's meritorious military service and his fierce pride. Later, at Johnston's court martial trial in 1811, Bligh would ridicule the account, saying he was sitting on the floor destroying official papers. He pointed out that he had braved the dangers of Cook's voyages on HMS *Resolution* and sea battles with Lord Nelson, and he was not about to disgrace the medals he wore 'by shrinking from death' and hiding under a bed. His servant supported this by testifying that Bligh was far too stout to fit under the bed; it was only a foot (30 cm) high and sagged in the middle to only 8 inches (20 cm) from the floor.[5]

After arresting Bligh, Major Johnston handed him a letter outlining the reasons for his dismissal as governor:

> I am called upon to execute a most painful duty. You are charged by the respectable Inhabitants of Crimes that render you to unfit to exercise the Supreme Authority another Moment in this Colony; and in that Charge all the Officers under my command have joined.[6]

Johnston informed Bligh that martial law had been proclaimed, and that for the time being, he was to act as the lieutenant governor of the colony. He also directed Bligh to leave the colony on the first available ship, and, until his departure, he would be under strict house arrest in Government House. Johnston then ordered soldiers to search the buildings for all Bligh's documents and papers. Thompson's farm reports and letters were prominent among his papers when they broke into Bligh's private desk. The seizure of these documents was important to Macarthur and the rebels who needed evidence to support their charge that Bligh was guilty of 'injustice, tyranny and oppression'.[7] The rebels believed the farm reports would prove that Bligh had sought to improve his private fortune at the expense of the Crown.

On the evening of the insurrection, Bligh's surviving public and private papers were scrutinised for incriminating evidence against him. Bligh's dinner guests and close associates were interrogated and released. The head of police in Sydney, Provost Marshall William Gore, was arrested and gaoled.[8] Macarthur's persistent accusations had convinced Major Johnston that the 'most shameful abuses had been practised' by Bligh in his use of the government stores and livestock. To confirm the misuse of public property he ordered the investigation of the officials Robert Fitz, Deputy Commissary;

James Wilshire, Deputy Commissary; John Gowen, Superintendent of Stores; William Baker, storekeeper at Green Hills; Andrew Frazier, baker and servant of Commissary Palmer; John Jamieson, Superintendent of Stock, and Andrew Thompson, Bligh's 'confidential Manager' of Blighton.[9]

That night the military celebrated their 'bravery' in Sydney streets with alcohol, bonfires and the burning of effigies. And Macarthur, self-proclaimed hero of the day, proudly paraded the streets in victory – he saw the night as recognition of his saving the colony. As a precaution against a counter-rebellion, the Corps tried to prevent news of the arrest reaching the inland settlements. Sentries were set up on roads to stop anyone going to Parramatta and Green Hills.[10] But suppressing the rapid spread of such momentous news was nigh on impossible and the Hawkesbury settlers quickly learnt of the overthrow, most likely from the soldiers stationed in Green Hills. In the district it caused great foreboding among 'every sober and industrious inhabitant, that so unfortunate an event had taken place as the *revolution*, which it was generally called'. They understood all too well what now lay ahead with John Macarthur and the NSW Corps back in control. Having sworn to defend Bligh at the risk of their lives, they debated among themselves what might be done to reinstate him as governor.[11] They were ready to fight but were unsure where and when to start.

In contrast to the settlers' despondency, the military stationed at the Green Hills barracks were jubilant. They celebrated Bligh's demise and inebriated men littering the streets for days.[12] Attempts to control them met with threats of violence and imprisonment.

A multitude of rebel reprisals soon followed. Fearing a counter coup, the Corps soldiers scoured the Hawkesbury district and confiscated farmers' firearms. The rebellion had given soldiers an inflated sense of power and they exerted it ruthlessly, justifying the firearm controls and arrests as necessary to maintain order in the district and to prevent the senseless shedding of blood. Without weapons the settlers were outgunned and outmanoeuvred, and they had to supress their 'very enraged state of Mind at the indignity' Bligh had suffered at the hands of Macarthur and the Corps.[13] The subjugation of the Bligh loyalists meant that the overthrow of the government of New South Wales went unchallenged by a much larger number of dissenting inhabitants. It was the only successful 'coup' to occur on Australian soil and would later be known as the

'Rum Rebellion' because of the role the NSW Corps played and their commitment to the rum trade.

Soon after the rebellion, the governor's arrest was lampooned in Sydney with a cartoon portraying him as a coward being dragged from under a bed by soldiers. Corps Sergeant Thomas Whittle, who had taken part in Bligh's arrest, had hired an unknown artist to depict this as a watercolour cartoon. Whittle had an axe to grind with Bligh after his house had been demolished for town improvements. Relishing an opportunity for revenge, he circulated the cartoon widely and proudly. This and other anti-Bligh images soon appeared in rebel shops and pubs boasting how 'respectable Inhabitants' had saved the colony from 'tyranny and oppression'.[14] The fact that only three weeks earlier 830 reputable and sober men had vowed allegiance to the governor was totally ignored.[15]

A cartoon by an unknown artist showing the arrest of Governor Bligh on 26 January 1808. It was intended to portray Bligh as a coward and is unlikely to be accurate.

Contrary to its intent, the Hawkesbury Loyalty Address may have contributed to Bligh's arrest by alerting the Corps that an organised settler block would back further restrictions on their businesses. It may have caused Corps Surgeon John Harris to declare that a mass uprising of settlers was nigh, and helped Macarthur convince the military that Bligh had to be arrested. It begs an intriguing question:

did Andrew Thompson's actions in organising the Loyalty Address inadvertently triggered the Rum Rebellion? It is a possibility.

No documentary record exists to tell us where Andrew was on the day of Bligh's arrest. However, it is almost certain he was in Sydney to witness Macarthur's *Parramatta* trial and he probably observed the storming of Government House and the celebration that followed. As one of the Hawkesbury leaders of the Bligh loyalists, he would have been devastated and may have attempted to return to Green Hills to meet with the settlers. However, the roads to the Hawkesbury district had been barricaded and, in any case, Thompson was instructed by the rebels that he would be interrogated the next day, and that he must remain in Sydney.

Watercolour painting of Government House at Sydney Cove in 1807. Governor Bligh and his daughter Mary were held under house arrest here in 1808-1809.

Bligh's arrest had immediate repercussions for Andrew Thompson. He was in a court battle with John Macarthur over the promissory note payment. Macarthur now effectively ran the colony and was capable of doing real harm to his enemies. Thompson's farms, granary, store and ships had contributed significantly to the demise of John Macarthur's, and the Corps', businesses. He knew that the rebels would now attempt to ruin him, just as they had tried earlier. With Bligh no longer able to protect him, there was a genuine possibility that he would be gaoled. These were serious concerns, quite apart from the complications he faced policing the Hawkesbury district which was now under a hostile military and rebel administration.

Macarthur had always claimed that Thompson's business successes were due solely to preferential treatment from Governors Hunter, King and Bligh. While both businessmen were among the wealthiest in the colony, Thompson had recently secured a land lease in central Sydney and the other had lost his. Macarthur saw this as definite evidence of fraudulent collusion with Bligh. His dislike of Thompson was exacerbated by his popularity in the colony, while he knew his own coterie of followers were there only to gain business and financial benefits. Now that Macarthur had the Blighton management records, Thompson anticipated he would attempt to use these to implicate him with Bligh in a charge of stealing from the Crown.

The rebels instructed Thompson to meet with them the next day at Government House to explain the management of the Blighton farm, which they believed was one of Bligh's most corrupt enterprises. Thompson realised that he would need to cooperate fully and openly. The rebels John Jamieson and Charles Grimes interviewed him on 27 January 1808, and possibly with Macarthur present as an observer. In responding to questions on his management of convict labour in the Hawkesbury district and on the Blighton farm, Thompson detailed his broader duties and how Magistrate Arndell oversaw them. He said that over 100 male convicts, fully provisioned, worked on different government projects at the Hawkesbury. Between 20 to 30 convicts worked at the Blighton farm supported by rations, and seven laboured at Mary Putland's farm. Thompson explained that he periodically drew supplies from the public store for use at Blighton, for which he had detailed account records. Additionally, he had paid for goods from the government store for his own use but also had credits with Commissary Palmer. Thompson stated he was in charge of 'Bligh's Private Concerns' at the Hawkesbury, and detailed the livestock drawn from and returned to the public herds on Bligh's behalf.[16]

Thompson informed the interrogators that he had received a large quantity of cedar on the public and the governor's account. With Bligh's permission, he had also taken cedar on his own account. Some of this cedar had been used to make pews for the new church at Green Hills. The recorded interrogation reads in part:

> The pew marked No.1 is built for the Governor. Andrew Thompson's name is marked on pew No. 2. The magistrates pew will come in about No. 14. The pew marked No. 2 was built by the public labourers and in part by the public timber.[17]

From a historical perspective, the recorded transcripts of these interrogations are extremely valuable – they reveal otherwise unknown information about the colony. One such detail is that they acknowledge that Bligh recognised Thompson as the leader in the Hawkesbury community by granting him pew No. 2 in the church. This was the seat next to the governor when he attended church service in Green Hills.

Responding to questions on the Blighton dairy, Thompson stated that payments into Bligh's account for the milk had been in grain worth about £70 to £80. In the last year he had deposited 2000 bushels of grain, from his own seven farms and from Blighton, into the granary under his own account. This is an impressive amount, and he explained that part came from Bligh's farm as re-payment for its initial purchase.

The interrogators then tried to implicate Andrew Thompson in the illicit trade of distilled spirits. He responded to questioning:

> I drew one hundred and ten gallons of prize spirits by Governor Bligh's permission, about two months ago, for which I am to pay about 8s per gallon, and have sold it in small quantities at from 18s to 20s per bottle. I have received during the last twelve months about three hundred gallons exclusive of the prize spirits. I have never had any Colonial distilled spirits to my knowledge in my house, within this last twelve months, or had any sold on my account.[18]

The 'prize spirits' was presumably the puncheon (cask) that had caused Thompson to be accused of illicit trading of spirits in December. The rebels were trying to connect him to a trade they had been unable to pursue because of Bligh's intervention.

The cross-examination of Thompson now took a different direction. It referred to the court case brought against Macarthur for the escape of a convict on the ship *Parramatta*. He told them that George Crossley, after consulting with the governor, had informed him 'that the charge against Mr. McArthur was liable to be punished by fine, imprisonment, or pillory, but that he thought it would not reach the pillory in this colony'. Thompson stated that the governor only occasionally consulted him 'on public affairs and some things of little consequence about the officers'. He told the interrogators that he had heard the rumour that Bligh 'preferred sitting down with an Hawkesbury settler than an officer' but was 'not certain Governor Bligh did not tell him so'.[19]

Continuing, he described the buildings on Bligh's farm erected by convicts, adding that 'I imagine the buildings would cost an individual upwards of a thousand pounds'. He told the interrogators that he had paid for the original purchase of Bligh's farm with his own promissory note of £100 that would be repaid with farm products, for which he held 'Governor Bligh's memorandum'. The questioning concluded with Thompson stating that he had received no specific instructions on how to manage the farm, other than 'I have been informed by Governor Bligh that the stock and articles drawn from the store were to be paid for, and he wished everything to be fair and honorable'.[20]

Thompson emphasised that point because of the time normally taken for the repayment of debts in the colony, and he believed Bligh would settle the account for the livestock and articles drawn from government stores 'in due course'. After all, Bligh had only acquired the farm twelve months prior, and the average duration for credit in the colony was six to twelve months. When the interview ended, Jamieson and Grimes admitted that Thompson had not provided them with anything new about the Blighton finances but, nevertheless, he had verified information that might be useful in justifying Bligh's arrest. They still hoped that further examination of the farm reports would reveal Bligh's corrupt intent, but the evidence so far suggested all managerial actions had been performed according to the orders Bligh had received from the Colonial Office.

The rebels continued to scour Bligh's official papers for evidence that he had amassed a private fortune at public expense. They made copies of all of the letters, official documents and Blighton farm reports, and these copies were authenticated by the newly appointed Justices of Peace, Charles Throsby and Captain Anthony Kemp. Many of Bligh's original documents were subsequently lost from the colonial files in Sydney, and the copies sent to England provide the only surviving historical record. The later court hearings in England would eventually show that the evidence gathered by the rebels was inconclusive and the charges of corruption against Bligh were dismissed. The huge volume of written material and witness statements submitted as evidence failed in their primary objective, but they provided long-term benefits for Australian history. They are a veritable goldmine of historical information that would have otherwise lost to posterity.

Andrew Thompson now awaited the retribution he was sure the rebels had in store for him. The judge advocate, along with all magistrates and civil officials, had been dismissed and replaced by Corps officers and rebel supporters. Though Johnston had no legal authority to appoint a new judge advocate, he offered the post to Captain Edward Abbott, a Corps officer who had taken no part in Bligh's arrest. Within three days of the offer Abbott declined the appointment.[21] Since the case for removing Bligh now appeared extremely weak and the penalty for treason was hanging, Abbott was not alone in having second thoughts about supporting the rebels. Also, inhabitants distrusted Macarthur and suspected that Johnston's motives for participating in the rebellion was more about personal ambition than a desire to remove a tyrant.

Oblivious to the weakness of their cause, rebels took revenge on known Bligh loyalists across the colony. Some were dismissed from their posts while others were arrested and sent in chains to remote prison camps. Andrew Thompson expected he would soon lose his chief constable position. The Parramatta chief constable, Francis Oakes, had already been sacked because he had reported to Bligh that Macarthur had resisted arrest, and this had resulted in Macarthur's prosecution. Barnaby Riley was chosen in his place. Riley had been Macarthur's gaoler days earlier and had taken a sword to Macarthur's cell in case he needed to protect himself.[22]

On 28 January, a day after Thompson's interrogation, several Corps supporters, ex-Corps officer Thomas Hobby, deputy commissary Robert Fitz and Thomas Biggers met at Thompson's pub in Green Hills to draft a letter congratulating Major Johnston for leading the overthrow of Bligh. After they had been 'heated with wine and spirits, they sallied-out to solicit signatures' from Green Hills inhabitants. At the risk of injury and recrimination many men were pressured into signing. Martin Mason, who had helped Andrew Thompson gather the 833 signatures for the settler's Loyalty Address, was harassed three times that day and was told if he did not sign, he would end up in the Sydney gaol.[23] Mason ignored the threats, but other Bligh supporters buckled. Under duress 66 men signed the letter after only weeks earlier backing Bligh in the Loyalty Address. Fearing for his life, Thomas Arndell, whom the rebels had already dismissed as magistrate, signed – something he deeply regretted and renounced for the rest of his life.[24]

Thompson had returned to Green Hills and from his farmhouse he saw Corps soldiers transporting cartloads of wood to their barracks and building a large pyre near wooden gallows. That night they lit a bonfire and burnt effigies of Governor Bligh and Provost Marshal Gore suspended from the gallows.[25] The township was now in pandemonium, and he was powerless to stop it.

Now that he had the authority to do so, John Macarthur wasted no time in rescheduling a trial to clear his name of the *Parramatta* convict escape charge. Whether these proceedings were legal or not was irrelevant. The court sat on 2 February with the newly appointed Charles Grimes as judge advocate, and, predictably, Grimes did not require the charges to be examined. Instead, he gave Macarthur unlimited time to question witnesses and speak directly to the jury. No one at the bench objected to the questions or refuted the evidence presented. Even when Captain Abbott reported the irregular proceedings in the court to Major Johnston, he allowed the trial to continue.[26] The questions Macarthur asked witnesses did not relate to the charges; most were intended to denigrate Bligh. Macarthur even referred to the Thompson promissory note case, saying that 'a verdict had been given by the Governor in my favour for £38 … I had not received a farthing of it, although many months had expired'.[27] He then asked Bligh's secretary Edmund Griffin why the Provost Marshal Gore had not put a verdict into effect that would enforce Thompson to pay the promissory note, as the government had not yet made the court judgement official. After a four-day hearing, the court predictably found Macarthur not guilty.

The same day that Macarthur's mock trial got under way, Andrew Thompson was dismissed as chief constable at the Hawkesbury. After 15 years of loyal service, he was to be replaced by Macarthur's agent, Richard Fitzgerald.[28] The posting would prove difficult for Fitzgerald. Andrew was a highly respected leader in the district and that made his duties as chief constable much easier – most inhabitants were willing to assist him if his duties got too onerous. The settlers, who still supported the imprisoned Bligh, resented the appointment of Macarthur's agent, and many declared they would not cooperate with Fitzgerald.

Shortly after the installation of the new chief constable,

Lieutenant Archibald Bell, the Corps commandant at Green Hills, was appointed magistrate of the Hawkesbury district. Evidently Bell needed someone with knowledge of the district to show him around. Rather than asking Thomas Arndell, the previous magistrate, or the new Chief Constable Fitzgerald, he approached the established farmer and businessman in Green Hills, Andrew Thompson. This may have been at the advice of Thomas Arndell, who had given Andrew many responsibilities in recent years. However, the interaction between Bell and Thompson was to have adverse consequences. Following their tour of the district, Bell was brought before a Court of Enquiry by Macarthur and reprimanded:

> for riding in Company with Andrew Thompson …, who had just been superseded as Constable, & whose services I had requested for the purpose of shewing me the District.[29]

Macarthur was certainly not going to allow any collusion between the rebels and Thompson, even if his local knowledge was invaluable. This reprimand frightened Bell and thereafter he excluded all emancipists from his association. He took the advice to extremes and later vigorously opposed the progressive emancipist policies of Governor Macquarie. In an 1823 government report Archibald Bell would describe Thompson as 'a very industrious & bustling character; but extremely avaricious and astute'.[30] It was an interesting assessment of Andrew coming from a supposed enemy and our knowledge of his vigorous entrepreneurship. When it came to business opportunities, Thompson let little stand in his way!

The rebels were now unrelenting in their pursuit of Bligh loyalists, and they used the courts as instruments of their political revenge. Former lawyer, George Crossley, who had helped Judge Atkins and Governor Bligh prepare the papers for the prosecution of Macarthur in the *Parramatta* escape, was sentenced to seven years labour in the Coal River (Newcastle) mines for acting as an attorney when ineligible because of a previous conviction for perjury in England.[31] Next in line was the ex-Provost Marshal William Gore who had arrested and imprisoned Macarthur. When committed to trial, Gore challenged the court's authority but was found guilty and sentenced to seven years labour at the coalmines. The emancipist Sir Henry Browne Hayes was sent to the mines for eight months hard labour for condemning the rebellion and warning Corps officers they would face capital punishment for their traitorous act.[32] Bligh was furious at the harsh treatment being meted out to his supporters and secretly wrote to Castlereagh in the Colonial Office:

> Thus, in terrorem, the Usurpers held up punishment to those who dared to speak in favor of my administration against their treasonable practices, and notwithstanding the illegality of their Courts.[33]

On hearing that the rebel court had sentenced George Crossley, Andrew expected a similar action to be soon taken against him, as both had been the principal authors of the settler's Loyalty Address. Loyalist settlers now expected multiple arrests across the district and wondered who would be the next? They still wanted to free Bligh, but without weapons or a courageous leader, it would be an unwinnable battle against soldiers and result in heavy loss of life.

However, the rebels had more pragmatic penalties in mind for Bligh's supporters. Johnston ordered all Hawkesbury settlers to immediately repay debts owed to the government store.[34] For small farmers carrying large debts from flood damage this was impossible. Johnston knew that the repayments would break the will of many farmers and distract the intentions of other settlers not in debt. This edict had Thompson in its sights, as he certainly carried major debts. Fortunately, only two weeks earlier, he had deposited grain in the government stores and received a credit of £55 from Commissary Palmer. He wanted to use this credit to offset the money he owed.[35]

On 12 February George Johnston appointed John Macarthur as a magistrate and the NSW Colonial Secretary. The latter position enabled Macarthur to oversee all of the colony's business dealings and to take lucrative commissions for doing so. His oversight also seriously diminished the flexibility of small farmers to sell their produce. Macarthur's control on the rebel administration was now complete – he would now make all of the major decisions for Johnston, even dictating his letters to the Colonial Office.[36] It returned to him the same dictatorial role he had assumed during the governance of Francis Grose and William Paterson from 1793 to 1795.

With the rebels now running the rum trade, the consumption of alcohol in the colony soared to heights reached prior to Bligh and King implementing their reforms. To prevent any obstacles to buying alcohol in the Hawkesbury district, the government storekeeper at Green Hills was replaced with a rebel sympathiser. The monopoly of Corps officers supplying imported goods to the stores was reinstated, and the trading enterprises of the merchants

Robert Campbell and Simeon Lord were effectively sidelined. The rebels raided the government cattle herd and distributed the best livestock to Corps officers and their supporters.[37] The removed animals were supposed to be paid for in grain, but no payments were ever recorded.

Farmers were now required to sell grain to the government stores at lower prices than before, and alcohol could be used as payment. Macarthur also promptly redistributed 300 convicts employed on public projects to work on the properties of his supporters.[38] But Macarthur overlooked the importance of rewarding all his backers. The pillaging of the government store and animal herd for himself and his close friends earned him new enemies, and one by one his erstwhile supporters began to desert him.

Under house arrest, William Bligh was prevented from meeting anyone outside Government House staff. Nevertheless he was secretly informed of atrocities on his supporters and on a growing opposition to the rebels. Bligh was instructed he could leave for England provided he made no attempt to reassume authority in the colony. But he was in no hurry to go anywhere and announced he would only depart if certain conditions were met. These included being given command of the warship HMS *Porpoise* anchored in the harbour and the return of his naval sword and confiscated papers. He also insisted that selected persons accompany him to England as witnesses at a future investigation on his dismissal. Throughout his negotiations with Johnston, Bligh repeated his demand to be reinstated as the rightful governor of the colony, and that the rebel leaders be arrested for high treason. He saw such demands as necessary to make it understood he did not accept the illegal overthrow of his government. Bligh also knew that his only real power in the colony resided in his command of HMS *Porpoise*, which had been the colony's principal naval support since 1807.

On 11 February Bligh was instructed by Johnston to board the local cargo ship *Pegasus*, owned by Simeon Lord, John Harris and Thomas Moore, soon to sail for England. He refused, declaring it not seaworthy for such a long journey. Repairs were made to the ship, but the three owners changed their minds about being responsible for removing Bligh and cancelled the arrangement. As the penalties of treasonable acts sank home and the promised rewards of the rebellion failed to materialise, support for the rebels was waned even in Sydney's elite business circles.[39]

In the meantime, Bligh had given Johnston a list of the thirteen men to accompany him to England. He requested that the requisite steps be taken for this to happen. His witness list was as follows.

Richard Atkins, Esq	Late Judge-Advocate
Thomas Arndell	Late Magistrate
Robert Campbell	"
John Palmer	"
James Williamson	"
William Gore	Late Provost-Marshal
Edmund Griffin	My Secretary
Reverend Henry Fulton	Late Chaplain
James Wiltshire	Commissary's Clerk
Nicholas Divine	Superintendent
Richard Rouse	"
Francis Oakes	"
Andrew Thompson	Chief Constable at Hawkesbury[40]

Johnston ordered Bligh to leave for England aboard other ships, but he refused them all. In these negotiations Macarthur and Johnston avoided agreeing to Bligh's conditions for leaving the colony, and especially to his insistence on taking command of HMS *Porpoise*.

The presence of Andrew Thompson on Bligh's list of witnesses clearly worried Macarthur. The rebels' allegations that the Blighton farm was a corrupt enterprise were critical to their case against Bligh, and Thompson must be prevented from refuting them at the trial. If he could not be stopped from accompanying Bligh, he must be publicly discredited. Macarthur contrived a way to accuse Thompson of financial fraud. Commissary John Palmer was due to pay Andrew Thompson £248 6s 10¼d (£22,000 today) for grain he deposited in the government store. The rebels had dismissed Palmer and they now refused to make the payment, claiming Thompson had used Bligh's grain and not his own. The note on the document reads: 'Incorrect – to produce his Bill and Voucher for carriage of Grain – the whole objectionable at present'.[41] The loss of several hundred pounds would have ruined most of the colony's farmers, but not Thompson. He was concerned about the fraud charge but knew it was a provocation he could not do much about at the moment. He decided to keep his head down and sort out the legalities of this payment later with a future legitimate administration when Macarthur was not in charge.

What followed then is one of the more bizarre acts of retribution. On 26 February John Macarthur issued a 'capias' of £10,000 (£875,000 in today's currency) on Andrew Thompson for damages. No details are given for the charge, other than a short notice in the court papers:

> *Special Meeting.*
> *Present: The Judge Advocate and Thos. Laycock.*
> *Capias: Mr. Mcarthur Esq sts. Mr Andrew Thompson*
>   *£10,000 - Damages*[42]

The capias was a bond that would have to be paid by Thompson if he did not attend in person a scheduled colonial court appearance. The reasons for the capias, the nature of the trial to which the capias applied, and why Thompson's presence was essential at this trial, were never specified. Macarthur was prepared to use any ploy to prevent Thompson from going to England and testifying for Bligh – he was a far too credible witness. Macarthur was famous for his legal manoeuvres but the use of such a bond was new. With the law courts under his control, Macarthur was free to make up his own rules. He had probably realised by now that the rebels' case against Bligh was flimsy and would be further weakened if Thompson were allowed to testify on the Blighton farm management. Under no circumstances should he be permitted to leave the colony.

The enormous sum of £10,000 levied in the capias was probably based on Thompson's estimated wealth – it was an amount intended to ruin him if he attempted to leave the colony. Indeed, it posed an enormous dilemma for Andrew. He had promised the settlers to defend Bligh in England, and if this stopped him from doing so, he would lose the respect of the community. For a man who had disgraced his parents, his honour was more important to him than his property. After all, wealth could easily be remade, but in his bitter experience regaining respect was much more difficult. It is also probable that Thompson had figured out, or been advised by his legal friends, that this capias would be impossible to enforce, especially if support for Macarthur continued to waver.

Thompson also faced more complicated problems returning to Britain. He was especially worried about the reception he would receive from his brother Walter. In all his years in the colony, he had received only two letters from Walter. The first informed him that his elder brother William and his wife had died, and that their four children were now living with him. Andrew had offered to adopt two of the children and have them grow up with him in New South Wales. Walter's second letter refused this offer.[43] With his father now deceased and his mother very old, Andrew was extremely anxious that the fragile link with his family had been lost, and there was no way to regain it.

The chaotic and predatory behaviour of the rebel administration was now widely ridiculed in the colony. It caused Thomas Arndell to bitterly regret his part in the congratulatory letter to George Johnston. Unaware of Arndell's participation in this letter, Bligh had added him to his list of witnesses to go to England. Embarrassed and scorned by Bligh's loyalists after being one of their leaders for years, Arndell desperately wanted to recant. On 6 March he smuggled a letter to Bligh, expressing a deep regret for having sided with the rebels. He told him it was a matter of enormous grief that the governor had been replaced by 'ambitious and discontented men who wish to govern this territory in a manner that will suit their own private advantage and gratify their avarice and lust of power' without honesty, morality or justice. These men had used the threat of violence to extort signatures from Bligh's supporters. Arndell confessed that he had signed the paper out of terror, which 'his heart and better judgement abhorred'.[44] This confession enabled Thomas Arndell to be reaccepted to the inner circle of Hawkesbury leaders.

On 23 March Johnston ordered Bligh to board Macarthur's whaling ship the *Dart* that would depart the colony on 1 April. Bligh was outraged at being asked to leave on a stinking whaler and refused but said he would sail on HMS *Porpoise* on that date provided he was in command of the ship. Two days later Bligh submitted the list of 15 men he wished to embark with him on HMS *Porpoise*. Thomas Arndell remained and two new men, George Crossley and George Dowling, had been added.[45]

Johnston agreed to Bligh's conditions, but he changed his mind two days later, reissuing the order for him to board the *Dart*. Bligh, of course, refused and the standoff continued for weeks. Bligh would not give up his demands and was patiently anticipating a response to his letters to the Colonial Office. He remained confident that the British government would eventually restore him to his lawful position. In the meantime, Andrew Thompson anxiously waited for news on when he was expected to depart for England on HMS *Porpoise*.

By late March 1808 serious disagreements were occurring among the rebels. Johnston challenged his disgruntled supporters to either put up or shove off, and he ordered the most troublesome to leave the colony. This put a temporary lid on the grumbles.[46] There were also rumours circulating that the settlers planned to assassinate John Macarthur, and that they were willing to sacrifice their lives for the cause.[47] The hopes of Bligh's supporters rose in April with the news that Lieutenant Colonel William Paterson would soon replace George Johnston. Paterson was willing to come from Van Diemen's Land to take charge and had requested a ship to bring him to Sydney. At the same time, he demanded that more supplies, troops and convicts be sent to Port Dalrymple (now Launceston).[48] Macarthur did not relish Paterson's return – they were sworn enemies who had once fought a duel – so the arrangements to send HMS *Porpoise* to Port Dalrymple proceeded slowly.

Since the rebellion, Andrew Thompson and others had been documenting the malpractices and corruption of rebels as evidence for convicting them later of treason. Bligh was kept abreast of misdeeds in the colony, especially of the plundering of the stores. He secretly informed the Colonial Office Secretary Castlereagh that rebels were shamelessly stealing items from the stores and from government herds. He also told Castlereagh that existing land leases in Sydney were being illegally renewed and that some rebel supporters had received new leases. The main benefactors of this largesse were the three ship owners, John Macarthur, Garnham Blaxcell and Henry Kable. They had stolen large quantities of goods for use on their ships; regularly removing quantities of ropes, metal, canvas, sails and clothing. In one instance Macarthur and Blaxcell had each taken two millstones and Kable one at a time when the Hawkesbury farmers were unable to grind flour because of a lack of replacement millstones. Also, Corps soldiers were stealing clothing from the government stores intended for convicts and they were 'almost left naked' in rags.

Bligh expressed disgust at Macarthur's brazen dishonesty. He had stolen ammunition from the stores and sent it to South Sea Islands to be used as barter for pork meat. This was then shipped to Sydney and used to undercut the Hawkesbury settlers' pork prices, and to increase his meat trading profits. All the vacant land on the banks of the Hawkesbury River had now been granted to rebel leaders, except for a small area where Government House stood. In less than six months Macarthur had made, in George Johnston's name, twelve land grants of 6814 acres, including 2000 acres to Johnston's son.[49] Those inhabitants who the rebels no longer trusted received no grants or benefits, even if they had previously backed the overthrow. Rebel support was ebbing away.

Encouraged by the likelihood of William Paterson taking command of the colony, some settlers assumed that the rebels were in retreat. On 11 April they wrote to Johnston objecting to John Macarthur being made Colonial Secretary. The letter stated that Macarthur was the source of constant quarrels in the colony and had 'violated the Law, violated public faith, and trampled on the most Sacred and Constitutional Rights of the British Subjects'. It pleaded for his dismissal: 'We most earnestly pray that the said John McArthur may be removed from the said Office of Colonial Secretary, from all other Offices, and from all Public Councils and interference with the Government of this Colony'.[50]

The letter was not signed. The unidentified writers, who probably included Andrew Thompson, knew that if Macarthur had their names, he would seek immediate retribution. Their caution was justified. Johnston was never going to dismiss Macarthur who was in reality the *de facto* leader of the rebels. Johnston ordered Chief Constable Fitzgerald at the Hawkesbury to find out who authored the letter and imprison them. Fitzgerald offered a free pardon and a passage to England to any convict who could provide information about the letter.[51] Considerable pressure was brought to bear on hundreds of the settlers who had signed the original Loyalty Address, and on convict servants to report on their masters, but not one came forward to claim the reward.

Undeterred by the failed attempt to demote Macarthur, the Bligh loyalists smuggled another letter onto HMS *Porpoise* before it sailed to bring Lieutenant Colonel Paterson from Port Dalrymple. The letter, with 21 signatories including Arndell, Thompson and Mason, pleaded for Paterson to restore legal government and order to the colony. They wrote that the rebel administration was in 'the hands of John McArthur', who was 'a very improper person' with 'a turbulent and troublesome Character', who was 'the principal agitator and promoter of the present alarming and calamitous state of the Colony'. They strongly protested that signatories for Bligh's arrest petition had been coerced by threatening individuals with imprisonment. The letter pledged to support Paterson 'at every hazard that is dear to Man, in restoring the Government and placing us again under the protection of the King and the Laws'.[52]

It was now widely believed in the colony that it was just a matter of time before Paterson would reinstate Bligh as governor. However, those who knew more about the Corps officers involved suspected otherwise. In any case, for the sake of the colony, Bligh had decided to return to England as soon as Paterson returned. A day after the departure of HMS *Porpoise* for Port Dalrymple, Bligh sent a message to the Colonial Office Secretary Castlereagh:

> How all these evils will end, and a restoration of peace take place in the Colony, it is impossible for me to say until Colonel Paterson arrives; but it is my duty to represent that I think it absolutely necessary I should return Home to show what must be effected for its Security.[53]

Despite the growing contempt for the rebels, it was unwise to show it in public. Some citizens claimed the rebellion had parallels with the French Revolution, and that the march on Government House and arrest of the governor was 'like a Roberspierrean [sic] party or a revolutionary tribunal'.[54] When William Gore was arrested, he later relayed to his distressed wife that the attitude of the arresting officer was in a 'true spirit of Jacobinical [sic] equality'.[55] The same spirit inspired the Irish convict Lawrence Davoren to write the satirical song *A New Song, Made in New South Wales on the Rebellion*. Davoren, a former attorney who was sentenced for life, arrived in the colony in 1793. By 1806 he had received a conditional pardon from Governor King and worked as a lawyer. However, in late 1806 he was found guilty of receiving two stolen promissory notes for £6 and £8 and sentenced to fourteen years at the Coal River mines. He had been asked by the rebel administration to prepare pamphlets denigrating Bligh for circulation in England, but he declined and instead threw his lot in with the loyalists. While working in the mines he would have met many men sent there after Bligh's arrest, and this would have inspired him to write his song to the tune of 'Health to the Duchess'.[56]

The song is historically interesting because it contains satirical ditties about men who participated in the rebellion. They include George Johnston, Joseph Foveaux, John Macarthur, alias 'Jack Boddice', William Minchin, William Lawson, John Harris and

William Paterson. Three judge advocates were also mocked: Charles Grimes, Anthony Kemp and Richard Atkins. Here are two of the song's nine verses:

> *The voice of rebellion resounds o'er the Plain*
> *The Anarchist Junto have pulled down the banner*
> *Which Monarchical Government sought but in vain*
> *To hold as the rallying Standard of honor,*
> > *The Diadem's here fled*
> > *From off the King's head,*
> *His Royal appointment by force they depose,*
> > *But the time it draws nigh*
> > *When magnanimous Bligh*
> *Will triumph with honour and prostrate his foes.*
> ....
> *These skellams all loyalty here have put down*
> *And the New Gallic School in its stead have erected,*
> *John Bull's would-be pupil, how dare he to frown*
> *His French education was too long neglected.*
> > *That Turnip head tool*
> > *Jack Boddice's fool*
> *Stepped into that station he dare not oppose*
> > *And the cub of a cook*
> > *His allegiance forsook*
> *To become "His Honor" new crimes to disclose.*[57]

Many words in the song have double meanings. In the second verse above, the word 'skellams' was Scottish for a rogue, whereas the phrase 'New Gallic School' refers to the French Revolution and Foveaux's ancestors. The 'turnip head' is George Johnston and 'cub of a cook' is Joseph Foveaux. The lampooning of John Macarthur as 'Jack Boddice' came from John being once a stay-maker's apprentice in his father's mercer business – hence the nickname Boddice.[58] The snobbish John Macarthur was in fact born into a less privileged family than many of the convicts he now spurned socially.

Andrew Thompson would have relished in the singing of 'The New Song' while entertaining his friends in the Red House. For a while at least, Bligh's supporters felt at liberty in the right company to express their feelings, and their collective hopes rose that the 'magnanimous Bligh' would seize 'the rights of the Crown' and vanquish his enemies.[59] It was an ambitious wish that would take considerable time to be fulfilled.

Chapter 14

LOYALIST RESISTANCE

Thompson had suffered some injury from the persons who succeeded to the government, on the suspension of Governor Bligh, and his fidelity to the legitimate authority of that officer had made him an object of their dislike and suspicion.[1]

Anticipating the eventual restoration of legitimate government, a group of Bligh loyalists compiled a detailed record of any rebel actions that might assist in later prosecutions. This included material that Andrew Thompson had collected over his fifteen years of policing. One such item was the statement of John Brennan, who had personally collected signatures for the congratulatory letter to Major Johnston for his role in Bligh's arrest. Brennan had a copy of the letter, and Thompson asked Thomas Arndell, who had signed the same letter under duress, to convince him to cooperate. In his reply to Thompson, dated 28 April 1808, Brennan sincerely repented for opposing Bligh after 'taking the advice of others, in doing which I ought not to have done'. He enclosed a copy of the congratulatory letter with the names of the 66 signatories. This was vital information, as it listed Bligh's opponents at the Hawkesbury. With the rebels still in control, it was too dangerous yet to act openly against these men, but the loyalists now knew whom to distrust. Thompson had the list delivered to Bligh though a sympathetic guard, and he then smuggled a copy on one of Campbell's cargo ships to be delivered to Sir Joseph Banks.[2]

Two weeks later, on 26 May, HMS *Porpoise* returned to Port Jackson only to reveal, much to the dismay of rebels and Bligh supporters alike, that Paterson had changed his mind and remained in Port Dalrymple. Paterson knew that with Bligh still in the colony he would be unable to assume legal control of the government, and that it would be far too dangerous for him to try and reinstate Bligh as governor without the Corps' backing.[3] He also knew that Lieutenant Colonel Joseph Foveaux was due to arrive in Sydney to take up duties on Norfolk Island, so why not let him sort things out. Paterson viewed the uprising as a political mess of John Macarthur's making and, since he loathed the man, he wanted nothing to do with it. Indeed, it is quite evident that if Paterson had been the Corps Commandant at the time of Macarthur's trial, Bligh's arrest would never have happened. This was well understood in the colony and the principal reason why Johnston and Macarthur were not enthusiastic about Paterson's return. They need not have worried; Paterson was enjoying his relaxed recuperative life in Van Diemen's Land and was quite content to let someone else sort out this mess. John Macarthur was nonplussed by Paterson's reticence. The arrival of Joseph Foveaux, with whom he was well acquainted, was more of a problem for him because he would be harder to manipulate than either Johnston or Paterson.

HMS *Porpoise* had a rough passage returning from Van Diemen's Land and had sprung major leaks that would take weeks to repair. Bligh was in no hurry to leave anyway and made good use of this delay preparing his case against the rebels, while his supporters continued to accumulate evidence on the malpractices happening across the colony. Bligh sent secret communications to the Colonial Office and on 30 June enclosed a copy of the settler's Loyalty Address of 1 January that had so unnerved Macarthur and the rebel group, adding:

> The Inhabitants lament in silence they cannot show their loyalty and affection through a fear of their lives. If I stood in need of a defence, I need not make a better of my government having been satisfactory than this, and the affectionate and dutiful Address presented to me on the first day of this Year.[4]

With the imminent arrival of Lieutenant Colonel Foveaux, Bligh plotted how he might be reinstated as governor. With HMS *Porpoise* in dry docks, Andrew Thompson realised that his return to England was weeks away and he spent this time making arrangements for how his businesses and farms would be managed in his absence. Without the police and bailiff duties, Andrew could concentrate on his own interests, which were all doing surprisingly well. He needed to ensure, as much as was possible in these uncertain times, that this continued during his absence. With his dismissal as chief constable, he was also no longer in charge of convict labour at the Hawkesbury. Thompson knew that in future he would not have access to assigned convict servants – those working at Blighton had been reassigned by Macarthur to rebel supporters. In any case, most of his own workers were either emancipists or ticket of leave men on wages, and there were always other male and female emancipists willing to work for him. There was one main concern for Thompson; the £10,000 capias lodged by John Macarthur requiring him to appear in court. But with no court hearing date set, he hoped it would not affect his departure.

On 15 May 1808, *The Sydney Gazette* resumed publication, with one radical change. It was now published under the aegis of the Colonial Secretary John Macarthur. This meant, of course, that he was no longer criticised by the newspaper as he frequently had been in the past. It was not an easy decision for George Howe to restart *The Sydney Gazette* under rebel control, and he deeply regretted 'the necessity of vying with the camelion [*sic*] its change of colour'.[5] However, the colony's inhabitants desperately needed some means of receiving news on colonial matters, even if it was censored and politically biased.

The first new issue of *The Sydney Gazette* reveals an interesting insight on Andrew Thompson's day-to-day life. Inhabitants with government receipts for grain or maize had been ordered to attend the Commissary Office in Sydney for reimbursement. 'Mr. Thompson' had made his way to the Commissary Office but on the way lost a receipt for 500 bushels of maize somewhere between Barrack Square and Simeon Lord's warehouse. He advertised his loss in *The Sydney Gazette*, offering a reward of one guinea Sterling (£1 1s) to the finder. The receipt was worth over £100. In the meantime, he stopped the payment at the Commissary's office.[6] Further reward notices never appeared, so presumably someone had handed in the receipt and received the one guinea – the amount a labourer would earn in a month.

Bligh was not confident that Joseph Foveaux would support him when he arrived, so he urgently sent off as many secret despatches as possible to England. There were only a few reliable couriers he could trust, and they might be shut down under a new more efficient Foveaux administration. He strongly believed that only his personal account of the overthrow would cause the Colonial Office to restore him as governor – if only he did not have to wait over a year for their response. Bligh considered Captain Richard Brooks, Master of the *Rose*, to be his most trustworthy courier to the Colonial Office.

Brooks was the business partner of the loyalist Robert Campbell, who was a part owner of the *Rose*. Since, in theory, Macarthur controlled all shipping in the colony, most captains were unwilling to carry anything to England that would affect their trading rights. Andrew Thompson was a shipper with three boats, but they were only involved in local trade to the islands and New Zealand. Even so, he once again put his 'oar in the water' for Bligh. On 19 June Captain Brooks advertised in *The Sydney Gazette* that the *Rose* would sail for England in five weeks and that anyone 'desirous of writing to their Friends, are requested to leave their letters with Mr. A. Thompson at the Green Hills, or with Captain Brooks, at Sydney'.[7]

Bearing in mind that John Macarthur censored the newspaper, this notice appeared to be an unexpected opportunity for anyone wishing to write to the British about the diabolical state of the colony, and to use Thompson as an intermediary. It would be five weeks before the *Rose* departed and by then Foveaux had arrived. Unwisely, Captain Brooks later refused to give passage to Captain James Symons, who was to carry dispatches for Foveaux to England. This refusal quickly resulted in the *Rose* being seized on charges of trading in violation of the East India Company's monopoly. The charge was, of course, just a ruse to force Brooks to take Symons, and prevent any settlers' letters being carried on the ship. Although Brooks could show he was licensed for this trade, he eventually agreed to carry Symons and another rebel supporter, John Blaxland, as passengers. After this pressure it was unsurprising that Brooks was heard using 'some highly disrespectful expressions against the present Government of the Colony'.[8] And, despite Bligh's demand that no one involved in the rebellion leave the colony, the *Rose* sailed on 11 September with Blaxland on board. But Captain Brooks had secret instructions, and on departing Port Jackson, Symons was thrown in the brig as a deserter and Blaxland was arrested at the Cape of Good Hope.[9]

Andrew Thompson's businesses were thriving, albeit at a less frenetic pace. On 17 July his vessel the *Governor Bligh*, had sailed into Port Jackson after three months in the north. It brought back a number of green turtles and a ton of sea cucumbers. The vessel's name alone was enough to provoke the anger of rebel supporters in Sydney, as it clearly publicised Thompson's allegiances. But apart from some indignation, no orders to change the ship's name were issued, and she sailed a month later with a gang of sealers for the southern isles of New Zealand.[10]

On 28 July, Lieutenant Colonel Joseph Foveaux arrived in Sydney aboard the transport ship *Sinclair*. He had been sent for a second time to take charge on Norfolk Island, and to oversee the transfer of all the island's inhabitants, who were mostly ex-convict settlers, to Van Diemen's Land. Foveaux was a capable man whose reputation has been tarnished by claims that in his previous administration of Norfolk Island he severely punished convicts and sold female convicts to free settlers.[11] Recent histories, however, assert that these claims are false.[12] Foveaux's arrival in Sydney raised the expectations for Bligh's reinstatement. Three loyalists, Commissary Palmer, Bligh's Secretary Griffin and Reverend Fulton planned to board the *Sinclair* and request that Foveaux come to Government House to talk with Bligh. But as soon as the ship docked in Sydney cove Macarthur and Johnston barred Bligh's men from boarding and spent the day explaining to Foveaux why they had arrested Bligh. Joseph Foveaux disembarked the next morning and met with Bligh at Government House, but the meeting was fruitless. He was unsympathetic and refused to reinstate him.[13]

Just four days after arriving in Sydney, Joseph Foveaux agreed to assume control of the rebel administration until Lieutenant Colonel Paterson could do so. Johnston and Macarthur had managed to convince him that the colony had been mismanaged and 'Captain Bligh has been acting on a settled plan to destroy and ruin the better Class of Inhabitants'.[14] In keeping with the social norms of the time, Foveaux did not question the right of the privileged inhabitants to rule over the majority. He probably shared the views of the colony's exclusives, but he did make a major change; he dismissed John Macarthur as Colonial Secretary. Foveaux's adjutant Lieutenant James Finucane took over these responsibilities.[15]

After Foveaux had time to hear the arguments of others, he could see that the evidence supporting the charge that Bligh was a 'corrupt tyrant' was decidedly slim. Realising it was too late to swap camps he tried, where possible, to make governmental decisions equitable to both sides. Colonial Secretary Finucane seriously doubted the claims that Bligh had tried to steal from the crown. After he had inspected Blighton farm he noted: 'He [Bligh] is charged by Colonel Johnston with having lavished vast sums of the public money' on his property. 'It appears to me, however, that very little money of any kind had been expended'. Instead of lavish buildings, he found a barn, sheep shed and pigsty.[16]

On 21 August, a month after Foveaux's arrival, the colonial schooner *Estramina* was sent to convey Lieutenant Colonel Paterson from Van Diemen's Land. On the same vessel, Bligh had secretly sent a letter to appeal to Paterson to come back to Sydney to rescue the colony.[17] Hope for Bligh's reinstatement once again flourished among the loyalists of the colony.

Thompson and many others rejoiced at Macarthur's loss of the Colonial Secretary post. However, with the capias still in force against him, Thompson avoided the possibility of disagreements with Foveaux. In any case, he expected Macarthur to eventually argue with Foveaux, and that Paterson's arrival would work in Bligh's favour. In the meantime, the industrious Scot kept his public activities to a minimum and assisted the Hawkesbury settlers where he could. A group of loyalists, led by local surgeon Martin Mason, continued to hold regular meetings at his Red House.

Despite Foveaux's administrative reforms, no attempt was made to reinstate Thompson as chief constable. In fact, he was about to be challenged in court over a transaction that had occurred when he held that post. Thomas Pitt, a free Hawkesbury settler, sued Thompson in August 1808 over the payment of a £50 promissory note made out to Thomas Jones in November 1807.[18] It is unclear how Pitt came into possession of this note, and it is quite likely that Macarthur was behind it all and used him as a proxy. Thomas Pitt had been a Bligh supporter but had switched sides after the rebellion and signed the letter congratulating Major Johnston.[19] Thompson realised that this court case was probably just another attempt to try and prevent him from returning to England with Bligh.

On 5 August the court met in judgement of this case, with Captain Kemp as the new acting judge advocate and Lieutenants Moore and Brabyn as magistrates. The defence pointed out that the promissory note had been made out to Thomas Jones without the usual words 'or bearer'. It expressed the obligation four months after 3 November 1807 'to pay Thos. Jones the sum of Fifty pounds Sterling Money for a horse named 'Roger' bought of him.'[20] The court was informed that when Pitt asked Thompson for payment, he had refused for two reasons: first the note was made out solely to Jones not to the bearer, and second, when Pitt requested payment

Thompson noticed changes and imperfections to the note that suggested it was a forgery or, at least, a copy. The two men had discussed this and Pitt 'appeared convinced the Note in question was imperfect and that he would return it thru' the channel he had it'. Other witnesses confirmed these discussions. It appears that when Thomas Pitt returned the note 'from whence he received it', the issuer refused to take it back. Pitt then took Thompson to court. Judge Advocate Kemp summed up the verdict: 'We have considered this case very attentively and, I own, with a great leaning and wish on my part that the same should turn out in favor of the Plaintiff, but the words of the Act are too strong'. The verdict was given in Thompson's favour, but Kemp made it quite clear he would have preferred to give it to the plaintiff.[21] Once again, he had won a case about a disputed promissory note. There would be further attempts to bring him down.

Thompson had much more on his mind than legal matters – he was about to build a large house on his plot in the centre of Sydney. Through the government administration 'grapevine' – as active then as it is now – he heard that Foveaux wanted to alter the lease arrangements for central land in Sydney, the same issue that had caused so much friction between Bligh and Macarthur. The acting lieutenant governor was advocating the conversion of leases into permanent grants if large sums of money were spent building houses on the leased land.[22] The land lease that Thompson had received from Bligh a year earlier already had a small house, in which Mrs Ellen Moore still resided.

The day after the promissory note court case concluded in his favour, Thompson registered the sale of the land and the transfer of the house, garden and premises from Mrs Moore for a sum of £40, with an additional £14 for 'Materials'.[23] Thompson immediately commenced building a large 'handsome' brick house with a detached kitchen, a stable, a coach house and a granary.[24] The land was close to the mouth of the Tank Stream and bridge, near the wharf and close to Government House. The area is now named Macquarie Place – it was then, and is now, premium real estate.

Living close to this house were many of Andrew and Ellen's friends, successful businessmen and ship owners who also had large farms at the Hawkesbury. Their female companions, mostly ex-convicts, were prominent women in their own right, though not necessarily members of the Sydney social set. Simeon Lord and his partner Mary Hyde lived in a large house next to the Tank Stream bridge. Mary was transported on a seven-year sentence in 1798 for stealing clothing and in 1801 received an absolute pardon. After the death of her partner John Black, a ship's officer, Mary became in 1802 the companion of Simeon Lord, a former partner of Black. Mary and Thomas Reibey were also neighbours of Andrew and Ellen. They were among Thompson's oldest friends at the Hawkesbury. The 15-year-old Mary Haydock arrived in 1792 on a seven-year sentence for stealing a horse and in 1794 married the ex-sailor Thomas Reibey. The young couple were early settlers on the Hawkesbury River, and over the years extended their landholdings. A year after Thompson launched his first boat on the Hawkesbury in 1802, Reibey commissioned his first grain cargo vessel. Later he added more ships to transport timber and coal from the Hunter River and do sealing in Bass Strait. In 1803 Thomas Reibey established a trading business on leased Sydney land where his family later resided.[25] After her husband's death in 1811, Mary Reibey became well known in the colony as a businesswoman and is featured on the 1994 Australian $20 banknote.

The removal of a corrupt administration was the rebels' principal reason for overthrowing Bligh. Now, under a rebel government, crime and corruption had become rampant in the colony, and there were no legal law courts or civil authorities to help combat it. Stealing was so common in Sydney that merchants defended their properties with private armed guards. Robert Stewart, a former Corps lieutenant, who had been freed from prison by the rebels had seized the brig *Harrington* and escaped with 50 convicts to the Philippines. Few of the absconded convicts were ever caught.[26] It was a farcical crime symptomatic of a colony administered by incompetent and dishonest officials, and a lax military. The need to re-instate a legitimate government was becoming urgent.

A major source of agitation for residents was the justice system – the courts were unpredictable and corrupt. Three of Thompson's workers had been hauled into court; one for stealing, the other two for murder. William Lindsey, a ticket of leave convict on a fourteen-year sentence, had kept Thompson's sheep for eight years and none had ever been lost. Shepherds often ran their flocks together on Nelson Common. It was alleged that Lindsey had stolen two sheep belonging to John Palmer's flock, a charge liable to the death sentence. Fortunately, Thompson's overseer William Mortimer vouched for Lindsey's honesty and good standing, and he was acquitted.[27] In rebel courts defendants needed strong support, otherwise a death sentence was 'only a whisper away'. Mortimer, who had been first assigned to Thompson as a convict servant, remained with his master as a freeman overseer after completing his sentence in 1803. Thompson's employees saw him as a just and fair man who paid wages promptly and treated his workers humanely.

In another court case two of Thompson's workers were charged with murdering John Brazil, an assigned convict working in his tannery at West Hill farm. On 28 August 1808, it was alleged that Brazil had gone with accomplices to rob the pigsty of Robert Richie on South Creek. In the darkness, Brazil had been mistaken as a servant of Richie and was shot dead by one of his accomplices. Brazil had shared a hut at the tannery with two other employees, the colonial born Robert Rope and convict Mark Eivers. On the night of the murder Rope and Eivers had been found asleep in their hut. The court was told that Rope was in the habit of carrying a musket to protect his master's property. This musket had recently been discharged and blood was found on his trousers. Rope and Eivers were charged with wilful murder; they pleaded not guilty and vigorously denied the charges. Both men 'produced good general characters' and in the absence of any substantive evidence of intent, they were summarily acquitted.[28] The rebel courts did not conform to any judicial standards, but they were not yet a 'kangaroo court'.

The Hawkesbury district was still the breadbasket of the colony but there was little appreciation of this by the rebel administration. Although Foveaux had removed Macarthur from controlling the district, the interests of the rebels remained focussed on amassing property and profits for the officers and business elite. The Hawkesbury settlers were bitterly disappointed in Foveaux and continued to keep Bligh informed of his administrative improprieties. The Green Hills surgeon Martin Mason told Bligh that the court was now 'fortified with villains' who lied under oath to protect their patrons. He assured Bligh that most settlers still supported him.

> The settlers collectively, and without exception (excepting a few who are employed as agents and pedlars, directly or indirectly, for the present magistrates and officers), are to a man decidedly in your

> favour, and highly approve of your administration ... and most earnestly wish for an opportunity to express their loyalty and gratitude.[29]

At a secret meeting in August 1808, the Hawkesbury loyalists agreed to send two delegates to the Colonial Office. The Surgeon Martin Mason and the Baulkham Hill settler George Suttor were asked to go to London and tell authorities about the 'rise and progress of abuses' under the rebels. They were to urge for a military force to reinstate Bligh and to bring justice to those guilty of the rebellion.[30]

Mason prepared to depart and as required by regulation, he placed a notice in *The Sydney Gazette* asking his creditors to submit their claims, and for debtors to make repayments.[31] This was a legal necessity to prevent men leaving the colony without settling their debts. However, in this instance, it also served to alert the rebels that a person who may cause problems in England was about to depart. This compliance with regulations cost Mason dearly. Foveaux's officials saw the notice and they were not about to allow anyone to reach London and lobby the British before they could.

Surgeon Mason had a small pharmacy shop in front of his premises in Green Hills. On 1 October 1808 Corps soldiers, led by Chief Constable Fitzgerald, raided the shop and discovered a still that Mason had used to produce medicine. The equipment was essential to Mason's practice and, while all his customers had known about the still for years, it was suddenly deemed to violate the prohibition on distillation. A week later, Foveaux issued a General Order in *The Sydney Gazette* announcing that in view of Mason's 'large family in very indigent circumstances' he would remit any further penalties for the breach of regulations. Nevertheless, the informer, Charles Thorpe, a convict on a fourteen-year sentence, received a pardon and a reward of £10 for informing the authorities. It was also published that Martin Mason had previously been dismissed as an assistant surgeon for misconduct.[32]

The accusation of misconduct was untrue and in a letter to Foveaux, Mason declared that:

> I left Government employment with clean hands and empty pockets. If unshaken loyalty to His Majesty's Governor be a crime, if that be misconduct, I plead guilty in an eminent degree.[33]

Martin Mason applied for a court hearing to clear his name, demanding a copy of the accusation concerning his still. This was refused. The case was never reviewed but a conviction was recorded, and the distillation plant confiscated. Mason was then refused permission to sail to England. He quite rightly protested against 'the scandalous libel' printed about him in *The Sydney Gazette* and claimed 'the object was something more than that of seizing' his small still when most other surgeons in the colony were operating much larger ones.[34] Even those unsympathetic to Bligh knew the real reasons for this conviction – it was to stop Mason from lobbying for the removal of the illegitimate government.

On 12 October the *Estramina* returned to Sydney Cove from her voyage to Port Dalrymple. And, once again, Paterson was not aboard. This time he had claimed poor health and that, in any case, the *Estramina* was inappropriate for his passage. He was obviously delaying his duties in Sydney for as long as possible. Foveaux was furious; he had expected by now to rid himself of this onerous responsibility. He may have also felt increasingly nervous about leading a rebel administration, which carried with it the prospect of being charged with treason. At short notice, he decided to return to England and planned to sail on the first ship leaving for London, the *Albion*, a whaler part-owned by Robert Campbell. However, the *Albion* Master, Captain Richardson, informed him that he could not be accommodated.[35] Whether this was true or not, is unknown – Campbell consistently refused to help the rebels and certainly considered Foveaux to be one of them. It may have also been precautionary; Captain Richardson was one of the men regularly conveying Bligh's secret dispatches to London.[36]

Foveaux changed his mind about leaving, or perhaps he had no choice. In any case, he resumed his duties running the colony. HMS *Porpoise* was refitted to sail for Van Diemen's Land to pick up Paterson. This time it would be a warship worthy of a lieutenant governor. Bligh's ambitions to command HMS *Porpoise* for his return to England were put aside for the moment, but he would press his demands with gusto when Paterson was installed.[37] Foveaux had had enough of his NSW governance duties and wanted Paterson to take over as soon as possible so he could go to Norfolk Island. This probably seemed like a wise strategic withdrawal.

Surgeon Martin Mason went back to Green Hills to settle his debts and he borrowed £185 from Andrew Thompson and £80 from Rowland Hassall, putting his house, land, crop and cattle up as security.[38] People in the district regularly sought loans from

Thompson because he gave liberal credits and generous repayment conditions. With no banks in the colony until 1817, private individuals or businesses gave loans. Thompson initially only offered credit to customers of his Hawkesbury store, but he later lent money for purchasing land, houses and ships.

His debtors came from all walks of life, emancipists, freemen and ex-military men – his earliest recorded loans were made in March 1808, only two months after the rebellion. The brothers William and James Jenkins were emancipist settlers who invested in the shipping industry and needed funds to build new vessels. They borrowed £244 with the security of their farm and existing ships. In the same month, Thompson loaned Thomas Either £37 secured by his farm, and John Bradbury £35. Isaac Moos required only £5 to buy a small plot of land, whereas rebel supporter ex-Corps Officer Thomas Hobby borrowed £400 using his large farm at Green Hills as security. William Chapman, who arrived on the *Pitt*, indentured his house and land in Sydney for the sum of £150, and ship owner Daniel McLeece borrowed £125 using his ship and house in Sydney as security.[39] In total, Andrew Thompson made eleven loans valued at £1363 (£121,300 today).

Based on later records of his accounts, all of these loans were repaid in full. There is no evidence that Thompson took legal action to recover his money, though John Bradbury and Thomas Hobby had to sell their farms to settle their debts.[40]

With Martin Mason's return to England blocked, loyalists sought other avenues to assist Bligh. On 4 November Hawkesbury settlers smuggled a letter to the Colonial Secretary claiming that the colony faced disaster with corrupt law courts, farmers being paid in rum for their grain and unable to support their families. The letter stated that this was a direct result of the Corps hegemony, and most farmers could not grow sufficient grain to feed themselves. They pleaded with Secretary Castlereagh to reinstate Bligh, adding that, while only a few of the larger landholders had signed this petition, many more wanted to but had been prevented by a 'system of terror'.[41] The principal author of the letter was the Hawkesbury settler George Suttor. Many others, including Andrew Thompson, supported the letter but did not sign it because there was a real possibility it would be intercepted.

In early December Judge Advocate Captain Kemp resigned.

Foveaux offered the position to several men, but all declined. As a last resort Richard Atkins was reappointed judge advocate on 13 December 1808. Atkins had been without an income since Bligh's arrest in January and was in debt again.[42] He and John Jamieson were the only Bligh supporters who agreed to work for the rebels after being dismissed. On 18 December George Suttor was brought to trial for impugning Foveaux's authority by refusing to participate in the recent muster. Denying the legality of the court he refused to plead guilty and was imprisoned for six months. At the same trial four other men arraigned for refusing to comply with the muster were sentenced to a month in gaol – among them was Martin Mason.[43] These sentences were meant to discourage anyone from defying Foveaux but, if anything, it hardened their resolve. George Suttor expressed his loyalty to Bligh in a letter from his prison cell.

> But when I reflect on what your Excellency and family have suffered, and still are suffering, I, as a humble individual, ought to bear my lot with humility and patience.[44]

Andrew Thompson and other loyalists did not offer the rebels an easy target for retribution, and they complied with the muster.

On Christmas Day 1808, *The Sydney Gazette* provided a glimpse into Thompson's private life with a notice about his missing pet:

> STRAYED, or stolen from a Farm belonging to Mr. A. Thompson, at Hawkesbury, a black Dog with white streak down the neck, white tip on the tail, which curls upwards in a small ring, answers to the name of Bumper. Any person restoring the said Dog to Mr. Thompson, at Hawkesbury or Sydney, will receive One Guinea Reward; but if detained after this notice the parties will be prosecuted in whose possession he may be found.[45]

The dog, Bumper, was Andrew Thompson's constant companion and his disappearance would have weighed heavily on him. He offered the large reward of a guinea (£1 1s) for the return of the dog and stated he would prosecute anyone found guilty of stealing his beloved pet.

On 31 December 1808, as Thompson had been alerted to in advance, Foveaux offered grants to those who built substantial buildings on their Sydney leases. Thompson received a grant of 1 acre 37½ perches (5000 square metres) with an annual government 'quit rent' (land tax) of £24 14s 3d – a sum that few in the colony could afford.⁴⁶ Foveaux converted the Sydney land leases to grants for five emancipists: Simeon Lord, Isaac Nichols, Andrew Thompson, John Driver and David Bevan. These men had 'laid out very large Sums of money in the erection of excellent dwelling houses, extensive Stores, and other substantial and useful buildings'.⁴⁷ Foveaux claimed that these houses would not 'disgrace the most fashionable square in London' and had cost several thousand pounds.⁴⁸ All these men, except Thompson, had signed Macarthur's petition to arrest Governor Bligh, though Simeon Lord had subsequently aligned himself with the Bligh loyalists. Obviously, Foveaux was hoping this generous conversion of leases would unite these powerful men behind his administration – the grants were a none-too-subtle enticement for their support. In a letter to the Colonial Office, Foveaux justified his action:

> The Justice of securing the permanent enjoyment of the fruits of their industry to persons who have speculated with such confidence and spirit upon the precarious tenure of a lease, and the policy of encouraging others to similar exertions, and thereby materially contributing to the extension and ornament of the town, are so obvious that I feel no necessity of enlarging on the motives which led me to the step I have taken in their favor.⁴⁹

Thompson's land grant not only encompassed Ellen Moore's plot of 19 perches (480 square metres) and the rest of the partitioned block, it also included the neighbouring block of William Chapman of 2 roods and 8½ perches (2238 square metres). In April 1808 Andrew had lend £150 to Chapman and his wife who, as security on the loan, had indentured their land in Sydney.⁵⁰ In November William Chapman had received a 100-acre land grant in Bankstown and was quite willing to transfer his Sydney lease to Thompson.

The turbulent year of 1808 closed for the colony with William Bligh and his daughter Mary still confined to Government House, and the rebels continuing to govern for the benefit of a select few. Andrew Thompson maintained his allegiance to Bligh but, as a prominent shipper and businessman in the community, he was increasingly rubbing shoulders with the Sydney exclusives. He may not yet have the social attributes to go with his wealth and influence, but his presence, and that of his companion Ellen Moore, in their grand new house at the centre of the Sydney business district was a matter of considerable conjecture. The most influential men in town may not agree with Andrew's political leanings but he had become too powerful for even rebel sympathisers to ignore or disrespect. Of course, this did not apply to John Macarthur who continued to voice his dislike for Thompson. However, since Macarthur rarely showed respect for anyone, including the governors, this was expected.

At the end of the year Captain John Porteous arrived from England to take command of HMS *Porpoise*. His presence in the colony increased Bligh's prospects of regaining control of the ship when it returned from Van Diemen's Land with Lieutenant Colonel Paterson.

Optimism was never in short supply inside Government House, nor among the Hawkesbury settlers.

Chapter 15

LOCAL HERO

In the calamitous floods of the river Hawkesbury, in the years 1806 and 1809, at the risk of his life, and to permanent injury of his health, he exerted himself each time, during three successive days and nights, in saving the lives and properties of those settlers whose habitations were inundated.[1]

New Year's Day 1809 offered fresh hope to Bligh supporters. HMS *Porpoise* had returned from Port Dalrymple with William Paterson, who was to take over the colony's administration. The hope that he might also reinstate Bligh soon vanished. As soon as the warship sailed into Port Jackson, a note from Colonel Foveaux was delivered warning Paterson that he might be kidnapped and imprisoned on HMS *Porpoise*. The rebels were clearly concerned at the intentions of the loyalists and of Bligh's naval authority over HMS *Porpoise* and commandant Captain Porteous. Taking no chances, Lieutenant Finucane boarded the ship before it reached the Cove and took Paterson by carriage into Sydney.[2]

William Paterson was not a well man and had become overly fond of spirits. Doubtless he would have preferred to stay in Port Dalrymple, but was eventually persuaded by Joseph Foveaux's envoy that, as the senior Corps officer, he should do his duty and return to Sydney. Paterson knew that the role of temporary lieutenant governor would be difficult administratively and politically. As a past commandant of the Corps, he understood better than most the pressures that would be brought to bear by the military and the rebels, and also by the Bligh loyalists for the restitution of a legal government. When Major Grose left the colony in December 1794 Paterson had acted as administrator until Governor John Hunter arrived. During his brief nine-month tenure Paterson granted 4965 acres of land to fellow officers and made no attempt to check their trading malpractices. In 1795 he returned to England where he informed Sir Joseph Banks on the plants and trees in New South Wales, and because of these contributions he was elected a Fellow of the Royal Society.

Paterson returned to Sydney in November 1799 to be Corps commandant and lieutenant governor to Governor King. In July 1801 he accused Lieutenant John Macarthur of disclosing the contents of a letter written by Mrs Paterson to Mrs Elizabeth Macarthur, and challenged him to a duel in which he was seriously wounded. Because of the duel, King sent Macarthur to England to be court martialled. Paterson recovered and pursued his botanical interests with studies of plants along the Hawkesbury River and the Hunter River further north. But he never fully regained strength and early in 1803 was relieved of his duties. In May 1804 Lieutenant Colonel Paterson was put in charge of the settlement founded at Port Dalrymple (Launceston) in Van Diemen's Land.

When William Paterson arrived in Sydney in early January 1809, Joseph Foveaux resigned immediately as administrator to enable a quick transfer of power. However, he and John Macarthur were still expected to play a role in the colony's governance. Macarthur was a bitter enemy of Paterson since their duel but knew he would be easier to manipulate than Foveaux. After several unsatisfactory meetings with Paterson, Foveaux announced on 5 January 1809 he would return to England. Sensing a split in the rebel camp, the anti-Macarthur faction lobbied Foveaux to stay on. He and Paterson eventually agreed on a governance arrangement – Paterson would officially govern the colony but would reside in Parramatta, while Foveaux would remain in Sydney as Corps Commandant and oversee the daily administration. The arrangement pleased Macarthur – he could easily access Paterson from his nearby farm and extract what he wanted from this often-befuddled man. Botanical studies became Paterson's main preoccupation.

However, the shared administrative arrangement left many in the colony uncertain of who was actually in control. At the very least, ex-Governor Bligh expected William Paterson to return his personal papers and property, but this did not happen. Moreover, Bligh assumed that Paterson would have the good sense to act on his entreaty that no person should leave the colony until sanctioned from England. Paterson failed to do this as well.[3] Bligh loyalists were exasperated – it had been at their urging that Paterson had returned. Many frustrated settlers wondered when the administrative nightmare would end, and help would finally arrive from England.

Two weeks after Paterson's arrival, Foveaux claimed he had found a discrepancy in Macarthur's accounts as Colonial Secretary.

Macarthur angrily disputed this but was ordered to repay the treasury £500 for goods appropriated for his own use. Other officials verified Foveaux's audit, but Macarthur considered the accusation a personal insult and demanded satisfaction from Foveaux in a duel. On the morning of 19 January 1809, the two men met at a secret location with their seconds, Finucane for Foveaux and Johnston for Macarthur. Macarthur won the toss of a coin and fired first. He 'took a very deliberate aim and was perfectly cool' yet missed his target. Foveaux then lowered his pistol and refused to fire. This was a scorching insult to Macarthur – not returning fire in a duel implied your opponent was not worth shooting at. Foveaux then informed Macarthur that he felt grossly offended for having been 'obliged to account in that manner' for opinions expressed in his role as administrator of the colony.[4] Johnston suggested the two men shake hands, and they reluctantly did so.

Macarthur had to repay the £500 and, from then on, he had no further contact with Foveaux, verbally or by letter. In keeping with prevailing etiquette, details of the duel were not published in *The Sydney Gazette*, but a poem on a fatal 1807 duel in Ireland was reprinted in the next edition. This probably gave Bligh's supporters some appreciation of the colony's ignoble equivalent.[5] In any case a full account of the early morning duel and the humiliation of Macarthur was widely circulated. Macarthur's colossal pride was, for a short time at least, severely deflated.

A week after arriving in Parramatta, William Paterson appointed Andrew Thompson to be the official auctioneer for the Hawkesbury district.[6] This was probably at the recommendation of Foveaux, who had farming experience in the area and knew that Thompson was the right man for the job. Although Joseph Foveaux saw himself as a gentleman, he was astute enough to realise that the distinctions of class and rank was quite different in New South Wales to those in Britain. His views became evident when he proclaimed on 31 July 1808 that his administration would be 'a system of the strictest economy, and the most impartial justice between persons of every description'.[7] Thompson had been cooperative with all previous administrators except Grose and Paterson (1792-1794), and Johnston and Macarthur. The Corps' antagonism towards Thompson lessened noticeably during Foveaux's administration and, although a known Bligh loyalist, he received a Sydney land grant in December 1808. Foveaux was shrewd. Thompson was influential in the Hawkesbury district and, while he would never join the rebel cause, blunting his rigid opposition might lead to better cooperation between the two camps.

Actions taken over this period also show that Foveaux's attitude towards rebels noticeably hardened following Paterson's arrival. Various administrative decisions indicate he had become aware of the danger the rebel leadership posed for him personally. He tried to make his actions beneficial to everyone in the colony; they were not dissimilar to those of Bligh. In particular he implemented measures that reduced the colony's economic burden on Britain, and in doing so he diminished Macarthur's influence and profits.

In October 1808 the ripening crops in the Hawkesbury district were soaked by continual rain. The river rose dangerously and then quickly subsided, but resulting poor harvests caused grain scarcities across the colony. Although Foveaux claimed that he supported the Hawkesbury farmers, his administration resisted buying grain for cash, preferring that goods be bartered from the government stores. This may have been necessary because of a coin shortage, but a lack of cash payments discouraged settlers from planting larger crops. They needed hard currency to settle their debts from previous flood losses and complained that merchants were making huge profits from the grain barter system while they did all the work.[8] It rained heavily again in 1809 and the prospect of other poor harvests loomed. This was just the beginning of the settlers' misfortunes.

Government stores opened for grain delivery in late January 1809, but little was received. Farmers had sown less wheat this season and in addition the crop yields were poor. An added problem was that private traders tried to entice settlers to sell their grain for spirits rather than taking it to the government stores. The impending grain shortfall forced Foveaux to reinstate Bligh's offer to give preference to growers who had signed up for the fixed 10s per bushel.[9] On 11 February, to the astonishment of the traders and Corps officers, Foveaux reaffirmed, and then enforced, Bligh's government prohibition on trafficking in spirits and forbade all barter of grain for rum. He ordered magistrates to enforce the law and issue penalties for any offence.[10]

For many years Thompson had consistently supported the government and sold his grain to their stores, however, he had not done so since the rebellion. This changed for the 1809 harvests, when Thompson's farms delivered 269 bushels of wheat, valued at £134 10s, to government stores.[11] Perhaps as a reward for doing so, Foveaux awarded Thompson in late February liquor licences for the Sydney and the Hawkesbury districts.[12] Other emancipists also became new licence holders, reducing the rebels' stranglehold on the spirit trade. Again, Macarthur was angry at the 'hostile attempts from that unprincipled man Mr. Foveaux'.[13]

William Bligh had now been imprisoned in Government House for a year. During this time the backing of the small settlers had not waned – if anything it had grown. The rebels were aware of this and feared that Bligh would soon receive military support from England. Bligh remained the Commander of all Royal Navy ships in the South Pacific, and Captain Porteous on HMS *Porpoise* still responded to his orders. Indeed, the rebels were worried that Porteous might intercede on the loyalists' side and forcibly release the governor. These concerns were heightened on 26 January 1809 when Captain Porteous refused to accept an order from Paterson to sail HMS *Porpoise* to Norfolk Island and transport its inhabitants to Van Diemen's Land.[14] This rebuttal of a direct order signalled to the colony that Bligh still held a major card in this political poker game. Paterson responded with the threat that unless Bligh relinquished command of HMS *Porpoise* and left the colony on the first available ship for England, he would be imprisoned in the military barracks' gaol. Bligh was not easily intimidated and flatly refused to give up his naval command or to voluntarily leave the colony. On 30 January Bligh was taken from Government House to the barracks in a one-horse chaise, with his daughter following behind. Mary remained in the barracks throughout his incarceration.[15]

With Bligh in military prison, the Corps officers attempted to loosen his grip on HMS *Porpoise* by offering land grants to Captain Porteous and the other officers on board. They gladly accepted the grants but remained loyal to Bligh. Paterson next threatened Bligh with a forced expulsion on the convict transport *Admiral Gambier*. This ship was soon to take John Macarthur and George Johnston to England. Bligh refused, declaring that sharing a ship with such scoundrels would be unthinkable.

On 4 February 1809 Bligh agreed to depart on HMS *Porpoise* provided his selected companions could accompany him, and that he and Mary would reside in Government House until then.[16] In return he agreed not to interfere in local matters. With command of

HMS *Porpoise* now assured, there was renewed hope among the loyalists that legitimate government was not far off. For Andrew Thompson and Bligh's other nominated travelling companions it meant that departure for England was imminent, and they had better start preparing for a long absence from the colony. Several days later the prospective travellers applied to Paterson for permission to leave the colony. Andrew moved to Sydney just in case he was called to board HMS *Porpoise* at short notice. Days passed and nothing happened.

On 20 February 1809, after a 13-month confinement, Bligh boarded HMS *Porpoise* as its Commander and the ship readied for departure. When Bligh left Government House and passed by the guardhouse, he claimed that the Corps officers ignored him but 'the Privates of the Guard turned out of their own accord, touching their Caps'.[17]

A critical clause in the Paterson–Bligh departure pact was that Bligh be allowed to take selected witnesses with him to England. Within a day of Bligh boarding HMS *Porpoise*, Paterson, at the insistence of Lieutenant Colonel Johnston, disallowed John Palmer from leaving with Bligh because he had refused to make requested alterations to his account books.[18] Bligh complained bitterly because Palmer was badly needed to verify his government's decisions. The remaining twelve witnesses, Andrew Thompson, Thomas Arndell, Richard Atkins, Robert Campbell, James Williamson, Reverend Henry Fulton, Nicholas Divine, Richard Rouse, Francis Oakes, George Dowling, William Gore and George Crossley were still waiting for Bligh's order to board HMS *Porpoise*. Days went by without a reply from Paterson on Palmer's release.

On 26 February 1809 Bligh ordered HMS *Porpoise* to weigh anchor and sail down the harbour to the channel leading to the Pacific Ocean and drop anchor.[19] Here the warship remained until early March waiting for the pact conditions to be complied with. If they were not agreed to, Bligh intended to block the departure of the *Admiral Gambier* with Johnston, Macarthur and others on board. These men wanted to arrive in England as soon as possible to lobby their case to parliamentarians for Bligh's overthrow. The blockade of HMS *Porpoise* prevented their ship from leaving the harbour.

Lieutenant Colonel Johnston was becoming increasingly nervous about the trial in England, and he demanded that four of Bligh's witnesses, Palmer, Atkins, Gore and Crossley, be prevented from leaving with Bligh and that they come with him on the *Admiral Gambier* as his witnesses. Johnston informed Paterson he would prefer that all of Bligh's witnesses accompany him but was told non-government employees could not be forced to do so. The four men he requested were, however, the 'principle [*sic*] Agents' of the ex-governor 'in the execution of the Oppressive and Tyrannical Measures' that had led to the rebellion. He urged that these four men be instructed to leave with him and support the charges against Bligh. Paterson declined, pointing out he had no authority to direct men to leave against their will.[20] Johnston now became increasingly desperate and ordered Richard Atkins to accompany him. He refused unequivocally, and Paterson again declined to intervene.[21]

Paterson's unwillingness to meet Johnston's requests coincided with an intriguing tribute being paid to Lieutenant Colonel Foveaux, which may have influenced his later decisions. *The Sydney Gazette* reported on 11 March 1809 that John Grono, Master of Thompson's *Governor Bligh* had discovered, while on sealing voyage to New Zealand, a new strait between the South Island and Stewart Island. This strait had been named Foveaux Strait and a nearby tip of the South Island, Windsor Point.[22] These names would have been at Thompson's instigation – he certainly knew how to massage the egos of officials and persuade them to lean in his direction.

On 17 March a group of Hawkesbury settlers boarded HMS *Porpoise* and presented Bligh with a letter of gratitude for his 'firm, upright and impartial administration'.[23] They warned Bligh that some rebels were demanding that he should be kept hostage in the colony and the pact with Paterson cancelled. Plans were already advanced for the Corps to board HMS *Porpoise* and to arrest him again.[24] Bligh thanked them and declared that no matter what happened he would remain in the area until he had received orders from the Colonial Office. To reinforce this promise he issued a proclamation to the masters of all ships in Port Jackson, forbidding the removal of any rebel from the colony. It listed the names of all Corps officers, and 15 civilian and public officials, including John Macarthur, Garnham Blaxcell, Gregory Blaxland, Richard Atkins, Robert Fitz, D'Arcy Wentworth and Thomas Hobby.[25]

Two days later the rebel administration charged John Palmer and Charles Hook with sedition for distributing Bligh's proclamation to ships' masters. Hook was sentenced to one month, and Palmer to three months, imprisonment with a £50 fine.[26] This proclamation reminded the rebels that Bligh was still a force to contend with, and some would have felt the noose tightening around their neck. He made it clear that anyone remotely connected with his overthrow would be prosecuted, and the frightening implications of a treason charge were starting to dawn on the less committed rebels – especially those who had not really benefited from the rebellion. With HMS *Porpoise* anchored at the harbour entrance, some rebels believed, probably correctly, that Bligh intended to board the departing *Admiral Gambier* and arrest their leaders.

Bligh realised his pact with Paterson was now defunct and that the rebels would not hesitate to arrest him again. He prepared to depart immediately without taking Palmer or any other witnesses with him. On 17 March 1809 HMS *Porpoise* weighed anchor and sailed through the Heads into the Pacific Ocean, parading up and down the coast in full sight of the Sydney residents. Two days later, she sailed south but, instead of setting a course west through the Bass Strait for England, headed south to Van Diemen's Land. Bligh was to keep his word about staying in the region. Paterson had reneged on their pact and Bligh felt no obligation to keep his promise to sail back to England. Two weeks after Bligh's departure George Johnston, John Macarthur and a group of rebel supporters departed for England on the *Admiral Gambier*.[27]

On 29 March HMS *Porpoise* docked in the harbour of Hobart Town, and Bligh sought the support of Lieutenant Governor David Collins. Bligh planned to stay in Hobart until assistance from England arrived and then sail back to Sydney. For the first three weeks Collins welcomed Bligh and his party. News that Bligh was in Hobart reached Sydney on 10 April and Foveaux immediately dispatched a ship with an order prohibiting all contact with Bligh or the provisioning of anyone aboard HMS *Porpoise*.[28] As lieutenant governor, Collins was obliged to comply with this order, but Bligh was not an easy man to deny and continued to press for official recognition. The relationship between the two naval colleagues strained and finally broke. Bligh reboarded HMS *Porpoise* and Collins forbade contact with the crew or any reprovisioning of the ship.[29] Many settlers forcibly sent from Norfolk Island to Hobart supported Bligh, and they secretly conveyed food out to the ship. Collins punished several for doing so.[30] Bligh responded with his usual bravado and resolve – he blockaded incoming vessels to the harbour and demanded provisions for his crew.[31] HMS *Porpoise* continued to obstruct incoming ships until it returned to Sydney in January 1810.

The departure of George Johnston and John Macarthur for England consolidated Foveaux's power in the colony. However, administering the rebel government had become increasingly difficult – Bligh's swaggering departure had eroded the confidence of the rebel supporters. Moreover, there was general agreement in the colony that those who had led the rebellion should not leave until the legality of Bligh's arrest was resolved, and that this constraint should have also applied to Macarthur and Johnston. Additionally, there was open hostility from Bligh supporters who had paid dearly for their loyalty with fines, imprisonment, foreclosures and incarceration at the Coal River mines. Others had endured abuse and humiliation from the Corps, theft of their property and injustice in the courts. Until Bligh's escape, these disenchanted inhabitants had remained silent in fear harming the governor but now their resentment was starting to boil over.

Paterson was apparently unaware of, or indifferent to, the increasing distrust of his administration. He continued collect plant specimens and to give land grants to benefit his supporters and bribe his detractors. The emancipist Henry Browne Hayes wrote to Lord Castlereagh at the Colonial Office about these malpractices.

> Paterson gets drunk at Government House at Parramatta, and Foveaux is left at Sydney to do as he likes. ... F. is king and supreme; P. is only a cypher. ... Oh, it has been charming times! ... Hang half this worthy set and it will be justice, for they have been the greatest robbers.[32]

Hayes was one of Bligh's supporters who had been sentenced to the Coal River mines for opposing the rebellion and was now back in Sydney under house arrest. He wrote that officers and favourites had been 'enriched by this republican Government' gifting thousands of acres of land, as well as 40,000 litres of spirits, since the rebellion. So many grants and leases had been issued that 'there is nothing left for any other Governor (when he arrives) to give'.[33]

Heavy rain fell across the farming districts at the end of April 1809 and continued into May. The soil moisture prevented crops from being sown, and the likelihood of another grain shortage boosted wheat prices. Paterson visited Green Hills on 1 May and judged that the conditions should not preclude a decent harvest.[34] A week earlier Thompson's farms had delivered 44 bushels of wheat to the government store, the largest delivery in April by any settler.[35] From the Government House in Green Hills Paterson would have seen Thompson's buildings in the government precinct; his white cottage, a retail store, a three-storey warehouse, a two-storey building and the brewery. On the other side of the South Creek, Thompson's Red House was the centrepiece of the Government House vista. This must have impressed Paterson, because a week later the Scot received a 14-year lease on 1 acre 43¼ rods (5140 square metres) of land where his brewery complex had been built.[36]

When Paterson departed Green Hills, the rain had eased and with it any concern about flooding. Whereas early rains had been patchy, later rainfalls in the Blue Mountains were heavy. These flooded the tributaries, and on 15 May 1809 a wild torrent of water inundated the Nepean and Hawkesbury Rivers submerging many buildings and crops along their banks and those of the South Creek.[37] Once again, settlers experienced the severe downside of farming in low-lying fertile valleys. These repeated losses forced some settlers to move out of the district to higher land where the lower soil fertility was compensated by the promise of a harvest each year without flooding. Farmers at the Hawkesbury in particular had incurred the frequent loss of houses, farm equipment and animals from flooding. Indeed, fortunes were being made in the retail trade from a constant need to replace everything damaged by floods. Thompson's retail store had certainly profited from these losses. Only a week after the flood, on 21 May, he advertised in *The Sydney Gazette* that his shop in Green Hills had for sale the following articles: woollen and linen drape, hosiery, cottons, silks, muslins, stationery, tea, coffee, sugar, rice, tobacco, drugs, tinware, saddles, harnesses, dressed leather, shoes and boots, salt, oil, tar as well as sheep and other stock. All purchases were payable in cash, but payments could be delayed until the next season's harvest. Thompson asked those who already had debts with him to settle these as soon as possible.[38] There is no record of him suing anyone who was unable to pay.

The 1809 floods had not finished yet. On 23 May the river rose at 4 ft *per hour*, and by the next day Green Hills and the surrounding districts were completely inundated.[39] Foveaux's secretary, James Finucane, reported that the Hawkesbury rose by 66 ft, 9 ft higher than the 1806 floods.[40] Lives were at risk and magistrates mobilised all available men and boats in a rescue effort that was reported in *The Sydney Gazette*.

> ... as long as assistance was found necessary, such persons as were fortunate enough to be provided with boats were employed in rescuing others who were in imminent danger; and on this occasion Mr. Andrew Thompson personally signalized himself, in an unremitting exertion of two whole days and nights continuance. About 4 on Saturday morning the water was at the highest, and remained tranquil for three hours, when it began very gradually indeed to fall. From the Green Hills, over the South Creek as far as Tuckwell's Lagoon near the Red House was a sheet of water, across which Mr. Thompson's accommodation boat conveyed persons to and fro; and all the lower situations down the River were laid entirely under water.[41]

Crews worked through the night, with distressed families firing guns to alert the rescue boats. It was reported that 'the unfortunate people were calling in the most piteous manner for relief. The shrieks of women and children filled the air'.[42] Soaking wet from two days and nights of rescue effort in boats, Thompson and others risked their lives on numerous occasions. Through their brave efforts not one life was lost.

Within days the flood levels dropped as rapidly as they had risen but the devastation was extensive. Almost all grain stored in the Green Hills government store had been lost, Thompson's cottage was damaged and most of his farmland on the South Creek flooded. Fortunately, some of his buildings were safe on higher ground. The toll bridge on the South Creek was not 'at all impaired by the late inundation, with the dreadful torrents it was opposed to'.[43] Thompson's overall property damage was tolerable, but he probably incurred major financial losses when other devastated settlers were unable to pay back their large loans and debts from purchases.

Foveaux quickly appreciated the enormity of the disaster and ordered convict assistance to the district to help clear and re-sow the land. On 1 June 1809 he visited the Hawkesbury to assess damage in the colony's largest grain growing region. He brought with him 150 convicts, 50 draught bullocks and their drivers, tools, seeds and provisions. A severe food shortage was now likely, and Foveaux's assistance helped many settlers replant their crops. Within two weeks up to 3000 additional acres of wheat were sown; much more than at any time previously.[44] During this recovery

Thompson helped feed hungry workers by delivering 500 lb of pork to the government store.[45] Nevertheless, the loss of the granaries meant that food shortages threatened the colony, and Paterson despatched a ship to Bengal to purchase wheat.[46]

On 19 May 1809 Lieutenant Colonel Macquarie, accompanied by his wife Elizabeth, departed from England for Sydney on the warship HMS *Dromedary*. Lachlan Macquarie was to be the fifth Governor of New South Wales and he brought with him soldiers of the 73rd Highland Regiment of Foot to replace the NSW Corps. Most of the soldiers were on board HMS *Hindostan* that was escorting HMS *Dromedary*. The news of the rebellion against Bligh had reached London in September 1808 but at that time the British government was preoccupied fighting the Peninsula War in Spain and containing Napoleon in Europe.

Macquarie had not been the initial choice as the next governor. In December 1808, the Colonial Office had selected Brigadier General Miles Nightingall to be governor, and Lieutenant Colonel Lachlan Macquarie as Commander of the 73rd Highland Regiment of Foot and lieutenant governor. However, in April 1809 Nightingall fell ill and the former lieutenant governor of NSW, Francis Grose, offered to replace him. Fortunately for the colony, Macquarie boldly put himself forward as governor. At first his self-nomination appeared to have failed and he attended a royal levée as the new lieutenant governor. However, the following day Lachlan was informed he would in fact be the next governor.[47]

Before departing England, the Colonial Office briefed Macquarie on the reforms badly needed in the colony: to restore confidence, improve morals, encourage marriages, improve education, prohibit the use of alcohol and increase agriculture. Colonial Secretary Castlereagh realised that these reforms had previously failed because of the lack 'of Example and Co-operation in the higher Classes of the Settlement'.[48] The instructions were similar to those given to Bligh and previous governors, but with the disbanding of the NSW Corps, Macquarie was expected to have a much better chance of implementing these reforms.

By the time the news of General Nightingall's initial appointment as governor had reached Sydney in July 1809, his replacement, Lachlan Macquarie, had already departed England. The first detachment of soldiers from the Scottish 73rd Highland Regiment of Foot was sent with 132 convicts on the *Boyd* reaching Port Jackson in August. The early arrival of the troops confirmed that Bligh's request for the NSW Corps to be replaced had been listened to but to everyone's dismay no regimental officers were on board and there were no warrants to arrest rebels. The troops bivouacked outside Sydney awaiting the rest of the regiment to arrive.[49] Until then, the rebels remained in charge of the administration.

With their departure imminent, the NSW Corps officers helped themselves to as much booty they could lay their hands on. The issuing of land grants by Paterson and Foveaux reached new highs with 403 allotments totalling 67,475 acres being granted. Before 1806 only 85,000 acres land had been granted in the colony. Arthur Phillip granted 3389 acres over five years and William Bligh, who did not believe in free land, granted only 2180 acres.[50] Governor Lachlan Macquarie was later to comment that William Paterson had been 'such an easy good natured thoughtless man that he latterly granted Land to almost every person who asked them, without regard to their Merits or pretensions'.[51]

The Hawkesbury settlers were just starting to recover from the devastating autumnal floods when, on 29 July, heavy rain set in again. The following day the Hawkesbury reached a record peak of 86 ft. The whole settlement was a dreadful scene of 'horror' and one uninterrupted sheet of water. Many Green Hills houses located where the river joined the South Creek were totally immersed. Only the government buildings and Thompson's property on the ridge of Green Hills were spared, and this dry island became the safe area for flood victims. Once again Andrew was called upon by Magistrate Bell to coordinate the rescue work. He and his men worked tirelessly in small boats to save families from drowning. Over several days and nights rescuers rowed their boats to find people stranded in the torrents of water. *The Sydney Gazette* editor George Howe heaped praise on the rescuers for their efforts:

> And I cannot omit to mention the active and indefatigable exertions of Messrs. Thompson and Biggers, to whom, under the direction of Divine Providence, many are indebted for their lives. Their fatigues were equal to their dangers, which were increased by the extreme darkness of the nights; during which their boats were repeatedly stove, and it was with difficulty they could with their crews preserve their lives. Many others who volunteered their exertions are also entitled to every praise.[52]

Help came too late for some. Five people sitting on top of their thatched roof drowned when it collapsed. Entire farms disappeared under water.

Part of a sketch showing the extent of the 1816 flood in Windsor. The floods in 1806 and 1809 were even higher. Andrew Thompson's Red House farm on the left side between the trees was not immersed in any of the floods.

All the newly sown crops were lost and so was stored grain salvaged from previous floods. Immediately on learning of the floods, Foveaux set out for Green Hills only to turn back because the roads were impassable.[53] Paterson ordered that everyone in the colony with a garden must raise vegetables to help food supplies, and he banned the export of flour or grain. The rebel administration then tried to increase the flour supplies by removing the monopoly on grain sales.[54] But these measures gave little relief to struggling settlers in remote areas where there were acute food shortages and the prices had ballooned. Even so, there were no petitions to the government for flood relief, as there had been in Hunter, King and Bligh's time. The settlers knew where the rebels and Corps officers' main interests lay, and they were not going to waste their time.

Because of his rescue efforts Andrew Thompson was acknowledged as the Hawkesbury's 'common Friend and Patron'. But his strenuous and prolonged exposure in the flood rescues had permanently affected his health.⁵⁵ Paterson rewarded Thompson for his extraordinary rescue work with a grant of 120 acres land on an island near the southern end of Pittwater Bay.⁵⁶ Governor Phillip had named the island Pitt Island, in honour of the British Prime Minister William Pitt the Younger. Andrew renamed it Scotland Island, and established a shipbuilding yard and salt works there, with houses for the workers. He had earlier relocated his salt works from Mullet Island after conflicts with the local Aborigines.

About the same time Thompson bought a 50-acre grazing farm on the Eastern Creek in the Parish of Melville, eight miles south of Green Hills, which he named Creek Retreat. The land was rented out to John Bowman.⁵⁷ On 24 August Andrew Thompson received another grant from Paterson, 1240 acres of land on the Cowpastures Road in Minto – the largest land grant he ever received. The allotment was 30 miles south of Green Hills in newly established pastures west of the Georges River and he named the property 'St Andrews' after Scotland's patron saint. Here he built 'an excellent farmhouse with suitable offices, garden, stock yards' and later purchased several neighbouring farms, 345 acres in total, to the southeast of St Andrews.⁵⁸

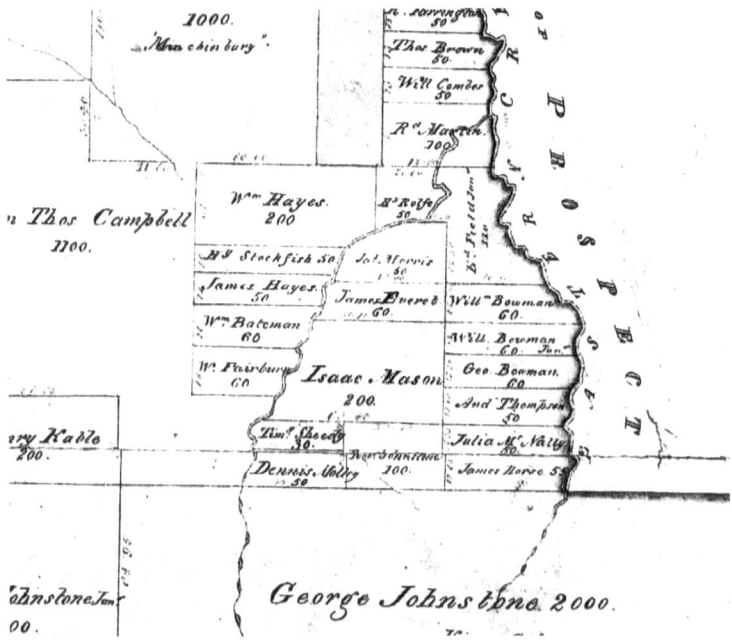

Part of a Melville parish map showing Thompson's 50-acre farm Creek Retreat on the Eastern Creek.

However, it was becoming increasingly evident that Thompson was a sick man. His lively stride and enormous vigour had gone, and he began to assign some of his duties and responsibilities to others. St Andrews farm was to be managed by emancipist Joseph Ward, another long-term employee who had risen from being a convict servant to a position of trust. A year later Governor Macquarie commended Ward and his wife as 'a very decent couple' who were careful to protect their 'good master's interests'.[59] In the 1970s a new suburb was established in the City of Campbelltown at this same location and it was named St Andrews to commemorate the first titleholder, Andrew Thompson.

Part of a Minto parish map showing Thompson's 1240-acre St Andrews farm. The 345-acre plot were smaller farms consolidated in 1815 by his executors, Antill and Moore.

Following the devastating series of floods in 1809, the Hawkesbury magistrate Bell reported to Foveaux, quite erroneously, that the damage there had been less than first thought, and that some crops were likely to recover.[60] In fact, the damage to most farms had been greater than the massive 1806 floods. To make matters worse, on 11 September heavy rain caused more crop losses in the area. All low land on South Creek farms was immersed including 'the whole of Mr. Thompson's spacious wheat plantation extending from the Creek Bridge to the Red House'.[61]

Because of Andrew Thompson's rapidly declining health he was urged in November 1809 to further lighten his workload. He reluctantly accepted this advice and progressively reduced his direct involvement in the Green Hills businesses. The 36-year-old Scot appointed John Howe, a fellow Scot and Bligh loyalist, as his business manager. Howe had arrived with his family in 1802 with a group of free Presbyterian settlers who settled on the Hawkesbury River at a place called Ebenezer. By the end of 1809 they had finished building their own Presbyterian Church. Thompson showed great confidence in him, and Howe became the first person allowed to make decisions on managing his businesses. On 3 December *The Sydney Gazette* announced the change.

> John Howe begs leave to inform the Public, that he keeps and carries on the extensive House and Business of Mr. Andrew Thompson, at the Green Hills, Hawkesbury, with every respectful attention, and has now on Sale a valuable Assortment of … at the most reduced Prices, for ready Payment only. All Persons indebted to A. Thompson are once more requested to make good their Payments without further delay.[62]

John Howe also became Thompson's personal secretary and one of the more onerous tasks assigned to him was the recovery of monies owed to Thompson. People across the colony were financially indebted to Andrew Thompson and their repayment conditions tended to be overly generous.

Chapter 16

FIRST EMANCIPIST MAGISTRATE

> *Mr. Thompson's intrinsic good qualities were appreciated by His Excellency the present Governor, who soon after his arrival here was pleased to appoint him a Magistrate, for which situation Mr. Thompson's natural good sense and a superior knowledge of the Laws of his Country peculiarly qualified him.*[1]

On 28 December 1809, HMS *Hindostan* and HMS *Dromedary* sailed into Port Jackson. On board HMS *Dromedary* was the new governor, Lieutenant Colonel Lachlan Macquarie and his wife Elizabeth. Also arriving were the remaining soldiers of the 73rd Highland Regiment of Foot, Lieutenant Governor Maurice O'Connell and the newly appointed Judge Advocate Ellis Bent. When the vessels dropped anchor, Joseph Foveaux came on board to welcome Macquarie, and William Paterson travelled from Parramatta to welcome the new governor on shore. The Sydney residents watched with a mixture of relief and delight at the pomp and ceremony displayed as the new governor, his wife Elizabeth and officials, and the two Scottish regiments of the 73rd of Foot marched up Grand Parade to Government House with military gun salutes and a brass band playing 'God Save the King'.[2] Macquarie was greeted by Lieutenant Governor Paterson, Lieutenant Colonel Foveaux, 'Gentlemen of the Settlement, and a great number of Inhabitants', who bowed as the couple passed down a corridor formed by the troops.[3] Among the welcoming party was the emancipist Andrew Thompson.

The Colonial Office had told Lachlan Macquarie to temporarily reinstate William Bligh as governor before officially taking over the position. On hearing that Bligh was on HMS *Porpoise* moored in Hobart Town harbour, Macquarie thought it propitious to assume the mantle of governor promptly and did so on 1 January 1810. Unfortunately, this deprived Bligh the satisfaction of being briefly reinstated.[4] But the rapid installation of Macquarie as governor was needed to bring stability and law to the colony. The Colonial Office had listened to ex-Governors Hunter, King and Bligh, and appreciated the parlous state of politics in the colony. They instructed Macquarie to arrest Major Johnston and send him back to England for trial. John Macarthur 'the leading Promoter and Instigator of the mutinous Measures' was to be arrested and charged with criminal acts against the government and was to be tried in the colony.[5] Johnston and Macarthur had already departed for England and would be arrested there. Macquarie was instructed to send the NSW Corps Regiment, with Lieutenant Colonel Foveaux, back to England where they would be disbanded. Colonel Paterson was to be allowed to return to Van Diemen's land if he so wished.

Joseph Foveaux, an active participant in the rebel administration, fully understood the precarious situation he was in and immediately set out to endear himself to the new governor. Initially he had no idea what instructions Macquarie had been given on the punishment to be meted out to the rebels – it well may be that his destiny lay at the end of a rope. But Foveaux was a resourceful man and he had been careful to play a reasonably conciliatory role in his later administration of the colony. He was confident enough to volunteer his services to the governor and lead him on a tour of the Sydney settlement. And, in truth, there was no one else who could do it more authoritatively. Macquarie listened carefully to Foveaux's advice on the 'true interests of the Colony' and those 'principal inhabitants' who could best assist the government.[6] Macquarie would have been cautious about taking advice from a Corps officer who had supported the rebels – the same men who had arrested the previous legal governor – but he needed to hear their side of the story before initiating the major reforms he had in mind.

It must have puzzled Macquarie to hear Foveaux speak so glowingly of the non-rebel emancipist settlers' contribution to the colony's prosperity. In particular, Foveaux claimed the emancipist farmers were largely responsible for the colony's self-sufficiency in food production, and that they created and excelled in many of the colony's business enterprises. He informed Macquarie of Andrew Thompson, an ex-convict who had become successful in the colony 'both as an individual, and an active and intelligent chief constable'. He may have also told him of the injustices Thompson had suffered because of his loyalty to Bligh and his opposition to Macarthur. Being an opponent of Macarthur was reason enough for Foveaux to recommend him, and since Macquarie was looking for 'those individuals who had remained steadfast in their loyalty and obedience' to previous governors, Thompson was quickly accepted by the governor as a man of influence who he could trust.[7]

During their tour of Sydney, the governor and his wife inspected the house intended for the newly arrived Judge Advocate Ellis Bent in which Richard Atkins was currently living. They considered the house a 'perfect pigstye' and quite unacceptable for the new judge.[8] Ellis Bent had been sent out to reform the colony's civil courts and his chronic ill health meant he was frequently sick on the voyage. Macquarie considered Bent's comfort and peace of mind vital to his administration, as he needed his advice in reconciling the divided colony. Finding a suitable house for the Bent family was a high priority. It was initially planned that the Bent family stay on board HMS *Dromedary*, but Foveaux knew of much better accommodation. Bent soon received a note from Macquarie saying: 'that Colonel Foveaux had got a Mr Thompson to lend us his house ready furnished for such time as we wanted it and that it was now ready for our reception'.[9] The family moved into Thompson's house on the same day and 'thought themselves very lucky in having so good a home on shore so soon'.

Part of a view of Sydney from the west side of the Cove around 1810. It shows the properties of the three prominent residents Reibey, Thompson and Lord, and the proximity of their land to the harbour and Government House.

In a letter to his mother, on 4 Mar 1810, Ellis Bent praised Andrew Thompson as the 'first man' in the colony:

> Mr Thompson came out a convict to this country but is now, I may say, one of the first men if not the first in the Colony. He possesses an amazing herd of cattle, a most extensive property at Hawkesbury where he generally lives. Besides, he has to the amount of £50,000 engaged in different pursuits. He has established a Tan yard where he manufactures leather from the skins of kangaroos and seals. He also has a Saltwork etc etc. He is a Bachelor and built the house at Sydney for his residence but has since determined to reside at the Hawkesbury where he also has a House.[10]

Admiring the grandeur of the house, Bent continued:

> The house is I assure you one of the prettiest in Sydney. The entrance is into a very good hall – having on each side of it a room of 17 feet square – on the same floor there is also a butler's pantry. Upstairs there are two good bedrooms, one of which is the nursery and three servant bedrooms and a good storeroom. There is a charming verandah both above and below. There are also extremely good cellars. The kitchen is not yet built but there is a small wooden house close to this and within the gates which serves that purpose very well. ... The House was only just finished, but in many of its requisites it was incomplete.[11]

Ellis Bent's letter to his mother provides us with some insights into Thompson's lifestyle in 1810. It describes the house as the prettiest in Sydney and, since it was available for long-term rental, it was apparently rarely used. Bent wrote that the building was unfinished but was well furnished and even had a nursery. Having a child's room suggests Andrew may have planned to have a family, but nurseries were common in large houses when big families were the norm. Significantly, Bent refers to Thompson as a bachelor who mostly resided at the Hawkesbury. This observation begs the question: where was Ellen Moore then, and were they still an occasional couple? Of course, Ellis Bent would not have been familiar yet with the living arrangements of the locals, however, with Simeon Lord as a neighbour he would soon learn of the many *de facto* couples in society. Clearly Ellen Moore now dwelt in another house and probably this is where Andrew stayed during his regular visits to Sydney.

Bent's letter to his mother is long and admirably detailed – he clearly set out to convey a visual image of the settlement and how his family was adjusting to this remote and fascinating place. Thompson's house was only 100 yards from the waterfront of Sydney Cove but had no fence; the property was open to the street and the Cove. Bent observed that 'This was extremely inconvenient as the Natives quite naked would come up to the very windows of the house'. Joseph Foveaux continued his efforts to find favour with the new governor and it was he who later 'supervised the works', enclosing the yard towards the Cove with a 6 ft cedar fence.[12]

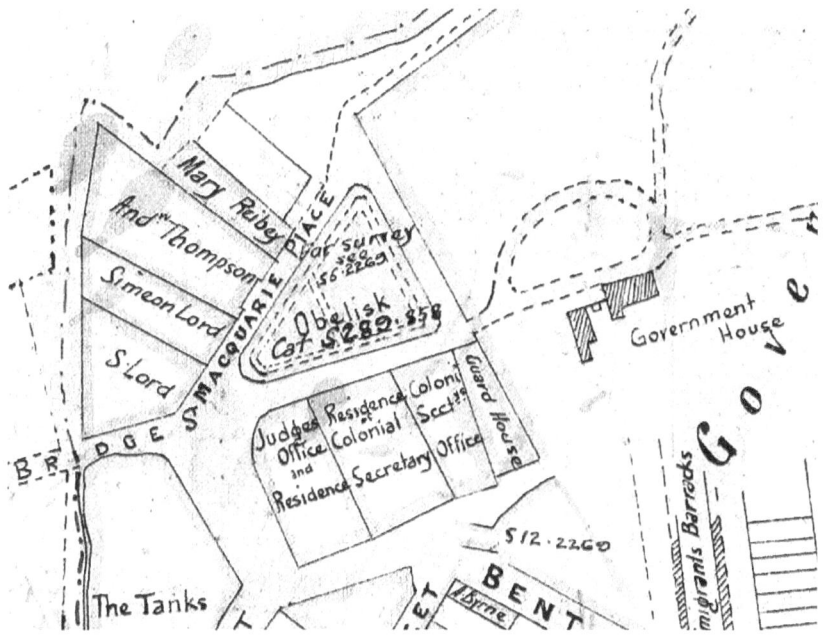

Part of a St James parish map in Sydney showing Andrew Thompson's property in Macquarie Place and the proximity of his land to Government House.

For the rental of his Sydney house Andrew received £152 12s per annum from the government.[13] A condition of the lease was that Thompson's servants, Joseph and his wife, should be retained on an existing joint annual wage of £36. The servant couple quarrelled incessantly but Bent realised it was difficult to get servants in the colony and replacing them might result in domestics 'ten times worse'. Joseph's wife was a good cook, and he was 'an excellent footman, very willing, quick, active, sober and honest too. He waits at Table very well, and cleans up his things and does his work'.[14] These servants would have enabled Andrew Thompson to live the life of a gentleman in town, where he was well known for lavish dinner parties in one of the finest houses in Sydney.

An archaeological dig in the 1980s discovered beneath the footpath of 11-15 Macquarie Place a vaulted brick cellar of a house that was constructed by Andrew Thompson in the early 19th century. It is 'a fine and rare example of traditional building technology' and reveals the nature of early colonial Georgian style buildings in central Sydney.[15]

Portrait of Lachlan Macquarie, the colony's fifth and longest serving Governor of New South Wales (1810-1822). A friend of Andrew Thompson, Macquarie was later a major beneficiary in his will.

On New Year's Day 1810 the 48-year-old Lachlan Macquarie was officially sworn in as the fifth Governor of New South Wales. Macquarie was born on the island of Ulva in the Scottish Hebrides. His father was a cousin of the last chieftain of the Macquarie clan, but his own family was poor and without land. They were tenants of the Duke of Argyll on the Isle of Mull and could not afford to stock the farm themselves. Upon his father's death in 1785, Lachlan and his brother Charles came under the care and guidance of Murdoch Maclaine, his mother's brother. Lachlan acknowledged that it was his uncle's generosity that had enabled his career in the military. Nevertheless because of his strict penurious upbringing Lachlan understood first-hand how it was to be deprived, and because his rise through military ranks had been through merit not privilege, the convicts and emancipists had found in this man a natural champion for their goal of equality.

In his first proclamation to the colony the new governor expressed His Majesty's greatest regret for the tumultuous and mutinous conduct against William Bligh. Macquarie was confident that the 'dissensions and jealousies' in the colony would now cease and give way for forgiveness, harmony and hope among all classes in the colony. He declared that his first task was to restore an orderly, lawful government and discipline in the colony. He was committed to the happiness of all inhabitants and promised that 'the honest, sober, and industrious Inhabitant, whether Free Settler or Convict, will ever find in me a Friend and Protector'.[16] Some in the audience may have thought this speech overly ambitious but he would prove to be an ardent egalitarian who meant what he said.

Macquarie was the first army officer in the colony's history to be in executive command of both the government and the military.[17] Past governors were naval men who had often struggled with uncooperative army and marine officers. Lieutenant Colonel Maurice O'Connell had been sworn in Lieutenant Governor, Captain Henry Antill as the Aide-de-Camp and Ellis Bent as the judge advocate. Macquarie instructed Foveaux to arrange the return of the NSW Corps regiments to England.[18] From their first meeting on 28 December 1809 on board HMS *Dromedary*, Foveaux had insisted that his superior officer Colonel William Paterson had been responsible for his rebel posting. The Colonial Office appears to have been unaware that Foveaux shared the rebel administration of the colony, otherwise they would have instructed that he be sent home under close arrest. Macquarie had received no such orders and he became progressively impressed with Foveaux's executive skills and by his previous administrative efforts.

Macquarie needed to quickly re-establish proper governance in the colony. Only four days after becoming governor he dismissed all public officers appointed by the rebels, including the Hawkesbury magistrate Lieutenant Bell and Chief Constable Fitzgerald. In the courts, he declared that all trials and investigations initiated after the rebellion to be null and void, that all convictions be quashed, and that any recent convict pardons revoked. Macarthur's capias bond of £10,000 against Thompson was deemed invalid. All grants and leases issued by the rebel administration were cancelled and landholders had to surrender the title deeds, with Macquarie reserving the right to ratify any he considered worthy. Despite the many serious misdemeanours committed in the past year, Macquarie disallowed legal action against the rebels who were magistrates, gaolers or constables, unless they had committed acts of oppression. Other transgressions would be punished in due course.[19]

In the second week of January Macquarie reinstated the first four of Bligh's principal civil officers, John Palmer, Robert Campbell, William Gore and Reverend Henry Fulton to their former positions. He also reappointed the former Sydney and Parramatta chief constables, John Redman and Francis Oakes. But Andrew Thompson was not reinstated as the Hawkesbury chief constable; a grander promotion was in train.[20]

Andrew Thompson was preoccupied with other issues. The edict to revoke all rebel grants had cancelled land grants and leases he had received from Paterson and Foveaux. In a letter to Macquarie on 10 January 1810 he sought his 'humane consideration' in the retention of the grants he had received for rescue efforts during the floods. He pointed out that as 'an Agriculturalist, Grazier, Manufacturer, Builder and Owner of Vessels etc in the interior' he had served other governors and had taken no part in Bligh's arrest. He had been suspended as chief constable because of this support.[21]

> Humbly implores your mercy and goodness to take your Humane consideration the case of your Petitioner and renew four Grants of Land annulled in the General Proclamation three of which was of old Occupancy on Leases Documents & given by former Governors – Namely Petitioners House and all his premises at Sydney on Quit rent of £24-13-9 per annum. His extensive Saltworks, Fisheries, Dock-yard, Buildings, and improvements at Pitt Water. His Brewery – Malt Houses, Yards, Work Houses & Buildings thereto, at the Hawkesbury – containing in all about 123 acres – and a remote new Grazing Farm of 1240 acres on which there us now about 1400 head of Stock, otherwise in want of Feed, and many people there at work – should your Excellency be pleased, Petitioner can show there is a capital employed by these upwards of £6000, and about 40 persons, towards increasing the internal resources of the Colony, by the manufacture and produce of essential necessities.[22]

Thompson argued that three of the grants had been given as renewal of former occupancies to 'encourage the spirit of preserving industry and being a principal part' of his property.[23] He asked that his record of service to the colony be considered in reviewing his case for the grants.

On his arrival in Sydney, Macquarie had been alerted to the

perilous state of the colony's granaries. Considerable grain had been lost because the wheat reserves were ruined by the 1809 floods and this season's grain crops had also been flooded. He was told that grain losses from floods in the Hawkesbury region had been huge for the past decade. As a military man Macquarie was well versed in making bold strategic decisions. He quickly concluded that the only practical solution to recurrent flooding was to relocate farms, houses and stock to higher ground. It was a radical idea and received a mixed reception from the settlers who at the time had many more immediate problems. Their financial losses from the most recent floods had been exacerbated by low prices being offered for the little grain that had been saved. The government stores gave only 9s per bushel whereas traders were selling grain for 23s per bushel in Sydney. Those farmers who still had any grain refused to sell it to the stores. Joseph Foveaux understood the settlers' frustration. He suggested to Macquarie that the government offer 12s per bushel of wheat under the same conditions that Bligh set in 1807; namely that farmers agree to sell next year's crop in the stores at a fixed price.[24]

On the same day Thompson submitted his plea to retain his grants, Macquarie requested that he and Lieutenant Bell meet with Hawkesbury settlers and urge them to sell their grain and potatoes to the government stores. Andrew had been in Sydney awaiting Bligh's return when he received Macquarie's request, and he immediately rode back to his Green Hills house.[25] Bell was reluctant to work with Thompson – the last time they collaborated he had been severely reprimanded. After that, Bell had avoided any further contact with the wealthy emancipist. Now, the governor's order left him no choice.

Over the next two days Bell and Thompson toured Hawkesbury farms and met settlers who still had grain. Bell reported to Macquarie on 12 January 1810 that 'the result of our exertions has exceeded our sanguine expectations' and the success resulted from 'the benefit of what personal influence I possessed'. The truth was probably quite different. It was Thompson's longstanding authority in the district and not Bell's influence that had convinced settlers to sell their grain to the government store. Foveaux understood this only too well and he almost certainly had recommended Thompson for this task. In any case, the two men raised 734 bushels of wheat, 323 bushels of barley and 108 cwt potatoes; one settler alone offered 2000 bushels of maize.[26] Thompson pledged 40 bushels of wheat and 40 bushels of barley. His actual contribution to the grain shortage was larger – he was feeding his 100+ employees with flour at no cost to the government. A week later the grain prices plummeted after the return of the *Marian* and the *Experiment* from Bengal with cargos of wheat.[27]

On 12 January, the same day that he received Bell's letter, Macquarie made Andrew Thompson the Magistrate for the Hawkesbury district. It was a momentous honour for Thompson – he was the first ex-convict to ever be appointed to the colony's judicial system. The promotion was awarded for much more than Thompson's recent success in gaining the cooperation of the Hawkesbury grain farmers. He had a long and impressive record of serving the colony and had already held positions of trust under Governors Hunter, King and Bligh. Clearly, these achievements had been noted by Macquarie and he recognised that, had it not been for Thompson's criminal record, Bligh or King would have made him a magistrate earlier. Nevertheless, it was a brave decision and set a precedent for the colony and, in all likelihood, for the British Empire. It would have far-reaching repercussions for the colony and for Macquarie. On 14 January 1810 *The Sydney Gazette* reported that:

> His Excellency the Governor has been pleased to appoint Mr. Andrew Thompson Justice of the Peace and Magistrate at the Hawkesbury, in the County of Cumberland; and he is accordingly to be respected and obeyed as such.[28]

The announcement may have come as a surprise to Thompson. Emancipists greatly outnumbered freemen in the colony and several already sat on the bench of the civil court. However, none had previously had the judicial authority to fine, flog or incarcerate an offender. Today, the decision to advance one of the most talented men in the colony seems obvious but prior to Governor Macquarie no one had had the courage to ignore the widely held belief that ex-convicts were incapable of fairly administering a legal system that had treated them so harshly.

For this reason alone, Thompson's promotion came as an enormous shock to many freemen and businessmen in Sydney. They would have expressed their indignation to Macquarie, and asked: are we to be judged now by an ex-convict? But the congratulatory letters coming from the farming districts would have far outnumbered any criticisms. Many would have seen the appointment as overdue and totally in step with having the best men administer the law. After all, Thompson had been doing this job for years at the Hawkesbury when the previous magistrate, Thomas Arndell, assigned such duties to him as chief constable. There was also awareness in Green Hills and the district, that Andrew's health was such that he could no longer hold the physically demanding post of chief constable. It was only fitting that he should be the magistrate – a job with similar responsibilities requiring the same fair-mindedness.

The Hawkesbury district residents had other strong reasons why they wanted Thompson to be their local magistrate. He was one of the wealthiest men in the colony and had been an influential business and community leader in the rural districts for years. Based on his time as chief constable, they were certain he would administer justice fairly. The magistrates Archibald Bell and Thomas Arndell had been ineffective – Bell was a rebel appointee and Arndell 'so much superannuated' that Thompson had to perform most of his duties.[29] The Scot, a free man since his pardon in 1797, was the right man for the job, and no one else in the district could match his abilities.

Making Andrew Thompson a magistrate had enormous political and social significance for the colony. With this appointment Macquarie was making it official that he would treat all free inhabitants equally, independent of their social status or occupation, or whether they came to the colony as transportees or freemen. In many respects, permitting an emancipist to make legal judgements was a watershed moment for the colony and heralded in an enlightened period of social and economic reforms. Macquarie wrote to the Colonial Office of his decision.

> Soon after my arrival here, I found Mr. Thompson to be, what he always had been, a man ever ready and willing to promote the public service, for this was the character he had obtained from all my predecessors. In consequence of his merits, and being the only person at that time in his neighbourhood fit to fill the office, I appointed him a Justice of Peace, and Chief Magistrate of the Districts of the Hawkesbury, where he had acted in that capacity, though not invested with the title of Magistrate, for eight years previously.[30]

The appointment of Andrew Thompson, and later the emancipist Simeon Lord, to a judicial post was not well received by the Colonial Office. The majority of the Tory government in Britain still thought of New South Wales as predominantly a penal colony, and they saw

Macquarie's actions as more akin to anarchy than a welcome step towards a society in which all inhabitants were equal under the law. The social shifts signalled by these emancipist appointments to the judicial bench shocked many in Britain, and Tory members of Parliament would eventually call for Lachlan Macquarie's blood.

William Bligh had not yet returned to Sydney on HMS *Porpoise* and was quite unaware of the rapidly unfolding events. Well before he had learnt that a new governor was coming from England, Bligh had devised a plan to reinstate himself. After all, he had waited two years without any word from the Colonial Office; it was time to return to Sydney and sort out these scoundrels. He had decided that, if necessary, he would board ships along the east coast of New South Wales to confiscate provisions and to solicit their involvement in the removal of the rebels.[31] In fact, by the time the communiqué announcing Macquarie's arrival was sent to Bligh on 9 January 1810, he was already sailing to Sydney.[32] HMS *Porpoise* reached Port Jackson on 17 January and, on finding HMS *Dromedary* and HMS *Hindostan* anchored in the Cove, Bligh assumed these to be the naval support that were there to reinstate him as governor. Military relief to remove the rebels had indeed arrived, but not in the way Bligh would have preferred.

As soon as HMS *Porpoise* dropped anchor Lieutenant Governor O'Connell came on board and informed William Bligh that Lachlan Macquarie had become governor in his absence. It was a dreadful shock for Bligh and, although he understood the circumstances, he was far from pleased. He was somewhat placated when he heard that the NSW Corps was to be disbanded and would soon leave the colony. The news that George Johnston was to be prosecuted in England, and John Macarthur court martialled, also helped to allay his disappointment. However, Bligh was dismayed to hear that his previous 'gaoler', Joseph Foveaux, now advised the new governor. One can be certain Bligh told Macquarie what a treacherous fellow Foveaux was, and that he should have nothing to do with him.

Bligh's ceremonial disembarkation from HMS *Porpoise* took place on 18 January 1810 accompanied by a 13-gun salute from the ship and the 73rd Highland Regiment of Foot. On shore, O'Connell welcomed Bligh, and troops accompanied William and Mary to Government House, where they dined with Governor Macquarie and his wife Elizabeth. Crowds of Bligh loyalists lined the streets to welcome their ex-governor; Andrew Thompson would have almost certainly been among them. Bligh and his daughter took residence in a rented house on Bridge Street beside the Tank Stream, and here they met their supporters to hear of the trials and tribulations of the past ten months. Bligh relished his return to Sydney, and soon recovered most of the official papers confiscated by the rebels. Macquarie personally returned his ceremonial sword.[33] A number of important documents were missing, presumably taken to England by Johnston and Macarthur to support their case for a rebellion.

Largely unnoticed during these celebrations was the arrival into Port Jackson of two of Andrew Thompson's ships; the *Governor Bligh*, mastered by John Grono, returning from New Zealand with 10,000 skins, and the *Speedwell* docked returning fifteen prisoners from the Coal River settlement. Thompson's fleet would soon be increased with two new ships, the sloop *Whale* and the 20-ton schooner *Geordy*, being constructed on Scotland Island.[34]

With the restoration of civil courts and the reinstatement of proper legal processes, Macquarie brought stability and efficiency to the colony. The grain farmers had hoped he would adhere to the policies of Bligh in assisting small farmers to increase food production. Macquarie gave assurances of support but failed to match the generosity of Bligh. He made it clear that his first priority was to heal the serious rifts between the business and farming communities, and he avoided overt favouritism to any sector. Under his competent management, the colony's economy gradually recovered from the dysfunction and chaos of the rebel era. Efficiency, reconciliation and industry became the cornerstones of this new age.

The new title of 'Magistrate' changed Andrew Thompson's social standing in the colony, and he was now entitled to be called 'Mr Thompson, Esq. (Esquire)'. This probably meant little to him, since for years he had earned all the respect he needed within the district. What was important to him now was to be able to perform his duties of magistrate well. Thompson knew that his judicial effectiveness depended on having an efficient chief constable to assist him. The dismissed rebel Chief Constable Fitzgerald had been unpopular with Hawkesbury settlers and Thompson needed someone who would get local support to replace him. On 23 January he recommended his long-time colleague Constable Matthew Lock as 'a very fit person' for the position.³⁵ Thompson trusted Lock even though he had signed the congratulatory letter to Johnston on Bligh's arrest.³⁶ Lock had done this under duress and later recanted, signing settler's petitions in Bligh's favour. In any case Thompson valued Lock's competency above his political views and his recommendation was accepted. The following day Macquarie appointed Matthew Lock as the next chief constable at the Hawkesbury.³⁷

On 16 February the 1810 annual muster was administered by Thompson started at Green Hills. Over several days everyone in the Hawkesbury district assembled at the chapel, which was also the magistrate's office, and provided personal details, livestock, crop yields and property. Lieutenant Governor O'Connell attended the muster and Thompson used the visit to show him around the district. On one occasion they crossed the Hawkesbury River and rode to Kurrajong on the lower slopes of the Blue Mountains. Here, Thompson renamed a hill called 'Kurry Jung' to be 'Mount Maurice', in honour of O'Connell.³⁸ However, this name change was never registered and soon disappeared. Thompson also showed O'Connell his own farms, as well as the two properties he managed for the Bligh family: the Blighton and Putland farms. The bachelor Maurice O'Connell was fond of the young widow Mary Putland and would have queried him about both of the farms and their owners. O'Connell would later invite Thompson to dine in his regimental mess – something that would have been impossible during the NSW Corps era. Andrew reciprocated by entertaining O'Connell at the Red House.³⁹

From the very outset of his term of office Governor Macquarie promoted morality, temperance and good public order. Before leaving England, he had met Reverend Marsden, who had been telling everyone who would listen of the immorality in the New South Wales colony and of the need for urgent reforms. Marsden's complaints probably led to the Colonial Office issuing specific instructions to Macquarie that included the need for regular church attendance, prohibition of work on Sundays, mandatory convict church parades, closing public houses during church services and the prosecution of brothel proprietors.⁴⁰

On 24 February 1810, Macquarie issued a proclamation condemning the 'Immorality and Vice so prevalent among the Lower Classes of this Colony' in which 'scandalous and pernicious' *de facto* relationships existed contrary to decency and good government. He advocated lawful marriage 'by every possible Means' and warned that cohabitation did not entitle a woman to any part of her partner's estate should he die without a will, no matter how long they lived together.[41] Macquarie declared

> his high Disapprobation of such Immorality, and his firm Resolution to repress, by every Means in his Power, all such disgraceful Connections; and publicly declares, that neither Favour nor Patronage will ever be extended to those who contract or encourage them.[42]

This announcement would prove to be an embarrassing double-edged sword for the governor. Both Andrew Thompson and Simeon Lord, who had recently received the governor's patronage as appointed Magistrates, were widely known as cohabiting with women who were not their wives. Macquarie had intended his proclamation to be for the 'Lower Classes', who Reverend Marsden assured him were the main offenders. He had not realised yet that 'class' was not as well defined in the colony as in Britain. Possibly Macquarie was not aware that Andrew Thompson, Simeon Lord and D'Arcy Wentworth were, by his definition, leading 'immoral lives', otherwise he may not have issued his proclamation; though it was unlikely to have affected his magistrate appointments. Macquarie later claimed he was obliged to issue his compromising 'Immorality' edict because of a common belief in Britain that all unmarried women in the colony were whores and most children were born out of wedlock. The Colonial Office had instructed him that such reforms should be implemented, and he had complied.

As far as can be ascertained from records, Macquarie's call for higher moral standards caused little reaction in the colony, even among the 'lower classes'. One can be certain that those opposed to emancipists becoming magistrates would have tried to make the most out of this apparent hypocrisy, but their criticisms never made the newspaper. There is little doubt that one of Macquarie's advisors, perhaps Foveaux, or even Thompson, would have quickly informed the governor that the codes of accepted conduct in New South Wales were much more pragmatic than in Britain. This seems to have been quickly accepted by Lachlan, possibly with Elizabeth's help, and his criteria for what was genuinely immoral certainly evolved from that point on.

In any case, Macquarie's insistence on the importance of

marriage would not have influenced Thompson's relationship with Ellen Moore. She was a Catholic and he was a Protestant, and quite independent of their wishes, the Church of England would not ordain their marriage. Simeon Lord took nine years to marry his long-term emancipist partner Mary Hyde. They were among many others in Sydney's 'upper classes' who lived immoral lives according to Marsden's standards. Even Joseph Foveaux, Macquarie's personal advisor, lived for many years in Sydney with a married woman before returning to England where they wed.

Three days after Macquarie's 'Immorality' publication, the Reverend Samuel Marsden returned to Sydney accompanied by Reverend Robert Cartwright, the new chaplain for the Hawkesbury. Marsden had been in England during Bligh's overthrow and returned to resume church duties in Parramatta and oversee his large landholdings. He planned to expand both his theological and business pursuits, not only in the colony but also in New Zealand. The governor welcomed the Reverend's return but showed no inclination to seek his advice. Marsden had expected to become a Parramatta magistrate again, but he was to be bitterly disappointed – Captain John Murray of the 73rd Highland Regiment of Foot had already been appointed. This was just the start of serious disagreements between Marsden and Macquarie.

Most free and emancipist settlers at the Hawkesbury lauded Thompson's appointment as magistrate, however, their enthusiasm was not shared by the demobbed Corps officers who retained official posts until their departure for England. One such officer was Lieutenant Bell who had been relieved as magistrate and then ordered to collaborate with Thompson. Bell found multiple excuses to avoid assisting the new magistrate, even when specifically ordered to do so. He held firm to his belief that no matter how wealthy an ex-convict was, he or she should not be allowed into the society of 'respectable persons'. All emancipists were taboo in his circles; he 'considered them as having been once tainted, unfit for associating with afterwards'.[43] Fortunately, Bell was soon to leave the colony.

But Archibald Bell was not alone in these prejudices. They were definitely shared by the naval surgeon Joseph Arnold, who had accompanied Lachlan Macquarie on the voyage to New South Wales. Arnold mixed freely in a Sydney society composed of wealthy merchants and military men. He wrote to his brother on these interactions and, while he did not mention Thompson's appointment as magistrate, he claimed Macquarie and his wife were considered stingy – whereas previous governors routinely held dinner parties, Macquarie 'keeps a shabby table, and very seldom has company'.[44] He also expressed surprise, considering the lowliness of their class, at the business successes of Thompson and Lord.

> Some of the convicts, (their time having expired) are now very rich. Mr Thompson who was sent here for theft twenty years ago has elegant town and country houses, several thousand acres of cultivated land, and employs 300 men the year round on his estates. Mr. Lord ... has built a house which he lives in that costs £20,000; but still these men are despised and any free settlers would not deign to sit at their tables.[45]

Arnold's use of the word 'despised' does not ascribe a dislike of the two men but a disdain for their low social status. This was an era when no amount of success in later life could reverse the stigma of 'low born' parents or a criminal charge. Not all of the upper or middle classes discriminated in this way but those insecure in their own social status often did. When successful men such as Thompson and Lord were shunned socially, it was based on the edict that 'money does not trump social superiority'. Invariably, most people who considered themselves superior in colonial society had low social standing in England. Although the barriers to an emancipist being accepted into society were high, they were not insurmountable. They could sometimes be bridged by business partnerships, marriages or romantic attachments. But the prevailing level of social discrimination against emancipists in the colony concerned Macquarie greatly. He wrote to the Colonial Office Secretary Castlereagh about the 'extraordinary and illiberal' policies adopted by previous governments with respect to emancipists:

> those men who had been originally sent out to this country as convicts, but who, by long habits of industry and total reformation of manners, had not only become respectable, but by many degrees the most useful members of the community. Those persons have never been countenanced or received into society.[46]

He pointed out that the colony would benefit from:

> conceiving that emancipation, when united with rectitude and long-tried good conduct, should lead a man back to that rank in society which he had forfeited, and do away ... all retrospect of former bad conduct.[47]

Macquarie's policies prioritised criminal reform and rehabilitation over punishment, and he believed the fastest route to a normal life was reintegration into a free society. He had been given no instructions by the Colonial Office regarding the treatment of emancipists, so his own beliefs determined his actions. Macquarie decided to set an example for the rest of the colony; he invited emancipists to dine at Government House. This kindled a new spirit of egalitarianism among the emancipists, but it caused a storm among the elite. Colonial social norms were shattered when the governor invited four emancipist men to dinner in Government House.

> The number of persons of this description whom I have yet admitted to my table consist of only four, namely, Mr. D'Arcy Wentworth, Principal Surgeon; Mr. William Redfern, Assistant Surgeon; Mr. Andrew Thompson, an opulent farmer and proprietor of land; and Mr. Simeon Lord, an opulent merchant.[48]

The invitation for Andrew Thompson to dine at Government House would not have included Ellen Moore. Women were rarely invited to such functions and, in any case, the social barriers with regard to *de facto* relationships still existed at this level. Andrew's first invitation to Government House probably followed the occasion he dined in the mess of the 73rd of Foot Regiment with Maurice O'Connell.[49] It is abundantly clear that Andrew Thompson and Lachlan Macquarie, along with Elizabeth, greatly enjoyed each other's company. Andrew was a frequent dinner guest of the governor, and they became close friends. For some of the Sydney elites, and in particular Reverend Samuel Marsden, the seating of an ex-convict at the governor's table was an unforgivable breach in social etiquette, and strongly worded complaints were soon being sent to the Colonial Office.

In March 1810 despite a marked decline in his health, Thompson was still involved in various business ventures. At this time a New Zealand shipping tragedy caused much anguish in the colony, and Andrew was called upon to help. Sydney merchants, and friends of Thompson's, Simeon Lord, Francis Williams, Alexander Riley and Thomas Kent had permission from Macquarie to create a settlement on the North Island of New Zealand to grow flax suitable for making cordage and canvas, with the possibility of a 14-year monopoly in trading. In November 1809 Lord had chartered the *Boyd* to take sealskins to England after loading ships' spars at

Whangaroa Harbour in New Zealand. On 10 March 1810 news reached Sydney that a tribe of Maoris had attacked the *Boyd* killing 70 crew and passengers and burning the vessel.[50]

Riley and Kent promptly quit the consortium, and Lord and Williams needed to find another ship and a new business partner. At the time Thompson's large vessel *Governor Bligh* was anchored in Sydney Cove having just returned from New Zealand.[51] On 12 March Lord informed Macquarie that Thompson had joined the scheme and made the *Governor Bligh* available, and that Foveaux had agreed to take flax samples with him to England aboard the *Experiment*.[52] While Thompson and Lord may have held different political views, their business collaborations remained unaffected. On 25 March 1810 the *Governor Bligh* sailed for New Zealand. When Foveaux returned to England with flax samples, the promotion of the scheme failed, and the New Zealand trade was never established.

In April 1811 the news that Andrew Thompson had been made a magistrate reached an astounded John Macarthur in England. He accused Joseph Foveaux, who had just returned to London, of 'being the principal cause of all the mischief that hangs over the Colony'.[53] Macarthur was outraged that Macquarie could have been so misled as to make the ex-convict Thompson a magistrate. Foveaux claimed he had 'cautioned Governor Macquarie respecting Thompson' but Macarthur, who detested all emancipists and Thompson in particular, did not believe him. Macarthur predicted the colony would plunge into the depths of iniquity if ex-convicts were allowed to sit at the governor's table:

> Is it possible, it is said, that Governor Macquarie can associate with, and bring to his table men who have been Convicts? who have amassed fortunes by the most infamous frauds, and have and continue to set the most shameful examples of dissoluteness and vice?[54]

Back in the colony William Bligh was finalising arrangements to return to England and give evidence at the trial of George Johnston. He had compiled extensive records on the mutinous behaviour of the rebels and continued to urge colonists to support the charges against Johnston and Macarthur. In early March 1810 he made a request to Macquarie for sixteen witnesses to accompany him to England but was told that several of the men were unavailable.

Judge Advocate Bent advised Macquarie that only those holding government appointments could legally be required to depart the colony. Macquarie agreed that, apart from John Palmer, William Gore, Reverend Henry Fulton and Richard Atkins, the decision to accompany Bligh must be left to the individuals. Robert Campbell, James Williamson, Francis Oakes, Nicholas Divine, George Suttor and Martin Mason opted to accompany Palmer, Gore, Fulton and Atkins on the voyage.[55] Thomas Arndell and Andrew Thompson declined to go.

The 37-year-old Thompson was now far too weak for the voyage, and there were other reasons why he did not want to return to England. The colony had given him a home where he was honoured and respected, and Governor Macquarie had shown him real friendship – much more than Bligh had ever done. Relations with Bligh had further strained since becoming a magistrate and being granted land by Foveaux and Paterson. Why should he risk such a long voyage when Bligh had never treated him as anything other than an employee?

And there were other compelling reasons why Andrew was reluctant to return to Britain. He now understood all too well that his prosperous life at the Hawkesbury would be a relatively brief one, as there was no known cure for his respiratory illness. He was also uncertain how Walter, his only surviving brother, would react to his return. The hostility of his family for a crime he committed as a boy worried him greatly, and a fractious reunion would be unbearable. He decided to spend 'the evening of his life where his manhood had been meritoriously exerted, [rather] than of returning to the land that gave him birth'.[56]

Despite being aware of Thompson's deteriorating health, the Reverend Marsden continued to publicly ridicule him. He criticised Thompson not only for being a magistrate and his 'immoral cohabitation' but also for his sharp business practices. As one of the largest woolgrowers in the colony, Marsden combined his efforts to 'save the souls' of Pacific Islanders and New Zealand Maoris with the trading of flax and timber from those islands. When Marsden learnt of the 14-year monopoly Lord, Williams and Thompson were seeking to export New Zealand flax, he was livid. This would stymy his own ambitions, and it gave him further reason to oppose the promotion of emancipists.[57] Even so, Marsden was prepared to overlook social barriers when it suited him, and he routinely did business with emancipists. In 1807 he hired the *Hawkesbury* from Thompson to take supplies to the Society Islands. Three years later Marsden had still not settled his bill of £444 (£35,000 today).[58]

Samuel Marsden's first serious boilover with Macquarie came when a new turnpike road was being planned from Sydney to Green Hills. The existing road was so bad that it often prevented produce from being taken by wagon to Sydney. Macquarie wanted a road and bridges built with tollhouses to pay for their repair and maintenance. It is quite likely that Thompson suggested this to Macquarie over dinner, even though such a road would compete with his own shipping interests on the Hawkesbury. Thompson understood the transport requirements of small settlers and grain farmers better than anyone; he had years of experience with his South Creek toll bridge and roads. On 31 March, Thompson received a letter from Macquarie's secretary, John Campbell:

> I am commanded by His Excellency the Governor to signify to you that he has been pleased to appoint you conjointly with Rev Mr Samuel Marsden and Simeon Lord Esq as Trustees and Commissioners for regulating and conducting all affairs & matters connected with the Turnpike road about to be established between Sydney and the Hawkesbury.[59]

Marsden agreed to join the Turnpike Road Trust before he knew who the other trustees were. He first saw their names in *The Sydney Gazette* on 31 March and was appalled to find that he had been officially placed in the company of two emancipists.[60] Although these were the wealthiest men in the colony, Marsden promptly told the governor that he would not associate with Thompson and Lord because of the 'immorality of their private lives'. He claimed that any connection with them was a dereliction of his sacred duties as senior chaplain.[61] Emphasising his disapproval of appointing magistrates 'who had been under the sentence of the law', Marsden claimed that to socialise with Thompson would 'lower his rank in society' and be 'attended with the most serious evils'.[62] Marsden's malice towards these two successful men was unbounded and he claimed that it was inconsistent 'with morality, religion or sound policy' to nominate ex-convicts as magistrates who were 'still living openly in profligacy'.[63]

Marsden's bigotry and hypocrisy infuriated Macquarie, just as it had Bligh, and he told him his refusal to join the trust was an act of civil disobedience.[64] Macquarie later observed that the morals of Marsden and his friends were far worse than those of Thompson and Lord:

> As to their looseness of morals, they were in that respect not worse, at least, than many of Mr. Marsden's most intimidate and particular friends, some of whom, who were even married men, have been guilty of the crime of seduction, and still Mr. Marsden continues upon very intimate terms with them.[65]

Macquarie promptly appointed surgeon D'Arcy Wentworth as the new trustee.[66] The three turnpike trustees Thompson, Lord and Wentworth quickly reached agreement and on 10 May 1810, James Harrex received the contract to build the new road from Sydney to the Hawkesbury.[67] Three days later, in a blunt unequivocal response to Marsden's outburst, Macquarie appointed another ex-convict to the judiciary; emancipist Simeon Lord and surgeon D'Arcy Wentworth were made magistrates for the Sydney area.

Marsden's opposition to ex-convicts on moral and social grounds might have been more convincing if he did not willingly collaborate with them in business matters. The Reverend was quite agile in separating the spiritual from the pecuniary, and it was only when his businesses were threatened that his attacks became vicious. Macquarie observed cynically that Marsden preached compassion to his parishioners but opposed their advance materially and socially.

At the end of April 1810, Bligh was ready to sail to England. Just prior to departure, he was surprised when Maurice O'Connell proposed marriage to his daughter. He was unaware of their friendship and disapproved the marriage. But Mary insisted on becoming engaged to Maurice and on 8 May they married and remained in Sydney. On 12 May Bligh sailed from Port Jackson on HMS *Hindostan*, part of a three-ship squadron with HMS *Dromedary* and HMS *Porpoise*.[68] On board HMS *Hindostan* were Bligh's witnesses for the court martial of George Johnston. The three ships also transported the disbanded NSW Corps, with Colonel Paterson and his wife aboard HMS *Dromedary*. The sickly William Paterson died on the voyage and was buried at sea.[69]

Captain William Bligh was one of the most controversial governors of New South Wales. A highly respected naval veteran, he lacked the political and diplomatic skills to have all segments of the community support his administration. Outspoken and proud, he was greatly admired by small settlers in the colony who he consistently helped but had less following in the larger settlements where he strictly regulated businesses. His eventual arrest and imprisonment by the military and Sydney elites was quite unjustified, as evidenced by the later court martial trial of George Johnston. This trial also revealed an unfortunate 'take-no-prisoners' trait in Bligh's character. If need be, the captain was willing to abandon friendly colleagues and employees in order to protect his own reputation. Andrew Thompson, who did not live long enough to witness it, would be such a victim of Bligh's ruthlessness.

On taking up the governorship Macquarie had done his best to smooth over frictions that remained in the community from the Bligh era but had personally found it hard to deal with the man himself. He wrote to his brother Charles: 'He had been a great plague to me ever since, and I am now heartily glad to get quit of him'. Although Macquarie found Bligh's temperament erratic and sometimes harsh, he had been unable to detect 'any crime or act of tyranny' that 'could in the smallest degree excuse or justify the rebellious and mutinous conduct' of those people who arrested Bligh and toppled the government.[70]

Chapter 17

A Remarkable Life

No finer stamp of early Australian manhood is to be found in the historical records of New South Wales than that exemplified by the hard-headed, shrewd young Scotchman, Andrew Thompson.[1]

By the autumn of 1810, Macquarie's steady administration and Bligh's departure for England gave much-needed tranquillity to Green Hills and the surrounding districts. The prolonged period of disruption caused by the rebel government had left the community exhausted and anxious, and the settlers now longed for a good grain-growing season devoid of floods, debts and political interference. In addition, a real sense of sadness had permeated the district with the realisation that Andrew Thompson, their long-time leader and benefactor, was seriously sick. His battle with acute respiratory failure was especially distressing for many who knew that this illness had resulted directly from his actions in saving their lives during the Hawkesbury floods. The tightknit settler community prayed for his recovery but most realised that he would not live much longer. Lung diseases were untreatable then, and usually fatal.

But there was always hope and Thompson was a fighter. As the champion of emancipist settlers and a bastion for the return of legitimate government, he deserved a miracle if anyone did. In the meantime, notwithstanding the debilitating consequences of lung failure, Thompson seemed determined to keep going. He resisted advice to slow down and rest, maintaining that there was much to do and not much time to do it in. He gave his magistrate duties top priority and continued to preside at the weekly sessions of the Hawkesbury court bench. He even presided over detailed coroner enquiries that followed several suicides and unexpected deaths in January, April and May.[2] Despite pleas from his friends and colleagues, he remained superintendent of government labour, cattle and public works, managing the distribution of convicts to settlers and their employment at public works. This included checking the identity of convicts who applied for a governor's pardon. He was even involved in the grim task of arranging the execution of James Davis.³ But inevitably these duties took their toll, and only after he realised his ability to make wise decisions was faltering, did he start to refer many matters onto Matthew Lock, just as Arndell had done when he was chief constable. By June, Andrew had become so debilitated that he needed to rest most of the time, and only made occasional appearances in court.

Few details of Thompson's decisions as the Hawkesbury Magistrate have survived. His court sittings were held in the chapel-schoolhouse next to his own premises in Green Hills. At one such court hearing in July, Magistrate Thompson fined Thomas Ivory and Charles Beasley £5 each for selling spirits without a licence.⁴ Beasley held a licence in Sydney but not in Green Hills and this charge was normally liable to a £20 fine.⁵ The case aroused interest because Thompson had been fined £100 in 1807 for a similar offence in Bligh's court. Three years on, he more fairly assessed this offence.

On 5 June 1810, Governor Macquarie renewed Thompson's two land leases in the government precinct of Green Hills for a further 14 years and confirmed the other land grants given by Paterson and Foveaux.⁶ Macquarie was in the process of reviewing all of the leases granted by the rebel administration and reclaimed many given to Corps officers and other men unworthy of 'such extraordinary Indulgences'. However, he renewed the grants of 'very deserving and Meritorious Persons'.⁷

By the close of July, Andrew was so weak that his movements were confined either to his white cottage or the upper floor of his storehouse. From here he conducted his business and magistrate duties and attempted where possible to participate in decisions about his farms and businesses. John Howe, to whom he regularly dictated letters, now managed his vast estate and four clerks kept the accounts of his many enterprises up to date. But Andrew's mind was far too active for him to properly convalesce, and he became increasingly frustrated by his fatigue, shortness of breath and painful coughing. The Hawkesbury surgeon James Mileham and the highly regarded Sydney surgeon and fellow emancipist William Redfern did as much as they could for him, but it was mostly palliative. A precise diagnosis of the illness is not recorded apart from acknowledging that his prolonged immersion in the 1809 floodwaters had 'laid the foundation for that illness'.[8] Governor Macquarie later recalled that during the 1806 and 1809 floods Andrew Thompson had 'at the risk of his life, and to permanent injury of his health' greatly exerted himself during his humanitarian rescue work. From the exposure of two days and nights in wet cold clothes, he had 'in the fulfilment of his duty caught a severe cold' from which he never really recovered.[9]

Confined to his bed, Andrew maintained an interest in as many of the activities in the district as he could. But by August his condition had deteriorated so badly that he was no longer allowed to 'meddle with business'.[10] Realising his end was near, Thompson set about putting his affairs in order. For years he had resisted pressing his debtors for the repayment of loans and promissory notes, but now his clerks began a series of actions in the Court of Civil Jurisdiction to put his books and estate in proper order. Writs for between £4 and £259 were issued against 33 settlers for unpaid promissory notes issued after the 1809 floods. His clerk James Smith appeared at the court hearings in August in his place. At three sessions in August 1810 Judge Advocate Bent awarded him £765 in 'Damages'. Since the account books kept by Thompson's clerks were not always correct, this was less than the amount claimed of £914.[11] In September Judge Advocate Bent awarded Thompson £361 of the £428 claimed.[12] The total amount returned to Thompson's estate was £1126 (£89,100 today).

In early September Thompson appeared to recover slightly and was able to 'take an airing in a chaise'.[13] But a week later his health lapsed again and, at the age of 37, Andrew Thompson resigned himself to soon departing the world of his adopted land, and he started to say farewell to close friends. It can be justly claimed that up to his final months, he had lived his short life 'as fast as the Yetholm weaver's shuttle' and had adhered to the motto *Industria Ditat*. On 4 October Andrew asked Constable Douglas to fetch John Howe, as he wished to alter his will again. Prior to redrafting the will, he asked Howe to record some details of his brothers, parents and his life in Scotland.

Thompson told Howe, who recorded the conversation verbatim, that when he 'was cast down', his brother William who 'would not look at him; [and] that he once went to see his brother after his failure, but he avoided him'. Howe then writes that 'Mr. Thompson at that time, from his youthful indiscretions, was not looked upon by his friends, and he then resided at Workington, in the north of

England'.[14] With increasing difficulty Andrew described what he knew of his Scottish family since he had been in the colony. These were matters that clearly caused him considerable distress, and he had no idea how they would treat any inheritance from his estate. Part of Howe's dictation reads:

> That his said eldest brother and his wife died, and left six children: that Mr. Thompson has another and only remaining brother, now or lately residing at Whitehaven, in the county of Cumberland, a manufacturer or merchant of Scotch muslin, &c. and employs about twenty or thirty looms; with him remain four of the children of his late brother. He, Mr. Thompson, had applied for two or more of his said brother's children, but their uncle, with whom they were, would not allow them to come.
>
> That Mr. Thompson's said brother had only corresponded with him twice. He believed Mr. Thompson was intended for the excise, till he made a breach in his conduct, after which time he was looked upon as an outcast goat, and went to Workington as above. He then corresponded from thence with his father and mother, though only very coolly on their side: that Mr. Thompson's mother is now an aged woman, and of course can be in want of but very little, if living; that he, Mr. Thompson, had turned it over attentively in his mind, in consequence of which he has sent for me, as he wished his relatives to enjoy what he was possessed of; viz. his brother at Whitehaven, and the four children of his eldest brother, with a provision for his mother (if she was now living); these were the only relatives he knew of, except a number of uncles, aunts, cousins, &c. which were usual in all families; that in case he should die with [within] days, or that the Lord should please to take him, Mr. Thompson wished a will to be written out by me, and he should order it to be filled up as he should settle in his mind by the time it was made out. I then proposed Smith should make out a rough copy for his approval, which he immediately ordered to be done.[15]

Of particular relevance in the drafting of the will was that Andrew's brother Walter had been raising the children of his eldest brother William and his wife since their deaths. Andrew 'had turned it over attentively in his mind' and he 'wished his relatives to enjoy what he was possessed of'. In particular he desired that Walter, the four orphaned children and his old mother in Yetholm, benefit from his estate. He asked Howe to make all possible haste in finalising the will, as time was short. This was done and Thompson made several more adjustments. Two days later, on 6 October 1810, Chief Constable Matthew Lock, Constable William Bladdey and the First

Fleet settler James Ruse witnessed his last will and testament.[16] Andrew appointed Captain Henry Antill, the Governor's Aide-de-Camp, and Magistrate Thomas Moore as executors of his will.

Thomas Moore was a shipwright who had known Andrew since arriving in the colony in 1796. Appointed as master shipwright by Governor Hunter, Moore was Thompson's neighbour in Sydney and shared his passion for ships and shipping. He was married to the ex-convict Rachel Turner, who arrived on the *Lady Juliana* in 1790. Rachel had initially been the partner of the First Fleet surgeon John White and bore him a child before he returned to England. Her now husband Thomas Moore had been a member of the court bench when John Macarthur sued Thompson for the payment of a promissory note. He had also signed the Hawkesbury settlers' Loyalty Address to Bligh in 1808. In May 1810 Governor Macquarie had appointed Moore as the magistrate for Georges River.[17]

The second executor, Captain Henry Colden Antill, was born in New York where his father had fought for the British in the American War of Independence. Antill was Macquarie's Aide-de-Camp, having served under him since 1796 in the 73rd Regiment of Foot. Antill knew Thompson from dinners at Government House and the military mess. With the same positive attitude of emancipists as the governor, Antill would have dined at the Red House in Green Hills when visiting the Hawkesbury. He was of a similar age to Thompson, and they had become friends. This, and the governor's trust in Antill's judgement, led Thompson to select him as someone who could handle the complexity of disposing of such a large estate. Later events proved that Antill was a good choice.

On 6 October, the same day Thompson signed the final version of his will, Macquarie initiated a beautification project in Sydney. The buildings opposite 'the Houses of Mr. Lord, Mr. Thompson, and Mr. Reibey' were demolished to make way for an open park area he named, rather vainly, 'Macquarie Place'.[18] Today it is known as Macquarie Place Park.

Thompson would never see the new park in front of his house. At the age of 37, Andrew Thompson Esq died in Green Hills on the morning of Monday, 22 October 1810.[19] One would like to believe that Ellen Moore was at his side during his final days but there is no record of it. The news of Thompson's death reached the governor after noon that day, and Macquarie chronicled the sad event in his journal:

> This afternoon between 1 & 2 O'Clock I recd. the melancholy accounts of the Death of poor Mr. Andrew Thompson Chief Magistrate at the Hawkesbury, where he died at 7 O'Clock this morning; an excellent worthy man, and much & justly regretted by everyone. He has left Capt. Antill his Executor.[20]

For three days Thompson's body lay at rest in his Red House on the West Hill farm just south of Green Hills, and many men in the community came to pay their last respects. Thompson's open casket was surrounded by flowers in the main room of the Red House – the same room where many mourners would have been entertained in much happier times.

The Church of England chaplain of Green Hills, Reverend Robert Cartwright, was asked to conduct the funeral service. Since taking up his duties in Green Hills six months earlier, Cartwright had frequently visited his sick parishioner. Macquarie later recalled that Thompson 'was on a term of intimacy with many of the most respectable gentlemen in the colony, and was much liked' and one of his friends was the 'excellent and worthy man, the Reverend Mr. Cartwright'. Macquarie later observed, when responding to character slights on Thompson in the Bigge Report, that Reverend Cartwright would not have considered him 'worthy of a funeral sermon if he had been so loose and so immoral a character'.[21]

In the ten months that Lachlan and Elizabeth Macquarie had known Andrew Thompson they had become close friends. Andrew was well liked by most people he socialised with, and he had quickly become part of the inner circle of Macquarie's acquaintances. The fact that they were both of Scottish birth (Lachlan was ten years older) probably helped to forge a common bond between the two men – though, paradoxically, Andrew had a more secure upbringing than Lachlan. Soon after Andrew's death Macquarie sent his Aide-de-Camp Captain Antill to Green Hills to arrange a burial plot. Months earlier Governor Macquarie had consulted Thompson on town planning for Green Hills, which included the location of a new church and burial ground well beyond the reach of floodwaters. The existing cemetery on the banks of the South Creek, west of Bridge Street, had often been inundated. Thompson had suggested a location, and this is where Antill was directed to look for a burial plot. Macquarie desired that the opening of the new cemetery be brought forward so that Andrew Thompson would be the first person to be buried there. A 'most beautiful' spot overlooking the

Hawkesbury valley with the Blue Mountains in the background was carefully chosen by Antill for Andrew's final resting place.[22]

At noon 25 October 1810 the casket of the 'much-lamented Gentleman' was taken from his house and ceremonially conveyed to the chapel in Green Hills. Many distinguished officers and gentlemen, both exclusives and emancipists, were among the large congregation at the funeral service delivered by Reverend Cartwright, who gave 'a very elegant and appropriate discourse upon the occasion to one of the most numerous and respectable congregations ever assembled there'.[23] Reverend Samuel Marsden was not among them.

After the church service, the congregation walked the 1.3 km to the new burial ground, known today as St Matthew's Cemetery. Reverend Cartwright led the procession followed by Surgeons Mileham and Redfern 'who had attended the deceased during the long and painful illness that brought to a conclusion an existence that had been well applied'. The bier with Thompson's coffin and the Chief Mourner Captain Antill, representing Governor Macquarie, followed. The pallbearers were William Cox, James Cox, Simeon Lord, Francis Williams, Thomas Arndell and Gregory Blaxland. A long train of men from the Hawkesbury district followed in succession. The remains 'of this true philanthropist were conveyed to the New Burial-ground', where the coffin was deposited in a vault in the presence of the mourners who 'felt the most sensible regret in taking their last farewell of him whose life had been devoted to the service of his fellow creatures'.[24]

Funeral protocol of the time discouraged women from attending the internment, and if they joined the procession, they remained outside the cemetery grounds. As a Catholic, Ellen Moore was not allowed to attend either the church service or the burial. This was an era when most women had to mourn the loss of a friend or family member at home. Many tears were shed during the ceremony and elsewhere in the district. Thompson was the man who had helped save many lives during the floods and, in doing so, had lost his own – it was seen as the ultimate sacrifice. Of equal importance, in better times, this young man had ensured the district's security as the chief constable and helped many setters when they were financially destitute. He had been such a large and beneficial figure of their lives that his passing created a void that few believed could be filled. Men and women in the district, particularly those employed on his many farms and businesses wondered: what was going to happen with his passing? Who would look after them now?

At the conclusion of the funeral service, Andrew Thompson's will was read out by his appointed executives Henry Antill and Thomas Moore.

> In the name of God, Amen, whereas I, Andrew Thompson of the Hawkesbury, one of His Majesty's Justices of the Peace for the County of Cumberland in the Territory of New South Wales, being weak in body but of perfect mind and memory, thanks be given unto God, therefore calling into mind the mortality of my body and knowing that it is appointed for all men once to die do make and ordain this my last Will and Testament all others being null and void, that is to say, First I give and recommend my soul into the hands of Almighty God that gave it and my body to the earth to be buried in decent Christian burial at the discretion of my Executors not doubting but at the General Resurrection. I shall receive the same again by the mighty power of God. And as touching my Estates and worldly goods wherewith it has pleased God to bless me in this life I give, demise and dispose of in the following manner and form, after all and every my just debts are paid.
>
> ITEM: To my beloved and only surviving brother, Walter Thompson of Whitehaven in the Country of Cumberland and Kingdom of Great Brittain [sic] and to the four orphan children left by my beloved brother, William Thompson deceased or to so many of them that are now living, I give and bequeath one half my real and personal property and in case of their decease to the next of kindred.
>
> ITEM: To Lachlan Macquarie, Esquire, Governor of this Territory, I give and bequeath one fourth my real and personal property.
>
> ITEM: To Simeon Lord, Esquire, Merchant of Sydney, I give and bequeath the other fourth of my real and personal property.
>
> ITEM: I also constitute, make and ordain, Captain Antle [sic] of the 73rd Regiment and Thomas Moore, Esquire, of Sydney, my sole executors for carrying this my last Will and Testament into execution.
>
> In Witness whereof I have hereunto set my hand and seal at the Hawkesbury aforesaid this sixth of October in the year of Our Lord one thousand eight hundred and ten.
>
> Andrew Thompson, J.P.
>
> Signed, sealed and declared by the said Andrew Thompson, Esquire, as his last Will and Testament in the presence of us the Subscribers.
>
> Matthew Lock, James Ruse, William Bladdey[25]

Thompson's final bequests are remarkable in a number of respects.

The presence of the Governor Lachlan Macquarie and the merchant Simeon Lord as major beneficiaries caused a sensation in the colony and was to have significant consequences for the governor. Specifically, the inclusion of these two men in the will, and not Andrew's partner, Ellen Moore, deserves some analysis. Men in Andrew's established situation usually left their estate to their nearest and dearest first, close relatives next, and other dependents and charitable concerns last. Andrew had bequeathed half of his huge estate to his family, most of whom he had never met, and the other half to men who would have never expected it and, for that matter, especially in the case of Simeon Lord, did not need it. Moreover, Thompson's last will and testament makes no mention of his close female companion and friend, Ellen Moore.

The bequests to Macquarie and Lord look oddly inappropriate. But Thompson had always been a shrewd man and a strategic planner, and one can be certain that he had chosen his beneficiaries with care. Why then the omission of Ellen Moore? There are probably two good reasons. Andrew's first priority was always going to be his relatives in Britain, and that is where most of his fortune was directed. He had shamed his family two decades previously and always wanted to repair his reputation at home by showing them the respect and success he had earned in New South Wales. Andrew would have known that financial achievement alone was unlikely to gain redemption in the eyes of his proud family; after all, criminals frequently made fortunes. He needed to demonstrate that he had earned acceptance in the highest social circles as well, and to this end, what could be more convincing than to have benefactors in his will with impeccable social qualifications such as the governor, who was a Scottish officer with traditional links to his clan.

The presence of the governor would demonstrate to a family who knew little of his life in New South Wales that he had become a person of honour and consequence in this new land. Andrew saw 'promotion by association' as essential, because, based on the abysmal communications with his brother Walter, it was likely that the family would reject his legacy if they judged it a dishonourable one. In fact the inclusion of Governor Lachlan Macquarie as a co-beneficiary served a dual purpose; it thanked Lachlan and Elizabeth for their generosity and friendship and, most importantly, it confirmed for his family that he had become a respected citizen, a successful farmer and businessman who was honoured at the highest levels of government for his service and endeavour.

But where did Simeon Lord fit into this strategy? Unquestionably Andrew would have pondered long and hard on how to include Ellen in the will without endangering his first priority: to be forgiven by his family. Arriving at an effective plan probably accounts for the numerous revisions of the will in his final days. His main worry was that including Ellen, a widowed catholic woman with whom he had 'lived in sin', in his will would be strongly disapproved of by his devout protestant family and this might negate the benefit of including the governor. And this is where Andrew and Ellen's wealthy Simeon Lord fitted his plan. Despite their different political inclinations, Lord was a friend and business partner of Thompson, and the neighbour of Andrew and Ellen in Sydney. He trusted Lord's financial integrity and knew that any agreement reached with him would be honoured. If part of his estate was bequeathed to Simeon Lord on the understanding that he passed a portion onto Ellen Moore as a pension, he could be certain it would happen. It is possible that Macquarie or Antill also knew of this arrangement and would ensure his wishes were carried out. This *de facto* pension is pure supposition of course, as there is no written record of it. Today such an arrangement seems a ridiculous way to ensure the financial security of a loved one but, considering the sensitivities of his family, it was probably the only way open to Thompson at a time when there were no banks or trustee facilities where long term pension assignments could be made.

Of course, it is also possible that Andrew gave money and property to Ellen Moore prior to his death. No documents have been found to support this, probably because he would have made sure it was never recorded. Evidence of Simeon Lord agreeing to a custodian role for Ellen Moore is purely circumstantial, but the argument for the existence of such a pact is compelling and provides a logical explanation for the will's unexpected beneficiaries. Why else would Andrew Thompson leave Simeon Lord such a substantial legacy and not even partially benefit his many other close friends and business colleagues?

There have been other attempts to explain Thompson's will. Byrnes suggests that Thompson had political motives for making Macquarie a major benefactor. He argues that Thompson wanted to reward the governor for his close friendship but, more importantly, he was determined to undermine John Macarthur's endeavours by strengthening the governor's resolve to promote emancipists as social and business equals. In fact, Macarthur himself attributes such devious motives to Thompson in a letter he wrote to his wife Elizabeth in April 1811. On hearing of the death of his emancipist adversary, he wrote from England:

> I think it an earnest of the interposition of Providence to save the colony from utter ruin. Never was there a more artful or a greater knave. How, how could Governor and Mrs. Macquarie be imposed upon as they have been? I think the last stroke, of leaving the Governor part of his property is by far the deepest he ever attempted, whether I view it as an act done in contemplation of death, or in expectation of raising himself to higher favour should he live.[26]

J. V. Byrnes claims that the inclusion of Macquarie in Thompson's will was principally to benefit Bligh, and to disadvantage Macarthur and the rebels in the upcoming trial of George Johnston. Byrnes envisioned that when the rebels returned to the colony after the trial, they would find 'that Macquarie was chained to his emancipist policy'.[27] This explanation of the beneficiaries is not believable. Thompson disliked Macarthur but malice was not part of his character – he was not a spiteful person in life, so why would he exhibit it in his dying days? One can be reasonably confident that Thompson was not remotely interested in John Macarthur on his deathbed; he had more important family matters to worry about. And, it is unsurprising that Macarthur assumed that Thompson's will was a conspiracy; he believed everyone was scheming against him. Indeed, the converse was much more likely to be true and Andrew never gave this troublemaker another thought.

On the day following the reading of the will, Thompson's business partner Francis Williams returned to Sydney and informed Governor Macquarie of his inheritance. Macquarie wrote in his journal:

> Mr. Fras. Williams Mercht. Sydney returned this day from Hawkesbury from attending the late Mr. Thompson's Funeral and gave me the first intelligence of that worthy good and most useful man having kindly and generously bequeathed to me one fourth of his whole Property; leaving another fourth to Mr. Simeon Lord Mercht. in Sydney, and the remaining Half equally divided between his only surviving Brother and four Nephews by another Brother deceased. The amount of Mr. Thompson's Fortune is very

uncertain; but it is supposed that after all his Debts are paid, and his affairs are properly arranged and adjusted that it may amount to about Twenty or Twenty five Thousand Pounds! – This indeed of leaving a part of his Fortune to me is a most extraordinary instance of Friendship & Gratitude![28]

The governor estimated that Andrew Thompson was worth between £20,000 and £25,000 in 1810 (almost two million pounds sterling today) meaning his own quarter share would be at least £5000. Macquarie saw in Thompson's legacy nothing other than 'Friendship and Gratitude' for him being restored to the society he had once belonged.

> Mr Thompson was born of a respectable family, who, from the time of his conviction, entirely discarded him from all intercourse with them. He felt so much gratitude for being restored to the society he had once forfeited, that in his will he bequeathed to me one-fourth of his fortune.[29]

On 27 October, a day after being informed about his inheritance, Macquarie finished his report to the Colonial Office Secretary, the Earl of Liverpool, to be dispatched in the *Atalanta* sailing for England. At the end of the report, he added a paragraph on the death of Andrew Thompson, 'a most respectable and Opulent Free Settler', whom he had appointed 'Chief Magistrate in the District of the Hawkesbury'. Macquarie pointed out that the executors were eager that Thompson's brother Walter, or one of his nephews, 'should immediately Come out to this Country and take the Charge and Management of his Effects'. Macquarie requested permission for Thompson's relatives be allowed to come to the colony as soon as possible, if one of them 'should make Application to that Effect to Your Lordship'.[30] Macquarie did not mention that he was also a benefactor of the will. He probably considered this a private matter that did not require disclosure under his commission.

The executors Antill and Moore wrote at the same time to Walter Thompson telling him of Andrew's death and asking that someone come to the colony to claim the inheritance. The *Atalanta* left Sydney shortly after and it was expected to take at least eight months to reach England; any reply would take at least eighteen months.

On 27 October editor George Howe published one of the longest obituary notices to appear in *The Sydney Gazette*. He had been an admirer of Andrew Thompson and gave a vivid picture of a worthy man who would be greatly missed in the colony.

> At Hawkesbury, Green Hills, on Monday the 22d Instant, after a lingering and severe illness, aged 37, Andrew Thompson, Esq. Magistrate of that District. In retracing the last twenty years of the Life of this exemplary and much lamented Character will not be held uncharitable to glance at the lapse from rectitude which in an early and inexperienced period of youth destined him to these Shores, since it will stamp a more honourable Tribute to his Memory to have it recorded, that from his first arrival in this Country he uniformly conducted himself with that strict regard to morality and integrity, as to obtain and enjoy the countenance and protection of several succeeding Governors; active, intelligent and industrious, of manners mild and conciliatory, with a heart generous and humane, Mr. Thompson was enabled to accumulate considerable property; and what was more valuable to him, to possess the confidence and esteem of some of the most distinguished Characters in this Country; the consciousness of which surmounted the private solicitude of revisiting his native Country, and led him rather to yield to the wish of passing the evening of his life where his manhood had been meritoriously exerted, than of returning to the land which gave him birth. Mr Thompson's intrinsic good qualities were appreciated by His Excellency the present Governor, who soon after his arrival here was pleased to appoint him a Magistrate, for which situation Mr. Thompson's natural good sense and a superior knowledge of the Laws of his Country peculiarly qualified him.
>
> Nor can we close this Tribute to his Memory without recurring to the important services Mr. Thompson rendered this Colony, and many of his fellow-creatures, during the heavy and public distresses which the floods at the Hawkesbury produced amongst the Settlers in that extensive District; Mr. Thompson's exertions were on a late occasion for two days and two nights unremittingly directed to the assistance of the sufferers, and we hasten to add, that in these offices of humanity, he not only exposed himself to personal danger, but laid the foundation for that illness which has deprived the World of a valuable Life.
>
> During the unfortunate Disturbances which lately disrupted this Colony, he, whose death we now lament, held on the even "Tenor of his Way," and acquitted himself with mildness, moderation, and wisdom, and when the ruthless Hand of Death arrested his earthly career, he yielded with becoming fortitude, and left this World for a better, with humble and devout resignation, and an exemplary confidence in the Mercies of his God![31]

Within days of Thompson's burial, the governor received a formal testimony from Hawkesbury settlers, expressing their deep regret at the death of Andrew Thompson 'which deprived them and that Settlement at large of their "common Friend and Patron"'. The settlers petitioned Macquarie to appoint Francis Williams as the new Magistrate.[32] Williams was Simeon Lord's business partner and husband of Lord's ward, Joanna Short who rented Thompson's Killarney farm since 1809. Macquarie was happy to 'receive so unequivocal a Testimony to the Rectitude of the late Mr. Thompson's general Conduct, both as a Magistrate and as a private Gentleman', but he had already appointed William Cox as Justice of the Peace and Magistrate for the Hawkesbury. Cox was the ex-Corps officer, who had been bankrupted in 1802 at the time Thompson managed his Argyle farm. He proved to be a good choice and quickly became popular in the community. Richard Fitzgerald took over Thompson's post as the Superintendent of Convicts, Cattle and Public Works.[33]

When Henry Antill and Thomas Moore commenced their execution of Thompson's wishes they were unaware of the full extent of his wealth, properties, loans, credits and debts. Thompson had selected his executors knowing they would protect the interests of his beneficiaries and administer the estate until his relatives in England could claim their share. To assist in this, John Howe remained as secretary to the Thompson estate, and the clerks were assigned to the difficult task of recovering outstanding debts. The executors initiated their duties on 3 November 1810 with a notice in *The Sydney Gazette*.

> ANDREW THOMPSON, Esq., late of Hawkesbury in this Territory, deceased, having by his last Will and Testament appointed us, the undersigned, to be the Executors, a Probate of his said last Will and Testament hath been duly obtained; this is therefore to require that all Persons having Claims on the Estate and Effects of the said Andrew Thompson, Esq. will present the same to Mr. John Howe at the Hawkesbury, or Captain Antill at Sydney, on or before the 1st day of December next ; and that all those who may be indebted to the said Estate will liquidate their Accounts respectively within the term above specified; in failure whereof legal measures must necessarily be resorted to, which it is jointly the wish of the Executors to avoid.
>
> (signed) H. C. ANTILL, THOS. MOORE, Executors.[34]

The notice caused many settlers to deliver the grain from their latest harvest to Thompson's store in Green Hills to pay off as much debt as possible. However, a large number of farmers remained in debt to the estate.

On 6 November 1810 Governor Macquarie and Elizabeth led a touring party on a seven-week inspection of all the farming areas in the colony. They wanted to visit all of the large estates and to meet with prominent farming families. Even before the trip commenced Macquarie was certain that some farms and residences would need to be relocated to less flood-prone areas to avoid further loss of lives, animals and crops. He urged the most recent flood victims to move to new towns on higher ground, and over the last few months he had made plans to establish new settlements. Captains Henry Antill and Thomas Cleaveland, Surgeon William Redfern and Surveyor James Meehan, their servants and wagons full of camping gear, accompanied the Macquaries on their tour.[35] When organising the trip, the governor had no idea that some of the farms he would visit partially belonged to him as a result of Thompson's bequest.

On 7 November the tour visited an area on the Georges River prone to flooding, and stayed with Thomas Moore, one of Thompson's executors. Here they surveyed the site for a new town to be named 'Liverpool' in honour of the Earl of Liverpool, the current Colonial Office Secretary. The next day the group traversed the Minto district and, after visiting several large farms, reached 'Mr. Thompson's Farm called St Andrews'. Macquarie stopped 'a little while there to look at this excellent farm belonging to our late worthy friend, which we found in excellent order and in a most improving flourishing state'. He judged this farm, and that of neighbour Dr Townson, to have the finest soil and best pasturage he had yet seen in the colony.[36] It impressed him so much, that he decided to come back two weeks later, on their return from the Cowpastures where the government herds grazed.

The tour group arrived at Thompson's St Andrews farm on 20 November and spent several days exploring the area. Elizabeth was 'much pleased with the beautiful situation of this farm, the picturesque scenes around it, and the great order and regularity in which the worthy deceased owner' had kept it. Thompson had only owned the farm for nine months before 'his much lamented death'. It had an excellent farmhouse with suitable offices, gardens and stockyards, 90 cattle and 1400 sheep, all managed by Joseph Ward and his wife. Macquarie thought that the cattle were 'in very high order and most excellent condition as I ever saw any cattle in, in any country I have visited'.

That evening the tour group was entertained with a plentiful dinner at St Andrews and they toasted the memory of their 'lamented departed friend Andrew Thompson'.[37] Macquarie wrote in his journal of his memories of their lost friend:

> ... and [I] could not help making the melancholy reflection how much more happy we should have been and felt ourselves here had the kind and valuable deceased owner of this estate been alive on it now to receive and entertain us under his hospitable roof! This reflection affected Mrs. M. and myself deeply, for we both had a most sincere and affectionate esteem for our good and most lamented departed friend Andrew Thompson. But alas! How vain are our regrets! He is lost to the world and to us forever, and we must console ourselves with the well grounded hope that he is happier now than if he had remained amongst us.[38]

The group now headed to farms in the Nepean and the Hawkesbury districts. On 30 November 1810 they arrived at Thompson's Agnes Bank farm at the junction of the Nepean and Grose Rivers. Here they set up camp at the Yarramundi Lagoon, which flows through Agnes Bank, and were to be joined by William Cox, the new Magistrate of the district. Macquarie and Elizabeth took a short horse ride around the beautiful lagoon, admiring this and the nearby Thompson farms of Wardle Bank and Glasgow.[39] The next day they went for the first time to Green Hills where Lachlan and Elizabeth were 'quite delighted with the beauty of this part of the country, its great fertility, and its picturesque appearance'.[40] The vista from Government House was dominated by Thompson buildings, which covered much of the precinct.

On Sunday 2 December 1810 Réverend Cartwright gave a church service in Green Hills attended by the governor and his touring party. After the service Lachlan, Elizabeth and Henry Antill rode to the new burial ground to visit the grave of their 'late worthy and highly esteemed good friend Mr. Andw. Thompson'. Macquarie apparently became very emotional at the 'loss we both very sincerely lament and deplore'. Macquarie told Antill that he approved of his choice of the burial site. But he said with regret that if his tour of Green Hills had been only a few months earlier they could have had Thompson's 'superior local knowledge and good sound sense and judicious advice' on their inspections. They stayed for half an hour at their 'friend's tomb', which Macquarie declared he 'intend[ed] to improve and render more elegant & conspicuous as a tribute of regard and friendship for his memory'.[41] He would keep his word.

After the cemetery visit, the three proceeded to Thompson's West Hill and Killarney farms. 'Both very good ones' Macquarie commented, but he observed that many of the settler's houses in the area were 'miserably bad' and were liable to be flooded.[42]

On 6 December, at a dinner in Green Hills, Macquarie delivered his now famous speech announcing the establishment of five new towns on land above the flood plains. He gave the name of 'Windsor' to a town that would replace Green Hills. The village in the Richmond district became the town of 'Richmond' and a settlement in the Nelson district would be called 'Pitt Town' after the 'late great William Pitt, the Minister who originally planned this Colony'. The Phillip district was to have a town named 'Wilberforce', to honour MP William Wilberforce, the famous British opponent of the slave trade. A new town in the Nepean and Evan district was to be called 'Castlereagh', to honour Lord Castlereagh, a past Secretary of the Colonial Office. He requested all his guests to encourage settlers to move their farms as quickly as possible to these places away from the threat of floods.[43]

The following morning Macquarie, Antill, Lord and Moore sailed down the Hawkesbury to Thompson's property on Scotland Island. Only two weeks earlier, the vessel *Geordy*, Thompson's most recent boat, had been launched from Scotland Island. The 18-ton ship was 'said to be one of the finest of her burthen ever built in the Colony'.[44] Sadly, her owner never saw her sail. Nor would he see the launch of his other vessel being build there, the sloop *Whale*.

In early January 1811 the governor's tour of the colony's rural areas drew to a close. During his Hawkesbury stay, Macquarie had surveyed the proposed new town sites and had fixed their locations. He wanted the layout for Windsor to be finalised before returning to Sydney. On Saturday 12 January, assembled residents and farmers from the district watched the erection of a board painted with the name 'Windsor' and markers for new streets were erected. Governor Macquarie named the main street of Windsor 'George Street' in honour of King George III and then declared that:

> The square in the present town I have named Thompson Square in honor of the memory of the good and worthy late Andrew Thompson Esqr. Justice of Peace & Principal Magistrate for this

district, and who may justly be said to be the father and founder of the village hitherto known by the name of the Green Hills; there being hardly a vestage of a single building here, excepting the Government Granary, when he first came to reside on the Green Hills ten years ago. I had a post erected this afternoon in Thompson Square, having a board nailed thereon with the name painted on it in large characters; a similar post and board having been previously erected at the eastern extremity of George Street to mark out that street as the main or principal one in the town of Windsor.[45]

Naming the main square of Windsor after Andrew Thompson was a singular honour for an emancipist, even for someone as famous as the recently deceased Windsor magistrate. Macquarie's decision departed from the long-entrenched practice of commemorating only members of Royalty, eminent politicians, senior members of government and distinguished patrons of the arts. In doing so Macquarie had set another precedent – it was the first time in the colony that an ex-convict had been recognised with such an honour.

Chapter 18

ANDREW'S LEGACY

> *For a man whose influence on this country's history was so powerful, this surely makes Thompson the most unique and intriguing figure in any country's records.*[1]

In early December 1810 the executors of Thompson's Will embarked on the massive task of settling an estate of seven separate farms and in Green Hills a white cottage, a retail store, two warehouses, a brewery, an inn and other buildings. In Sydney, his large dwelling house had to be sold. There were also many personal effects, herds of farm animals, a toll bridge over the South Creek, a leather tannery, a salt works and a shipbuilding yard on Scotland Island, and four seaworthy cargo ships. In accordance with Thompson's instructions everything was to be sold and the money divided among the beneficiaries.

The executors decided some of the assets could be disposed of promptly, while the sale of the larger properties should await the authorisation of the family beneficiaries in Britain. Buildings and farms were to be leased until the executors had their approval. It was quickly realised that the settlement of such diverse holdings would be complex, however, nobody would have appreciated just how complicated it would prove to be. Neither Antill nor Moore could have foreseen the obstacles posed by the remoteness of the family or their reticence to even respond to the executor's letters. This added to the difficulties of disposing of such a huge property portfolio, and to the complexity of resolving the large number of debts and loans. The recovery of Thompson's loans alone clogged up colonial courts for years, and settlement negotiations with the family would not be satisfactorily concluded for decades.

Many people in the colony, both settler-farmers and businessmen, had borrowed heavily from Thompson, sometimes without collateral or time constraints. While the Sydney exclusives tried to exclude Andrew from their social circles, they did not hesitate in borrowing from the wealthy emancipist, and he apparently gave them loans willingly. Thompson's complete credit portfolio did not survive, but we have a fragmentary record of the trials and tribulations the executors faced in recovering many loans. For this reason, assessing the total money owed and recovered for the estate is almost impossible. Just the unpaid promissory notes alone brought before the court in 1812 totalled £4200 (£332,300 today), though not all of this was recovered.[2] Andrew himself had also taken out major loans for the commissioning of his ships and a number of these were outstanding. One thing is certain, Antill and Moore would have regretted on more than one occasion taking on this mammoth settlement task.

Several of the early transactions went smoothly. The first sale of property took place on 15 December 1810 in Sydney, just a week after Macquarie, Lord and Moore had set out from Windsor to inspect Thompson's property on Scotland Island.[3] Thompson's ship the *Governor Bligh* was auctioned along with some of his effects at Lord's warehouse. It returned an impressive sum of £1754. The *Governor Bligh* was bought by Simeon Lord and Francis Williams in order to continue their trading in flax from New Zealand.[4]

Another sale of property was held in Windsor on 27 December, when William Gaudry auctioned items from Thompson's warehouse and furniture from his inn. The properties included tools for shoemakers, blacksmiths and carpenters, hemp and flax, leather, medicines, and shoes. The furniture auctioned comprised beds, sofas, tables, chairs, chests of drawers, tables and household goods. Also sold were six small boats, saddles, bullocks, horses, pigs, wagons and carts. This three-day auction returned £1947.[5] These two initial auctions alone recouped £3701 for the estate (£301,200 today). Shortly after the sloop *Speedwell* was sold to William Johnston.[6]

On 17 January 1811 more of Thompson's ships and effects went under the hammer at Lord's warehouse in Sydney. Included were the schooner *Geordy* and the sloop *Whale*, a number of horses, household furniture and several tons of salt. Henry Kable junior, who had already purchased Thompson's sloop *Hawkesbury*, now bought the *Whale* and the *Geordy*. The latter was purchased jointly with the auctioneer William Gaudry, Kable's brother-in-law.[7]

On 11 February John Howe, as the newly appointed Hawkesbury auctioneer, held a seven-day sale of Thompson's property and effects at Windsor. It was reputed to be the largest auction yet held in the colony with 613 lots going under the hammer. There were an astonishing variety of items; the first day sale included mixed merchandise: frying pans, bedding and blankets, window curtains, women's shifts and frocks, shoemaker's tools, tanned leather for shoes and harnesses, 148 pair of shoes, shoe soles, saddles, tobacco and a large quantity of salt. In the following days livestock, wagons, carts, saddles and harnesses were auctioned. Eighteen horses were sold at prices from £52 to £120, and twelve oxen fetched between £26 and £47 each. The 613 sheep were sold for 14s per head and 41 goats went for 15s each. The average sale price for the 113 pigs on offer was £2 each, while a good sow fetched £16 and a boar £9. There was a variety of material for builders and tradesmen: window glass, paint, brimstones, copperas, nails, ploughs, agriculture tools, casks, razors, 1700 gunflints, sheets of tin, knives, wafers, kangaroo skins, buffalo hides, lead pipes, paint, a variety of timber and bricks. Household items were sold as well: iron pots, paper, handkerchiefs, shawls, needles, twine and medicine, dishes, decanters and wine glasses, knives and forks. The seven-day auction returned £3827 (£311,400 today).[8] Purchasers were required to pay a deposit of 25% in cash or wheat at government price, and the balance over the next six months.[9]

The seven-day Windsor auction also offered two-year leaseholds on some of Thompson's properties. The executors intended these leases to span the time needed for the family in England to respond to their inheritance. Leases were also available for Thompson's buildings in the Windsor government precinct: 'a good Dwelling House, Stores, Granaries, Cellars, Stabling, and Warehouses'; for the brewery, the South Creek toll bridge, and for six of his seven farms – West Hill including Moxham farm and the tannery, Agnes Bank, Wardle Bank, Glasgow, Killarney and Creek Retreat – as well as the salt works and ship building yard on Scotland Island.[10] Most properties were leased promptly, but others took months. Francis Williams renewed his tenancy at Killarney farm for £23 annually and rented the storehouse at Windsor for £140. William Stephens leased a house in Windsor for £12 and Henry Kable, who had already leased the brewery for ten months, renewed his lease for £245 per year. The toll bridge was leased by John Gray, Agnes Bank farm by Joseph Nobbs for £80, Creek Retreat farm by James Blund for £12 and West Hill farm by Matthew Everingham. The government renewed the lease for Ellis Bent on Thompson's Sydney house for £152 per year.[11] The large farm of St Andrews at Minto, with its extensive pastoral holdings, was not leased and remained under the executors' control. The farm, managed by Joseph Ward, was to be used for raising cattle and sheep as a source of meat for the colony.

Andrew Thompson had always resisted using court action to recover debts and he often gave loan extensions. His lenient policies gained him the reputation of being a 'true philanthropist' and a 'Common Friend and Patron'.[12] But this changed with approaching death; in June 1810 33 debtors were taken to court and had to settle their accounts by 1 December. It was now the responsibility of the executors to collect the money and by the court designated deadline only six of the 33 settlers had paid £68. In February 1811 further court action was taken against the remaining 27 defaulters, as well as another sixteen debtors; this action returned £1438 to the estate. Judge Advocate Bent issued writs to eighteen defaulting debtors, ordering the Provost Marshal Palmer to confiscate and auction their grain and animals to raise the money owing.[13]

This way of recovering debt may seem unduly harsh but in the absence of a banking system, property seizure was standard practice in the colony. The governor could, however, limit debt recovery if it was excessive. Traders and moneylenders routinely resorted to repossessions, especially after floods when debt collectors took farmland as repayment. Litigation over debts was frequent and it often overwhelmed the courts. After the 1809 flood, for example, the emancipist Henry Kable sued many Hawkesbury settlers for non-payment of their debts and, as a result of court actions, 51 farm plots were transferred to his name.[14]

On 1 May 1811 Lachlan and Elizabeth Macquarie revisited Windsor to finalise the town's layout of streets and the town square. Once again, painted boards were erected with the newly assigned names. In the last three months Macquarie had made surprisingly few entries into his diary even though he was a prolific chronicler, but, at the close of the first day in Windsor, he sensitively recorded:

> I laid out the Town of Windsor in regular Streets, and formed the open area immediately to the Westward of the Government Domain and the late Mr. Thompson's Premises into a Square. The main or principal Street extending from this Square to the new Township, I have called George Street in honor of His Majesty;

> the new Square I have named Thompson Square, to commemorate the memory of the late Andrew Thompson Esqr., the great Promoter of this Town – and who may justly be called its Founder.[15]

A week later, the Windsor cemetery was officially opened.[16] Until then, Andrew Thompson's grave had been the only one at the site.

Henry Antill, who had just been promoted to the rank of Major, bore most of the responsibility as an executor of Thompson's estate. In the second half of 1811, another 31 men were sued for failing to pay their debts before the deadline. Most of these were promissory notes made out to Thompson, but there were also litigants who were in debt for items bought at recent auctions. In one court sitting Judge Advocate Bent awarded the executors £891 (£70,500 today).[17] The same court issued writs against other debtors to settle immediately or be charged by the provost marshall. Since the annual wage of a labourer was only £10, even a debt of £4 was difficult for many to repay.

An advertisement in *The Sydney Gazette* in November 1811 called for prompt payment of debts to the Thompson estate.[18] The executors soon realised that many settlers devastated by floods had nothing left to settle debts. Moreover, the confiscated property of others attracted no buyers and some items needed to be stored in the same warehouse that contained Thompson goods passed in at auction. To liquidate these, John Howe held another auction at Windsor on 30 November 1811. The auction made £626 for the estate.[19] Much of the furniture from the Red House had been passed in at auction because it was too fancy or too expensive for a settler's wooden house, but it was quite suitable for a governor and was bought for the Government House in Windsor.[20] It meant that whenever Lachlan and Elizabeth Macquarie visited the district, they used the furniture Andrew Thompson had once cherished.

Major Antill was still struggling with his executor's role in April 1811. He gave some insights into his dealings in a letter to John Howe.

> In answer to Mr. Gilberthorpe's request, you may acquaint him that if he wishes to rent the granary from Mr. Everingham he may do so without any fear from me of having his grain seized as I trust Mr. Everingham will pay his rent like an honest man and not put me to the trouble of distraining. …

> I can give Mr. Gaudry no more time. Whenever he is sent for he makes the same excuse. He has had plenty of time. Mr. Kable the same. They seem to contract debts without any wish to discharge, and if we go on at this rate, we shall not realise any prosperity by them for twenty years. I had a letter from Mr. Bell, who, with the rest, pays me with excuses – instead of money. Mr. Robinson the same. ...
>
> A Mr. Hayes came to me yesterday respecting a debt due to him of upwards of £50, but whose name is not down in the lot (list) Smith gave me. Let me know by any opportunity what his balance is, as he (Hayes) says he is willing to receive it in wheat. ... Milward says that he can only pay £40 a year for his debts. I suppose we must take this if we can get no more. Having nothing more to add at present, I have enclosed to you Morley's agreement and Jones's - also. These are all I have of his. Mr. Abbott refuses still to settle for the pigs.[21]

Clearly Antill shared Thompson's sympathy for settlers and a distaste of 'gentlemen debtors' who always had excuses not to pay. In fact, there was an increasing number of 'gentlemen' who had purchased expensive items from the estate and reneged on payment. William Gaudry and Henry Kable jun. were two such defaulters. They had jointly purchased the *Geordy*, and when Gaudry defaulted Antill secured a mortgage on his house in Sydney. He threatened to confiscate the house unless £424 was paid off within six months. The house was eventually seized and in 1813 William Gaudry was also compelled to sell the *Geordy*. Henry Kable had also reneged on payments and eight years later Antill made him sell property in Windsor and elsewhere, to settle his debts.[22]

A recurrent problem for Thompson's executors was the realistic estimation of the retrievable value of the estate. Without it any proportioning of funds to beneficiaries was almost impossible. One impediment to valuing the estate was the uncertainty of Thompson's own liabilities. Antill paid off any debts he was confident were valid, but he contested claims where the loan or payment records were insufficient. Thompson had routinely borrowed funds to finance land acquisitions and building projects, and also to construct ships. Because there were no financial institutions, moneylenders were private individuals who often did not like to publicise their usury practices. Some were merchants in England, but Simeon Lord also lent money to Thompson and the executors paid £4000 owed to him.[23] Despite Antill's diligence, on three occasions the Thompson estate was sued for unpaid debts. It lost two of these actions, paying £945 to two plaintiffs but won a third for £384.[24] In 32 cases executors were awarded £665 for unpaid promissory notes.[25]

The executors also found it hard to retrieve debts from small settlers affected by floods. If these men delivered their grain to the government store, the cash they received was rarely used to repay debts to the deceased estate. To enforce this, Antill instructed indebted settlers to take their grain directly to a Windsor storehouse he partially rented from Francis Williams, and from here he sold it to the government store.[26] Because Governor Macquarie was a beneficiary of the will, and had a vested interest in these transactions, he 'never took any charge or share in the management of the estate of Mr. Thompson'. Grain was commonly used for currency exchange and in late 1812, Antill delivered 3139 bushels of wheat into the government stores at Windsor and Sydney with a value of £1425 (£102,100 today).[27]

Two years had now passed since Andrew Thompson's death. The ship *Atalanta* had reached England in July 1811 with a letter informing the Thompson family of Andrew's death and their inheritance.[28] Antill and Moore estimated it would take at least two years before a reply could be expected. When no response had been received by August 1812, they decided to sell some of Thompson's buildings and rent out his farms for a further year, so as to allow the family to properly take possession of their inheritance. In September 1812 the premises adjacent to Thompson's brewery were leased to the government for an annual rent of £135. The main building would serve a dual purpose; the ground floor would be a military barracks and the top floor a hospital. The other buildings were used as the courthouse and a gaol.[29]

The government was also interested in Thompson's storehouse and other premises on Thompson Square. These included his white cottage, retail store, warehouse, offices, stables and coach house. On the advice of two builders, John Howe valued these at £1844. The governor sought the opinion of three other men, who valued them at £1500. Richard Fitzgerald, now the Windsor government storekeeper, was instructed to bid for Thompson's buildings at the upcoming auction.[30] On 9 November 1812 all of Thompson's remaining Windsor properties were auctioned: the granary, the

Thompson Square buildings, the brewery with malt house, a kiln, the granary and brewing utensils, a two-storey building with eight tenements of two rooms each, and two small building plots. Extended rents were also offered on the South Creek toll bridge, and the salt facility and shipbuilding yard on Scotland Island.[31]

Richard Fitzgerald acting on behalf of the government successfully bid £1500 for the granary and surrounding premises.[32] This was one of the few sales. The bids for the brewery failed to reach the reserve price. Antill eventually accepted the offer of Richard Woodbury, who had previously made beer for both Andrew Thompson and Henry Kable, to continue brewing for another year at the lower rent of £100.[33]

A recent photo showing Andrew Thompson's grave (front) in the St Matthew's cemetery Windsor. It was the first burial in the cemetery. The original gravestone was elevated on the four stone pillars.

In early 1813, true to his promise of two years ago, Governor Macquarie commissioned a large tombstone for Andrew Thompson's grave at St Matthew's cemetery. It was engraved with a heartfelt epitaph written by Lachlan. His words reflect genuine grief and recall aspects of Thompson's life, bravery and illness. In July 1813 Lachlan and Elizabeth were present for the laying of the tombstone on Thompson's grave.

SACRED to the MEMORY
of
ANDREW THOMPSON ESQUIRE

> Justice of the Peace and Chief Magistrate of the Hawkesbury a Native of Scotland Who at the age of 17 Years was sent to this Country who from the time of his arrival he distinguished himself by the most persevering industry and diligent attention to the commands of his Superiors. By these means he raised himself to a state of respectability and affluence which enabled him to indulge the generosity of his nature in assisting his Fellow Creatures in distress more particularly in the Calamitous Floods of the river Hawkesbury in the Years 1806 and 1809 and at the immediate risque of his life and permanent injury of his health he exerted himself each time during three successive Days and Nights in saving the lives and Properties of numbers who but for him must have Perished.
>
> In consequence of Mr Thompson's good Conduct Governor Macquarie appointed him a Justice of the Peace. This act which restored him to that rank in Society which he had lost made so deep an impression on his grateful Heart as to induce him to bequeath to the Governor one fourth of his Fortune. This most useful and valuable Man closed his Earthly career on the 22nd Day of October 1810 at His House at Windsor of which he was the principal Founder in the 37th Year of his age with the Hope of Eternal Life.

From respect and esteem for the Memory
of the deceased
this Monument is erected by
LACHLAN MACQUARIE GOVERNOR
of New South Wales
A.D. 1813[34]

Originally the tombstone was elevated as an altar on the four pillars; today these pillars flank the tablet.[35] It has undergone several restorations to improve legibility of the inscription, the last in 2010. Today it is only just readable.

Throughout his term of office Lachlan Macquarie continued to promote egalitarian principles across the colony. His determination to rehabilitate convicts rather than punish them, and to promote emancipists, was doggedly resisted by exclusives in the colony. Samuel Marsden was among those who complained bitterly to the Colonial Office, and the topic of convict treatment and social distinction became issues that were hotly debated in Britain's parliament. In 1812, the British government set up a Parliamentary Select Committee to enquire into the transportation of convicts and the efficacy of their punishment. In late June 1813 Macquarie received their report and accepted the recommended reforms to the law courts and for trial by jury. However, he strongly rejected the criticism of his social acceptance of emancipists and that ex-convicts should not serve on a 'petty and Grand Jury'. He wrote bitingly to the Colonial Office that free settlers who opposed emancipists having equal social standing should reconsider coming to the colony at all.[36]

> It has been My Invariable Opinion, and Upon that Opinion I have Acted ever since I Came to this Colony, that, Once a Convict had become a Free Man, either by Servitude, Free Pardon, or Emancipation, he should in All Respects be Considered on a footing with every other Man in the Colony, according to his Rank in Life and Character. In Short, that no Retrospect Should in any Case be had to his having been a Convict.[37]

In March 1814 Elizabeth Macquarie gave birth to a son after many miscarriages. He was named Lachlan and two months later the governor proudly informed his brother Charles in Scotland of the happy event. He added a less happy note to the letter, telling Charles that his bequest from the Thompson estate was likely to be small.

> I am sorry to tell you that all my fine expectations of greatly increasing my private fortune from poor, good Andrew Thompson's legacy have vanished into air. At one time I expected to receive about £7,000 – the £5,000 – then £3,000 – but now I really do not think I shall ever pocket £500 from that good man's legacy.[38]

Macquarie's guess at the value of his bequest was overly pessimistic, but at the time the sale of the estate was slow and so was the recovery of loans. Also, Macquarie had little knowledge of the extent of Thompson's holdings and no appreciation of his other revenue sources – yearly rents for buildings and farms; grain and meat delivered to stores, livestock sold from farms and loans eventually recouped. It would take over 15 years to finally settle the estate. An estimate of its value from known auctions, grain sales and yearly rentals exceeded £24,000 in 1819. The final assessed value may have been much higher. Additionally, the courts recovered loans valued at over £4500. How much of this was needed to pay Thompson's debts and cover executor expenses is uncertain, but it was at least £5000. The best estimate of the recovered value of the estate is between £20,000 and £25,000. Lachlan would have received a quarter of this, and when the Macquaries returned to Britain in 1822 a significant amount of their property and wealth remained in the colony. Elizabeth had shares in the recently founded Bank of New South Wales valued at £500, and there were 263 cattle in her name on Henry Antill's property at Picton. Since each cow was worth £20, it could be surmised that the Macquaries were worth over £6000 in colonial assets and a significant portion of this probably came from the Thompson settlement.[39]

In any case, Governor Macquarie had far more pressing issues to deal with in 1815 than worrying about Thompson's bequest. Judge Advocate Ellis Bent, who had arrived in the colony with Macquarie, initially collaborated well with him but by 1814 Bent had started to object to his egalitarian policies. Bent permitted three emancipists qualified in law to practise in the Court of Civil Jurisdiction but only if attorneys without a criminal past were unavailable. Emancipists were only allowed to be specially appointed agents for plaintiffs or defendants who needed their services. Two of these men, George Crossley and Edward Eagar, acted for Thompson's executors in 20 debtors' cases and recovered £858.[40]

Ellis Bent's opposition to Macquarie's emancipist policies hardened with the arrival of his brother Jeffery, who was the first Supreme Court Justice in the colony. Because of Jeffery's extremely conservative views, the Bents began to support Samuel Marsden's strong opposition to the advancement of emancipists in society. Jeffery Bent defied Macquarie's request for emancipist attorneys to be allowed to serve in the Supreme Court, and he blocked court sittings for five months until a lawyer from England arrived and a more auspicious building was found for the Supreme Court. The Bent brothers became so obstructive that Macquarie informed the Colonial Office that he would quit unless they were replaced. The brothers were eventually recalled but by then the sickly Ellis had died.[41] Jeffery returned to England and heavily criticised Macquarie in British parliamentary circles. Macquarie remained largely indifferent to these criticisms and where possible he continued to help emancipists progress in business and society.

At the close of 1814, four years after Thompson's death, no word had yet been received from Walter about the inheritance. Antill and Moore wrote again pleading for either an acceptance or a refusal of the bequest. The serious concerns Andrew Thompson had long harboured about Walter not accepting his attempt to seek reconciliation with his family were indeed well founded – so far they appeared to view the inheritance from a convict relative as quite unworthy of their consideration.

Walter Thompson was still a bachelor working as a draper in the small town of Workington on the west coast of England. He had adopted the orphaned children, John, Robert, Jean and Margaret, when his brother William had died twelve years earlier. On the ground floor of Walter's house was a shop and he had another shop in Whitehaven, eight miles to the south. Both boys John and Robert worked in his stores, and in 1812 John moved permanently to Whitehaven where he married and would raise nine children.[42]

Walter was a successful fabric merchant, but he was by no means wealthy enough to ignore the inheritance. His reluctance to respond to the executors' letters suggests he had not forgiven Andrew for the shame and disgrace his theft had brought on the Thompson family. Walter had only communicated with Andrew twice in eighteen years; once to tell him of William's death and again to refuse his offer to adopt two of the children. He had declined Andrew's offer in the full knowledge that the children would have led a more prosperous life in the colony. Walter's refusal of help was probably because of pride, but religion may have also played a part. It would seem that the same concerns were dictating the response to Andrew's second, posthumous, much larger offer.

Of course, the prejudices against transported convicts prevalent in England in the early 19th century could well have had a bearing on the acceptance of the inheritance. The textile and church communities in Workington might have been critical of Walter if he accepted money from his convict brother. The New South Wales colony was invariably portrayed in the English press as a place of immorality and depravity – a reputation that suited the Tories who wanted the penal settlement to be seen this way in order to deter criminals. In reality, life in the colony, even for convicts, was reasonably good and many had a better standard of living than those in rural England. The Thompson family would not have known this, and since his brother William later had become a minister in a Scottish Church just north of Glasgow, there may have been serious religious concerns that their erstwhile relative's earnings had been acquired dishonestly, and that accepting it would be sinful.[43]

By 1815 the executors had still not received an answer from Walter Thompson about the bequest and, with Macquarie threatening to soon leave the colony, there was added pressure for them to finalise the settlement. They agreed that additional properties must be sold. The Glasgow farm on the Nepean River had already been bought by Thomas Wayham in the previous year.[44] In January 1815 two auctions were organised, and because of past non-payments, promissory notes and grain were not permitted as payment.[45] Prior to the auction John Howe was instructed by the executors to purchase the brewery for the government. Constable William Bladdey, Thompson's old friend who had witnessed his will, acted as Howe's proxy and bought the brewery, land and the nearby cottage for £500. The brewery would become a general hospital for up to 50 patients.[46] Months later Agnes Bank farm was sold for £500 to John Campbell, Macquarie's secretary, and Killarney farm to Edward Redmond.[47]

Debts owed to Thompson's estate were now pursued vigorously in the courts. The arrival in late 1816 of the new Judge Advocate John Wylde enabled Antill to launch a series of court actions. Later, lawyer Thomas Amos was engaged to recover debts in the Supreme Court presided over by the new Judge Barron Field.[48] In an article *Andrew Thompson: Macquarie and the Thompson Legacy*, J. V. Byrnes is very critical of Macquarie accepting Thompson's bequest and of the ruthless way executors sought to recover monies owed to the estate. For reasons that appear to be strongly influenced by the Bigge Report, he portrays the governor as a rapacious opportunist and declares that 'Macquarie's reputation as the greatest champion of the emancipists is only another Australian legend'.[49] There seems very little justification for this conclusion, especially if they are based on the intentionally prejudicial comments and disputed findings published in the 1822 and 1823 Bigge Reports.

By 1817 the concerns of the British Tory government with Macquarie's enlightened treatment of convicts and emancipists were reaching a crescendo. The repeated complaints from Sydney exclusives of Macquarie's promotion of emancipists received an increasingly receptive ear at the Colonial Office and many politicians in Britain were starting to question if the convict transportation system was fit for purpose. The stories of ex-convicts making fortunes in the colony and of governors assisting and benefiting from this largesse was certainly not the image the British Tories wanted to portray of a penal colony. It was expensive to transport convicts to Sydney, and if convicts expressed willingness and indeed a desire to make the journey, it was no longer an effective deterrent to petty crime! Macquarie's administration was deemed to be far too generous – lawmakers in Britain wanted a sentence of transportation to be feared by the criminal class, not welcomed. Despite being an excellent administrator Macquarie's reputation had been ruined in the eyes of many British politicians. What is more, he had now been in the office for eight years, much longer than previous governors. Macquarie realised that he had lost the respect of the Colonial Office and on 1 December 1817 he resigned.[50] It would take another four years before the replacement governor arrive in Sydney.

With Macquarie's resignation, the executors Antill and Moore knew that Thompson's estate had to be settled immediately. In September 1818 Antill tried to sell the remaining properties through Simeon Lord's auction house at Macquarie Place. Lots were offered without a reserve price, with buyers needing to make immediate cash purchases. The Green Hills barracks were sold to Samuel Terry for £120 and Scotland Island to Robert Murray but the rest remained unsold. A year later John Campbell bought West Hill farm for £450, his second farm from the estate.[51]

British parliamentarians on both sides of the political divide were becoming increasingly opposed to transportation being a remedy to overcrowded gaols. On his return to England, Jeffery Bent assisted MP Henry Gray Bennet to vilify both the governance of the NSW colony and the role of Lachlan Macquarie. This led to the creation of a 'Select Committee on the State of Gaols in London' in 1819 headed by the Colonial Office Secretary, Henry Bathurst. Nine years after his death, Andrew Thompson's life in the colony was examined by this committee to try and understand why he was so successful. They heard evidence from past residents such as Alexander Riley, secretary to Colonel Paterson, Jeffery Bent and John Macarthur Junior. Riley's views on Thompson's appointment as magistrate were commonly held by the Sydney exclusives.

> The appointment unquestionably materially lessened the respect of the inhabitants towards the magistracy; and it was viewed by the mercantile connections of the colony abroad, and by every stranger who visited it, in the same light.[52]

When questioned if Thompson was a person who had 'redeemed his character from the original stigma' of being a convict, Riley replied:

> He was certainly a man of much industry and enterprise, and in that point of view had been considered of service to the colony.[53]

Nevertheless, in his opinion Thompson's reputation was not 'sufficient to perform the duty of a magistrate'. When asked what the offence for which Thompson had been transported, Riley showed how little he actually knew about the young Scot.

> I have understood for setting some property on fire in Scotland; I have heard it stated that his original offence was comparatively trivial to that of persons who are sent in general to New South Wales, and that he was, I believe, very young at the time.[54]

Of course, Andrew is unlikely to have disclosed much about his juvenile crime to anyone in the colony, it was a lifelong source of embarrassment to him. Riley espoused even more nonsense when he claimed Thompson had many illegitimate children.[55] Riley's attempts to ridicule Thompson went on and on; all his evidence was aimed at denigrating Governor Macquarie's emancipist policies.

As part of the enquiry by the 1819 Select Committee on the State of Gaols, John Bigge was sent out to Sydney to report back on all aspects of the NSW government administration. The Colonial Office seriously doubted if transportation provided a cost-effective way of punishing convicts and deterring crime, and they instructed Bigge to examine the governance of the NSW colony with this in mind. They commissioned him to find out if transportation was the 'severe Punishment' intended, and whether it was 'an Object of real Terror to all Classes of the Community'.[56] Secretary Bathurst believed the Botany Bay Scheme had worked initially because of the perceived remoteness and harshness of the colony, but if this were no longer true, convict transportation was not a deterrent to crime. The official brief given to Commissioner Bigge clearly implied that Macquarie was the main cause of this change in perception.

Bathurst had replied to Macquarie's resignation letter by asking him to postpone his decision. But this letter had been lost in transit, and when Commissioner John Bigge arrived in Sydney Macquarie had still not heard from Bathurst. The unexpected appearance of an official who, according to his brief, seemed to have authority over him confounded Macquarie. He had governed the prospering colony successfully for a decade, and he expected a positive and deferential interaction with the Commissioner. But Commissioner Bigge criticised both Macquarie's humanitarian treatment of convicts and his advancement of emancipists. He even went as far as opposing the new appointment of the emancipist surgeon William Redfern to the position of magistrate. Bigge declared that emancipist magistrates endangered the colony, and that Andrew Thompson and Simeon Lord should not have been appointed.

Portrait of Simeon Lord, Thompson's friend and a major beneficiary of his will.

Portrait of Major Henry Colden Antill, an executor of Andrew Thompson's estate.

The extensive notes Bigge gathered from his interviews portray a vivid picture of the jealousies and prejudices of the time. They are full of inaccuracies and unverified statements intended to vilify Macquarie. Information on Andrew Thompson and his estate were seen by Bigge as central to his study of Macquarie's administration. He visited Thompson's tombstone to read what Macquarie had said of the man and even questioned whether Thompson's rescues of flooded settlers were humanitarian or 'self-interest in supplying them with his own goods'. Bigge inferred that Thompson's 'claim to the praise of great humanity' was 'questionable'.[57] John Macarthur, who had returned to the colony, heavily influenced Bigge's final report and his views were often used as Bigge's own conclusions, many being only gossip, hearsay and lies. M. H. Ellis writes in his book *Lachlan Macquarie* that in Bigge's report 'Both in the recording of "evidence" and of findings there is slovenliness. The reports teem with error from end to end'.[58]

To belittle Andrew Thompson's reputation, Bigge made adverse entries on his parents, his private and immoral life, his businesses, his dining at the governor's table, his flood rescues, his appointment as magistrate, the turnpike road trusteeship and his will. Bigge searched for evidence that the governor, as a beneficiary of Thompson's estate, had somehow misappropriated funds. He found nothing, but his reports are loaded with implications of collusion and preferential treatment. Even Henry Antill was required to give evidence to Bigge on what Macquarie and Lord had gained from the estate, the reasons why Thompson's buildings had been bought by the government, and if grain sold from Thompson's estate had received preferential treatment by the government store. The unimpressed Antill kept his answers brief and provided as little personal information as possible – he made every effort to protect both Thompson's and Macquarie's reputation.[59] Bigge departed the colony for England in February 1821, and his first report was presented to the British Parliament in July 1822.

Lachlan Macquarie's health was failing, and Bigge's depressing visit had increased his desire to return to Scotland as soon as possible. After a decade of leadership, he was weary of defending what he saw as self-evident rights and he submitted another resignation letter in February 1820.[60] In March 1821 Macquarie received confirmation from Bathurst that this had been accepted but was asked to await the arrival of his successor.[61]

Governor Macquarie had never considered himself a reformer, but his policies were progressive and well before their time. Conservatives in the colony and in Britain saw him as a radical who needed to be reined in quickly. His influence on the colony's growth and prosperity had been colossal and, during his administration, building construction had advanced the infrastructure of the colony beyond recognition. Importantly, under his guidance the political astuteness of many emancipists had matured, and they now demanded fair and equitable treatment as a right. Any attempt to reverse these rights, either from within or from without the colony, would meet with fierce resistance. Andrew Thompson had played a major part in their political aspirations and was recognised as being a leading figure in their democratisation.

Lachlan Macquarie would soon leave the colony, but his Aide-de-Camp Henry Antill would remain. In 1818 he had married Eliza Wills, the daughter of an emancipist. In December 1820 the last property of the Thompson's estate, St Andrews farm, went under the hammer at Lord's auction rooms and was sold for £1300 to James Chisholm.[62] The settlement of the Thompson estate had been frustratingly slow for everyone involved. Despite countless court actions, many debts remained unpaid and ten years after Thompson's death only a fraction of the estate's value had been distributed to the beneficiaries.[63]

Little is known of Ellen Moore during these intervening years. She was still 'single' in 1821, having her own mantua business in Sydney, making elaborate dresses, coats and hats for the society ladies.[64] One wonders why she was still working at the age of 54? Of course, the Thompson estate had only been partially settled by then and Simeon Lord may not have been able to pass on much to Ellen, assuming that a pension for her was implicit in Thompson's settlement arrangements. Whatever the reason, this industrious lady preferred doing business than sitting home – it was this energy and spirit that had attracted Andrew Thompson in the first place. In the 1822 Muster, Mrs Moore is shown as a 'housekeeper' in Sydney but a year later Governor Brisbane granted her a land lease in Pitt Street where, in the 1825 Muster, she is listed again as a 'dressmaker'.[65] Ellen was one of the few women in the colony to have received two land leases – an honour only possible if she had an unblemished personal and business reputation. In 1825 the Thompson estate was finally settled, and Simeon Lord received his full bequest. By August 1826 Mrs Moore had become part of Sydney society and is recorded as donating money to the School of Industry for the education of female servants.[66] Ellen died on 12 November 1826 at the age of 59 at her Pitt Street house and was buried at the catholic St Mary's cemetery in Sydney. Her death was announced in *The Sydney Gazette* three days later. Ellen left an estate large enough to require two executors to oversee its settlement.[67]

The sixth Governor of New South Wales, Sir Thomas Brisbane, arrived unexpectedly on 14 November 1821 while the incumbent was on an official visit to Port Macquarie in the north. Brisbane quickly assumed office and on 12 February 1822 Macquarie and his family were ceremonially escorted to the transport ship *Surry* by his old regiment and military bands. Sydney, the city that Macquarie had largely built, was festooned in flags and the shore lined with cheering crowds as they proceeded to the docks. When Macquarie boarded the *Surry*, a 19-gun salute rang out in his honour. *The Sydney Gazette* newspaper captured the sentiments of the colony, reporting 'Never did Sydney Cove look so attractive and gay, as upon this occasion; and the shores were lined with spectators innumerable ... Australia saw her Benefactor, for the last time, treading her once uncivilized and unsocial shores and felt it too; – the parent and the child must endure the parting pang!' Macquarie had dedicated eleven industrious years of his life to the colony, and he was deeply moved by the occasion.[68]

The Macquaries reached London in July 1822 at the same time Bigge's first report was tabled in the House of Commons. Lachlan lost no time in seeing Colonial Secretary Bathurst, but he withheld comment on Bigge's report until all versions had been tabled a year later. The Report was critical of his liberal policies and would eventually lead to major changes to the British penal system. It advised increasing convict punishments to a level where even the hardest criminals in Britain would fear transportation. It also reversed Macquarie's policies on convict rehabilitation, emancipist rights and public works expenditure.

In December 1822 Lachlan and Elizabeth Macquarie went on a grand tour of Europe. While in France in July 1823 Lachlan Macquarie wrote his response to the findings of the Bigge Reports in which he delivered a lengthy rebuttal to Bathurst of 'Bigge's false, vindictive, & malicious' accounts and conclusions.[69] In response to the charge that he appointed 'improper persons to be magistrates' Macquarie stated he had selected men he 'considered most fit to fill that important office'. He added that he thought it highly inappropriate that a decade after his death, Andrew Thompson's name was so unfairly maligned.

> In his [Bigge] reverting to the birth, education and character of Mr.

Andrew Thompson, ten years after his death, he ought, in justice to me, to have gone back a little further, and to have condemned all my predecessors in office for their partiality to that person and the trust they reposed in him. I found him in the situation of chief constable, being then the principle [sic] man at the head of the police department at Windsor: Mr. Arndell, though nominally a magistrate, being superannuated. In the various services he performed for the government, I never heard of a complaint against him. He was on term of intimacy with many of the most respectable gentlemen in the colony, and was much liked: in the number of friends I may mention that excellent and worthy man, the Reverend Mr. Cartwright, who was then the resident chaplain at Windsor, and would not have considered him worthy of a funeral sermon if he had been so loose and so immoral a character.[70]

Macquarie also commented on the concerns of Andrew Thompson's family, and that neither the passage of time nor Andrew's subsequent advancement eased their sense of disgrace:

> ... although he had in an evil hour fallen under the lash of the law, he was by birth far removed from the dregs of society, and of honest though humble parents; as may be inferred from the indignation of his family, and their sense of disgrace by his temporary lapse, which no time could mitigate, nor any atonement on his part assuage. Some estimate of their character may be formed from the pride with which they disdained even to assist in realising the property which he bequeathed to them, although invited by me to depute one of their number to New South Wales for that purpose; a species of self-denial which would probably have cost many of their superiors a struggle.[71]

Macquarie's letter written in 1823, thirteen years after Andrew Thompson's death, indicates clearly the difficulties encountered reaching a final settlement of his will. Walter had still not written to Antill to claim his portion of the estate, despite being personally invited by Macquarie to do so. However, Walter had not specifically declined the inheritance either. His indecisiveness had caused legal problems in transferring the deeds of the estate's sold properties requiring the authorisation of all beneficiaries. It was essential that the Thompson family made a decision.

Macquarie wrote another letter to Walter. The contents of the letter are unknown, but it was certain to have expressed his esteem, appreciation and friendship towards Andrew. This intervention drew a response and, fifteen years after it was initially offered, the family agreed to accept the half share of the disgraced brother's estate. It took the personal intervention of Lachlan Macquarie, as Andrew Thompson's past governor and friend, to convince them that he had been a highly respected member of the colony, and that accepting his bequest was by no means a shameful act.

Lachlan and Elizabeth Macquarie returned from Europe in August 1823 and went to live on the Scottish Isle of Mull. Lachlan died on 1 July 1824 aged 62 while in London defending himself against Bigge's charges. Sadly, he never received the accolades in Britain he so richly deserved for his diligent and industrious governorship of New South Wales. In contrast, he is held in the highest regard in Australia for his leadership, energy and humanity, and is often cited as the 'Father of Australia'.[72]

On 25 August 1825, brother Walter, nephews John and Robert and niece Jean corresponded with Henry Antill and signed a letter accepting the inheritance of Andrew.

> Names of the Parties: Walter Thompson of Whitehaven in the Country of Cumberland Mercer Robert Thompson of Workington in the said County Mercer John Thompson of Whitehaven aforesaid Mercer and Jean Thompson of Workington aforesaid Spinster to H. C. Antill of Hawkesbury in the Country of Cumberland New South Wales
>
> Description of the Lands or Property conveyed: To sell and absolutely dispose of and convert into money all and every the manors messuages farms lands tenements and hereditaments estate and effects situate in the said County of Cumberland and Territory of New South Wales belonging and appertaining to us are entitled under or in pursuance of the will of the said testator Andrew Thompson deceased or wherein we or any or either of us have or hath or any person or persons in trust for us or any of us have or hath any estate or interest whatsoever for such price or prices sum or sums of money or other equivalent and by such ways and means as our said Attorney may deem most reasonable and prudent And on such sale or sales being effected for us and each and every of us and in our and each and every of our names and name and as our and each and every of our acts and deeds by all due proper and necessary instruments or conveyances to convey and dispose of the said manors messuages tenements lands hereditaments estate and effects to the person or persons who may happen to become the purchaser or purchasers thereof[73]

There is no indication that Walter ever forgave his brother. The decision to accept the inheritance may well have been influenced by the younger family members, and Walter had agreed for their sake.

One of the nieces, Margaret, had died in 1821 aged 25, and Walter may have decided that the others should benefit from Andrew's legacy. There is no record of how the inheritance was accredited to the family but presumably it was paid to Walter and proportioned to the two nephews and the niece. The surviving niece, Jean, was still a spinster at the age of 33, but a year after accepting the bequest she married – her increased dowry may have helped her find a husband. Walter Thompson lived only three more years and died in Workington aged 62. His estate in 1828 had an assessed value of £14,000. Walter's house and shop went to John and the rest of the estate was divided between John, Robert and Jean.[74]

Robert never married and remained in the business in Workington. John successfully expanded his Whitehaven draper business and was able to send three of his boys to university.[75] His son John became a medical doctor, Charles a solicitor, and William studied theology at Oxford. In 1840 William was an ordained minister in the Church of England and he eventually rose in the church hierarchy to become the Archbishop of York in 1862.

It is entirely possible that Andrew Thompson's inheritance had benefited his nephew John's family in their careers. Gaining degrees at prestigious universities was costly and usually only affordable by the wealthy and privileged. Possibly John had made his own fortune, but the inheritance money would certainly have helped. Whatever the reasons, Andrew would have had cause to be proud that his successful life had finally allowed some closure on the disgrace of his youthful conviction.

The final value that Andrew Thompson's estate may never be known. The settlement process was long and tortuous, and a complete record of the accounts has not been found. It is possible that they were never completely and coherently recorded, despite Antill and Moore's strenuous efforts. Even if Thompson's estate was only worth £20,000, the family in England would have benefited by £10,000 in 1825 (almost one million pounds in today's currency).

Thompson Family Tree

John THOMPSON
b. 1725, Yetholm
& Agnes HILSON
b. 1733, Sprouston

Children of John THOMPSON & Agnes HILSON:

- **Margaret THOMPSON** — b. 1761, Yetholm; d. 1770, Yetholm
- **William THOMPSON** — b. 1762, Yetholm; d. 1801, Glasgow
  & Jean YOUNG — b. 1759, Yetholm; d. 1802, Glasgow
- **Walter THOMPSON** — b. 1765, Yetholm; d. 1828, Workington
- **John THOMPSON** — b. 1767, Yetholm
- **Robert THOMPSON** — b. 1770, Yetholm; d. 1773, Yetholm
- **Andrew THOMPSON** — b. Feb 1773, Yetholm; d. 22 Oct 1810, Windsor

Children of William THOMPSON & Jean YOUNG:

- **John THOMPSON** — b. 1787, Yetholm; d. 1878, York
  & Isabella THOMPSON — b. 1787, Whitehaven; d. 1847, Whitehaven
- **Robert THOMPSON** — b. 1789, Yetholm; d. 1840, Workington
- **Jean THOMPSON** — b. 1793, Glasgow
  & Thomas MARTIN
- **Agnes THOMPSON** — b. 1794, Glasgow; d. 1795, Glasgow
- **Margaret THOMPSON** — b. 1796, Glasgow; d. 1821, Workington
- **Walter THOMPSON** — b. 1799, Glasgow

(Walter THOMPSON married 1802)

Children of John THOMPSON & Isabella THOMPSON:

- **Jean THOMPSON** — b. 1812, Whitehaven; d. 1879, Whitehaven
- **Ann THOMPSON** — b. 1814, Whitehaven; d. 1823, Whitehaven
- **Agnes THOMPSON** — b. 1816, Whitehaven; d. 1819, Whitehaven
- **William THOMPSON** — b. 1819, Whitehaven; d. 1890, York
- **John THOMPSON** — b. 1821, Whitehaven; d. 1866, Whitehaven
- **Walter Home THOMPSON** — b. 1823, Whitehaven; d. 1848, Whitehaven
- **Isabella THOMPSON** — b. 1826, Whitehaven; d. 1897, Whitehaven
- **Edward THOMPSON** — b. 1828, Whitehaven; d. 1873, Paris
- **Charles Robert THOMPSON** — b. 1831, Whitehaven; d. bef 1878

Epilogue

Andrew Thompson was one of the most remarkable men in colonial New South Wales. His progression from a boy transportee to chief constable, businessman, ship owner, brewer, emancipist magistrate, and the friend of governors, places him at the forefront of Australian pioneers. He was also an emancipist leader who contributed greatly to the economic and political development of the colony in its earliest years. Acknowledging this is critical to help refute early histories that portray transportees in largely negative roles. Recent well-researched histories increasingly show that the converse was often true.

Thompson's life and work is acknowledged today in various places. The suburb of *St Andrews* in Campbelltown is named after his farm, *Andrew Thompson Drive* is in McGraths Hill at the site of his West Hill farm and there is a *Thompson Street* on Scotland Island. Governor Macquarie proclaimed Andrew Thompson to be the 'Founder of Windsor' and named the Windsor central park *Thompson Square* after him. Today it is the oldest town square in Australia and the historic heart of the old Green Hills village.

The square has gained prominence recently because it is now traversed by roads leading to a new concrete bridge replacing the old bridge over the Hawkesbury River. The recent construction of the new Windsor bridge and its access roads required the excavation of a historical part of the town containing many of the foundations of early colonial buildings, including some that Andrew Thompson had built in the old government precinct. Significant archaeological evidence of the early colonial period has certainly been lost. For this reason, residents lobbied for years in an attempt to stop the new bridge being built on such an important historical site, when an equally effective crossing site existed out of Windsor further along the Hawkesbury River. Sadly, these determined efforts failed.

Fortunately, Andrew Thompson did not witness the desecration of what artifacts remained of the earliest European settlers. As an avid bridge builder himself, well read in history and the classics, he probably would have ruefully observed

Industria ditat sed eget praeterita.*

---

* Industry enriches only when one respects the past

Acknowledgements

Recent research into early colonial history has benefitted greatly from electronic access to 18th and 19th century material in British and Australian libraries and archives. Staff in these institutions have also assisted in tracking down the more elusive historical documents and maps. The Mitchell Library and the State Archives and Records of New South Wales provided the bulk of official records, letters, dispatches and records referred to in this book, and the NSW Land Registry Services has supplied all historical maps and land transactions. The National Records of Scotland and The National Archives (UK) rendered documents on Thompson's trial and his family, and the Borthwick Institute for Archives in York (UK) supplied details of Andrew's brother, Walter Thompson. I am much indebted to J.V. Byrnes 1958 thesis of Andrew Thompson – it is a solid body of work considering his investigations were done without electronic access to libraries.

Most of the original historical material obtained in researching this biography came from the digitised archives of newspapers, books and documents accessed over the Internet. In this endeavour, the web service TROVE at the National Library of Australia (NLA) has been especially helpful. The everyday details of colonial life have been extracted from early newspapers, government gazettes and publications stored electronically by the NLA library. I also wish to thank the State Library of Western Australia for electronic access to the British newspaper collection.

The illustrations in this book include sketches, drawings and paintings of early landscapes and portraits. These have been sourced as digital online images from the State Library of New South Wales, the Mitchell and Dixon Libraries, the National Library of Australia, the NSW Land Registry Services, the National Gallery of Australia, the Yale Center of British Art, the Wellcome Library and the National Maritime Museum in Britain. I gratefully acknowledge and thank these institutions for this extremely valuable service.

Many people have helped me write Andrew Thompson's biography. I especially want to recognise the valuable advice of Elizabeth and Graeme Watson from the Yetholm History Society. They generously assisted me during a visit to Yetholm in 2019 and

ACKNOWLEDGEMENTS

explained how life was in the Border villages in the 18th century. I also received historical assistance from the Heritage Hub in Harwick Scotland. I am also grateful to Elly Todhunter of the Heritage Group in Workington England for details on the extended Thompson family who resided there and in Whitehaven.

I am indebted to numerous people for comments and feedback on early drafts of the manuscript, especially to Brian McMahon, Ruth Guss and Robert Hall. Special thanks go to Brian for his expert comments when he was particularly busy in the UK working from home during the Covid-19 shutdown. A big thank you to Timo Wöstefeld for his technical assistance in producing the book cover.

As always, my friends and family have been essential in bringing this book to fruition. Without their encouragement and support during the lengthy research and preparation stages of the writing – a task that seemed interminable – the story may never have been finished. No one is more responsible for this biography being printed than my husband Syd, whose efforts on many fronts have been absolutely invaluable.

BIBLIOGRAPHY

ARCHIVES AND RECORDS

HLRV	Historical Land Records Viewer, New South Wales
HRA	Historical Records Australia
HRNSW	Historical Records of New South Wales
NAI	National Archives of Ireland
NGA	National Gallery of Australia
NLA	National Library of Australia
NMS	National Museum Scotland
NMM	National Maritime Museum, England
NRS	National Records of Scotland
SANSW	State Archives & Records of New South Wales
NRS 897	Colonial Secretary, letters received
NRS 898	Colonial Secretary, special bundles
NRS 899	Memorials to the Governor
NRS 935	Colonial Secretary, copies of letters sent
NRS 938	Colonial Secretary, copies letters sent & received
NRS 1150	Convict Indent
NRS 1213	Colonial Secretary, Grants and Leases
NRS 1215	Land Grants and Pardons
NRS 2659	Court of Civil Jurisdiction
NRS 4518	Despatches to Secretary of State
NRS 5607	Coroners' Inquest
NRS 13836	Land grants and leases
SLNSW	State Library of New South Wales
DX	Dixson Library
ML	Mitchell Library
TNA	The National Archives, England
WL	Wellcome Library, England
YCB	Yale Center of British Art

PRIMARY SOURCES

Atkins, Richard, *Journal of Richard Atkins*, 1791-1810, NLA: nla.obj-570654388.

Baird, John, *Parish of Yetholm, The New Statistical Account of Scotland*, Vol III, William Blackwood and Sons, Edinburgh, 1845.

Baird, William, *Memoir of the late Rev. John Baird*, James Nisbet & Co, London, 1862.

Banks, Joseph, *The Letters of Sir Joseph Banks: A Selection, 1768-1820*, ed. Neil Chambers, Imperial College Press, London, 2000.

Bartrum, J, *Proceedings of a General Court-Martial ... for the trial of Lieut.-Col. Geo. Johnston, Major of the 102d Regiment, late the New South Wales Corps, on a Charge of Mutiny, ... for deposing, on 26th January 1808, William Bligh, Esq*, Sherwood, Neely and Jones, London, 1811.

Bigge, John, *Report of the Commissioner of Inquiry into the State of the Colony of New South Wales*, House of Commons, 5 Aug 1822.

BIBLIOGRAPHY

Bigge, John, *Report of the Commissioner of Inquiry on the Judicial Establishment of New South Wales and Van Diemen's Land*, House of Commons, 21 Feb 1823.

Bigge, John, *Report of the Commissioner of Inquiry into the State of Agriculture and Trade in the Colony of New South Wales*, House of Commons, 13 Mar 1823.

Blackie, William, *Parish of Yetholm, The Statistical Account of Scotland*, Vol XIX, Edinburgh, 1797.

Bligh, William, *Account of the Rebellion of the New South Wales Corps*, ed. J. Curry, The Banks Society, Colony Press, Malvern, 2011.

Bent, Ellis, *Judge Advocate Ellis Bent, Letter and Diaries 1809-1811*, ed. Paula Jane Byrne, Desert Pea Press, Sydney, 2012.

Collins, David, *An Account of the English Colony in New South Wales*, Vol I - II, ed. B. Fletcher, Royal Australian Historical Society, Reed, Sydney, 1975.

Colquhoun, Patrick, *A Treatise on the Police of the Metropolis*, London, 1806.

Davoren, Lawrence, *A New Song: Made in New South Wales on the Rebellion*, ed. G. Mackaness, Australian Historical Monographs, Vol. XXXIII, Sydney, 1951.

Douglas, Robert, *General View of the Agriculture of the Counties of Roxburgh and Selkirk*, Richard Phillips, London, 1798.

Finucane, James, *Distracted Settlement: New South Wales after Bligh*, ed. Anne-Marie Whitaker, Miegunyah Press, Melbourne, 1998.

Groome, Francis, *Ordnance Gazetteer of Scotland, A Survey of Scottish Topography, Statistical, Biographical and Historical*, Vol IV, Edinburgh, 1885.

Harris, Alexander, *Settlers and Convicts, or Recollections of Sixteen Year's Labour in the Australian Backwoods*, C. Cox, London, 1847.

Bladen, F. M. (ed.), *Historical Records of New South Wales*, Vol I - VII, Government Printer, Sydney, 1892-1901.

House of Commons, *Report from the Select Committee on the State of Gaols*, 12 Jul 1819.

Howard, John, *The State of the Prisons in England and Wales*, Warrington, printed by J. Johnson, C. Dilly and T. Cadell, 4th ed., London, 1792.

Howe, George, *New South Wales Pocket Almanack and Colonial Remembrancer*, Government Press, Sydney, 1806.

Hunter, John, *An Historical Journal of Events at Sydney and at Sea 1787-1792*, ed. J. Bach, Royal Australian Historical Society, Angus and Robertson, Sydney, 1968.

Jeffrey, Alexander, *The History and Antiquities of Roxburghshire*, Vol III, Thomas Clark, Edinburgh, 1859.

Macquarie, Lachlan, *Lachlan Macquarie, Governor of New South Wales, Journals of his Tours in New South Wales and Diemen's Land 1810-1822*, Trustees of the Public Library of New South Wales, Sydney, 1956.

Macquarie, Lachlan, *A Letter to the Right Honourable Viscount Sidmouth in Refutation of Statements made by the Hon. Henry Grey Bennet, MP*, Richard Rees, London, 1821.

Macquarie, Lachlan, *Copy of a Report by the late Major General Macquarie, on the Colony of New South Wales, to Earl Bathurst; in July 1822*, Government Printer, London, 1828.

Macquarie, Lachlan, *Extract of a Letter from Major General Macquarie to Earl Bathurst, in October 1823; in Answer to certain Part of the Report of Mr. Commissioner Bigge, on the State of the said Colony*, Government Printer, London, 1828.

Marsden, Samuel, *An Answer to the Calumnies in the late Governor Macquarie's Pamphlet*,

BIBLIOGRAPHY

Hatchard and Son, London, 1826.

Noah, William, *Voyage to Sydney in the Ship Hillsborough 1798-1799 and A Description of the Colony*, Library of Australian History, Sydney, 1978.

Sinclair, John, *The Statistical Account of Scotland*, Vol I & XIX, Edinburgh, William Creech, 1796-1797.

Tench, Watkin, *Sydney's First Four Years*, ed. L. Fitzhardinge, Angus and Robertson, Melbourne, 1961.

Thompson, George, *Slavery and Famine, Punishment for Sedition: An Account of New South Wales and the Miserable State of the Convicts*, J. Ridgway, London, 1794.

Watson, Frederick (ed.), *Historical Records of Australia*, Vol I - X, Library Committee of the Commonwealth, Government Printer, Sydney, 1914 - 1917.

SECONDARY SOURCES

Abbott, J. H. M., *The Governor's Man*, The Bookstall Company, Melbourne, 1919.

Antill, Loftus C. and James M., *Andrew Thompson's Executors*, Journal Royal Australian Historical Society, 1962, Vol 48, Pt 5, pp. 394-396.

Atkinson, Alan, *The Europeans in Australia. Vol. 1, The Beginning*, Oxford University Press, Melbourne, 1997.

Barkley-Jack, Jan, *Hawkesbury Settlement Revealed: A new look at Australia's third mainland settlement 1793-1802*, Rosenberg, Dural, 2009.

Bateson, Charles, *The Convict Ships, 1787 – 1868*, Brown, Son & Ferguson, Glasgow, 1959.

Baxter, Carol, *Muster and Lists, New South Wales and Norfolk Island*, Volumes: 1800-1802; 1805-1806; ABGR in association with Society of Australian Genealogists, Sydney, 1988,1989.

Bennett, Rachel E., *Capital Punishment and the Criminal Corpse in Scotland, 1740-1834*, Palgrave Macmillan, eBook, 2018.

Bertie, Charles, *Governor Macquarie*, Journal Royal Australian Historical Society, 1930, Vol 16, Pt 1, pp. 22-51.

Bowd, Douglas Gordon, *Macquarie Country: A History of the Hawkesbury*, Library of Australian History, Sydney, 1979.

Byrnes, John Valentine, *An outcast goat, or, The life and times of Andrew Thompson*, Thesis (M.A.) University of Sydney, 1958.

Byrnes, John Valentine, *Andrew Thompson, 1773-1810, Part 1 – To the Arrival of Macquarie*, Journal Royal Australian Historical Society, 1962, Vol 48, Pt 2, pp. 105-141.

Byrnes, John Valentine, *Andrew Thompson, 1773-1810, Part 2 – Macquarie and the Thompson Legacy*, Journal Royal Australian Historical Society, 1962, Vol 48, Pt 3, pp. 161-207.

Clark, Manning, *A History of Australia, Vol. 1: From the Earliest Times to the Age of Macquarie*, Melbourne University Press, Carlton, 1979.

Clark, Manning, *Manning Clark's History of Australia*, abridge M. Cathcart, Melbourne University Press, Carlton, 1997.

Cobley, John, *Sydney Cove 1791-1792*, Angus and Robertson, Sydney, 1965.

Cobley, John, *Sydney Cove 1793-1795, The Spread of Settlement*, Angus & Robertson, Sydney, 1983.

Cobley, John, *Sydney Cove 1795-1800, The Second Governor*, Angus & Robertson, Sydney, 1986.

BIBLIOGRAPHY

Corr, Barry, *Pondering the Abyss: a study of the language of settlement on the Hawkesbury Nepean Rivers*, 2016, www.nangarra.com.au.

Currey, C. H., *The Brothers Bent*, Sydney University Press, Sydney, 1968.

Currey, C. H., *Andrew Thompson's Will*, Journal Royal Australian Historical Society, 1963, Vol 49, Pt 3, pp. 221-224.

Dando-Collins, Stephen, *Captain Bligh's other mutiny: The true story of the military coup that turned Australia into a two-year rebel republic*, Random House, Sydney, 2007.

Dillon, Harry & Butler, Peter, *Macquarie: From colony to country*, William Heinemann, Sydney, 2010.

Ellis, M. H., *Lachlan Macquarie: His Life, Adventures and Times*, Angus & Robertson, Sydney, 1969.

Ellis, M. H., *John Macarthur*, Angus & Robertson, Sydney, 1973.

Evatt, H. V., *Rum Rebellion: A Study of the Overthrow of Governor Bligh by John Macarthur and the New South Wales Corps*, Angus and Robertson, Sydney, 1943.

Fletcher, Brian, *The Hawkesbury Settlers and the Rum Rebellion*, Journal Royal Australian Historical Society, 1968, Vol 54, Pt 3, pp. 217-237.

Forbes, Catherine, Barkley-Jack, Jan, *Spring Hill Conservation Management Plan*, 2003.

Ford, Geoffrey Eric, *Darkinung Recognition, An Analysis of the Historiography for the Aborigines from the Hawkesbury-Hunter Ranges to the Northwest of Sydney*, Thesis, University of Sydney, 2010.

Frost, Alan, *Botany Bay Mirages*, Melbourne University Press, Carlton, 1994.

Frost, Alan, *Botany Bay: The Real Story*, Black Inc., Melbourne, 2012.

Frost, Alan, *Arthur Phillip, 1738-1814, His Voyaging*, Oxford University Press, Melbourne, 1987.

Gapps, Stephen, *The Sydney Wars*, NewSouth Publishing, Sydney, 2018.

Gladstone, Hugh, *Thomas Watling, Limner of Dumfries*, Hunter, Watson & Co, Dumfries, 1938.

Hall, Annegret, *In For The Long Haul, The First Fleet Voyage and Colonial Australia: The Convict Perspective*, ESH Publication, Nedlands, 2018.

Hall, Annegret, *Doctor Redfern: Mutineer, Convict, Medical pioneer, Rights Activist*, ESH Publication, Nedlands, 2023.

Hardy, Bobbie, *Early Hawkesbury Settlers*, Kangaroo Press, Kenthurst, 1985.

Hawkesbury City Council, Lukas Stapleton Johnson & Partners, *Thompson Square Conservation Management Plan*, Windsor, 2018.

Higginbotham, Edward, *Historical and Archaeological Investigation of Thompson Square, Windsor, NSW*, Camperdown, 1986.

Hill, David, *The Making of Australia*, William Heinemann, Sydney, 2015.

Hill, David, *Convict Colony: The remarkable story of the fledging settlement that survived against the odds*, Allen & Unwin, Crows Nest, 2019.

Hughes, Robert, *The Fatal Shore, A History of the Transportation of Convicts to Australia 1787-1868*, The Folio Society, London, 1998.

Jack, Ian & Barkley-Jack, Jan, *St Matthew's Windsor: an Anglican Landmark celebrating 200 Years*, Rosenberg, Dural, 2016.

Karskens, Grace, *The Colony: A History of Early Australia*, Allen & Unwin, Crows Nest, 2010.

Karskens, Grace, *The Rocks, Life in Early Sydney*, Melbourne University Press, Carlton, 1997.

BIBLIOGRAPHY

Karskens, Grace, *People of the River*, Allen & Unwin, Crows Nest, 2020.
Keneally, Thomas, *The Commonwealth of Thieves*, Random House, Sydney, 2005.
Kieza, Grantlee, *Macquarie*, ABC Books, Sydney, 2019.
Macarthur Onslow, Sibella, *Some early records of the Macarthurs of Camden*, Angus & Robertson, Sydney, 1914.
Mackaness, *The Life of Vice-Admiral Bligh*, Angus and Robertson, Sydney, 1951.
Mundle, Rob, *Bligh, Master Mariner*, Hachette Australia, 2010.
Murray, Robert & White, Kate, *Dharug & Dungaree: The History of Penrith and St Marys to 1860*, Hargreen, City of Penrith, 1988.
Ritchie, John, *Lachlan Macquarie: A Biography*, Melbourne University Press, Carlton, 1986.
Ritchie, John, *The Evidence to the Bigge Reports, New South Wales under Governor Macquarie*, Vol I & II, Heinemann, Melbourne, 1971.
Sharp, Andrew, *The World, the Flesh and the devil: The Life and Opinions of Samuel Marsden in England and the Antipodes, 1765-1838*, Auckland University Press, Auckland New Zealand, 2016.
Shaw, A. G. L., *Convicts & the Colonies, A Study of Penal Transportation from Great Britain & Ireland to Australia & other parts of the British Empire*, Melbourne University Press, Carlton, 1978.
Thomson, Ethel H., *The Life & Letters of William Thomson, Archbishop of York*, John Lane, London, 1919.
Walker, F., *Andrew Thompson: A Remarkable Colonist*, Journal Royal Australian Historical Society, 1937, Vol 23, Pt. 2, pp. 149-152.
Wannan, Bill, *Very Strange Tales: The Turbulent Times of Samuel Marsden*, Landsdown Press, Melbourne, 1962.
Watson, Graeme, *The Song of the Smugglers by Robert Gray, The Yetholm Poet*, Culver Press, Yetholm, 2017.
Whitaker, Anne-Maree, *Joseph Foveaux, Power and Patronage in Early New South Wales*, UNSW Press, Sydney, 2000.
Yetholm History Society, *Yetholm Past and Present*, Culver Press, Yetholm, 2017.
Yetholm, Roxburghshire Monumental Inscriptions III, Border Family Historical Society Publication, 1997.

ELECTRONIC SOURCES

Ancestry	ancestry.com.au
Australian Dictionary of Biography	adb.anu.edu.au
Biographical Database of Australia	bda-online.org.au
Findmypast	findmypast.com.au
Historical Land Record Viewer, NSW	hlrv.nswlrs.com.au
National Archives, UK	nationalarchives.gov.uk
National Library of Australia	nla.gov.au
National Records of Scotland	nrscotland.gov.uk
Scotland's People	scotlandspeople.gov.uk
State Archives & Records NSW	mhnsw.au/collections
State Library NSW	sl.nsw.gov.au
State Library of WA	slwa.wa.gov.au
Trove	trove.nla.gov.au
Yetholm History Society	yetholmhistorysociety.weebly.com

NOTES

CHAPTER 1 – GREAT EXPECTATIONS

1. Dickens, Charles, *Great Expectations*.
2. *The Sydney Morning Herald*, 24 Dec 2002.
3. NRS: Old Parish births and baptisms – Parish 811, Ref 20 66 Yetholm.
4. Baird, *New Statistical Account of Scotland*, pp. 159, 163.
5. Blackie, *Statistical Account of Scotland*, pp. 610-611; Baird, *New Statistical Account of Scotland*, p. 170.
6. Elizabeth Watson, Yetholm History Society.
7. Yetholm, *Roxburghshire Monumental Inscriptions*, p. 40.
8. TNA: IR 1/65, p. 55; NRS: Trial papers, Aug-Sep 1790, JC26/1790/38.
9. Blackie, *Statistical Account of Scotland*, p. 613.
10. Yetholm History Society, *Yetholm Past and Present*, p. 32.
11. Jeffrey, *History and Antiquities*, pp. 241-254.
12. Blackie, *Statistical Account of Scotland*, p. 613.
13. Baird, *New Statistical Account of Scotland*, p. 172.
14. Blackie, *Statistical Account of Scotland*, p. 614.
15. Howard, *State of Prisons*, p. 196.
16. Baird, *New Statistical Account of Scotland*, p. 174.
17. Blackie, *Statistical Account of Scotland*, p. 613.
18. NMS: 000-100-002-277-C.
19. Thompson to Howe, 4 Oct 1810, in Macquarie, *Letter to Bathurst*, 1823, p. 67.
20. NRS: Summons declaration, 25 Aug 1790, JC26/1790/38/2; Thompson to Howe, 4 Oct 1810, in Macquarie, *Letter to Bathurst*, 1823, p. 67.
21. Byrnes, *An outcast goat*, p. 12.
22. NRS: Summons declaration, 25 Aug 1790, JC26/1790/38/2.

CHAPTER 2 – A MOST HEINOUS CRIME

1. NRS: Judge Hailes to Laird of Niddrie, 4 Dec 1791, GD247/192/4.
2. Douglas, *View of the Agriculture*, p. 207.
3. NRS: Case papers, 31 Aug 1790, JC26/1790/38/1.
4. NRS: Summons declaration, 25 Aug 1790, JC26/1790/38/2.
5. NRS: Case papers, 31 Aug 1790, JC26/1790/38/1.
6. NRS: Case papers, 31 Aug 1790, JC26/1790/38/1; Summons declaration, 25 Aug 1790, JC26/1790/38/2.
7. Howard, *State of Prisons*, pp. 195-196.
8. NRS: Summons declaration, 25 Aug 1790, JC26/1790/38/2.
9. Ibid.
10. NRS: Summons declaration, 25 Aug 1790, JC26/1790/38/2.
11. Ibid.
12. Colquhoun, *Treatise on Police*, pp. 437-440.
13. Bennett, *Capital Punishment*, pp. 32, 45-46, 70.

NOTES

14 Howard, *State of Prisons*, p. 202.
15 Groome, *Gazetteer of Scotland*, pp. 329-332.
16 Ibid.
17 NRS: Case papers, 31 Aug 1790, JC26/1790/38/1; 'Thompson' is written as 'Thomson' in the trial papers. Andrew countersigned the papers with 'And^w Thompson'.
18 Ibid.
19 Ibid.
20 Ibid.
21 Ibid.
22 NRS: Case papers, 31 Aug 1790, JC26/1790/38/1.
23 NRS: Criminal charges, 4 Sep 1790, JC26/1790/38/3; NRS: Advocate letter & witnesses, 8-9 Sep 1790, JC26/1790/38/4.
24 NRS: Advocate letter & witnesses, 8-9 Sep 1790, JC26/1790/38/4.
25 Thompson to Howe, 4 Oct 1810, in Macquarie, *Letter to Bathurst*, 1823, p. 67.
26 Byrnes, *An outcast goat*, p. 21.
27 NRS: Judiciary Court, 21-22 Sep 1790, JC12/21 f.81-85.
28 Bennett, *Capital Punishment*, pp. 32, 70.
29 *The Scots Magazine*, Vol 52, Sep 1790, p. 463.
30 NRS: Witnesses, 1790, JC26/1790/38/5.
31 NRS: Judiciary Court, 21-22 Sep 1790, JC12/21 f.81-85.
32 Ibid.
33 Bennett, *Capital Punishment*, p. 32.
34 NRS: Judiciary Court, 21-22 Sep 1790, JC12/21 f.81-85.
35 Ibid.
36 Stephen, Leslie, *Dictionary of National Biography*, XIII, London, 1888, p. 404.
37 NRS: Judiciary Court, 21-22 Sep 1790, JC12/21 f. 81-85.
38 Byrnes, *An outcast goat*, pp. 22-23.
39 *The Scots Magazine*, Vol 52, Sep 1790, p. 463.
40 NRS: Judge Hailes to Laird of Niddrie, 4 Dec 1791, GD247/192/4.
41 Ibid.
42 Ibid.
43 TNA: Dundas to Roxburghe, 7 Feb 1792, HO 13/8, p. 389.
44 Thomas, Hugh, *The Slave Trade*, p. 549.
45 NRS: William Thompson vs John Rae, 18 Jan 1791, CS271/15824.
46 *The Sydney Gazette*, 27 Oct 1810.
47 Thompson to Howe, 4 Oct 1810, in Macquarie, *Letter to Bathurst*, 1823, p. 67.

CHAPTER 3 – BEYOND THE SEAS

1 Dundas to Phillip, 5 Jul 1791, HRNSW, I, ii, p. 496.
2 Convict indents, SANSW: NRS 1150, [SZ 115], Fiche 623; TNA: HO 11/1.
3 Phillip to Sydney, 13 Feb 1790, HRNSW, I, ii, p. 305.
4 Phillip to Nepean, 17 Jun 1790, HRNSW, I, ii, p. 350.
5 *The Scots Magazine*, Vol 48, pp. 525, 541 and Vol 49, p. 247.
6 *The Chester Chronicle*, 18 Mar 1791.
7 *The Norfolk Chronicle*, 26 Feb 1791.
8 *The Evening Mail*, 2 Feb 1791.

NOTES

9. *The Public Advertiser*, 5 Jan 1791.
10. *The Northampton Mercury*, 30 Sep 1786.
11. British Library: *Fortitude*: The ship was built in 1780 and was originally named *Fortitude*; Batson, p. 124.
12. *The Northampton Mercury*, 9 Apr 1791; The Hereford Journal, 25 May 1791.
13. *The Stamford Mercury*, 1 Apr 1791.
14. *The Kentish Gazette*, 31 May 1791.
15. *The Times*, 9 and 14 Jun 1791.
16. Gladstone, *Thomas Watling*, p. 16.
17. *The General Evening Post*, 12 Oct 1790.
18. Officers' Report, 30 Jun 1791, HRNSW, II, p. 451.
19. Noah, *Voyage to Sydney in the Hillsborough*, pp. 12-13.
20. Ibid.
21. JW to Grenville, 21 Jun 1791, HRNSW, II, pp. 450-451.
22. Dundas to Treasury, 23 Jun 1791, HRNSW, II, pp. 449-450.
23. Bateson, *Convict Ships*, p. 124; Officers' Report, 30 Jun 1791, HRNSW, II, p. 451.
24. Phillip to Dundas, 2 Oct 1792, HRSNW, I, ii, p. 649.
25. Dundas to Phillip, 5 Jul 1791, HRNSW, I, ii, p. 496.
26. SANSW: NRS 1150, [SZ115], Fiche 623; NRS 1155, [2/8273], Reel 2426; TNA: HO 11/1; Return of Officers, 20 Oct 1791, HRNSW, I, ii, p. 526.
27. Manning to Macaulay, 24 Oct 1791, HRNSW, I, ii, pp. 526-528; Soldiers' letter, 13 Dec 1794, HRNSW, II, p. 815.
28. Manning to Macaulay, 24 Oct 1791, HRNSW, I, ii, pp. 526-528.
29. Grose to Nepean, 22 Oct 1791, HRNSW, I, ii, pp. 525-526; Manning to Macaulay, 24 Oct 1791, HRNSW, I, ii, pp. 526-528.
30. Noah, *Voyage to Sydney in the Hillsborough*, pp. 30-31.
31. Manning to Macaulay, 24 Oct 1791, HRNSW, I, ii, pp. 526-528.
32. Small-Pox on Pitt, 12 Jan 1792, HRNSW, II, p. 792.
33. Ibid.
34. Grose to Nepean, 22 Oct 1791, HRNSW, I, ii, p. 526.
35. Manning to Macaulay, 24 Oct 1791, HRNSW, I, ii, p. 528; Soldier's letter, 13 Dec 1794, HRNSW, II, p. 815.
36. SANSW: Return of Convicts from Pitt, 12 Oct 1792, NRS 4518, [4/1634].
37. SLNSW: Bligh's Providence Logbook, 27 Nov 1791, SAFE/A564/1.
38. SANSW: Return of Convicts from Pitt, 12 Oct 1792, NRS 4518, [4/1634].
39. SLNSW: Bligh's Providence Logbook, 22 Dec 1791, SAFE/A564/1.
40. Hunter, *Historical Journal of Events at Sydney and at Sea*, pp. 190-191.
41. SANSW: Return of Convicts from Pitt, 12 Oct 1792, NRS 4518, [4/1634].
42. Hunter, *Historical Journal of Events at Sydney and at Sea*, pp. 190-191.
43. Cobley, *Sydney Cove 1791-1792*, p. 219.
44. Phillip to Dundas, 19 Mar 1792, HRNSW, I, ii, p. 595.
45. Ibid.

CHAPTER 4 – A NEW START

1. Byrnes, *An outcast goat*, p. 23.
2. Collins, May 1790, Mar 1791, *Account of the English Colony*, I, pp. 90, 130.

NOTES

3. Collins, May 1792, *Account of the English Colony*, I, pp. 177-178; Tench, *Sydney's First Four Years*, p. 249.
4. Grose to Nepean, 2 Apr 1792, HRNSW, I, ii, p. 613.
5. Cobley, *Sydney Cove 1791-1792*, 21 May 1792, p. 261.
6. State of the Settlements, 18 Mar 1792, HRNSW, II, pp. 465-467.
7. Collins, Jul 1790, *Account of the English Colony*, I, p. 103.
8. Soldier's letter, 13 Dec 1794, HRNSW, II, p. 817.
9. Thompson, *Slavery and Famine*, pp. 6-8.
10. Collins, April 1792, *Account of the English Colony*, I, p. 173.
11. Bigge, *State of the Colony*, 1822, pp. 80-81.
12. Collins, April 1792, *Account of the English Colony*, I, p. 170.
13. SLNSW: SAG 55-56, 90.
14. Phillip to Nepean, 29 Mar 1792, HRNSW, I, ii, pp. 610-613.
15. Phillip to Nepean, 28 Mar 1792, HRNSW, I, ii, p. 610.
16. Collins, October 1792, *Account of the English Colony*, I, p. 200.
17. Macquarie, *Letter to Sidmouth*, 1821, p. 36.
18. Phillip to Sydney, 15 Apr 1790, HRNSW, I, ii, p. 329; Phillip to Nepean, 15 Apr 1790, HRNSW, I, ii, p. 330.
19. Collins, Oct 1792, *Account of the English Colony*, I, p. 203; Phillip to Nepean, 16 Oct 1792, HRNSW, I, ii, pp. 669-670.
20. Collins, Dec 1792, *Account of the English Colony*, I, p. 211.
21. Phillip to Dundas, 26 Oct 1793, HRNSW, II, p. 75; Governor Phillip and his Successor, 30 Dec 1793, HRNSW, II, p. 813.
22. Macquarie, *Letter to Sidmouth*, 1821, p. 36.

CHAPTER 5 – THE YOUNG CONSTABLE

1. Macquarie, *Letter to Sidmouth*, 1821, p. 36.
2. Collins, Dec 1792, *Account of the English Colony*, I, 213-214.
3. Ibid.
4. Grose to Lewis, 22 Oct 1792, HRNSW, I, ii, p. 673.
5. Dundas to Phillip, 14 Jul 1792, HRNSW, I, ii, p. 632.
6. Collins, Dec 1792 and Feb 1793, *Account of the English Colony*, I, pp. 213-215, 224.
7. Collins, Jan 1793, *Account of the English Colony*, I, pp. 219-220.
8. Collins, Jul 1793, *Account of the English Colony*, I, p. 251.
9. Grose to Dundas, 16 Feb 1793, HRNSW, II, pp. 13-15.
10. Macquarie, *Letter to Sidmouth*, 1821, p. 36; Ritchie, *Bigge Report*, II, p. 97.
11. Collins, Dec 1792, *Account of the English Colony*, I, p. 209.
12. Collins, May 1792, *Account of the English Colony*, I, pp. 177-178.
13. Collins, *Account of the English Colony*, I, pp. 330, 354-355.
14. Karskens, *The Colony*, pp. 93-97.
15. Thompson, *Slavery & Famine*, p. 7.
16. SLNSW: SAG 55-56, 90.
17. Collins, Nov 1792, *Account of the English Colony*, I, p. 205; Tench, *Sydney's First Four Years*, pp. 257-258; George Barrington, Australian Dictionary of Biography.
18. Collins, *Account of the English Colony*, I, pp. 304, 337.
19. Collins, June 1793, *Account of the English Colony*, I, p. 249.

NOTES

20. Tench, 7 Mar 1789, *Sydney's First Four Years*, pp. 144-145.
21. Corr, *Pondering the Abyss*, p. 387; Collins, 1794, *Account of the English Colony*, I, pp. 292, 329.
22. Collins, Dec 1793, *Account of the English Colony*, I, p. 275.
23. Grose to Dundas, 31 Aug 1794, HRA, I, p. 483.
24. Atkins, 13-17 Mar 1795, *Journal of Richard Atkins*, p. 56.
25. Collins, Dec 1794, *Account of the English Colony*, I, p. 337.
26. State of the Settlements, 21 Mar 1795, HRA, I, pp. 492-493.
27. Corr, *Pondering the Abyss*, p. 42.
28. Paterson to Dundas, 15 Jun 1795, HRA, I, p. 499; Collins, May 1795, *Account of the English Colony*, I, pp. 348-349.
29. Corr, *Pondering the Abyss*, p. 433; Barkley-Jack, *Hawkesbury Settlement*, pp. 113, 295.
30. Cobley, *Sydney Cove 1793-1795*, p. 281.
31. Hunter to Portland, 25 Oct 1795, HRA, I, pp. 533-534.
32. Return of Land Grants, 25 Sep 1800, HRA, II, p. 566.
33. Government and General Order, 29 Feb 1796, HRA, I, p. 689.
34. Government and General Order, 2 Oct 1795, HRNSW, II, p. 322.
35. Government and General Order, 22 Mar 1796, HRNSW, III, p. 36.
36. Yarwood, A. T., *Samuel Marsden*, Australian Dictionary of Biography.

CHAPTER 6 – NEW-FOUND FREEDOM

1. Bowd, *Macquarie Country*, p. 121.
2. General State of Districts of Settlement, 20 Aug 1796, HRA, I, p. 596.
3. Collins, Feb 1797, *Account of the English Colony*, II, p. 16; Barkley-Jack, *Hawkesbury Settlement*, p. 229.
4. Government and General Order, 18 Jun 1796, HRNSW, III, pp. 54-55.
5. Collins, Jan 1796, *Account of the English Colony*, I, pp. 338-340.
6. Hunter to Portland, 20 Aug 1796, HRNSW, III, p. 80; Return of public buildings, 25 Sep 1800, HRNSW, IV, pp. 151-152.
7. Hunter to Portland, 30 Apr 1796, HRA, I, pp. 566-567; Government and General Order, 29 Jun 1796, HRNSW, III, p. 57.
8. Macquarie, *Letter to Sidmouth*, 1821, p. 36.
9. Livestock, 1 Sep 1796, HRA, I, p. 664.
10. Cobley, *Sydney Cove 1795-1800*, p. 456.
11. Hunter to Portland, 30 Apr 1796, HRA, I, pp. 566-567.
12. Government and General Order, Nov 1796, HRNSW, III, pp. 165-166, 182-183.
13. Ritchie, *Bigge Report*, II, p. 97.
14. Barkley-Jack, *Hawkesbury Settlement*, p. 347.
15. Government and General Order, 22 Feb 1796, HRNSW, III, pp. 25-26.
16. SANSW: Absolute Pardon, 17 Oct 1797, NRS 1215, Reel 773.
17. Collins, Sep 1796, *Account of the English Colony*, I, p. 410
18. Hunter to Portland, 10 Jan 1798, HRA, II, p. 117.
19. Ibid.
20. Settlers' Statement to Hunter, 19 Feb 1798, HRA, II, pp. 136-140.
21. Report Marsden and Arndell, 2 Mar 1798, HRA, II, pp. 140-146.

NOTES

22. Portland to Hunter, 22 Feb 1797, HRA, II, p. 7.
23. SANSW: Harris vs Kemp, 10 Jun 1799, NRS 2659, [2/8150].
24. Government and General Orders, 31 Dec 1800, HRNSW, IV, p. 279.
25. Trial for murder of two natives, 2 Jan 1800, HRA, II, p. 406.
26. Barkley-Jack, *Hawkesbury Settlement*, pp. 302-304.
27. Trial for murder of two natives, 2 Jan 1800, HRA, II, pp. 403-422.
28. Ibid.
29. Barkley-Jack, *Hawkesbury Settlement*, p. 307.
30. Trial for murder of two natives, 2 Jan 1800, HRA, II, pp. 403-422.
31. Ibid.
32. Hobart to King, 30 Jan 1802, HRA, III, pp. 366-367.
33. Ibid.
34. Hunter to Portland, 1 May 1799, HRA, II, p. 354-355; Collins, Mar 1799, *Account of the English Colony*, II, p. 143.
35. Ibid.
36. SANSW: 1 Oct 1799, NRS 13836, [7/446], Reel 2560; HLRV: Grant Register, 1 Oct 1799, Serial 2, p. 320. SANSW: Windsor town map, SZ 529.
37. HLRV: Grant Register, Serial 1, p. 130.
38. Hunter to Portland, 7 Jan 1800, HRA, II, pp. 433-434.
39. General Order, 19 Nov 1799, HRA, II, p. 592.
40. Expenses of Farming at Hawkesbury, 14 Jan 1800, HRA, II, pp. 435-436.
41. Hawkesbury Settlers to Hunter, 1 Feb 1800, HRA, II, pp. 445-446.
42. Hunter's Reply to Hawkesbury Settlers, 8 Feb 1800, HRA, II, p. 450.
43. Hunter to Portland, 20 Mar 1800, HRA, II, p. 474.
44. P.G. King to J. King, 3 May 1800, HRA, II, p. 505.
45. King to Grose, 30 Jan 1794, HRNSW, II, pp. 103-104; King to Dundas, 10 Mar 1794, HRNSW, II, pp. 135-168.
46. Statement for all Inhabitants in NSW, 25 Sep 1800, HRNSW, IV, p. 160.
47. Baxter, *1800-1802*, pp. 13, 189.
48. Government and General Order, 10 Jul 1800, HRNSW, IV, p.115; King to Hunter, 6 Jul 1800, HRA, II, p. 656.
49. General Orders, 1 Oct 1800, HRA, II, p. 622.
50. Government and General Order, 13 Nov 1800, HRNSW, IV, p. 255.
51. Hunter to Portland, 12 Nov 1796, HRA, I, p. 667.
52. *The Sydney Gazette*, 10 Jul 1803.

CHAPTER 7 – ENTREPRENEUR

1. *The World's News*, 19 Dec 1925.
2. King to Portland, 10 Mar 1801, HRA, III, p. 10.
3. Ibid.
4. Petition of Hawkesbury Settlers, Jun 1801, HRA, III, pp. 134-135.
5. King's General Order, 23 Jun 1801, HRA, III, pp. 135-136.
6. SANSW: 9 Aug 1803, NRS 1213, [9/2731, p. 134], Fiche 3268; Soar's land to Thompson, 9 Aug 1803, NRS 1213, [9/2731, p. 31], Fiche 3267.
7. Baxter, *1800-1802*, pp. 112, 115.
8. Macquarie, *Letter to Sidmouth*, 1821, p. 36.
9. King to Portland, 8 Jul 1801, HRA, III, pp. 111-112.

NOTES

10. P.G. King to J. King, 21 Aug 1801, HRA, III, p. 246.
11. King to Portland, 5 Nov 1801, HRA, III, pp. 276-286.
12. P.G. King to J. King, 8 Nov 1801, HRA, III, p. 325.
13. King to Johnston, 18 Feb 1803, HRA, IV, p. 216.
14. Shaw, A.G.L, *Philip Gidley King*, Australian Dictionary of Biography.
15. King to Portland, 10 Feb 1801, HRA, III, p. 48.
16. *The Sydney Gazette*, 6 Mar 1823.
17. HLRV: Grant Register, 9 Aug 1803, Serial 3, p. 115; Pitt Town parish map, AO MAP 263.
18. Government and General Orders, 25 May 1802, HRNSW, IV, p. 771; SANSW: Windsor map, SZ 529; NLA: Windsor map, nla.obj-229922176.
19. Government and General Orders, 25 May 1802, HRNSW, IV, p. 771.
20. *The Sydney Gazette*, 8 Dec 1805, 9 Mar 1806.
21. SLNSW: Old Register, 1 Apr 1802, Vol 1, p. 24, RAV/DISC10/1615.
22. *The Sydney Gazette*, 26 Jun and 7 Aug 1803.
23. Baxter, *1800-1802*, p. 80.
24. Return of Government Stock, 8 Apr 1804, HRA, IV, p. 625.
25. King to Portland, 1 Mar 1802, HRA, III, p. 438; King to Hobart, 9 May 1803, HRA, IV, p. 123.
26. Addresses from Settlers, 29 Mar 1803, HRA, IV, pp. 502-503.
27. Ibid.
28. King to Hobart, 9 May 1803, HRA, IV, p. 85.
29. Barkley-Jack, *Hawkesbury Settlement*, pp. 154-155.
30. *The Sydney Gazette*, 26 Mar 1803; Schooners and Sloops, 28 Feb 1804, HRA, IV, p. 515.
31. *The Sydney Gazette*, 8, 15, 29 May 1803.
32. *The Sydney Gazette*, 25 Sep, 23 Oct 1803.
33. *The Sydney Gazette*, 23 Oct, 4, 25 Dec 1803.
34. King to Hobart, 1 Mar 1804, HRA, IV, pp. 454-455.
35. *The Sydney Gazette*, 1 Jan 1804.
36. *The Sydney Gazette*, 19 Feb, 1 Apr 1804.
37. *The Sydney Gazette*, 26 Aug, 2 Sep 1804.
38. Return of Schooners and Sloops, 28 Feb 1804, HRA, IV, p. 515.
39. Macquarie, *Journal of his tours*, p. 26.
40. *The Sydney Gazette*, 12 Aug 1804.
41. SANSW: 1 May 1804, NRS 13836, [7/445], Reel 2560.
42. HLRV: Grant Register, 11 Aug 1804, Serial 3, p. 108.
43. SANSW: 11 Aug 1804, NRS 1213, [9/2731, pp. 138, 146], Fiche 3268; HLRV: Castlereagh parish map, AO MAP 203.
44. SANSW: 11 Aug 1804, NRS 1215, Reel 1913; HLRV: Pitt Town parish map, AO MAP 263.
45. *The Sydney Gazette*, 12 Aug 1804 and 20 Jan 1805.
46. SLNSW: Hassall's Parramatta store sales book, 23 Jul, 7 Aug, 7-8 Nov 1804, CY 1213, pp. 100, 105, 151, 152.
47. Buildings depicted in 1807 watercolour by G.W. Evans, SLNSW: SPF/3550.
48. SANSW: Auction, 11 Feb 1811, NRS 898, [ML C197 pp. 1-17], Reel 6040.
49. SANSW: 22 Jul 1812, NRS 2659, [5/1108], case 114.
50. *The Sydney Gazette*, 29 Apr, 8 Jul 1804, 6 Jan 1805, 19 Jan, 13 Apr 1806.

NOTES

51 Steven, Margaret, *Robert Campbell*, Australian Dictionary of Biography.
52 *The Sydney Gazette*, 21 Oct 1804.
53 *The Sydney Gazette*, 20 Nov 1803, 25 Mar 1804.
54 *The Sydney Gazette*, 11 Nov 1804.
55 *The Sydney Gazette*, 2 and 9 Dec 1804, 6 Jan, 5 May 1805.
56 *The Sydney Gazette*, 18 Aug 1810.
57 *The Sydney Gazette*, 9 Dec 1804.
58 *The Sydney Gazette*, 2 Dec 1804.
59 *The Sydney Gazette*, 1 Dec 1805.
60 Byrnes, *An outcast goat*, pp. 126-127.
61 *The Windsor and Richmond Gazette*, 24 Sep 1898.
62 *The Sydney Gazette*, 27 Oct 1810.
63 Ibid.
64 Bigge, *State of the Colony*, 1822, p. 82.
65 Ritchie, *Bigge Report*, II, p. 218.
66 *The Sydney Gazette*, 9 Dec 1804.
67 Byrnes, *An outcast goat*, p. 345.

CHAPTER 8 – CHIEF CONSTABLE

1 Macquarie, *Letter to Sidmouth*, 1821, p. 37.
2 *The Sydney Gazette*, 27 Oct 1810.
3 Result of General Muster, 12 Jul 1804, HRNSW, V, p. 431.
4 Government and General Order, 19 Feb 1802, HRA, III, p. 473.
5 Harris, *Settlers and Convicts*, p. 126.
6 Howe, *Almananck*, pp. 37-51.
7 Government and General Order, 14 Jan 1804, HRA, V, pp. 74-75.
8 *The Sydney Gazette*, 28 Oct 1804.
9 *The Sydney Gazette*, 5, 19 Mar 1803.
10 *The Sydney Gazette*, 25 Sep, 9 Oct 1803.
11 *The Sydney Gazette*, 5, 19 Mar 1803.
12 *The Sydney Gazette*, 19 Mar 1803.
13 Johnston to Paterson, 9 Mar 1804, HRA, IV, pp. 569-570; King to Hobart, 12 Mar 1804, HRA, IV, pp. 563-564, 566; *The Sydney Gazette*, 11 Mar 1804.
14 Population, 11 Aug 1804, HRNSW, V, p. 431.
15 *The Sydney Gazette*, 25 Mar 1804.
16 Court Martial, 8 Mar 1804, HRA, IV, pp. 573-576.
17 *The Sydney Gazette*, 1 and 8 Apr 1804.
18 Rowland, E. C., *Royal Australian Historical Society*, Vol 30, Pt 3, pp. 157-195.
19 Hardy, *Early Hawkesbury Settlers*, pp. 117-118.
20 *The Sydney Gazette*, 15 Jan 1804.
21 Ibid.
22 King to Hobart, 14 Aug 1804, HRA, V, p. 99.
23 *The Sydney Gazette*, 19 May 1805.
24 *The Sydney Gazette*, 26 May, 2, 30 Jun 1805.
25 *The Sydney Gazette*, 22, 29 Sep, 6 Oct 1805.
26 *The Sydney Gazette*, 3, 17 Jun 1804.

NOTES

27 *The Sydney Gazette*, 17 Jun, 1, 15 Jul 1804; King to Hobart, 14 Aug 1804, HRA, V, pp. 17-18.
28 King to Hobart, 20 Dec 1804, HRA, V, pp. 166-167.
29 Corr, *Pondering the Abyss*, p. 588.
30 King to Camden, 30 Apr 1805, HRA, V, pp. 306-307.
31 *The Sydney Gazette*, 28 Apr 1805.
32 Government and General Orders, 27 Apr 1805, HRNSW, V, p. 596; *The Sydney Gazette*, 21 Apr 1805.
33 *The Sydney Gazette*, 12 May 1805.
34 Ibid.
35 Ibid.
36 *The Sydney Gazette*, 9 Jun 1805.
37 *The Sydney Gazette*, 15 Sep 1805.
38 *The Sydney Gazette*, 22 Dec 1805.

CHAPTER 9 – SETTLER'S SURVIVAL

1 Marsden to King, 26 Mar 1806, HRNSW, VI, p. 827.
2 Government and General Order, 1 Oct 1800, HRNSW, IV, p. 221.
3 Camden to King, 31 Oct 1804, HRA, V, p. 161.
4 King to Camden, 20 Jul and 1 Nov 1805, HRA, V, pp. 510, 576.
5 King to Cooke, 6 Jan 1806, HRA, V, p. 632.
6 Hobart to King, 30 Nov 1803, HRA, IV, p. 428.
7 King to Hobart, 14 Aug 1804, HRA, V, p. 116.
8 *The Sydney Gazette*, 23 Jun 1805.
9 SANSW: Macarthur vs Thompson, 27 Oct 1806, NRS 2659, [2/8149].
10 King Papers, 2 Jan 1806, HRNSW, VI, pp. 1-2.
11 Phillip to Sydney, 15 May 1788, HRNSW, I, ii, p. 124.
12 *The Sydney Gazette*, 22 Dec 1805.
13 Notice, 14 Sep 1804, HRNSW, VI, p. 187.
14 Public Labour of Convicts, 15 Mar 1806, HRA, V, p. 665.
15 *The Sydney Gazette*, 8 Dec 1805, 30 Mar 1806.
16 Arndell to King, 1-25 Mar 1806, HRNSW, VI, pp. 823-825; Inundation at the Hawkesbury, Mar 1806, HRNSW, VI, after p. 64.
17 Ibid.
18 *The Sydney Gazette*, 30 Mar 1806.
19 Ibid.
20 Ibid.
21 *The Sydney Gazette*, 6, 13 Apr 1806.
22 *The Sydney Gazette*, 30 Mar 1806.
23 *The Sydney Gazette*, 31 Aug 1806.
24 *The Sydney Gazette*, 6 Apr 1806.
25 Inundation at the Hawkesbury, Mar 1806, HRNSW, VI, after p. 64; Marsden to King, 26 and 28 Mar 1806, HRNSW, VI, pp. 54, 826-827.
26 King to Marsden, 27 Mar 1806, HRNSW, VI, p. 828.
27 King to Camden, 7 Apr 1806, HRA, V, pp. 698-699.
28 *The Sydney Gazette*, 30 Mar 1806.
29 SLNSW: King family papers, Vol 8, 5 Apr 1806, CY 906, p. 207.

NOTES

30. SANSW: Macarthur vs Thompson, 27 Oct 1806, NRS 2659, [2/8149].
31. *The Sydney Gazette*, 17 Nov 1805, 16 Feb 1806.
32. Return of Private Colonial Vessels, 12 Aug 1806, HRNSW, VI, p. 128.
33. *The Sydney Gazette*, 6 Apr, 25 May 1806.
34. SLNSW: Wardle Bank and Glasgow, Old Register, 28 May, 1 Jun 1806, Vol 1, p. 138, RAV/DISC10/1615. Moxham farm was included in Thompson's 918 acres estate in the 1806 Muster and became part of the 150 acre West Hill farm.
35. Byrnes, *An outcast goat*, p. 159.
36. Bigge, *State of the Colony*, 1822, p. 81.
37. Ibid.
38. King to Camden, 15 March 1806, HRA, V, pp. 654, 668.
39. *The Sydney Gazette*, 11 May 1806.
40. Ibid.
41. Macquarie to Bathurst, 27 Jul 1822, HRA, X, pp. 690-691.
42. SLNSW: John Howe evidence before Bigge, CY 1562, p. 728.
43. Bartrum, *Johnston trial*, p. 123.
44. *The Sydney Gazette*, 11 May 1806.
45. Introduction, HRA, VI, p. xi; SLNSW: Camden to Banks, 18 Apr 1805, SAFE/Banks Papers/Series 59.01.
46. Inhabitants, 12 Aug 1806, HRNSW, VI, p. 132; Baxter, *1805-1806*, pp. xvi-xvii.
47. TNA: General Muster, Aug 1806, HO 10/37, p. 16.
48. Ibid.
49. Baxter, *1805-1806*, pp. 128-129.

CHAPTER 10 – ELEANOR

1. SLNSW: Thomas Moore evidence before Bigge, 1820, CY 1562, p. 757.
2. Baxter, *1805-1806*, pp. 146-147.
3. A. G. L. Shaw, *Convicts and the Colonies*; L. L. Robson, *The Origin of the Women Convicts Sent to Australia*; Robert Hughes, *The Fatal Shore*; Sian Rees, *The Floating Brothel*.
4. Bigge, *State of the Colony*, 1822, p. 81.
5. SLNSW: Thomas Moore evidence before Bigge, 1820, CY 1562, p. 757.
6. White, Charles, *Early Australian History: Convict Life in New South Wales and Van Diemen's Land*, 1889.
7. House of Commons, *Select Committee on Gaols*, p. 55.
8. Byrnes, *An outcast goat*, p. 265.
9. NAI: Petition for mitigation of sentence, 20 May 1800, PPC 529, PPC 3814.
10. *The Belfast Newsletter*, 18 Dec 1798.
11. NAI: Petition for mitigation of sentence, 20 May 1800, PPC 529, PPC 3814.
12. Ibid.
13. Bateson, *Convict Ships*, pp. 158-159, 326.
14. Ibid.
15. King to Portland, 10 Mar 1801, HRA, III, p. 9.
16. Baxter, *1800-1802*, p. 26.
17. TNA: General Muster, Aug 1806, HO 10/37, p. 107.

NOTES

18. HLRV: Grants issued Town Allotments, Register 19, p. 292.
19. Karskens, *The Rocks*, pp. 80-81.
20. Barkley-Jack, *Hawkesbury Settlement*, pp. 388-389.
21. *The Windsor and Richmond Gazette*, 18 Jan 1924.

CHAPTER 11 – BAILIFF OF BLIGHTON

1. *The Windsor and Richmond Gazette*, 9 Oct 1914.
2. Address to Bligh, 14 Aug 1806, HRNSW, VI, pp. 165-166.
3. *The Sydney Gazette*, 17 Aug 1806.
4. SLNSW: Settler's Address, Sep 1806, SAFE/Banks Papers/Series 40.109.
5. Ibid.
6. Byrnes, *An outcast goat*, p. 168.
7. *The Sydney Gazette*, 31 Aug 1806.
8. *The Sydney Gazette*, 16 Nov 1806.
9. SANSW: Macarthur vs Thompson, 27 Oct 1806, NRS 2659, [2/8149].
10. Ibid.
11. Ibid.
12. Government and General Order, 1 Nov 1806, HRNSW, VI, p. 198.
13. SLNSW: Bligh to Banks, 5 Nov 1806, SAFE/Banks Papers/Series 40.070.
14. Proclamation, 3 Jan 1807, HRNSW, VI, p. 236.
15. Regulations of Vessels, 4 Oct 1806, HRNSW, VI, pp. 193-195.
16. *The Sydney Gazette*, 30 Nov 1806.
17. *The Sydney Gazette*, 14 Dec 1806.
18. Bligh to Windham, 7 Feb 1807, HRA, VI, p. 123.
19. Commentary, HRA, VI, p. 731.
20. SLNSW: Bligh to Banks, 7 Feb 1807, SAFE/Banks Papers/Series 40.071; *The Sydney Gazette*, 8 Feb 1807.
21. *The Sydney Gazette*, 8 Feb 1807.
22. SLNSW: Settlers to Bligh, 29 Jan 1807, SAFE/Banks Papers/Series 40.115.
23. *The Sydney Gazette*, 8 Mar 1807.
24. Evatt, *Rum Rebellion*, p. 11.
25. Bligh to Windham, 7 Feb 1807, HRA, VI, p. 122.
26. Castlereagh to Bligh, 31 Dec 1807, HRA, VI, p. 201.
27. Government and General Order, 14 Feb 1807, HRNSW, VI, p. 253.
28. Castlereagh to Bligh, 31 Dec 1807, HRNSW, VI, p. 400.
29. SLNSW: Settlers to Bligh 25 Feb 1807, SAFE/Banks Papers/Series 40.116.
30. *The Sydney Gazette*, 6 Jun 1806, 12 Jul 1807.
31. Barkley-Jack, *Hawkesbury Settlement*, pp. 301-303; Karskens, *People of the River*, pp. 416-417.
32. *The Sydney Gazette*, 16 Mar 1806.
33. *The Sydney Gazette*, 1 Feb 1807.
34. SANSW: NRS 2659, [5/1103].
35. Byrnes, *An outcast goat*, p. 187.
36. SANSW: Blighton reports, Feb–Jun 1807, NRS 897, [4/1721, pp. 192-205], Reel 6041.
37. *The Sydney Gazette*, 1, 15 Mar, 14 Jun 1807.
38. *The Sydney Gazette*, 12 Apr 1807.

NOTES

39 *The Sydney Gazette*, 4 May 1811.
40 SANSW: Blighton reports, Feb–Jun 1807, NRS 897, [4/1721, pp. 190, 191, 197-199, 202-204], Reel 6041.
41 Thompson to Bligh, 26 Mar 1807, HRNSW, VI, pp. 262-263.
42 SLNSW: Wentworth papers, 1 Apr 1807, CY 699, p. 185.
43 *The Sydney Gazette*, 12 Apr 1807.
44 *The Sydney Gazette*, 24 Oct 1812.
45 Building is shown in the 1807 watercolour, possibly by G. W. Evans, SLNSW: SPF/3550; SANSW: 1812 Windsor town map, SZ 529.
46 Ritchie, *Bigge Report*, II, p. 218.
47 Government and General Order, 2 May 1807, HRNSW, VI, p. 266.
48 Thompson to Bligh, 27 May 1807, HRA, VI, pp. 371-372.
49 SANSW: Blighton report, May 1807, NRS 897, [4/1721, pp. 201-204], Reel 6041.
50 Thompson to Bligh, 27 May 1807, HRA, VI, pp. 371-372.
51 Ibid.
52 *The Sydney Gazette*, 28 Jun 1807.
53 Thompson to Bligh, 30 Jun 1807, HRA, VI, pp. 367-368.
54 Trial of John Macarthur, 2 Feb 1808, HRNSW, VI, pp. 485-488.
55 Ibid.
56 Ibid.
57 *The Sydney Gazette*, 8 Mar 1807.
58 Evatt, *Rum Rebellion*, pp. 107-109.
59 Byrnes, J.V., *George Howe*, Australian Dictionary of Biography.

CHAPTER 12 – THE LOYALIST

1 Settler's Address to Bligh, 1 Jan 1808, HRA, VI, pp. 373-374.
2 Bligh to Windham, 31 Oct 1807, HRA, VI, pp. 188-190.
3 Government and General Order, 23 Jul 1807, HRNSW, VI, p. 276.
4 *The Sydney Gazette*, 16 Aug 1807.
5 SLNSW: Blighton reports, Jul-Aug 1807, NRS 897, [4/1721, pp. 207-209], Reel 6041.
6 Examination of Thompson, 27 Jan 1808, HRNSW, VI, pp. 450-451.
7 Thompson to Bligh, 16 Oct 1807, HRA, VI, p. 361.
8 Banks, *Letters of Banks*, p. 261.
9 Thompson to Bligh, 16 Oct 1807, HRNSW, VI, pp. 307-308.
10 John Blaxland, 16 Oct 1807, HRNSW, VI, pp. 308-312.
11 Gore to Castlereagh, 31 Oct 1807, HRNSW, VI, p. 371.
12 Bligh to Windham, 31 Oct 1807, HRA, VI, pp. 155-156, 714-715.
13 Grimes to Macarthur, 13 Jan 1808, HRNSW, VI, pp. 413-414; Macarthur to Grimes, HRNSW, 14 Jan 1808, VI, p. 417
14 Bartrum, *Johnston trial*, p. 148.
15 HLRV: Grants issued Town Allotments, Register 19, p. 292; NLA: Plan of Sydney, 31 Oct 1807, MAP F 105A.
16 SLNSW: Old Register, 18 Sep 1808, Vol 2, No 27, RAV/DISC10/1615.
17 SLNSW: Harris to Mrs King, 25 Oct 1807, CY 906, pp. 243 - 244.
18 SLNSW: Bligh to Banks, 10 Oct 1807, SAFE/Banks Papers/Series 40.72.

NOTES

19 Ibid.
20 Bligh to Windham, 31 Oct 1807, HRNSW, VI, p. 355.
21 Allars, K.G., *George Crossley*, Australian Dictionary of Biography.
22 SLNSW: Bligh to Banks, 10 Oct 1807, SAFE/Banks Papers/Series 40.72.
23 Bligh to Windham, 31 Oct 1807, HRA, VI, pp. 150, 152.
24 Introduction, HRA, VI, p. xx.
25 Bligh to Castlereagh, 30 Apr 1808, HRNSW, VI, pp. 609-610.
26 Trial of Macarthur, 2 Feb 1808, HRNSW, VI, pp. 466, 471-472.
27 Trial of Macarthur, 2 Feb 1808, HRNSW, VI, pp. 476, 510.
28 Macarthur to Bligh, 29 Dec 1807, HRNSW, VI, pp. 395-396.
29 Mackaness, *Life of Vice-Admiral Bligh*, pp. 397-398.
30 Bartrum, *Johnston trial*, pp. 85-86.
31 Ibid.
32 Bartrum, *Johnston trial*, p. 50.
33 Ibid.
34 Ibid.
35 Byrnes, *An outcast goat*, p. 227.
36 Thompson to Bligh, 19 Dec 1807, HRA, VI, pp. 364-367.
37 Ibid.
38 Declaration Thompson, 19 Dec 1807, HRA, VI, p. 366.
39 Bligh to Castlereagh, 30 Jun 1808, HRA, VI, p. 524.
40 Evatt, *Rum Rebellion*, p. 141.
41 Gore to Castlereagh, 27 Mar 1808, HRNSW, VI, pp. 551-552.
42 Thompson to Bligh, 1 Jan 1808, HRA, VI, p. 373.
43 Bartrum, *Johnston trial*, pp. 186, 122.
44 Settler's Address to Bligh, 1 Jan 1808, HRA, VI, pp. 373-374.
45 SLNSW: Settlers to Bligh, 1 Jan 1808, SAFE/Banks Papers/Series 40.92.
46 Grimes to Macarthur, 13 – 14 Jan 1808, HRNSW, VI, pp. 414, 416-417; Bartrum, *Johnston trial*, pp. 56-57.
47 Bartrum, *Johnston trial*, p. 399; Evatt, *Rum Rebellion*, pp. 150-151.
48 Trial of Macarthur, 25 Jan 1808, HRNSW, VI, pp. 422-428; Atkins to Bligh, 26 Jan 1808, HRNSW, VI, pp. 431-433.
49 Bligh to Johnston, 26 Jan 1808, HRNSW, VI, p. 433.
50 Johnston to Castlereagh, 11 Apr 1808, HRNSW, VI, pp. 578-579.
51 Johnston to Gaol Keeper, 26 Jan 1808, HRNSW, VI, p. 433; Macarthur to Johnston, 26 Jan 1808, HRNSW, VI, p. 434.
52 Bligh to Castlereagh, 30 Apr 1808, HRA, VI, p. 432.

CHAPTER 13 – REBELLION

1 Byrnes, *An outcast goat*, pp. 237-238.
2 Bligh to Castlereagh, 30 Apr 1808, HRA, VI, pp. 421, 430-432; Bartrum, *Johnston trial*, pp. 9, 166.
3 Gore to Castlereagh, 27 Mar 1808, HRNSW, VI, p. 558.
4 Bartrum, *Johnston trial*, pp. 9, 25.
5 Bartrum, *Johnston trial*, pp. 379, 391.
6 Johnston to Bligh, 26 Jan 1808, HRA, VI, p. 241.
7 Bartrum, *Johnston trial*, pp. 9-10, 143.

NOTES

8 Examination, 26 and 27 Jan 1808, HRNSW, VI, pp. 435-446.
9 Johnston to Castlereagh, 11 Apr 1808, HRA, VI, pp. 214-215.
10 Bligh to Castlereagh, 30 Apr 1808, HRA, VI, p. 432.
11 Bartrum, *Johnston trial*, pp. 122-123.
12 Ibid.
13 Bligh to Castlereagh, 30 Apr 1808, HRA, VI, p. 438.
14 Bartrum, *Johnston trial*, p. 114; Neville, Richard, *Australiana*, 1991, 13 (2), pp. 38-42.
15 Bartrum, *Johnston trial*, p. 143; Johnston to Bligh, 26 Jan 1808, HRA, VI, p. 241; Settler's Address to Bligh, 1 Jan 1808, HRA, VI, p. 373.
16 Examination of Thompson, 27 Jan 1808, HRNSW, VI, pp. 450-451.
17 Ibid.
18 Ibid.
19 Ibid.
20 Ibid.
21 General Order, 27 and 30 Jan 1808, HRA, VI, pp. 271-272.
22 Macarthur Onslow, *Macarthurs of Camden*, p. 151.
23 Bartrum, *Johnston trial*, pp. 122-123.
24 Bartrum, *Johnston trial*, pp. 483-484; Settlers to Johnston, 30 Jan 1808, HRNSW, VI, pp. 458-459.
25 Bartrum, *Johnston trial*, p. 122.
26 Introduction, HRA, VI, pp. xxxiii-xxxiv.
27 Trial of Macarthur, 2 Feb 1808, HRNSW, VI, p. 489.
28 General Orders, 2 Feb 1808, HRA, VI, p. 272.
29 Ritchie, *Bigge Report*, I, p. 90.
30 Ritchie, *Bigge Report*, I, p. 92.
31 Johnston to Castlereagh, 11 Apr 1808, HRA, p. 214.
32 Bligh to Castlereagh, 30 Jun 1808, HRA, VI, pp. 535-536.
33 Ibid.
34 Government and General Order, 6 Feb 1808, HRNSW, VI, p. 511.
35 SANSW: 20 Jan 1808, NRS 897, [4/1722, p. 53], Reel 6041.
36 General Order, 12 Feb 1808, HRA, VI, p. 274; Bartrum, *Johnston trial*, p. 419.
37 Johnston to Castlereagh, 12 Apr 1808, HRA, VI, p. 408-409.
38 Johnston to Castlereagh, 11 Apr 1808, HRA, VI, p. 219.
39 Bayly to Bligh, 19 Mar 1808, HRA, VI, p. 249.
40 Bligh to Johnston, 17 Feb 1808, HRA, VI, p. 254.
41 SANSW: Mar 1809, NRS 897, [4/1722, p. 56] Reel 6041.
42 Byrnes, *An outcast goat*, p. 243.
43 Thompson to Howe, 4 Oct 1810, in Macquarie, *Letter to Bathurst*, 1823, p. 67.
44 Arndell to Bligh, 6 Mar 1808, HRNSW, VI, pp. 532-533.
45 Bligh to Johnston, 23 - 25 Mar 1808, HRA, VI, pp. 257-260.
46 Johnston to Castlereagh, 11 Apr 1808, HRA, VI, p. 220.
47 Deposition of Captain Kemp, 11 Apr 1808, HRA, VI, p. 397.
48 Paterson to Johnston, 12 Mar 1808, HRNSW, VI, pp. 536-537.
49 Bligh to Castlereagh, 30 Apr, 30 Jun 1808, HRA, VI, pp. 439-440, 524; Palmer to Bligh, 31 Aug 1808, HRA, VI, p. 605; Commentary, HRA, VI, p. 722.
50 Settlers to Johnston, 11 Apr 1808, HRA, VI, pp. 572-573.
51 Bligh to Castlereagh, 10 Jun 1809, HRA, VII, p. 148.

NOTES

52. Settlers to Paterson, 18 Apr 1808, HRA, VI, pp. 573-574.
53. Bligh to Castlereagh, 30 Apr 1809, HRA, VI, pp. 435-440.
54. Bartrum, *Johnston trial*, p. 26.
55. Gore to Castlereagh, 27 Mar 1808, HRNSW, VI, p. 559.
56. Davoren, *A New Song*, pp. 13-32.
57. Ibid.
58. Ibid.
59. Ibid.

CHAPTER 14 – LOYALIST RESISTANCE

1. Bigge, *State of the Colony*, 1822, p. 81.
2. SLNSW: Brennan to Thompson with Address to Johnston, 28 Apr 1808, SAFE/Banks Papers/Series 40.106.
3. Bligh to Castlereagh, 30 Jun 1808, HRA, VI, p. 528.
4. Bligh to Castlereagh, 30 Jun 1808, HRA, VI, pp. 539, 542.
5. *The Sydney Gazette*, 15 May 1808.
6. Ibid.
7. *The Sydney Gazette*, 19 Jun 1808.
8. Finucane to Brooks, 1-3 Sep 1808, HRA, VI, pp. 648-651.
9. Memorial by Blaxland, 26 Oct 1809, HRNSW, VII, p. 227.
10. *The Sydney Gazette*, 17 Jul and 21 Aug 1808.
11. Fletcher, B. H., *Joseph Foveaux*, Australian Dictionary of Biography; Holt, Joseph, Memoirs, II, London, 1838; Robert Jones, *Recollections of 13 years in Norfolk Island and Van Diemans* [sic] *Land*, 1823.
12. Whitaker, *Joseph Foveaux*, p. 2.
13. Bligh to Castlereagh, 31 Aug 1808, HRA, VI, p. 588-589.
14. Foveaux to Paterson, 16 Aug 1808, HRA, VI, p. 633.
15. Proclamation, 31 Jul 1808, HRNSW, VI, p. 701.
16. Finucane, *Distracted Settlement*, 5 May 1808, pp. 80-81.
17. Bligh to Paterson, 31 Aug 1808, HRA, VI, p. 590.
18. Byrnes, *An outcast goat*, p. 263-264.
19. SLNSW: Brennan to Thompson with Address to Johnston, 28 Apr 1808, SAFE/Banks Papers/Series 40.106.
20. Byrnes, *An outcast goat*, p. 263-264.
21. Ibid.
22. Foveaux to Castlereagh, 10 Sep 1808, HRA, VI, p. 663.
23. SLNSW: Old Register, 18 Sep 1808, Vol 2, No 27, 28, RAV/DISC10/1615; HLRV: Parish map of St James, AO MAP 349.
24. *The Sydney Gazette*, 24 Oct 1812.
25. Walsh, G.P., *Mary Reibey*, Australian Dictionary of Biography.
26. Commentary, HRA, VI, p. 740.
27. *The Sydney Gazette*, 28 Aug 1808.
28. *The Sydney Gazette*, 28 Aug, 2 Oct 1808; SANSW: 23 Aug 1808, NRS 5607, [2/8286, pp. 29-36], Reel 2232.
29. Mason to Bligh, 20 Aug 1808, HRNSW, VI, pp. 702-703.
30. Ibid.
31. *The Sydney Gazette*, 4 Sep 1808.

NOTES

32. *The Sydney Gazette*, 16 Oct 1808.
33. Bartrum, *Johnston trial*, pp. 461-463.
34. Bartrum, *Johnston trial*, p. 130.
35. Finucane, 18-21 Sep 1808, *Distracted Settlement*, pp. 65-66.
36. Bligh to Cooke, 8 Nov 1808, HRA, VI, p. 691.
37. Bligh to Castlereagh, 28 Oct 1808, HRA, VI, pp. 674-675.
38. SLNSW: Old Register, 5 Nov 1808, Vol 2, No 49, RAV/DISC10/1615.
39. SLNSW: Old Register, Mar – Nov 1808, Vol 2, No 25B, 25C, 25D, 26, 29, 30, 44, RAV/DISC10/1615.
40. SLNSW: Old Register, 21 Dec 1809, Vol 5, No 662, RAV/DISC10/1615; *The Sydney Gazette*, 22 Oct 1809.
41. Settlers' Petition to Castlereagh, 4 Nov 1808, HRNSW, VI, pp. 802-804.
42. Government and General Order, 13 Dec 1808, HRNSW, VI, p. 812.
43. *The Sydney Gazette*, 18 Dec 1808.
44. Suttor to Bligh, 1 Jan 1808, HRNSW, VII, p. 4.
45. *The Sydney Gazette*, 25 Dec 1808.
46. SANSW: 31 Dec 1808, NRS 1213, [9/2731, p. 216], Fiche 3268.
47. Foveaux to Castlereagh, 20 Feb 1809, HRA, VII, p. 4.
48. Private letter from Foveaux, 10 Sep 1808, HRNSW, VI, p. 752.
49. Foveaux to Castlereagh, 20 Feb 1809, HRA, VII, p. 4.
50. SLNSW: Old Register, 8 Sep 1808, Vol 2, No 27, 29, RAV/DISC10/1615.

CHAPTER 15 – LOCAL HERO

1. Macquarie, *Letter to Sidmouth*, p. 37.
2. Finucane, 1 Jan 1809, *Distracted Settlement*, pp. 70-71.
3. Correspondence, Jan 1809, HRA, VII, pp. 33-35.
4. Finucane, 19 Jan 1809, *Distracted Settlement*, pp. 73-74.
5. *The Sydney Gazette*, 22 Jan 1809.
6. Government and General Order, 21 Jan 1809, HRNSW, VII, p. 8.
7. *The Sydney Gazette*, 31 Jul 1808.
8. Settlers to Castlereagh, 4 Nov 1808, HRNSW, VI, pp. 802-804.
9. *The Sydney Gazette*, 18 Dec 1808.
10. Government and General Order, 11 Feb 1809, HRNSW, VII, p. 25.
11. SLNSW: 11-25 Feb 1809, NRS 898, [9/2673, pp. 7, 10, 13, 14], Reel 6040.
12. *The Sydney Gazette*, 26 Feb, 5 Mar 1809.
13. Macarthur Onslow, *Macarthurs of Camden*, p. 203.
14. Correspondences, Jan 1809, HRA, VII, pp. 36-39.
15. Correspondence Paterson to Bligh, 30 Jan – 1 Feb 1809, HRNSW, VII, pp. 12-14; Fulton to Castlereagh, 23 Mar 1809, HRNSW, VII, pp. 86-87.
16. Paterson to Bligh, 2 Feb 1809, HRNSW, VII, p. 16; Agreement between Bligh and Paterson, 4 Feb 1809, HRNSW, VII, pp. 17-18.
17. Bligh to Castlereagh, 10 Jun 1809, HRA, VII, pp. 123-124.
18. Paterson to Bligh, 22 Feb 1809, HRNSW, VII, p. 45.
19. Finucane, 17-18 Mar 1809, *Distracted Settlement*, pp. 77-78.
20. Johnston and Paterson, 1-2 Mar 1809, HRA, VII, pp. 57-58.
21. Atkins to Johnston, 4 Mar 1809, HRA, VII, p. 63; Paterson to Johnston, 17 Mar 1809, HRA, VII, p. 64.

NOTES

22 *The Sydney Gazette*, 12 Mar 1808.
23 Hawkesbury Settlers to Bligh, 17 Mar 1809, HRNSW, VII, pp. 78-79.
24 Bligh to Castlereagh, 10 June 1809, HRA, p. 124.
25 Proclamation by Bligh, 12 Mar 1809, HRA, VII, p. 73.
26 Fulton to Castlereagh, 23 Mar 1809, HRNSW, VII, p. 87.
27 *The Sydney Gazette*, 2 Apr 1809.
28 Paterson's Proclamation against Bligh, 19 Mar 1809, HRA, VII, p. 74.
29 Bligh to Castlereagh, 10 June 1809, HRA, VII, pp. 125-128.
30 Collins's General Order, 24 Jun 1809, HRA, VII, p. 165; Bligh to Castlereagh, 8 Jul 1809, HRA, VII, p. 161.
31 Collins to Paterson, 6 Aug 1809, HRA, VII, pp. 175-176.
32 Hayes to Castlereagh, 13 Oct 1809, HRNSW, VII, p. 217.
33 Ibid.
34 *The Sydney Gazette*, 7 May 1808.
35 SANSW: 22 Apr 1809, NRS 898, [9/2673, p. 33], Reel 6040.
36 SANSW: 9 May 1809, NRS 1215, Reel 2505.
37 *The Sydney Gazette*, 21 May 1809.
38 Ibid.
39 *The Sydney Gazette*, 4 Jun 1809.
40 Finucane, 2 Jun 1809, *Distracted Settlement*, p. 83.
41 *The Sydney Gazette*, 4 Jun 1809.
42 Finucane, 28 May-2 Jun 1809, *Distracted Settlement*, pp. 81-83.
43 *The Sydney Gazette*, 18 Jun 1809.
44 Government and General Order, 30 May 1809, HRNSW, VII, pp. 156-157; *The Sydney Gazette*, 25 Jun 1809.
45 SANSW: 17 Jun 1809, NRS 898, [9/2673, p. 55], Reel 6040.
46 Paterson to Castlereagh, 9 Jul 1809, HRA, VII, p. 167.
47 McLachlan, N.D., *Lachlan Macquarie*, Australian Dictionary of Biography.
48 Castlereagh to Macquarie, 14 May 1809, HRA, VII, pp. 81-82.
49 *The Sydney Gazette*, 2 Jul, 20 Aug 1809.
50 Introduction, HRA, VII, p. xix; King to Windham, 12 Aug 1806, HRA, V, p. 773; Return of Land Grants, 25 Sep 1800, HRA, II, p. 566; Ryan, *Land Grants*, p. 191.
51 Macquarie to Liverpool, 13 Nov 1812, HRA, VII, p. 549.
52 *The Sydney Gazette*, 6 Aug 1809.
53 Ibid.
54 Government and General Order, 8 Aug 1809, HRNSW, VII, p. 204.
55 *The Sydney Gazette*, 3 Nov 1810.
56 HLRV: Grant Register, 11 Aug 1809, Serial 4, p. 94; Parish map of Narrabeen, AO Map 259.
57 HLRV: Registered by executors as a land grant, 17 Aug 1819, Serial 11, p. 124; Book E, No 737; Parish map of Melville, AO Map 331.
58 SANSW: 24 Aug 1809, NRS 1215, Reel 2505; Macquarie, *Journal of his tours*, pp. 13-14. The 345 acres were consolidated in 1815 into one grant in the name of Thompson's executors, Antill and Moore. HLRV: Grant Register, 10 Jun 1815, Serial 8, p. 51; Parish map of Minto, AO Map 250.
59 Macquarie, *Journal of his tours*, p. 14.
60 *The Sydney Gazette*, 13 Aug 1809.

NOTES

61 *The Sydney Gazette*, 24 Sep 1809.
62 *The Sydney Gazette*, 3 Dec 1809.

CHAPTER 16 – FIRST EMANCIPIST MAGISTRATE

1 *The Sydney Gazette*, 27 Oct 1810.
2 *The Sydney Gazette*, 7 Jan 1810.
3 SLNSW: Macquarie's Memoranda, 31 Dec 1809, SAFE/A 772.
4 Proclamation, 1 Jan 1810, HRA, VII, pp. 226-227; Macquarie to Castlereagh, 8 Mar 1810, HRA, VII, p. 218.
5 Castlereagh to Macquarie, 15 May 1809, HRA, VII p. 87.
6 Finucane, 24 Jan 1810, *Distracted Settlement*, p. 92.
7 Bigge, *State of the Colony*, 1822, p. 81.
8 Byrne, Paula, *Letters & Diaries of Ellis Bent*, p. 127.
9 Byrne, Paula, *Letters & Diaries of Ellis Bent*, pp. 128-130.
10 Ibid.
11 Ibid.
12 Ibid.
13 *The Sydney Gazette*, 18 Apr 1812.
14 Byrne, Paula, *Letters & Diaries of Ellis Bent*, p. 137.
15 NSW Office of Environment & Heritage, www.environment.nsw.gov.au/heritageapp/ViewHeritageItemDetails.aspx?ID=2424811.
16 *The Sydney Gazette*, 7 Jan 1810.
17 Introduction, HRA, VIII, p. xiv.
18 *The Sydney Gazette*, 7 Jan 1810.
19 Proclamation, 4, 11 Jan 1810, HRA, VII, pp. 227-231.
20 Government Order, 7, 10 Jan 1810, HRNSW, VII, pp. 266, 268.
21 SANSW: 10 Jan 1810, NRS 899, [4/1822, No 307], Fiche 3009.
22 Ibid.
23 Ibid.
24 Government and General Order, 10 Jan 1810, HRNSW, VII, pp. 267-268.
25 SANSW: 10 Jan 1811, NRS 935, [4/3490B, pp. 15-16], Reel 6002.
26 SANSW: 12 Jan 1811, NRS 897, [4/1723, pp. 98-99], Reel 6042.
27 *The Sydney Gazette*, 21 Jan 1810.
28 *The Sydney Gazette*, 14 Jan 1810.
29 SLNSW: Macquarie to Bigge, 18 Jan 1821, BT 26, CY 1466, p. 5743.
30 Macquarie, *Letter to Sidmouth*, p. 37.
31 Bartrum, *Johnston trial*, p. 31.
32 SLNSW: Macquarie's Memoranda, 9 Jan 1810, SAFE/A 772.
33 SLNSW: Macquarie's Memoranda, 17-26 Jan 1810, SAFE/A 772; *The Sydney Gazette*, 21 Jan 1810.
34 *The Sydney Gazette*, 21 Jan 1810, 5 Jan 1811.
35 SANSW: 23 Jan 1810, NRS 897, [9/2736, p. 41], Reel 6042.
36 SLNSW: Brennan to Thompson with Address to Johnston, 28 Apr 1808, SAFE/Banks Papers/Series 40.106.
37 *The Sydney Gazette*, 28 Jan 1810.

38 Macquarie, *Journal of his tours*, p. 26.
39 Ritchie, *Bigge Report*, I, pp. 90-91.
40 *The Sydney Gazette*, 4 Feb 1810.
41 *The Sydney Gazette*, 24 Feb 1810.
42 Ibid.
43 Ritchie, *Bigge Report*, I, p. 89.
44 SLNSW: Arnold to his brother, 25 Feb 1810, CY 339, pp. 311-312.
45 Ibid.
46 Macquarie to Castlereagh, 30 Apr 1810, HRNSW, VII, pp. 356-357.
47 Ibid.
48 Ibid.
49 Ritchie, *Bigge Report*, I, pp. 90-91.
50 Lord to Macquarie, 27 Jan 1810, HRA, VII, pp. 294-295; Campbell to Lord, 2 Feb 1810, HRA, VII, p. 296; *The Sydney Gazette*, 10 Mar 1810.
51 *The Sydney Gazette*, 21 Jan 1810.
52 Correspondence, 12 Mar 1810, HRA, VII, pp. 298-299.
53 Macarthur Onslow, *Macarthurs of Camden*, pp. 215-216.
54 Ibid.
55 Macquarie to Castlereagh, 30 Apr 1810, HRA, VII, p. 247; Bligh to Banks, 11 Aug 1810, HRNSW, VII, p. 405.
56 *The Sydney Gazette*, 27 Oct 1810.
57 Byrnes, *An outcast goat*, pp. 298-299.
58 SLNSW: Hassall's Parramatta store sales book, 7 Jul 1810, CY 1213, p. 207.
59 SANSW: 31 Mar 1810, NRS 935, [4/3490B, p. 160], Reel 6002.
60 *The Sydney Gazette*, 31 Mar 1810.
61 Ritchie, *Bigge Report*, II, pp. 94-95; Bigge, *State of the Colony*, 1822, p. 83.
62 Marsden, *An Answer to Calumnies*, pp. 4-6.
63 Byrnes, *An outcast goat*, p. 308.
64 Marsden, *An Answer to Calumnies*, pp. 4-6.
65 SLNSW: Macquarie to Bigge, 18 Jan 1821, BT 26, CY 1466, p. 5740.
66 *The Sydney Gazette*, 7 Apr 1810.
67 SANSW: 10 May 1810, NRS 897, [4/1723, pp. 298-301], Reel 6042.
68 SLNSW: Macquarie's Memoranda, 8-12 May 1810, SAFE/A 772.
69 Bligh to Banks, 11 Aug 1810, HRNSW, VII, pp. 404-405.
70 Bertie, *Governor Macquarie*, p. 27.

CHAPTER 17 – A REMARKABLE LIFE

1 *The World's News*, 19 Dec 1925.
2 SANSW: 30 Jan 1810, NRS 897, [9/2736, pp. 46-47], Reel 6042; 7 Apr, 8 May 1810, NRS 898, [4/1819, pp. 433-434, 661-666], Reel 6021.
3 SANSW: Apr-Sep 1810, NRS 935, [4/3490C, pp. 55, 77-78, 89, 129-130, 135, 174, 176], Reel 6002.
4 Byrnes, *An outcast goat*, p. 308.
5 *The Sydney Gazette*, 17 Feb 1810.
6 SANSW: 5 Jun 1810, NRS 899, [4/1822, No 307a], Fiche 3009.
7 Macquarie to Castlereagh, 30 Apr 1810, HRA, VII, p. 268.
8 *The Sydney Gazette*, 27 Oct 1810.

NOTES

9. Macquarie, *Letter to Sidmouth*, pp. 37-38.
10. SANSW: Underwood vs Antill, 24 Jul 1812, NRS 2659, [5/1108], case 114.
11. SANSW: 22-24 Aug 1810, NRS 2659, [5/1103], case 289-296, 301-303.
12. SANSW: 13 Sep – 2 Oct 1810, NRS 2659, [5/1103], case 326, 355-356, 358-362, 364, 366-375; NRS 2659, [5/1104], case 1, 4, 61.
13. SANSW: Underwood vs Antill, 24 Jul 1812, NRS 2659, [5/1108], case 114.
14. Thompson to Howe, 4 Oct 1810 in Macquarie, *Letter to Bathurst*, 1823, p. 67.
15. Ibid.
16. The original document held in the Mitchell Library could not be located by library staff. It was last accounted for in the 1980s and is either lost or misplaced. The only surviving full transcript of the Will is from J.V. Byrnes *An outcast goat*, p. 315. A partial, unclear image of the original Will is in Byrnes, *Andrew Thompson, Part 2*, p. 167.
17. Loane, M. L., *Thomas Moore*, Australian Dictionary of Biography.
18. *The Sydney Gazette*, 6 Oct 1810.
19. *The Sydney Gazette*, 27 Oct 1810.
20. SLNSW: Macquarie's Memoranda, 22 Oct 1810, SAFE/A 772.
21. Macquarie, *Letter to Bathurst*, 1823, p. 31.
22. Macquarie, *Journal of his tours*, p. 27.
23. *The Sydney Gazette*, 3 Nov 1810.
24. Ibid.
25. Byrnes, *An outcast goat*, p. 315; Byrnes, *Andrew Thompson, Part 2*, pp. 166-167.
26. Macarthur to his wife, 21 Apr 1811, HRNSW, VII, p. 527.
27. Byrnes, *An outcast goat*, p. 316.
28. SLNSW: Macquarie's Memoranda, 26 Oct 1810, SAFE/A 772.
29. Macquarie, *Letter to Sidmouth*, p. 38.
30. Macquarie to Liverpool, 27 Oct 1810, HRA, VII, p. 347.
31. *The Sydney Gazette*, 27 Oct 1810.
32. *The Sydney Gazette*, 3 Nov 1810.
33. *The Sydney Gazette*, 27 Oct 1810.
34. *The Sydney Gazette*, 3 Nov 1810.
35. Macquarie, *Journals of his tours*, pp. 1-2.
36. Ibid.
37. Macquarie, *Journals of his tours*, pp. 12-14.
38. Ibid.
39. Macquarie, *Journals of his tours*, p. 23.
40. Macquarie, *Journals of his tours*, pp. 27-28.
41. Ibid.
42. Ibid.
43. Macquarie, *Journals of his tours*, p. 32.
44. Macquarie, *Journals of his tours*, p. 32; *The Sydney Gazette*, 24 Nov 1810.
45. Macquarie, *Journals of his tours*, pp. 42-43.

CHAPTER 18 – ANDREW'S LEGACY

1. Byrnes, *An outcast goat*, p. 306.
2. SANSW: NRS 2659 [5/1103-1108].
3. *The Sydney Gazette*, 8 Dec 1810.

NOTES

4. *The Sydney Gazette*, 29 Dec 1810; Byrnes, *Andrew Thompson*, Part 2, p. 172.
5. *The Sydney Gazette*, 15 Dec 1810; Byrnes, *Andrew Thompson*, Part 2, p. 172.
6. *The Sydney Gazette*, 5 Jan 1811.
7. *The Sydney Gazette*, 5 Jan, 9 Feb 1811; Hainsworth, R.D., *Henry Kable*, Australian Dictionary of Biography.
8. SANSW: 11-18 Feb 1811, NRS 898, [ML C197, pp. 1-18], Reel 6040.
9. *The Sydney Gazette*, 19 Jan 1811.
10. *The Sydney Gazette*, 22 Dec 1810, 19 Jan 1811.
11. *The Sydney Gazette*, 9 Feb, 2 Mar 1811, 18 Apr 1812; SANSW: 11-18 Feb 1811, NRS 898, [ML C197, pp. 4, 14], Reel 6040; SLNSW: Howe evidence before Bigge, 15 Dec 1820, BT 2, CY 1562, pp. 719, 728.
12. *The Sydney Gazette*, 3 Nov 1810.
13. SANSW: 1 Feb 1811, NRS 2659, [5/1105], case 19-59.
14. Hardie, *Early Hawkesbury Settlers*, p. 154.
15. SLNSW: Macquarie's Memoranda, 1 May 1811, SAFE/A 772.
16. *The Sydney Gazette*, 11 May 1811.
17. SANSW: 15 Jul, 28 Oct, 5 Nov 1811, NRS 2659, [5/1106], case 74-77, 80-87, 240-241, 244-246, 251, 289-301.
18. *The Sydney Gazette*, 9 Nov 1811.
19. *The Sydney Gazette*, 16 Nov 1811, 15 Apr 1927.
20. SLNSW: Antill to Wentworth, 4 Mar 1812, CY 699, p. 75.
21. *The Sydney Gazette*, 15 Apr 1927.
22. *The Sydney Gazette*, 31 Jul, 11 Sep 1813, 21 Aug 1819.
23. TNA: Antill evidence before Bigge, 1822, CO 201/128.
24. Byrnes, *Andrew Thompson, Part 2*, pp. 180; SANSW: Feb-Jul 1812, NRS 2659, [5/1107-1109].
25. SANSW: 24-30 Jul, 3 Nov 1812, NRS 2659, [5/1108], case 130-137, 143-151, 196, 198, 222-223, 385-396.
26. Macquarie, *Letter to Bathurst*, 1823, pp. 32-33, 67-68.
27. Ibid.
28. Macquarie to Liverpool, acknowledged 28 Jul 1811, HRA, VII, p. 341.
29. SLNSW: Wentworth police fund report, 30 Sep 1812, CY 417, p. 20; Higginbotham, *Thompson Square*, p. 19.
30. SANSW: 7 Nov 1812, NRS 935, [4/3491, p. 355], Reel 6002.
31. *The Sydney Gazette*, 24 and 31 Oct 1812.
32. SLNSW: Wentworth police fund report, 30 Dec 1812, CY 417, p. 28.
33. SLNSW: Howe evidence before Bigge, 15 Dec 1820, BT 2, CY 1562, p. 728.
34. Transcript of gravestone, visit in 2018.
35. Jack & Barkley-Jack, *St Matthew's*, p. 99.
36. Macquarie to Bathurst, 28 Jun 1813, HRA, VII, pp. 775-776.
37. Ibid.
38. Macquarie to his brother Charles, 28 May 1814, SLNSW: MLMSS 82.
39. SANSW: 31 Oct 1823, NRS 898, [SZ 1049, p. 2], Reel 6040; 1825, NRS 899, [4/1843A, No 498, pp. 259-262], Fiche 3142; *The Sydney Gazette*, 1 Sep 1825.
40. SANSW: Jan–Aug 1813, NRS 2659, [5/1109], case 13, 195,196, 334; Feb–May 1814, NRS, [5/1110], case 212-213, 235, 339, 378, 381-390.
41. Macquarie to Bathurst, 1 Jul 1815, HRA, VIII, p. 621; Bathurst to Macquarie, 18 Apr 1816, HRA, IX, p. 107.

NOTES

42 TNA: PROB 11/2018/302; Cumberland Directory, 1811.
43 Thomson, *William Thomson*, Archbishop of York, p. 3.
44 HLRV: Old System Records, Appl. No. 38827.
45 *The Sydney Gazette*, 7 Jan, 25 Feb 1815.
46 *The Sydney Gazette*, 4 Nov 1815.
47 Byrnes, *Andrew Thompson*, Part 2, p. 197.
48 Byrnes, *Andrew Thompson*, Part 2, p. 201.
49 Byrnes, *Andrew Thompson*, Part 2, p. 205.
50 Macquarie to Bathurst, 1 Dec 1817, HRA, IX, pp. 495-501.
51 *The Sydney Gazette*, 22 Aug 1818, 5 Jun 1819; SLNSW: Kitchen to Bigge, 29 Jan 1821, BT 26, CY 1466, p. 5942-5943; J. E. Manning papers, A 5350.
52 House of Commons, *Select Committee on Gaols*, pp. 55-56.
53 Ibid.
54 Ibid.
55 Ibid.
56 Bathurst to Bigge, 6 Jan 1819, HRA, X, pp. 4-8.
57 Bigge, *State of the Colony*, 1822, p. 81.
58 Ellis, *Lachlan Macquarie*, p. 513.
59 TNA: Antill evidence before Bigge, 1822, CO 201/128.
60 Macquarie to Bathurst, 29 Feb 1820, HRA, X, pp. 291.
61 Bathurst to Macquarie, 15 Jul 1820, HRA, X, p. 314.
62 *The Sydney Gazette*, 30 Sep 1820; SLNSW: Moore evidence before Bigge, 1821, BT 2, CY 1562, p. 756; HLRV: Old System Records, Appl. No. 37278.
63 SLNSW: Moore evidence before Bigge, 1821, BT 2, CY 1562, pp. 755.
64 TNA: Muster 1816, HO 10/4; Muster 1820, HO 10/14; Muster 1821, HO 10/17.
65 TNA: Muster 1822, HO 10/36; Muster 1825, HO 10/20; SRNSW: 30 Jun 1823, NRS 13836, [7/485], Reel 2704.
66 *The Sydney Gazette*, 1 Apr 1826.
67 SLNSW: SAG 7, No 77; *The Sydney Gazette*, 15 Nov 1826, 5 Sep 1827.
68 SLNSW: Macquarie's Memoranda, 12 Feb 1822, SAFE/A 775; *The Sydney Gazette*, 15 Feb 1822.
69 SLNSW: Macquarie's Memoranda, 14 Jul 1823, SAFE/A 772.
70 Macquarie, *Letter to Bathurst*, 1823, p. 31.
71 Ibid.
72 *The Monitor*, 27 Jan 1827.
73 HLRV: Old System Records, 12 Aug 1825, Book E, No 367.
74 TNA: PROB 11/2018/302; *Cumberland Pacquet*, 29 Jan 1828; Borthwick: Walter Thompson, Prerogative Court York, 1828.
75 Thomson, *William Thomson*, Archbishop of York, p. 4; Whitehaven Parish: www.whitehavenparish.org.uk/about-us/st-nicholas-centre/guided-tour/william-thompson86th-archbishop-of-york.php

INDEX

Abbott, Edward, 74, 187, 188
Aborigines, 57, 58, 61, 64, 67, 74, 76, 103, 106, 110, 112, 116-119, 228
    Charley, 118
    Gadigal, 57
    Major White, 75
    Terribandy, 75
    Yaragowhy, 118
Abraham, Esther, 141
Active, ship, 54
Admiral Gambier, ship, 218-220, 221
Agnes Bank farm, 95, 129, 269, 274, 284
Agnew, James, 47
Aitkin, John, 8, 9, 11-13, 16-18, 20-23, 25, 26
Albion, ship, 209
Amos, Thomas, 284
Andrew Thompson Drive, 294
Anna Josepha, ship, 86, 121
Anne, ship, 138
Antill, Henry, 229, 237, 258-260, 263-279, 282-292, *See* Thompson, estate settlement
Archer, Mary, 75, 76
Argo, ship, 121, 122
Argyll, Duke of, 236
Arndell, Thomas, 65, 71, 108, 115, 116, 118, 124, 127, 141, 144, 146, 151, 153, 175, 176, 179, 184, 187, 189, 192, 194, 196, 199, 219, 241, 250, 255, 260, 291
Arnold, Joseph, 246, 247
Atalanta, ship, 265, 278
Atkins, Richard, 43, 44, 60, 61, 63, 108, 109, 115, 141, 143, 145, 162, 168-170, 176-178, 189, 192, 198, 211, 219, 220, 233, 250
Atlantic, ship, 49, 113
Australian banknote, 206
Baker, William, 153, 157, 181
Balmain, William, 156
Banks, Joseph, 131, 147, 163, 167, 168, 199, 214

Barrington, George, 54, 55, 65, 69
Bass Strait, 94, 155, 206, 221
Bathurst, Henry, 285-288, 290
Baxter, William, 129
Bayliss, Joseph, 129
Bayly, Nicholas, 153
Beasley, Charles, 255
Bell, Archibald, 189, 226, 229, 237, 239-241, 246
Bellasis, George, 87
Bennet, Henry Gray, 285
Bent, Ellis, 231, 233, 234, 237, 256, 275, 282
Bent, Jeffery, 282, 285
Bevan, David, 128, 212
Bigge, Thomas, 135, 136, 259, 284, 286-288, 290, 292
Biggers, Thomas, 95, 125, 127, 187
Black, John, 206
Bladdey, William, 257, 261, 284
Blaxcell, Garnham, 128, 146, 169, 195, 220
Blaxland, Gregory, 164, 220, 260
Blaxland, John, 164, 202
Bligh Sound, 101
Bligh, William, 39, 40, 120, 122, 131, 132, 143-244, 246, 249, 250-255, 258, 264
Blighton farm, 149, 154-166, 171-175, 184-186, 192, 193, 200, 203, 244, *See* Thompson, bailiff
Blue Mountains, 66, 223, 244, 260
Blund, James, 274
Botany Bay, 28, 30, 31, 45, 53
Botany Bay Scheme, 28, 31, 286
Bowman, John, 144, 176, 228
Boyd, ship, 226, 248, 249
Brabyn, John, 178, 204
Bradbury, John, 210
Braddick, John, 97
Brazil, John, 207
Brennan, John, 199
Brisbane, Thomas, 289, 290
British House of Commons Select Committee, 136, 281, 285

INDEX

Brooks, Richard, 201, 202
Brown, David, 67, 74, 75, 78, 106
Bryan, Thomas, 115
Buccleuch, Duke, 23
Burman, Richard, 106
Burns, Robert, 5, 104, 105
Butler, William, 75
Byrnes, John Valentine, 8, 19, 23, 102, 105, 129, 136, 154, 172, 263, 264, 284
Camden, Lord of, 121
Campbell, John, 251, 284, 285
Campbell, Robert, 98, 158, 170, 175, 176, 179, 191, 192, 201, 209, 219, 238, 250
Campbelltown, 229, 294
Cape of Good Hope, 202
Cape Town, 39, 40, 48
Cape Verde, 36
Cartwright, Robert, 246, 259, 260, 269, 291
Castle Hill farm, 110, 111, 130
Castlereagh, 116, 270
Castlereagh, Lord of, 137, 151, 190, 195, 197, 210, 222, 225, 247, 270
Chalker, William, 125, 126
Chapman, William, 166, 210, 212
Chisholm, James, 289
Cleaveland, Thomas, 268
Clifton, Richard, 115
Coal River, 94, 107, 112, 189, 197, 222, 243
Collins, David, 40, 42, 48, 51, 52, 58, 61, 62, 93, 94, 108, 141, 221
Colonial Office, 121, 134, 138, 152, 161, 162, 168, 169, 186, 190, 194, 201, 212, 225, 231, 237, 241, 242, 244, 245, 248, 281, *See* Home Office
Cook, James, 131
Cornwallis farm, 93, 100, 114
Cosdale, William, 93
Cowpastures, 117, 121, 151, 228, 268
Cox, James, 153, 260
Cox, William, 90, 260, 267, 269
Creek Retreat farm, 228, 274
Crossley, George, 132, 144, 151,
168, 175, 176, 185, 189, 190, 194, 219, 220, 282
Cummings, William, 144, 176
Cunningham, Philip, 111, 112
Dalton, Elizabeth, 108
Dart, ship, 194
Daveney, Thomas, 53
Davis, James, 255
Davoren, Lawrence, 197
de facto relationships, 134, 141, 245, 248
Dickens, Charles, 1
Divine, Nicholas, 192, 219, 250
Dixon, James, 87
Dore, Richard, 75, 108
Dorlong, Dominicus, 40
Doubtful Sound, 101
Douglas, George Sir, 24
Dowling, George, 194, 219
Driver, John, 212
Duke of Clarence, ship, 40
Dundas, Henry, 25, 35, 36
Dunkirk, hulk, 30
Dyer, George, 54
Eagar, Edward, 282
East India Company, 32, 87, 92, 202
Eastern Creek, 228
Ebenezer, 230
Either, Thomas, 210
Eivers, Mark, 207
Elizabeth Island, 101
Ely, John, 40
Estramina, ship, 204, 209
Evans, George, 153
Everingham, Matthew, 274
Experiment, ship, 240, 249
Faa, Johnnie, 5
Field, Barron, 284
Finucane, James, 203, 214, 216, 223
First Fleet, 28, 34, 41, 50, 61, 79, 108, 123, 134, 258
Fitz, Robert, 180, 187, 220
Fitzgerald, Richard, 53, 87, 113, 114, 132, 188, 189, 196, 208, 237, 243, 267, 278, 279
Floods, 38, 76-79, 84, 85, 88, 104, 106, 120, 124-128, 133, 145, 146, 160, 190, 214, 217, 222-224, 226,

327

INDEX

227, 229, 238, 239, 254, 256, 260, 266, 268, 270, 275-280
Foveaux Strait, 220
Foveaux, Joseph, 34, 39, 51, 52, 56, 141, 167, 197- 209, 211, 212, 214-218, 220-224, 226, 227, 229, 231-233, 235, 237-239, 242, 245, 246, 249, 250, 255
Francis, ship, 36, 66, 92, 99
Frazier, Andrew, 181
Freebody, Simon, 75
French Revolution, 8, 27, 197, 198
Fulton, Henry, 87, 146, 176, 179, 192, 203, 219, 238, 250
Gannan, Patrick, 110
Gaudry, William, 273, 277
Geordy, ship, 243, 270, 273, 277
Georges River, 228, 258, 268
Gibbons, Matthew, 144
Gillespie, John, 8
Glasgow farm, 129, 269, 274, 284
Goodall, William, 74
Gore, William, 176, 179, 180, 188, 189, 192, 197, 219, 220, 238, 250
Governor Bligh, ship, 155, 202, 220, 243, 249, 273
Gowen, John, 181
Gray, John, 274
Green Hills, 58, 61, 65-70, 77, 85, 88-97, 100-106, 110, 112, 116-118, 120, 122, 129, 132, 147-149, 153, 155-157, 174, 179, 181, 183-190, 202, 207-210, 223, 224, 226-228, 230, 239, 241, 244, 251, 254, 255, 258-260, 266-272, 294
Grierson, George, 137
Griffin, Edmund, 179, 188, 192, 203
Griffiths, Jonathan, 94
Grimes, Charles, 184, 186, 188, 198
Grogan, Christopher, 138
Grono Bay, 101
Grono, John, 93, 99-101, 140, 155, 220, 243
Grose, Francis, 34, 38, 43, 49-53, 55, 58-60, 63, 67, 77, 80, 169, 174, 190, 214, 216, 225
Hailes, Lord Judge - Sir David Dalrymple, 21-26

Harrington, ship, 206
Harris, John emancipist, 72, 73, 157
Harris, John surgeon, 166, 176, 178, 182, 191, 198
Hassall, Rowland, 96, 209
Hawkesbury district, 30, 61, 65, 67, 72-74, 78, 81, 82, 85, 104-107, 112 -116, 120, 121, 123, 136, 148, 149, 159, 181, 184, 189, 190, 207, 216, 217, 240, 241, 244, 260, 269
Hawkesbury River, 29, 57-60, 65, 66, 76, 88, 92, 93, 97, 100-102, 108, 110, 112, 116, 117, 119, 124, 127, 148, 149, 196, 206, 215, 223, 230, 244, 294
Hawkesbury settlers, 61, 64, 70, 77, 78, 84, 108, 120, 144, 145, 147, 150, 152, 170, 173-175, 181, 190, 195, 204, 207, 210, 213, 217, 220, 226, 239, 251, 258, 266, 275
Hawkesbury, ship, 94, 101, 119, 128, 155, 273
Hawkesbury, Lord of, 29
Haydock, Mary, 206
Haydon, William, 154
Hayes, Henry Browne, 189, 222
Hervey, James, 105
Highland Regiment, 73rd of Foot, 225, 226, 231, 242, 248, 258
Hill, Richard, 78
HMS *Assistant*, ship, 39
HMS *Bounty*, ship, 131
HMS *Buffalo*, ship, 79, 81, 143
HMS *Dromedary*, ship, 225, 231, 233, 237, 242, 252
HMS *Hindostan*, ship, 225, 231, 242, 252
HMS *Porpoise*, ship, 131, 191-200, 209, 213, 214, 218-222, 231, 242, 252
HMS *Providence*, ship, 39
HMS *Reliance*, ship, 61
HMS *Resolution*, ship, 131, 180
HMS *Sirius*, ship, 39
Hobart Town, 94, 221, 231
Hobart, Lord of, 76, 94, 116, 122
Hobby, Thomas, 74, 75, 151, 153,

INDEX

176, 187, 210, 220
Hodgkinson, Thomas, 75
Hogg, Abraham, 12
Holding, Lawrence, 110
Home Office, 30, 34-36, 41, 48, 62, 72, 78, 79, 81, 82, 84, 86, *See* Colonial Office
Hook, Charles, 220
Hope, ship, 93, 94, 101, 128
Howard, John, 6, 15
Howe, George, 92, 102, 160, 201, 226, 265
Howe, John, 19, 230, 255-257, 267, 273, 276, 278, 284
Howell, John, 95
Hunter River, 93, 206, 215
Hunter, John, 39, 49, 60-72, 77-81, 86, 108, 121, 167, 214, 215, 227, 231
Hunter, ship, 86
Hyde, Mary, 141, 205, 246
Ikin, Obadiah, 118
Irish convicts, 56, 110-112, 138
Irish Rebellion, 110
Ivory, Thomas, 255
Jamieson, John, 110, 181, 184, 186, 211
Jedburgh, 15, 105
Jedburgh Abbey, 14, 15
Jedburgh trial, *See* Thompson, Andrew
Jenkins, James, 210
Jenkins, William, 210
Johnston, George, 87, 111, 141, 143, 170-180, 187, 188, 190-200, 203, 204, 216, 218-222, 232, 242-244, 249, 252, 253, 264
Johnston, William, 273
Jones, Thomas, 204
Jordan, William, 26
Kable, Henry, 93, 94, 101, 128, 163, 179, 195, 273, 274, 275, 277, 279
Karskens, Grace, 53
Kean, Bridget, 115
Kearns, Matthew, 132
Kelly, John, 92, 93
Kelso, 10, 13
Kemp, Anthony, 73, 74, 178, 186,

198, 204, 205, 210
Kent, Thomas, 248, 249
Kerr, George, 11, 12, 21
Killarney farm, 95, 98, 140, 153, 267, 270, 274, 284
Killarney Lakes, 140
Killarney Racecourse, 153
King George III, 148, 152, 270
King George, ship, 128
King James V, 5
King James VI, 5
King, Anna Josepha, 132, 140
King, Philip Gidley, 30, 49, 76, 79-95, 101, 110, 112, 114, 116, 117, 120-132, 138-145, 165-170, 177, 184, 190, 197, 215, 227, 231, 240
Lady Juliana, ship, 258
Larra, James, 97
Lawson, William, 178, 198
Laycock, Thomas, 178, 193
Lindsey, William, 206, 207
Lion, hulk, 30, 32
Liverpool, Earl of, 265, 268
Lock, Matthew, 107, 125, 243, 244, 255, 257, 261
Lord, Simeon, 98, 113, 114, 122, 132, 139, 141, 158, 163, 166, 179, 191, 201, 205, 206, 212, 234, 241, 245-252, 258-264, 267, 270, 273, 277, 285, 287-289
Macarthur, Elizabeth, 145, 215, 264
Macarthur, John, 51-53, 56, 60, 62, 63, 72, 73, 79, 82, 83, 86, 87, 113, 114, 121, 122, 135, 143-146, 151, 152, 154, 158, 160, 161, 169, 170, 174, 177, 178-185, 187-190, 192-207, 213-222, 232, 242, 243, 249, 258, 264, 288
Macarthur, John Junior, 285
Maclaine, Murdoch, 236
Macquarie Place, 205, 235, 236, 258, 285
Macquarie, Charles, 236, 281
Macquarie, Elizabeth, 225, 231, 242, 248, 259, 268, 269, 280
Macquarie, Lachlan, 85, 135, 189, 225, 226, 229, 231-294
Mann, David, 87

329

INDEX

Manning, Edward, 36, 37, 38
Marian, ship, 240
Marsden, Samuel, 63, 67, 71, 73, 74, 83, 108, 110, 127, 129, 134, 135, 139, 140, 143, 149, 155, 244-246, 248, 250-252, 260, 281, 282
Mason, Martin, 175, 176, 187, 196, 204, 207-211, 250
McDougal, William, 21
McGraths Hill, 88, 294
McKellar, Neil, 74
McLane, Mary, 110
McLaughlane, Thomas, 110
McLeece, Daniel, 210
Mealing, John, 115
Meehan, James, 87, 167, 268
Melville, Parish of, 228
Metcalfe, James, 75
Mileham, James, 255, 260
Milford Sound, 101
Miller, William, 115
Milton, John, 105
Minchin, William, 178, 198
Minto, 228, 229, 268, 275
Moore, Eleanor (Ellen), 136-141, 165, 166, 205, 206, 212, 234, 246, 248, 258, 260, 262, 263, 289 *See* Thompson, companion Eleanor Island, 101, 140
Moore, Thomas, 135, 136, 146, 176, 191, 229, 258, 265, 267, 268, 270, 273, *See* Thompson, Andrew
Moore, William, 178, 204
Moos, Isaac, 210
Morris, John, 126
Mortimer, William, 206
Moxham farm, 98, 128, 274
Mulgrave Place, 58
Murray, John, 246
Murray, Robert, 285
Muster, 62, 81, 85, 91, 132, 134, 139, 289
Nancy Sound, 101, 140
Nancy, ship, 93, 94, 101
Nelson Common, 95, 153, 206
Nelson, Horatio, 161
Nepean River, 95, 116-118, 121, 127, 129, 148, 151, 223, 269, 284
Neptune, ship, 106
New Zealand, 101, 140, 202, 203, 220, 243, 246, 248-250, 273
Newgate prison, 32, 34, 105
Nichols, Isaac, 132, 212
Nightingall, Miles, 225
Noah, William, 33, 37
Nobbs, Joseph, 274
Norfolk Island, 39, 49, 72, 80, 86, 87, 107, 110, 123, 199, 203, 209, 218, 221
NSW Corps, 34, 35, 39, 44-67, 71-75, 80, 82, 85-90, 95, 96, 105, 110-113, 116, 118, 120-123, 131, 132, 143, 147, 152-154, 158, 160, 162, 168-170, 174-183, 187-191, 197, 199, 200, 206, 208, 210, 214-220, 222, 225-227, 232, 237, 242, 244, 246, 252, 255, 267
O'Connell, Maurice, 231, 237, 242, 244, 248, 252
Oakes, Francis, 187, 192, 219, 238, 250
Old Hawkesbury Road, 89, 95, 98
Palmer, Charles, 109
Palmer, George, 275, 276
Palmer, John, 85, 94, 109, 125, 132, 151, 175, 176, 179, 184, 190, 192, 203, 206, 219, 220, 238, 250
Parramatta, 41-63, 66, 69, 70, 74, 76, 83, 89, 96, 97, 108-112, 119, 127, 129, 132, 143, 159, 162, 170, 177, 178, 181, 187, 215, 216, 222, 231, 238, 246
Parramatta, ship, 169, 170, 174, 177, 183, 185, 188, 189
Paterson, William, 60-65, 86, 174, 190, 195-200, 203, 204, 209, 213-223, 226, 228, 231, 232, 237, 238, 252
Peacock farm, 88
Perkins, James, 115
Phillip, Arthur, 29, 30, 35, 36, 41-55, 57, 61, 62, 81, 94, 164, 226, 228
Pitt Town, 270
Pitt, ship, 23, 24, 32-44, 47, 48, 51, 52, 54, 66, 67, 109, 115, 141, 210

INDEX

Pitt, Thomas, 144, 176, 204
Pitt, William, 270
Pittwater Bay, 228
Plymouth, 30, 31
Port Dalrymple, 195-197, 199, 209, 214, 215
Port Jackson, 29, 40, 42, 53, 57, 79, 93, 199, 202, 214, 220, 226, 231, 242, 243, 252
Port Macquarie, 290
Porteous, John, 213, 214, 218
Portland Head, 116
Portland, Duke of, 72, 79
Portsmouth, 24, 28, 30, 32-34, 36
Powell, Edward, 75
Putland, John, 131, 164
Putland, Mary, 131, 132, 154, 179, 184, 218, 242, 244, 252
Queen Mary Stuart, 15
Rae, John, 13, 21, 26, 27
Randall, Thomas, 166
Redfern, William, 248, 255, 260, 268, 287
Redman, John, 238
Redmond, Edward, 284
Reibey, Mary, 126, 206
Reibey, Thomas, 126, 206, 258
Richardson, Cuthbert, 209
Richie, Robert, 207
Richmond, 270
Richmond Common, 95
Rickerby, Thomas, 67, 69, 72, 75, 128, 145
Riley, Alexander, 136, 248, 249, 285, 286
Riley, Barnaby, 187
Rio de Janeiro, 36, 38, 138
Rope, Robert, 207
Rose, ship, 201, 202
Rouse, Richard, 192, 219
Rowley, Thomas, 113
Roxburghe, Duke of, 10, 25
Royal Admiral, ship, 40
Rum Rebellion, 151, 161, 177, 182, 183
Ruse, James, 258, 261
Rushton, Thomas, 129
Ryan, John, 78

Scottish convicts, 28, 30, 47
Shaw's Creek, 118
Sheehy, Marcus, 138
Sherwin, Ann, 141
Sherwin, William, 141
Shortreed, Robert, 18
Simpson, Francis, 110
Sinclair, ship, 131, 203
Smith, James, 154, 256
Soare, John, 67, 69, 75, 85
Soare farm, 85
South Creek, 65-67, 77, 88, 89, 93, 95, 98, 107, 117, 124, 127, 128, 130, 132, 148, 155, 207, 223-226, 230, 251, 259, 272, 274, 279
Speed, John, 154
Speedwell, ship, 99, 100, 101, 114, 128, 155, 243, 273
Speedy, ship, 79, 94
Spital, John, 115
St Andrews farm, 228, 229, 268, 269, 275, 289
St Andrews in Campelltown, 294
St James Fair, Kelso, 10, 11
Sterne, Lawrence, 105
Stewart, Robert, 206
Stogdell, John, 81
Story, George, 6
Surprise, ship, 93
Surry, ship, 290
Suttor, George, 176, 208, 210, 211, 250
Sweet, George, 8
Sydney, 44, 52, 70, 76, 111, 117, 122, 126, 139, 165, 166, 183, 200- 206, 210, 215, 226, 231, 232, 233, 238, 239, 240, 242, 243, 251, 252, 258, 263-265, 272, 278, 285, 289
Sydney Cove, 25, 29, 30, 33, 40, 42, 44, 45, 52, 57, 123, 169, 183, 209, 235, 249, 290
Symons, James, 202
Tench, Watkin, 55
Terry, Samuel, 285
Thackeray, William, 1
The Chester Chronicle, 30
The Evening Mail, 30

INDEX

The Public Advertiser, 31
The Scots Magazine, 23
The Stamford Mercury, 32
The Sydney Gazette, 92, 93, 101, 102, 104, 109, 112, 117, 125, 127, 144, 147, 155, 157, 160, 161, 201, 202, 208, 209, 211, 216, 220, 223, 224, 226, 230, 240, 251, 265, 267, 276, 290
Thompson & Thomson families, 4
Thompson, Agnes, 2, 4, 6, 9, 13, 23, 24, 26, 93, 95, 257

Thompson, Andrew
Absolute pardon, 68
arrival in NSW, 42
arrival in Parramatta, 45
auctioneer appointment, 216
bailiff of Blighton, 39, 149, 154-160, 163, 164, 166, 167, 171-175, 181, 184-186, 200
birth, 2
Bligh's witness in Johnston trial, 192, 219, 250
brewery, 129, 130, 148, 187, 223, 272, 274, 278, 279, 284
capias, 193
Chief Constable, 85, 106, 188
Chief Magistrate, 240, 241, 243, 245, 254, 255, 280
companion, 135, *See* Moore, Eleanor
Constable in Green Hills, 65
Constable in Toongabbie, 52
death and grave, 258-260, 269, 276, 279, 287
excise officer, 5, 8, 257
estate settlement, 229, 258, 261, 265-268, 272-278, 282-285, 288-293, *See* Antill, Henry
flax and hemp crops, 123
flax scheme NZ, 249, 250
flood rescues, 77, 124, 125, 126, 127, 224, 225, 226, 227, 287
Green Hills buildings, 77, 96, 148, 223, 255, 272, 274, 278
illness, 8, 230, 241, 254, 255, 256
illicit spirit charge, 170

interrogated by rebels, 184-186
Jedburgh gaol, 9-31
Jedburgh indictment, 12, 13
Jedburgh trial, 14, 16, 18-22
library, 104
Loyalty Address, 175, 176, 182, 187, 190, 196, 200, 258
Parramatta storeman, 48
promissory note, Macarthur, 145, 146, 160, 188
promissory note, Pitt, 204, 205
Red House, 88-90, 96, 104, 148, 157, 198, 223, 224, 227, 230, 244, 247, 258, 259, 276
Registrar of Agreements, 82
salt works Mullet Island, 101, 117, 119, 228
salt works Scotland Island, 119, 228, 243, 270, 272-274, 279, 285, 294
shipbuilding, 92
stone-mason gang, 46
Superintendent of Labour, Cattle and Public Works, 254
Sydney land lease, sale and grant, 165, 167, 205, 211, 212 234, 235, 275
tannery, 155, 207, 272, 274
toll bridge, 88- 90, 98, 124, 127, 224, 230, 251, 272, 274, 279
turnpike trustee, 251, 252
voyage on *Pitt*, 28, 32-41
weaver's apprenticeship, 6, 8
Will and Testament, 256-263, 272

Thompson Sound, 101, 140
Thompson Square, 270, 271, 276, 278, 279, 294
Thompson Street, 294
Thompson, Charles son of nephew John, 293
Thompson, George, 53
Thompson, Gillespie & Sweet, 8, 27
Thompson, Jean niece, 283, 292, 293
Thompson, John, 2 -13, 17, 23, 24, 26

INDEX

Thompson, John nephew, 283, 292, 293
Thompson, John son of nephew John, 293
Thompson, Margaret, 3
Thompson, Margaret niece, 283, 293
Thompson, Robert, 2, 3
Thompson, Robert nephew, 283, 292, 293
Thompson, Walter, 2, 6, 8, 11, 13, 18, 193, 194, 250, 257, 261, 262, 265, 278, 283, 284, 291-293
Thompson, William, 2, 4, 6, 8-13, 16-18, 20, 21, 26, 27, 257, 261, 283, 284
Thom(p)son, William son of nephew John, 293
Thomson, James, 105
Thorpe, Charles, 208
Timms, William, 75
Toongabbie, 43, 51-58, 61, 65, 67, 68, 106, 109, 110, 113, 163
Turner, Rachel, 258
Turner, Walter, 10-13, 16, 17, 21, 27
Tweeddale, Marquis of, 3, 5
Tweedie, William, 38
Tyler, Thomas, 95, 149
Underwood, James, 93, 94, 163
Usher, Thomas, 12, 17
Van Diemen's Land, 40, 93, 195, 200, 203, 204, 209, 213, 215, 218, 221
Verdie, Eleanor, 8, 18, 21, 23
Vinegar Hill, 111
Waaksamheyd, ship, 39, 40, 48, 148
Walker, John, 26
Ward, Joseph, 229, 268, 275
Wardle Bank farm, 129, 269, 274
Watling, Thomas, 32, 40, 44
Wauchope, Laird of Niddrie, 3, 23, 24
Wayham, Thomas, 284
Weaver, 4, 5, 6, 7, 10, 27
Webb, James, 93
Wentworth, D'Arcy, 158, 162, 179, 220, 245, 248, 252
West Hill farm, 88, 89, 93, 95, 98, 128, 155, 156, 207, 259, 270, 274, 285, 294
Whale, ship, 243, 270, 273
White, John, 40, 141, 258
Whitehaven, 257, 261, 283, 292, 293
Whitehouse, James, 65
Whittle, Thomas, 182
Wilberforce, 270
Wilberforce, William, 270
Wilcox, Samuel, 65
Williams, Francis, 248, 249, 250, 260, 264, 267, 273, 274, 278
Williamson, James, 179, 192, 219, 250
Wills, Eliza, 289
Wiltshire, James, 181, 192
Wimbow, John, 75
Windham, William, 151, 168, 169
Windsor, 53, 65, 130, 227, 270-280, 291, 294
Woodbury, Richard, 130, 279
Workington, 19, 20, 256, 257, 283, 292, 293
Wright, Henry, 100
Wright, Isobel, 26
Wright, Richard, 133
Wylde, John, 284
Yarramundi Lagoon, 95, 269
Yetholm, 3-13, 16-18, 20-22, 26, 27, 68, 69, 94, 173, 256, 257
  Gypsies, 5, 20
  Kirk Yetholm, 2-5
  Town Yetholm, 2-6, 9, 11, 16
York, Henry, 77, 85
Youler, Abraham, 154
Young, Jean, 8

www.ingramcontent.com/pod-product-compliance
Lightning Source LLC
Chambersburg PA
CBHW032026290426
44110CB00012B/691